Reflections on Science and the Human Material Condition
Essays toward Critique, Evaluation, and Praxis

To Barbara, Katie + the great folks in The ICC

Curtis V. Smith
2017

Reflections on Science and the Human Material Condition
Essays toward Critique, Evaluation, and Praxis

Morteza Ardebili
Charles Reitz
Mehdi S. Shariati
Curtis V. Smith
Stephen Spartan

2016

Contents

Introduction: *Building Theory and Practice for an Alternative World System*

Part One: *Critical Theoretical Investigations—Philosophies of Science and Social Science*

Chapter One: Reorienting Socio-Economic Theory—
A Critique of Ontological Foundations
    Morteza Ardebili   1

Chapter Two: The Structure of Scientific Practice—
Toward a Resolution of the Problem of Relativism
in Heterodox Economics and Sociology
    Morteza Ardebili   13

Chapter Three: *Rival Philosophies of Science and Debates on the Constitution of Society*
    Curtis V. Smith   57

Part Two: *Science and Historical Materialism—History, Labor, and Ethics*

Chapter Four: *Historical Materialism—A Philosophical Examination*
    Morteza Ardebili   73

Chapter Five: *Materialism and Dialectics in Science and Philosophy— Nature, History, and Knowing*
    Charles Reitz   103

Chapter Six: *The Labor Theory of Ethics and Commonwealth*
    Charles Reitz   143

Part Three: *Political Economy, Pedagogy, and Praxis*

Chapter Seven: *The Political Economy of Predation and Counterrevolution*
    Charles Reitz and Stephen Spartan   181

Chapter Eight: *Surplus Over-Appropriation and the Reproduction Crisis of the Roman Empire*
    Stephen Spartan   217

Chapter Nine: *Imperialism, Militarism, and U.S. National Debt: "Socializing" the Costs of Globalization*
    Mehdi S. Shariati   237

Chapter Ten: *Latin America's March toward Democracy: Challenging the Hegemon*
    Mehdi S. Shariati   277

Chapter Eleven: *Comprehensive Sustainable Development as a Counter-Hegemonic Strategy?*
    Mehdi S. Shariati   301

Chapter Twelve: *Global Capitalism and Radical Opposition—Marcuse's 1974 Paris Lectures*
    Charles Reitz   339

Chapter Thirteen: *Education* As *Alienation; Education* Against *Alienation*
    Charles Reitz   351

Chapter Fourteen: *Decommodification & Liberation: Social Labor's Aesthetic Form: Commonwealth*
    Charles Reitz   377

Chapter Fifteen: *The Commonwealth Counter-Offensive: Political Economy, Pedagogy, Praxis*
    Charles Reitz   395

About the Co-Authors   423

Morteza Ardebili
Charles Reitz
Mehdi S. Shariati
Curtis V. Smith
Stephen Spartan

Introduction:
Building the Theory and Practice for an Alternative World System

The co-authors of this volume are dedicated to a re-thinking of the material human condition and are united in their emphasis on the roles of theory and science in scholarly research. A common thread in the studies we present here is our desire to improve global human living conditions. We highlight objective economic and social potentials which make greater equality, justice, and abundance attainable, though these real alternatives are now held back by entrenched political forces.

We are attempting to address what we see as a current crisis in economic theorizing and in sociological theory more generally. We see this crisis as rooted in philosophy. Therefore, we shall frequently examine here the relationship between knowledge claims and the ontological claims that condition them. Scientific practice cannot occur without ontology, that is without suppositions about cause and effect, the dynamism of the physical world, the nature of historical and sociological factors with regard to social behavior.

INTRODUCTION

In our *Part One: Critical Theoretical Investigations—Philosophies of Science and Social Science*, Morteza Ardebili undertakes the foundational philosophical task of elucidating the ontological assumptions of mainstream economic theory, especially its tendencies toward positivism, hermeneutics, mathematical deductivism, and critical realism. His work inquires into the prevailing philosophies of science and social science, and examines contemporary crises in social science research and teaching, His essay on "The Structure of Scientific Practice" develops the critical philosophical foundations capable of assessing the scientific claims of positivism, post-positivist hermeneutics, critical realism, and historical materialism.

Curtis V. Smith is concerned that relativism raises serious questions about the legitimacy of science. Smith's work resonates with that of Ardebili; he elaborates the comparative treatment of philosophies of science and discusses also their implications for debates regarding the constitution of society. As they conclude, if the nature of science changes when paradigms shift, then we cannot really speak of a history of science or its development through continuity or discontinuity. If the nature of science does *not* change when we change paradigms, then we must still ask, what is science, or to put it another way, how shall we scientifically evaluate the nature of scientific practice?

In our *Part Two: Science and Historical Materialism—History, Labor, and Ethics*, Morteza Ardebili furnishes a critical evaluation of historical materialism as a philosophy of science and social science. This is a *critical philosophical* examination and clarification of Marx's historical materialism, rather than any kind of partisan affirmation or denunciation of Marx's ostensible politics. Marx's system was intended to be a *scientific* one, and may well be evaluated utilizing the heuristic perspective Ardebili developed in

INTRODUCTION

Chapter 2, above, on the Structure of Scientific Practice.

Charles Reitz's line of inquiry is separate, yet related to, those of Ardebili and Curtis V. Smith. Reitz extends a foundational critique of philosophical perspectives in early natural scientific and social theory, and offers an historical account of the emergence of modern tendencies toward materialism and dialectics in both science and philosophy. He examines also pertinent controversies surrounding the nature of dialectics in the Marxist frame.

Reitz has been constructing a philosophical analysis of labor and the human condition, and has in this regard developed what he presents here as a labor theory of ethics and humanism. Working out *a labor theory of economics* (our critical political-economy paradigm) begins with the realization that labor is a resource, an asset, not a cost. Humanity reproduces itself socially through the process of labor. There has been a global history of human modes of labor, and in each case labor is a social process. For the longest period of human history labor was a communal project of social beings to meet human needs. Human brains and hands are not only tools of labor but the products of labor. The basic economic challenge is: how do we generate and sustain the flourishing of human existence and culture? How do we, and the world, work together best? What are the purposes of labor and production—meeting communal human needs, accumulating unbounded private property? Philosophy's deep and systemic moral and political questions involve the nature of the good life and the good society. What are our highest abilities— speech, cooperative social action, caring, intellectual and emotional empathy, wisdom? How does economics help us reclaim our common humanity?

Our *Part Three: Political Economy, Critical Pedagogy, and Praxis*, from the start pursues the reorientation of economic theory that has so far been argued as necessary. Two perspectives in economic thinking are compared and contrasted: 1) the *mainstream (neo-classical) paradigm* in which individuals are taken as the fundamental unit of investigation and analysis, with *individuals* existing as isolated units within a mass, and which are studied according to empiricist and positivist perspectives on the world, and 2) the *critical political-economy paradigm* in which *systems* are taken as the fundamental unit of investigation and analysis. Charles Reitz and Stephen Spartan build upon a Marxian and a Marcusean philosophy of labor to construct a countervailing theoretical force against the mainstream paradigm and obtain a critical theoretical perspective on the capitalist crises of over-accumulation and workforce austerity.

Increasing exploitation is occurring today through the "race to the bottom" as global capitalism scours the world for the lowest wage labor markets and presses domestic labor for steep cuts. Policies of the World Bank, the International Monetary Fund, and NAFTA (North American Free Trade Agreement) have led to structural adjustments that exemplify policies that dis-proportionately hurt the poor. In the U.S. the current recovery, devoid of job growth, is a further indicator of a distorted political economy in which taxpayer-government subsidies to finance capital have permitted a redistribution of wealth to the advantage of the largest banks and high income individuals—reducing the global payroll.

Reitz and Spartan address the over-appropriation crisis of U.S. capitalism today and develop a political-economic model of capital accumulation and workforce remuneration to obtain a critical theoretical perspective. The structure and dynamics of the value production process are made visible here in their material form. We see the over-appropriation of capital and the intensifying maldistribution of wealth in the U.S. as grounded in these relationships and at the root of the system's recurring recessions and economic depressions.

The analysis of Reitz and Spartan focuses on the complex and pivotal underlying structures of economic oppression and exploitation that are too often overlooked (sometimes actively suppressed) by analysts, policy makers, commentators, and educators when examining both the causes and the impacts of imperial corporate globalization. Their purpose is essentially pedagogical: to provide suggestions for inclusion in lesson plans that can help students understand the origins of economic inequality, the nature of capitalism's recurring crises, and the socialist logic of commonwealth production and ownership. They do this through a discussion of patterns of wealth and income distribution and other specific examples that can be intellectually and politically powerful tools for teachers in several interrelated disciplines—political science, sociology, economics, history, and ethics, as well as logic and critical thinking. They hope to mobilize students, faculty, and the general public to root out the conditions, educational and otherwise, that serve to perpetuate the undemocratic realities of political and cultural life (including neocolonial terror wars) deriving from the capitalist world's unfair and unequal social division of labor and wealth. They point out that realigning the social order to conform with the highest potentials of our economy and human nature requires the decommodification of certain social resources: health care, child care, education, food, transportation, housing—and the decommodification of work itself, through a guaranteed income policy.

Mehdi S. Shariati examines the U.S. national debt and proposes that key sources are to be found in the political and military imperatives structured into the accumulation dynamics of global capitalism. Four historically overlapping and essential components of the accumulation process will be analyzed: globalization, imperialism, militarism, and social imperialism. Accumulation strategies are at the same time projects involving the internationalization of capital and production which in turn involve imperialism and militarism on a global scale. He investigates the contemporary economic crisis in terms of neoliberalism's austerity politics as the social cost of globalization with the attendant consequences of increasing U.S. imperialism and militarism. In addition, Shariati builds a context for a critical analysis of U.S. corporate and military involvement in Latin America, which helps us appreciate the strategy of comprehensive sustainable development that has emerged from counter-hegemonic struggles for freedom and independence in the global South.

The key analytical categories of critical political economy (social formations, state formations, modes of privilege) are further developed and utilized by Stephen Spartan to recognize the contemporary relevance of the economic crises of the Western Roman Empire in terms of the analogous problems of over-accumulation and the non-reproduction of the U.S. mode of production.

Today capital is armed with its own theory; labor is not yet armed with its own theory. The main problem as we see it is to develop an alternate vision for labor. Real structured interconnection exists in our economic lives. Theory may be called critical *only* if it penetrates beneath empirical economic facts and discerns generative economic, social, and cultural structures that are neither obvious nor apparent.

The purpose of higher education is to understand social reality as a basis for social action. How does such an understanding occur? Scholarly explanation is tasked with generating valid, if also testable and fallible, claims to knowledge. Within many top-tier research institutions today the tacit, yet primary, purpose seems to be the reproduction of the given political-economic system with its many inequalities

INTRODUCTION

and injustices.[1] "Free spaces" for critical thinking there may be limited, but they can be found. Nonetheless, it is gravely difficult there to counteract an almost mandatory compliance with neoconservative corporate operationalism. Such is the current state (and future?) in much of higher education.

Within this nation's community colleges there has been positioned a greater concentration of first generation academics than anywhere else in academe. Among them is a greater proportion of PhDs and union activists than ever before. Fewer of them have the inherited elitist worldviews of the sons and daughters of earlier generations of academics, who also tend to teach at the more prestigious strata of the postsecondary system. It has been our good fortune to have collaborated closely with such committed teaching associates who have understood that science and learning have an obligation to furnish the community with truthful socio-economic and political assessments, and who have themselves struggled to liberate the progressive educational potentials (within their institutions, but structurally blocked from materialization) throughout their careers.

---

[1] See the now classic treatments by: Thorstein Veblen, *Higher Learning in America: A Memorandum on the Conduct of Universities by Business Men*, (New York: Cosimo, [1918] 2005); David Norman Smith, *Who Rules the Universities*, (New York: Monthly Review Press, 1974); Jennifer Washburn, *University, Inc. The Corporate Corruption of Higher Education* (New York: Basic Books, 2006); Curtis V. Smith, "The Decline of Shared Governance in Higher Education," *Kansas City Kansas Community College e-Journal*, Vol, 3, No. 2 October 2009; and Henry A. Giroux, *Neoliberalism's War on Higher Education*, (Chicago: Haymarket Books, 2014); Samuel Bowles and Herbert Gintis, *Schooling in Capitalist America* (New York: Basic Books, 1977).

Our joint efforts here are undertaken in the current period of economic crisis, change, and danger. These conditions of insecurity and risk make it imperative that the "roots of crisis" be understood and combatted. Our work is intended as a deeper exploration and inquiry into the necessity of *a humanist commonwealth alternative:* an alternative political economy through which humanity may govern itself best.

MORTEZA ARDEBILI
Chapter One

Reorienting Socio-Economic Theory:
A Critique of Ontological Foundations

The British social theorist, Tony Lawson, has made a significant contribution to understanding the nature of the social sciences generally, and to the discipline of economics specifically, from a critical realist philosophical perspective. Lawson's 2003 *Reorienting Economics* is a synthesis, clarification, and constructive extension of his previous contributions.[1] Before giving an overview of the book, I need to present an important general argument that is presupposed by Lawson's particular argument. The general argument is about the significant role that the conception of reality (i.e. ontology) plays in the process of production of knowledge overall, and Lawson's particular argument is about his contention that the discipline of economics should adopt the critical realist ontology as the foundation of its scientific practice. It is important to mention at the outset that the two arguments (i.e. the general and the particular) have an asymmetrical and logically necessary relation. The relation is logically necessary, because acceptance of the proposition, that the discipline of economics should adopt the critical realist ontology, logically requires a prior realization that a

---

[1] Tony Lawson, *Reorienting Economics* (New York and London: Routledge, 2003). Unless otherwise noted page numbers below refer to this volume.

philosophical ontology indeed undergirds any scientific practice. The logical relation between the two arguments is, at the same time, asymmetrical, because the realization that scientific practice is impossible without an ontological commitment does not necessarily entail that the critical realist social ontology must be accepted. Still, there is sufficient evidence that the critical realist social ontology is among the more suitable for social sciences (see also my critical examination of historical materialism, in chapter 5 below). In fact this distinction and clarification is necessary, because some of Lawson's critics, conflating the two arguments, have seemingly assumed that by rejecting Lawson's particular argument they have also rejected the general one. This assumption cannot be accepted. Given the logical priority of the general argument to the particular one, no critic's attempt at rejecting the critical realist ontology can be accepted until the critic has accepted the general argument that scientific practice is indeed impossible without an ontological commitment. If this is accepted, then a productive engagement between the critical realists and their critics would be possible only if the critics enter the critical engagement with an alternative social ontology—the intellectual illumination would be the result of the clash between the two conceptions of social reality and their consequences for scientific practice of production of knowledge. Now, if the critics do not accept the general argument, then they are compelled to put forth an argument as to how a science can be intelligibly practiced without an ontological commitment. To the best of my knowledge the latter argument has not been made by the critics. Now I turn to the general argument.

The general argument hinges on the insight that the scientific practice of the production of knowledge is unavoidably based upon certain ontology even though those engaged in such practice may not be not conscious of it. As

Rom Harré has stated: "To use the concept of a thing it is necessary to assume the existence of one's 'things' even when they are not being observed or detected."[2] This means, given that members of the scientific community, regardless of their ontological commitment, believe (indeed must believe) that what they study is "real" (it would be absurd to claim otherwise), it becomes incumbent upon them to clearly describe the ontology upon which their research program is based. The fact, moreover, that both the social and the natural scientific ontologies presuppose a philosophical ontology, indicates that the scientific practice of the production of knowledge has an indispensable philosophical dimension. A denial of the philosophical dimension of science will not cause this dimension to evaporate into thin air. As Andrew Collier has aptly stated: "... the alternative to philosophy is not no philosophy, but bad philosophy."[3]

Actually, social ontology does much more than underlaboring in social science. Indeed, social ontology, located at the foundation of the social scientific practice, broadly delimits every aspect of the practice of production of knowledge of objects of study. Since it is the nature of the object of study that determines[4] the research methods

---

[2] Rom Harré, *The Philosophies of Science* (Oxford: Oxford University Press,1972) p. 20.
[3] Andrew Collier, *Critical Realism: An Introduction to Roy Bhaskar's Philosophy* (London: Verso, 1994) p. 16.
[4] In this essay the word "determine" is always used in a broad and categorical sense. For example, the statement that it is the nature of the object of study that determines the research methods employed to study it, means that the totality of methods suitable for studying a given object of study are assumed to fall within a category whose boundaries are determined by the nature of object of study in question. Of course the concepts "category" and "nature" here are theoretical concepts and are ultimately grounded in our conception of reality.

employed to study it, and since it is the social ontology (within which the objects of study of the social sciences are embedded) that determines what we consider the nature of the object of study to be, it follows that our social ontology broadly sets the boundary for the types of research methods selected as well. Thus, while one conception of reality may predispose us to take only the perceivable properties of an object of study as an indication of its existence, another conception may orient us to take an object of study as real even if it is not directly perceived or detected (e.g. the magnetic field, social structures, human intelligence, etc.).

One important implication of this for scientific theorizing is that what we take the social reality to be, that is, our social ontology, delimits the manner in which we theorize the objects of study. And now if we add to this the fact that our observations are always theory dependent, it becomes clear that our theories as well as our scientific observations are ultimately ontology-dependent.

It should become clear, given what I have said so far, that *the scientific practice of production of knowledge of reality has an internal conceptual structure*. (I develop this insight in detail in the chapter which follows). Within this conceptual structure, the various components (i.e. ontology, epistemology, theory, and research methods) are not only internally related, but they are also stratified and differentiated in terms of the specific roles they play in the process of production of knowledge. Indeed, given the foundational role of social ontology within the conceptual structure of scientific practice in social science, various research programs, schools of thought, paradigms, etc. could be classified in terms of the ontology that they presuppose.

Currently, in the social sciences, three broadly conceived paradigms could be recognized—paradigms within which social sciences are practiced: positivism, hermeneutics, and critical realism. Each of these paradigms is based upon its own philosophical ontology which grounds its own social ontology, and each has its own criterion of "being" or "reality" of entities or objects of study. For positivism: to be is to be perceived, for hermeneutics: to be is to be meaningful, and for critical realism: to be is to be able to do. While the three paradigms have the same structure and the same structural components, what distinguishes them from one another and, hence, what distinguishes their specific mode of theorizing, their specific pattern of explaining the social phenomena, their specific logic for constructing research techniques, etc., are the differences that exist among their ontologies.

A significant implication emanating from the recognition of the structure of scientific paradigms is that, in every paradigm, the specifically defined components of the structure must be consistent with its ontology. For example, if the shared social ontology of a research community is constituted by atomistic individuals and atomistic groups with no necessary/internal relations among them, then it would be inconsistent to represent these relations that have been presumed not to exist in reality, as logical relations in theory. For scientific theory to do its job properly, the logic employed in thought must represent the logic one assumes to exist in social reality (i.e. the onto-logic).

Therefore, the established peer evaluation of the concrete research projects in terms of the propriety of the manner in which objects of study are theorized, research methods constructed, and data selected, must be expanded to also include the important task of examining the internal consistency of the entire process of production of knowledge. Finding a scientific paradigm internally consistent does not necessarily mean that knowledge produced within it is valid.

What it rather means is that if upon examination a paradigm is found to be internally inconsistent, the paradigm in question must no longer be considered a legitimate conceptual framework for scientific production of knowledge. The point being made here is that genuine evaluation of research projects will not be possible unless the determining role of ontology within the conceptual structure of scientific practice is taken into account. Thus, given the significant role of ontology within the conceptual structure of scientific practice, the description of the social ontology in every research program becomes an important obligation of every scientific community. If this is not done by the scientific community in question (e.g. the mainstream economists), then, the reason/justification for the manner in which the objects of study are theorized, explanations rendered, data selected, etc., would remain ungrounded and, hence, becomes an exercise in conventionalism at best. Thus, Lawson's suggestion that *the discipline of economics must take an ontological turn* is fully understandable and justified.

Lawson's *Reorienting Economics* consists of four parts that include ten essays (chapters), three of which have been previously published. Part I, "The Current Orientation of the Discipline and the Proposed Alternative," contains three chapters. In the first chapter, Lawson argues that the discipline of economics "is not in too healthy a condition." Lawson contends, is that there is "a mismatch" in modern economics between "its method of analysis and the nature of the material it seeks to illuminate." In other words, the mismatch is between the method of "mathematical deductivist modelling" of modern economics and "the social world in which we actually live" (p. xxiii). To correct this situation, that is, to enable the discipline to realize its potentially successful explanatory power, Lawson argues, the modern discipline of economics must turn away from its formalistic method and adopt critical realism as its social ontology.

To arrive at this social ontology, in the second chapter, Lawson starts with the generalized aspects of human actions and raises a transcendental question about the conditions of possibility of these actions. In other words, Lawson asks, how social reality must be constituted in order for the generalized human practices to be possible. Starting with "the intelligibility principle" which states that "all actual practices, whether or not scientific, and whether or not successful on their own terms, have explanations" (p. 33), Lawson answers his transcendental question of constitution of social reality with a cogent transcendental argument—an argument that clearly describes the nature of social reality from a critical realist perspective.

The third chapter of his book provides an extensive review of the critical realist social ontology as a more suitable foundation for the discipline of economics and its theorization. According to Lawson, critical realists take social systems to be inherently structured, stratified, and open, with the possibility of spontaneous closure in social sciences generally absent. Hence, any reliance on methods of mathematical-deductivist theorizing of social phenomena, which presupposes a closed system, is necessarily bound to generate non-viable explanations. This is in addition to the fact that, in every act of mathematical-deductivist theorizing, economists must ignore, contradict, and violate their own atomistic social ontology with which they start their research project, by constructing in their theoretical abstraction a totally different society whose atomistic state of affairs are presumed to be connected by a logical scaffold.

The domain of the theoretical abstraction of modern mainstream economics represents a fictitious world that does not resemble the one that its practitioners begin their research with, let alone illumine the one within which the structures of social relations of production, distribution, and consumption are empirically manifested through unequal distribution of wealth, power, and prestige. The argument for critical realist ontology as a more suitable foundation for the discipline of economics is followed by Lawson's Part II, "Possibilities for Economics," wherein the distinct role of the critical realist social ontology in explaining economic phenomena, in examining the suitability of evolutionary metaphor in economic theorizing, and in identifying the discipline of economics as a distinct social science are explored.

In Part III, "Heterodox Traditions of Modern Economics," Lawson discusses three heterodox schools of thought (i.e. post-Keynesian, institutional, and feminist) in three separate chapters. Lawson defines the term "heterodox," generically, as qualifying "those who systematically oppose a set of doctrines currently held to be true and in some sense fundamental by majority or dominant opinion within a particular community" (p. 165). Specifically, Lawson argues that heterodox economists reject the "fundamental feature" of the orthodox or mainstream economics that the models of "mathematical-deductivist modelling are essential to all serious theorizing" and in doing so, Lawson argues, heterodox economists, "implicitly at least, are taking a view on the nature of social reality" (p. 165). Lawson contends that Keynes himself is involved with ontological considerations and his "ontological commitments are indeed sufficiently similar to those underpinning modern post-Keynesianism" and similar to those "systematized within critical realism" (p. 173).

The institutionalist and feminist heterodox schools of thought, according to Lawson, reject the mainstream project for its a priori and "ungrounded universalising" approach. Lawson examines Thorstein Veblen's theory of institutional economics in the second chapter of Part III. While Lawson clearly distinguishes his critical realist perspective from

Veblen's institutionalism, he nonetheless contends that "in referring to evolutionary method and science, Veblen, in effect, is advancing a thesis that is largely ontological in nature" (p. 185). This ontology specifically, Lawson argues, "is one of non-teleological causal processes, of cumulative causal sequence" (p. 187). Lawson provides a detailed review and analysis of the anti-universalizing position of the feminist standpoint epistemology that figures prominently in the former. Lawson correctly suggests that feminist theorizing must be as reflexive about its ontology as it is about its epistemology. In fact, adoption of the critical realist social ontology as the foundation of feminist theorizing would accomplish at least three tasks for the feminist theorists: (1) it would enable them to retain the epistemological relativism of their insight that peoples' perspectives on society derive from their enduring experiences that are generated by the positions that they occupy in social structures; (2) it prevents their epistemological relativism from slipping into ontological relativism (and, hence, into judgmental relativism[5]) by providing a relational/structural conception of social totality which would explain why certain experiences are generated by certain positions in social structures in the first place; and, (3) it would enable them, by virtue of knowledge generated in #2, to advance their project of emancipation through structural elaboration or transformation.

Finally, the last part of Lawson's book, Part IV, consists of one chapter, "An Explanation of the Mathematising Tendency in Modern Mainstream Economics." Lawson starts the chapter with a question: If the modern mathematizing project of modern mainstream economics has not been successful in shedding light on the world in which we live,

---

[5] *Judgmental relativism* connotes the view that all philosophical perspectives are equally valid.

how can we account for its "rise, and continuing, dominance" of the discipline? To suggest an explanation, Lawson undertakes the development of his earlier thesis. In this thesis, Lawson states that the high esteem in which the Western culture holds the idea of science and its rigorous practice is at least partially responsible for the domination of the modern economics by mathematics. In other words, "it is this culturally based idea of science (or serious study) as necessitating mathematics that drives the mathematising project on in economics" (p. 250). Employing the Darwinian evolutionary model and the natural selection metaphor, with certain insightful changes in the prevailing use of this metaphor, Lawson provides some understanding as to "why the cultural perception of the ubiquitous role of mathematics came to play a bigger role in influencing developments within the economics academy at a certain point in twentieth century" (p. 273).

Insofar as my reading of *Reorienting Economics* is concerned, Lawson has clearly demonstrated that the mathematical-deductivist theorizing of the modern mainstream project makes the project internally contradictory and, hence, unacceptable. This is the case because such theorizing contradicts the methodological individualist social ontology that is presupposed by the practitioners of the mainstream project. Furthermore, if the general argument about the determining role of social ontology within the structure of scientific practice, as presented above, is correct, then, it would seem, the reason for the discipline of economics being in such a disarray, "especially [for] its lack of empirical/explanatory successes combined with the widespread experience of theory/practice inconsistencies" (p. 32), is not merely because of its mathematical-deductivist mode of theorizing. More foundationally, it is because of its false social ontology. Now, if such a conception of reality is false, that is, false in the sense that it does not represent the social reality the way in which it is actually constituted, then the discipline that is founded upon it will not be able to exhibit a genuine explanatory power, no matter what mode of theorizing is adopted—mathematical-deductivist or otherwise. Thus, before opting for a mode of theorizing or thinking about selecting research methods, given the foundational role that social ontology plays in scientific practice of production of knowledge, it is imperative that the discipline of economics gets its social ontology right. This is why, I believe, Lawson's argument, that the discipline of economics should adopt a critical realist social ontology, is a forceful argument.

Chapter One: Morteza Ardebili

MORTEZA ARDEBILI
Chapter Two

The Structure of Scientific Practice:
Toward a Resolution to the Problem of Relativism in Heterodox Economics and Sociology

In opposition to the theoretical, methodological, and pedagogical perspectives of the *orthodox* economics, a *heterodox* movement in economics has emerged. Based upon the belief that "orthodox economics as taught and practiced in the late 20th century has become vapid, exclusionist, and detached from its social and political milieu," and seeking to foster "intellectual pluralism and a sense of collective purpose and strength among" the heterodox economists, the International Confederation of Associations for Pluralism in Economics (ICAPE) was founded in 1993.[1] The movement has been further strengthened by a number of pleas to reform the education and practice of economics from students, with the support of the educators, in Paris, Cambridge, Kansas City, and Massachusetts. The ICAPE's first international conference on "The Future of Heterodox Economics" was held at the University of Missouri-Kansas City, in the summer of 2003.

Given the centrality of the term *pluralism* in name of this new organization, it is important, at the outset, to differentiate the two different senses of pluralism in this

---

[1] Please see, www.econ.tcu.eduleconlicare/main.html

context. On the one hand, pluralism refers to an academic receptiveness that encourages both the proliferation of new ideas and open-minded dialog among the heterodox economists in order to produce an integrated knowledge of the economic institution. On the other hand, pluralism refers to the state of intellectual affairs where plural perspectives exist but dialog among them is neither sought nor sustained because they are seen as incommensurate. Both definitions entail their own specific consequences.

The first definition of pluralism requires a set of agreed-upon epistemic criteria for theory appraisal and a mechanism for integrating the knowledge of economic activities. The second definition of pluralism is embedded in post-positivist philosophy which has also generated the problem and puzzle of relativism. Such a philosophy, as discussed below, would fragment the entire contingent of heterodox economists into separate groups where each group would pursue its own perspective and practice its own methodology. While the first definition would lead to an integrated heterodox community, the second one, entailing the fragmentation of the community, would preserve the hegemony of the orthodox economics.

The purpose of this essay is to discuss 1) the problem of pluralist relativism that the post-positivist philosophy of science has generated; 2) develop a non-relativist structure of scientific practice: a) as a means for comparison and critique of different conceptions of science; b) as a mechanism for generating an integrated knowledge of the objects of study; and c) as a potential framework for an interdisciplinary production of knowledge. Lastly, I shall indicate the tasks of self-clarification the heterodox economists' rival sociological perspectives have yet to undertake. In a subsequent chapter in this volume on the human material condition I shall try to advance the discourse on the scientific underpinnings of economics and social science through a critical examination of historical materialism.

The Need for Philosophical Reflexivity. The post-positivist philosophy of science emerged in opposition to, and through a sustained critique of, the inherent theoretical and philosophical features of positivism. The post-positivist phase is characterized by certain conceptual novelties that have also generated the puzzle of relativism. The post-positivist relativism, combined with the breakdown of the positivist consensus, has given rise to a state of crisis in almost every discipline of social sciences. The crisis is manifested in the genesis of a plurality of diverse theories and methodologies, and of a multiplicity of theoretical and methodological debates, and also in the fact that there is no agreement within the community of the social scientists on the proper mode of conceptualizing, or on a suitable methodology for generating knowledge of the social phenomena. In spite of their common position against positivism and/or the positivist theories (e.g., neoclassicism in economics, functionalism in sociology, behaviorism in psychology and in political science, etc.), there is little reflexivity on the part of the social science community about the fact that their scientific practice is taking place within the post-positivist phase of the philosophy of science.

The presence of philosophical reflexivity would generate awareness in the community about the strengths and the weaknesses of post-positivist theory. Its absence has resulted in the acceptance, and at times the celebration of, the theoretical and methodological pluralism that characterizes the status quo. In short, the positivist consensus in the social sciences has broken down and now three rival conceptions of science prevail: positivism (still dominant in many disciplines of the social sciences), hermeneutics (present during the positivist phase, but reemerged as a legitimate conception of science in the post-positivist phase), and the newly emergent critical realism. In addition to these rival conceptions of science, a plurality of relativist perspectives, such as feminist standpoint epistemology, social constructivism, post-structuralism, and postmodernism, has contributed to the crisis (see Sayer 2000). The three opposing conceptions of science along with the relativist perspectives have, to varying degrees, penetrated and fragmented almost every discipline of the social sciences.

Post-positivism is constituted by a set of interrelated and generally agreed-upon principles that have produced relativism. The post-positivist relativists, standing on the shoulders of such thinkers as Wittgenstein, Hansen, Quine, Feyerabend, Toulmin, Kuhn, and others who have been instrumental in ushering in the post-positivist phase, remain self-righteously committed, each to his own theory, which is thought to form the core philosophical principles of post-positivism itself. The anti-relativists, on the other hand, employing an historical/transcendental rationality, and/or ignoring the principles that are germane to relativism, have concluded that the latter is irrational, contradictory, nonsensical, etc. (e.g., Bhaskar 1978, 1979, 1986; Harris 1992; Norris 1996, 1997; and Sayer 2000). Thus, the problems that relativism has produced remain unresolved. Given the fact that anti-relativists agree that regress to positivism, theory-neutrality, and absolutism are unacceptable, the only way for them to transcend the post-positivist relativism is directly to confront the principles of post-positivism that are responsible for generating the relativist impasse.

The post-positivist philosophy contains three foundational theses. The first and most important thesis is that reality (both natural and social) is non-transparent. According to this thesis, contrary to the positivist notion that we have direct epistemic access to reality (the principle of theory-neutrality), our knowledge of reality is always mediated by a conceptual entity variously labeled as conceptual scheme, frame of reference, a paradigm, etc.[2] On this thesis, the very categories in terms of which we think or pose questions about reality are located within socio-historically produced conceptual entities. The first thesis entails a second one: that observation and experience are theory-laden. These theses together have fixed the significance of the conceptual dimension of science and have established the important distinction between reality and our conception of it. Kuhn added a third thesis (1962). Integrating his predecessors' insights about the conceptual dimension of science and arguing from the history of science, Kuhn reasoned that, contrary to what positivists believed, the development of science and accumulation of knowledge is neither linear nor continuous. Science develops and knowledge accumulates, Kuhn argued, within a series of succeeding *incommensurable paradigms*. That is, discontinuity best characterizes the development of science.

Given the incommensurability thesis—which includes the idea that the criteria of truth, theory-appraisal, rationality, evidentiary support, are all internal to paradigms—and given that there is no Archemedean point outside history from which to compare scientific paradigms, it must follow that the knowledge generated by the incommensurable paradigms is equally acceptable. The *judgmental relativism* entailed in the latter statement is precisely the problem that the post-positivist philosophy of science has generated and this problem must be taken seriously. Judgmental relativism, more specifically, states that if one adopts the theses 1) that the scientific practice of production of knowledge of reality is always mediated by a conceptual framework (ontological and

---

[2] Since these terms refer to the same thing (i.e., conceptual entity), for stylistic reasons, I will use them interchangeably.

epistemological relativity) and 2) that conceptual frameworks are incommensurable (ontological and epistemological relativism), then *it must follow* that 3) the knowledge generated within the incommensurable conceptual frameworks offers no (rational) means of preferring one claim over another, each being equally acceptable.

That thesis 1 plus thesis 2 leads us to thesis 3 becomes the single most important "puzzle" of the post-positivist phase of the philosophy of science. Of course, this is not a puzzle for the relativist social scientists that accept all three theses. It is, rather, a puzzle for the anti-relativists and those who accept the first thesis, or the first two theses, and strongly reject the judgmental relativism that is entailed by the first two theses. In other words, if one does not accept the first two theses, one would have to develop an alternative or revert to the positivist notion of theory neutrality. If one, however, accepts the first two theses, one cannot reject judgmental relativism simply because it leads to "irrationalism" (Bhaskar 1979, 73)—this is precisely the point of the puzzle. Thus, to arrest disciplinary fragmentation, to move the social sciences out of the crisis, and, finally, to pave the way for a conceptually integrated social science, it is critical that the post-positivist puzzle of relativism be resolved.

It is critical to note that the thesis of judgmental relativism is not external to science and scientific judgment; it is at the core of theory-choice, the accumulation of knowledge, and development of science. Given the three incommensurable conceptions of science (e.g., positivist, hermeneutic and realist), does this mean that in every succeeding account of science, the nature of science itself as a distinct set of theoretical and actual practices of production of knowledge is fully replaced by something completely different? If the answer to this question is *yes*, then we must accept the idea that with every new conception of science the definition and nature of science and scientific practice represents a complete break. If so, we cannot talk about the history of science, let alone its continuity and discontinuity. If the answer is *no*, that the definition and nature of scientific practice does not completely change, would it not make sense to ask: what is this thing called science of which different accounts may be given? This question implies that in every conception of science there are two features that must be distinguished: one is the unchanging nature of science and the other is the changing conception of it. But before discussing these two features we should raise the following question: what are *the conditions of possibility and intelligibility* of science as a set of interrelated theoretical and practical endeavors such that these may lead to the production of non-relativist knowledge of reality?

If the intelligibility of objects, practices, or other things is made possible by means of the conceptual categories in terms of which we think of those objects and practices, then, this is a philosophically *transcendental question* to be answered by a transcendental argument. The search for this argument has led me to propose a set of *categories, together with the internal relations among these categories, that constitute the conceptual structure of science*. Furthermore, while these categories and relations constitute the conditions of possibility of the conceptual structure of science, the content of the categories simultaneously constitutes conditions of intelligibility for the scientific community. Thus, I argue that the conceptual structure of science is stable and *inherent* in every historically emergent conception of science (i.e., in every paradigm, conceptual scheme, conceptual framework, etc.), yet the *content* of these categories, by virtue of their location within paradigms, is subject to socio-historical transformation. Moreover, given the internal and necessary relations between the theory and practice of science (and between the theoretical and actual practices of scientists), it follows that, in science,

Diagram 1.

The Structure of Scientific Practice

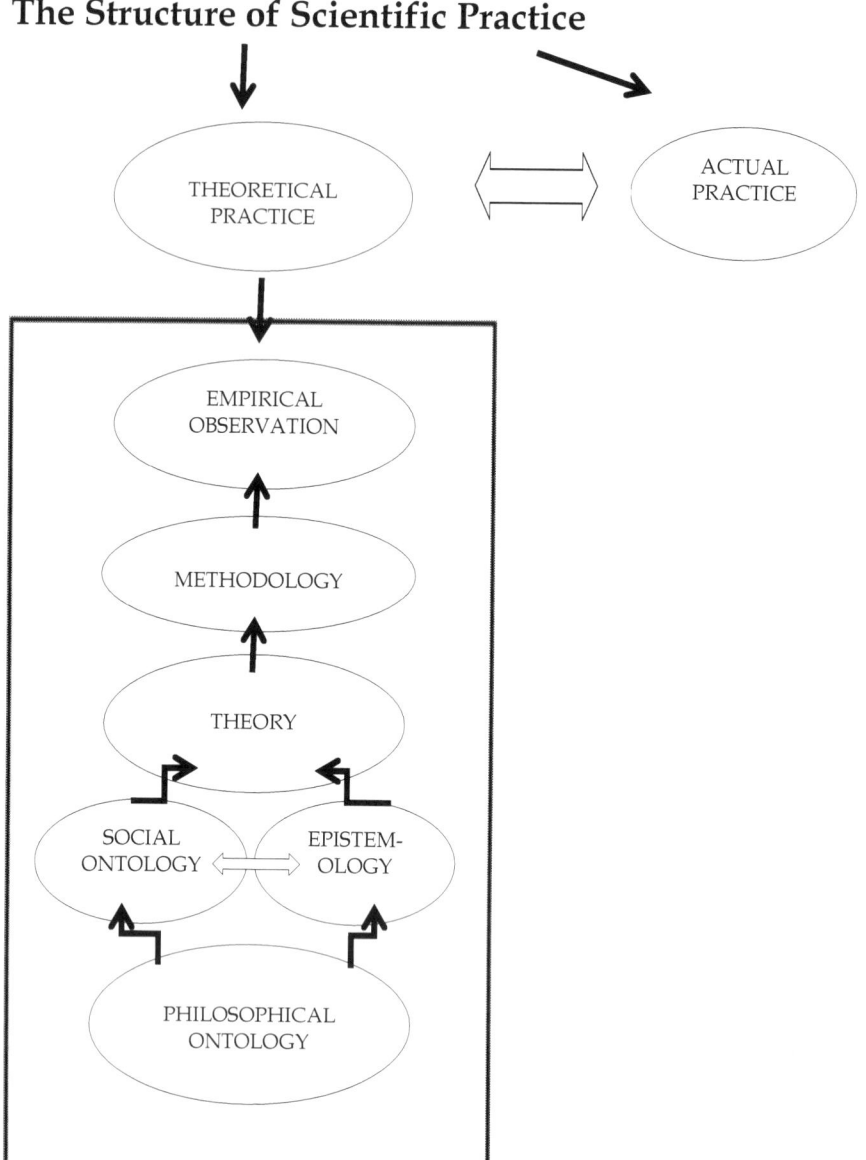

both the conceptual structure is *activity-dependent* and the actual practice of science is *concept-dependent*. I call this mutual dependency the "the dialectic of scientific practice." That is, while it is the conceptual structure of science that makes the scientific practice intelligible, it is the scientific practice that makes the production of knowledge possible. Thus, the structure of scientific practice is an *ideational* but *real* structure (see Bhaskar 1997). It is real because its causal efficacy is manifested through the methodical and intentional activities of production of knowledge of the members of the scientific community. Finally, while the structure and actual practices are mutually dependent (i.e., the dialectic of practice), they are not mutually reducible.

The Structure of Scientific Practice. In order to examine critically the foundations of heterodox economics as well as the rival theories of social science, it is absolutely crucial to understand what I am delineating here as the *Structure of Scientific Practice* (SSP). I take the structure of scientific practice to mean a heuristic philosophical device that can aid in the authentic production of knowledge. Therefore, I now turn to the elucidation of this structure. See **Diagram 1.**

I argue that the conditions of possibility and intelligibility of science presuppose two distinct, mutually irreducible, yet internally connected dimensions of the *conceptual* and *actual*. My primary focus here is on the internal structure of the conceptual dimension of science which I call the structure of scientific practice. The SSP consists of four distinct and vertically constituted categorical strata: the *metatheoretical* (*ontological* and *epistemological*) at the bottom, followed by the *theoretical, methodological and* (at the surface) the *phenomenal* or *empirical*. Within this structure, each layer presupposes the one below it (see Collingwood 1972).

The *Basic* and *Formative Element* of the Structure of Scientific Practice. *I group the ontology and epistemology of scientific practice together under the heading of metatheory,* and see metatheory as the foundational and formative element in the Structure of Scientific Practice. This is for two main reasons. First, ontology and epistemology are inseparably linked, not only as abstract philosophical categories, but also as concrete disciplinary assumptions and criteria. Secondly, as I have argued, since every discipline is identified by its broad object of study ontologically constituted, and since it is the nature of the object of study constituted as such that determines the nature and the possibilities of its investigation, it follows that *the metatheory determines the other levels of the structure I propose* (the *theoretical*, the *methodological* and the *phenomenal*). The metatheory also fundamentally grounds within itself the entire process of scientific practice.

Ontology may be broadly defined as a philosophical description of the nature of reality in general. Embedded in this, is an ontology of the social domain undergirding the social sciences. This consists in a theoretical description of the nature and constitution of social reality. The determinate objects of study (e.g., crime, unemployment, homelessness, etc.) of every social scientific practice (the practice of the production of knowledge) must be grounded in the broader object of study of the social scientific disciplines (i.e., society).

The legitimacy of every discipline, together with the possibility of a meaningful production and accumulation of knowledge within it, is contingent on a clear and shared conception of this object of study by its practitioners. Here, a theoretical description of the social ontological categories becomes necessary and broadly determines how the discipline develops. As Frisby and Sayer have written, "How society is conceived, or even the terms on which it is not conceptualized, crucially affects our conception of how to proceed with sociological analysis and investigation" (Frisby and Sayer 1986, 9). Put more strongly, scientific practice is impossible without an ontological commitment.

Epistemology is the second condition of the possibility of understanding social scientific practice. Its task is to elucidate in what the knowledge of social reality consists. Once we formulate a knowledge-claim about social reality, we must, invoking our epistemological criteria, be able to answer the ineluctable question: how do we know that which we claim to know is the case? Thus, within the SSP, epistemology and ontology go hand in hand.

In the process of production of scientific knowledge, the first step is to introduce a knowledge claim. A knowledge claim could range from a single propositional statement (a single simple hypothesis) to a very elaborate book-long theory. Regardless of their form or length, what all knowledge claims have in common is the fact that they all share two things: one is a claim to know something (an epistemological claim) and the other is the object of the claim itself (an ontological claim).

Scientific practice cannot be sustained without certain ontological assumptions, and neither can it proceed without the specification of certain epistemological criteria. For example, the statement "the revolution in Iran was the result of the country's rapid modernization" is a discursive presentation of a knowledge claim. The author of this statement is claiming that the revolution in Iran was *caused by* the country's rapid modernization (the epistemological claim). In doing so, the author is simultaneously presenting an object for the claim (Iran) to which the phenomenon of modernization has "occurred" (the ontological claim). Before examining the epistemological claim, I want to firmly establish the fact that *in science and scientific practice the epistemological and ontological claims are inseparably linked*, despite the fact that they may be studied separately in the discipline of philosophy.

Similar to the structure of the production of use values, the structure of scientific production also consists of such material categories as raw materials, tools/instruments, and labor. Just as in the production of use values the change in the quantity and quality of the content of these categories do not alter the categories themselves, the same is as true in the production of scientific knowledge. In the same vein, just as in the production of use values the types of the tools/instruments employed in production are determined by the kind of natural resources used as the raw material, the same is true in the production of scientific knowledge. Thus, the structure of scientific practice and it components remain the same in every scientific discipline even though the realities with which they deal are different. In this manner in a discipline like economics or sociology where there are different metatheories (located within different paradigms), the same structure of scientific practice will be in force. Hence, I suggest that *it is the difference in the nature of metatheories, embedded within different paradigms, that make paradigms incommensurable.*

Finally, it is the examination of the metatheoretical dimension of these divergent paradigms that will disclose their strengths and limitations. *A paradigm with a defective metatheory will not generate scientific knowledge.* What I am calling "The Structure of Scientific Practice" is not presented as some sort of master key here. It is not intended to exempt the scholars from creative thinking and tedious work. If anything, it requires more work—work that is more systematic and more rigorous.

SSP *Mid*-Layer #1: *Theory*. Perhaps it will not be an exaggeration to state that there is no consensus among scholars as to what a scientific theory *is* in the social sciences. A cursory review of the theory and method books in the social sciences reveals that the concept "theory" has been defined in different ways by different authors. The diversity in the definition of the concept of theory is not a problem for us at this stage of the argument. Hence, a generic definition of theory will be sufficient for my discussion of *this "middle component" of scientific practice*. But before discussing theory, I should mention that, regardless of what kind of definition is given to the concept "theory," it is basically a knowledge claim and it must be treated as such.

The necessity of the category "theory" for production of scientific knowledge derives from the capacity of the scientists' reason and imagination to generate explanation for the objects of study. But before a scientific theory can generate explanation for its object of study, the latter must be represented in thought. For a scientific theory to do so, however, not only the object of study, but more importantly, the domain that grounds the object of study (i.e. the social ontology) in itself must be assumed to exist; that is, to be real. For it is this domain that determines the existential properties of the objects that are found in that domain, and without a general knowledge of such properties, no genuine theoretical explanation can be formulated. Thus theorization of any object of study presupposes a domain (or domains) of reality (i.e., ontology) whose objects constitute the objects of study of a given scientific community. The reason that, in theorizing an object of study, the question of domain does not usually enter the consciousness of most scientists is because such question is rarely raised in the social sciences. The Humean ontology of the positivists, for example, forbids them to entertain any entity as an object of study other than those that, by virtue of occupying the domain of the "actual" (i.e., occupying time/space), lend themselves to our senses. That is, for an entity to be considered an object of study of a scientist in the first place, that object must be considered "real" in terms of the ontology of the paradigm in question. This is because no scientific community has the license to issue knowledge-claims about the objects that the ontology of the community's paradigm does not consider it to "exist." In addition to the fact that theorizing an object of study is contingent upon the certification of the object as "real" by the ontology of the paradigm in question, the concepts in terms of which the object of study are theorized must derive from (must be rooted in) the ontology of the paradigm as well. This brings out an important point: not only is the observation of the object of study theory-laden, but the theories themselves are also ontology-laden. Ontology grounds the very thesis of observation being theory-laden in science. This means that while the scientists are free to use their imagination to theorize, their theorizing, nevertheless, is both constrained and enabled (i.e., broadly determined) by the ontology of the paradigm within which they operate. Thus, theorizing in science is absolutely impossible outside of a conceptual framework; that is outside of the SSP.

Theorization as a scientific practice includes formation of theoretical concepts and the creation of a certain theoretical syntax among the concepts; the latter (the theoretical syntax) is the manner in which the concepts of the theory are arranged. Since every sociological theory represents in thought a social reality or a segment of it, the concepts of the theory should derive from the reality that has been presupposed by the ontology of the theory in question. If there is a concept within a theory that cannot be accounted for ontologically (that is, the theory does not locate the concept within its ontological domain), then the heavy burden of explanation is on the shoulders of the theoretician to explain why some unreal thing has been invoked to explain something that is real. Many sociologists import concepts into their theories that are not considered real by their ontologies by simply calling those concepts "abstract." It is as if calling a concept abstract would give them the license to change their ontological assumptions as they proceed.

So, the concepts within our theories are essentially located within the reality that is posited by the ontology of our paradigm. What about the other component of theories, namely, their theoretical syntax? Actually, to be more specific, every theory has two theoretical syntaxes: the *synchronic* syntax and the *diachronic* syntax. The former, specified within the ontology of the theory, is a cross-section of reality which represents a spatial arrangement of the theoretical concepts (i.e., a constellation of concepts). The latter, the diachronic syntax, is the theoretical assertion of the movement, and possible transformation of, these concepts over time.

Before moving to a discussion of the methodological level, two important points must be mentioned. First, even the nature of the theoretical syntaxes is determined by the paradigms within which the theories are located. Second, a paradigm may contain a large number of theories that may appear on the surface to be different from one another. The criteria that enable us to determine whether two theories belong to the same or to two different paradigms are the metatheoretical assumptions inherent in the theories. Indeed, it is these criteria that also enable us to categorize the existing theories within the disciplines of economics and sociology.

SSP *Mid*-Layer #2: *Methodology*. In the social sciences generally, and in sociology and economics more specifically, the term *methodology* is often used synonymously with the application of research methods and techniques. *Methodology here, however, as a middle level component of the structure of scientific practice,* is considered primarily as involving a deliberate philosophical discourse on *creation and employment of the research procedures and techniques that are suitable for the investigation of the object of study*. Methodology, then, is not an unreflective application of the existing quantitative or qualitative methods. It consists, rather, in a very detailed process which includes: 1) an examination of the concrete object of study proposed in the theory vis à vis the broad conception of reality that is assumed by the paradigm; 2) an analysis of the epistemological criterion so that a concrete epistemological range could be created. This range will then constitute the perimeter within which specific techniques shall be created for the investigation of the intended object of study; and 3) the creation of a set of techniques which would be capable of translating the *phenomenal/empirical* material into a "language" readable by the theory, but also capable of linking and mediating the two levels of specific theory and general ontology.

It is important to mention that, by virtue of its critical mediating status, methodology has two inseparable dimensions: the conceptual and the practical. The conceptual dimension of methodology—the dimension which includes the paradigmatic logic in terms of which the research techniques are constructed—involves a reflexive determination of the ontological features and epistemological criteria with regard to which the appropriate research techniques must be constructed. Because method incorporates both the features of the ontological domain (which determine the existential properties of the objects of study) and epistemological criteria (which determine the suitability/validity of the method of inquiry), the constructed techniques are grounded within the metatheory of the paradigm. Furthermore, it is the latter determination that is responsible for the idea that theory and methods are related. The conceptual dimension of methodology in every paradigm instructs its research techniques in a specific paradigmatic orientation towards the outside—practical—world. In other words, the actual practice of science is concept-dependent and its theoretical activity is application-dependent.

Surface **SSP** *Layer: the Empirical or Phenomenal. The empirical or phenomenal level is the one that lends itself to our senses both directly and indirectly, and is the surface element of the structure of scientific practice.* By "directly," I mean the direct sensual recording of the phenomena, and by "indirectly," I mean recording of the social phenomena by means of certain instruments or measures. Observing a bird through a binocular and determination of crime rates are two examples of indirect observations. It is important to note, however, that is constituted as "data" or "facts", though they may be empirical or phenomenal, are determined by the theory, which itself is determined by the paradigm in question.

To recapitulate briefly where we stand: in terms of the intellectual history, we are located in the post-positivist period. It is a period which is characterized by a voluminous body of literature which, subjecting positivism to devastating critiques, heralds the death of positivism. But somehow positivism (as a scientific paradigm) has managed to survive. This survival is evidenced by the strong grip that positivism still has on the scientific practices within the social science disciplines. I believe there are three important reasons for the survival of positivism and, until these reasons are simultaneously addressed, positivism will continue to dominate the disciplines of social sciences. These reasons are:

1) The post-positivist attack on positivism has been mainly led by the philosophers; to the extent that the social scientists have drawn from the resources of philosophy to attack positivism in their own disciplines, their attacks have been at best partial; that is, their attack has not aimed at positivism in its totality.

2) The attack on positivism in the social sciences has taken place either in the absence of an alternative paradigm, or from the perspective of a paradigm which has been either underdeveloped or is outright defective.

3) The post-positivist literature itself, despite its numerous valuable insights, has either ramified into dead ends, or has generated philosophical problems that have made the positivist counterattacks more forceful. It is within this intellectual setting that I have approached this project.

To address the crisis in social and economic theory, then, I had to devise a new perspective that could enable me to: 1) remedy the three above-mentioned problems involved in the criticism of positivism, 2) use this new perspective to critique other philosophical paradigms in sociology and economics, and 3) transcend the problems of the post-positivist literature (i.e., relativism, anti-scientism, epistemological nihilism), while incorporating insights into a new perspective.

A new perspective emerges as a combination of a rigorously delimited notion of the Kuhnian paradigm and my transcendental analysis of the structure of scientific practice. Grounding the latter in the former, I present a new concept of paradigm as follows: Paradigms are the broadest incommensurable intellectual totalities within which the structure of scientific practice is located. I present this new conception of paradigm as a means by which the existing paradigms in sociology may be more adequately evaluated. I also propose that the SSP developed here is the structure that the practice of science in every discipline must follow. Indeed, it is the acceptability of the SSP as a transcendental mode of the practice of science that makes the critical evaluation of purportedly scientific paradigms possible. Moreover, it is important to keep the subtle point in mind that while, in my view, the practice of science may vary from one paradigm to another, the structure of this practice does not. Furthermore, I do not necessarily subscribe to Kuhn's idea of the paradigmatic development of science. However, I do not necessarily reject the possibility of such development in one discipline either. Finally, I argue that the multiple paradigms existing in sociology were originally philosophical paradigms whose appropriation by sociologists requires a good deal of both sociological and philosophical attention.

Before going any further, I should distinguish my notion of paradigm from those of two scholars who have employed the concept in their analyses of the social sciences. David Thomas (1979) uses a revised Kuhnian notion of a paradigm in his examination of the status of social science. In his "working definition" of paradigm, he includes what he calls "the metaphysics of a scientific theory (that is, including its ontology) together with the central theoretical statements and concepts of the theory." As he says,

> my rough, working definition makes the notion of paradigm equivalent to the central concepts and ideas of a scientific theory. It would be wrong to include what I have called methodological elements within this notion. For methodology—the principles of scientific reasoning and validation—is not specific to any particular paradigm. (Thomas 1979, 162-63).

Thomas's notion of paradigm does not include epistemology, nor does it include a methodological component which, in my view is in error. Furthermore, Thomas rejects Kuhn's claim that every scientific discipline must have one exclusive paradigm. He says, "I will suggest ... that it is harmful from a scientific point of view for a social science to be dominated by an exclusive paradigm" (Thomas, 163). The problem with a multiplicity of paradigms dominating a discipline is that knowledge will not be cumulative. It is this very condition in sociology that, I maintain, has led to a crisis.

Sociology, A Multiple Paradigm Science by George Ritzer (1980) has employed the concept of paradigm to "reanalyze the status of contemporary sociology" (Ritzer 1980, 2). Ritzer develops his own definition of paradigm as follows:

> A paradigm is a fundamental image of the subject matter within a science. It serves to define what should be studied, what questions should be asked, how they should be asked, and what rules should be followed in interpreting the answers obtained. The paradigm is the broadest unit of consensus within a science and serves to differentiate one scientific community (or sub-community) from another. It subsumes, defines, and interrelates the exemplars, theories, and methods and instruments that exist within it. (Ritzer 1980, 7)

Based upon this definition, Ritzer introduces three paradigms in sociology: "The Social Facts Paradigm," "The Social Definition Paradigm," and "The Social Behavior Paradigm." There are several problems with Ritzer's argument. First, Ritzer's categorization of the sociological theories ignores any specific ontological assumptions that different theories may have. Second, and related to the first problem is the fact that, Ritzer does not present any argumentation justifying his omission of the Kuhnian notion of incommensurability in his definition of paradigm. The direct consequences of these two problems are seen in:

1) the arbitrary and descriptive nature of Ritzer's sociological paradigms: "In my view, the paradigms are nothing more than descriptions of the way sociologists

currently practice their craft. As such, there can be changes by those sociologists who desire to alter the way in which sociology is currently practiced." (Ritzer 1980, 32);

2) the inclusion of contradictory perspectives within a paradigm (e.g., functionalism and the conflict perspectives are located in the social fact paradigm); and

3) the logical fallacy that "the political character of the struggle between paradigms for preeminence within a field" (Ritzer 1980, 15) entails "the irrationality of sociological enterprise" (Ritzer 1980, 32) and that: "[i]rrational factors enter into the emergence of any paradigm."

4) the belief that the competing paradigms can be "bridged," "reconciled," and "simultaneously used."

Another problematic aspect of Ritzer's book is the fact that the methodologies presented in each paradigm are not grounded in their respective paradigms. That is to say, he does not present any argument as to why certain methods are used in a given paradigm. Finally, neither one of the two scholars whose works I have examined here make any mention of the practice of science that I have illustrated in the preceding pages. At this point, the stage is set for my evaluation of the philosophical paradigms undergirding the three sociologies.

In this exercise, I will perform the following operations: 1) I will examine the totality of each paradigm in terms of the SSP (i.e. by examining its metatheory [ontology and epistemology], its theory, its methodology, and its handling of empirical/phenomenal data). This will constitute an immanent critique (i.e., examining the internal consistency and coherence of each paradigm), plus subject each SSP level of the paradigms to a critical philosophical analysis. 2) I will probe to see to what extent a paradigm under examination is capable of accommodating the valuable and plausible insights that other paradigms have generated. 3) I will give a few examples of the scholarly works which instantiate the paradigm in question.

The Positivist Paradigm. Positivism, both as a term and as a philosophy of science, has been a subject of numerous interpretations and criticism. Indeed, controversy "over positivism begins immediately as *positivism* is used, for there are so many different understandings about how the term can and should be used." (Halfpenny 1982, 11). Thus, it is imperative that I make it clear at the outset what my object of study is and how I will study it. In this section, I am not particularly interested in the career of the term *positivism*, nor am I interested in investigating the genealogy of "positivism" as a brand of contemporary philosophy of science. What I am interested in is a critical examination of the positivist paradigm as a totality; a paradigm within the philosophy of science which was constructed by a number of philosophically-minded scientists and mathematicians directly and indirectly associated with the "Vienna Circle." It is my belief that despite the devastating critique of positivism, it has not been conclusively demonstrated that positivism must be abandoned as a philosophical paradigm. I want to elucidate here exactly why it is not ultimately tenable. To do so I will address it from the perspective that I have developed in this essay, namely, the philosophically transcendental notion of SSP. Contrary to the prevailing mode of critique of positivism, according to which certain aspects of positivism, such as theory, confirmation, explanation, laws, etc., are selected and critically examined (e.g., Suppe 1977, Brown 1977, Caldwell 1982), my critique of positivism is structural. Specifically, I show that the problems positivism has generated are perfectly understandable, mainly because its metatheory (that is, its ontology and epistemology) is constructed from two contradictory and irreconcilable philosophical traditions: empiricism and rationalism. Once the untenability of the metatheoretical level of the positivist paradigm is clearly understood, its problematic nature at the other levels of analysis will follow.

The Positivism of the Vienna Circle. As is well-known, the Vienna Circle was originally a discussion group which was formed by a number of scientists and mathematicians of similar philosophical persuasion in 1923. The regular weekly meetings of this group in an institute of Vienna University continued from 1924 to 1936. Over the years the membership in this group consisted of such individuals as Gustav Bergmann, Rudolf Carnap, Herbert Feigl, Philipp Frank, Kurt Gödel, Hans Hahn, Viktor Kraft, Karl Menger, Marcel Natkin, Otto Neurath, Olga Hahn-Neurath, Theodor Radakovic, Moritz Schlick, and Friedrich Waismann. In 1929, the Circle printed its manifesto entitled "The Scientific Conception of the World: Vienna Circle" and organized its first international congress at Prague. Subsequent congresses, propagating the Circle's scientific worldview, were held at Konigsberg, Copenhagen, Prague, Paris, and Cambridge in the 1930s. In 1930 the journal *Erkennitnis*, co-edited by Carnap, Neurath, and Hahn, started its publication and proved to be an important outlet for the ideas of the members of the Circle. In addition to the names of its members, the Appendix to the manifesto contains two categories of names: "those sympathetic to the Vienna Circle" and "leading representatives of the scientific world-conception." The latter category includes Albert Einstein, Bertrand Russell, and Ludwig Wittgenstein. Russell and Wittgenstein had profound intellectual influence on its members.

With death of some members by 1930 and the subsequent rise of Nazism, which forced some members into exile, the Vienna Circle was gradually undone. In 1930 Feigl left for the United States, in 1931 Carnap went to Prague and then to the United States in 1936. In 1934 Hans Hahn died and Neurath fled to the Netherlands. In 1936 Schlick, who conducted the Circle's meetings, was murdered by an insane student; his death brought the Circle's meetings to an end. Under the leadership of Neurath, however, the cooperation of the scattered members produced more congresses and publication until 1939.

The manifesto contains the clearest statement of the aims and objectives of the Vienna Circle:

> We have characterized the scientific world-conception essentially by two features. First it is empiricist and positivist: there is knowledge only from experience, which rests on what is immediately given. This sets the limits for the content of legitimate science. Second, the scientific world-conception is marked by application of certain method, namely, logical analysis. The aim of scientific effort is to reach the goal, unified science, by applying logical analysis to the empirical material. (Neurath 1973, 309)

The preceding paragraph, very clearly, characterizes the Viennese positivists' scientific world-conception as a combination of empiricism, positivism, and logical analysis. Incidentally, it is this combination that has prompted others to call this brand of philosophy "logical positivism" or "logical empiricism." On the empiricist feature, the paragraph unequivocally states that scientific knowledge derives only from sense experience (i.e., that is "immediately given"), and also that the very legitimacy of science is so determined.

What about the "logical analysis" feature? The significance of the logical analysis for the logical positivists is immense. Indeed, logical analysis is an inherent part of the scientific world-conception, since, not only it distinguishes the scientific world-conception from conventional philosophy, but it also enables the logical positivists to comb through the problems of traditional philosophy, separating them into masked or "pseudo" problems and *genuine* problems that could be transformed into "empirical problems" subject "to the judgment of experimental science." Thus, the task of the scientific world-conception as a positivist philosophy "lies in this clarification of problems and assertions" and the method "of this clarification is that of logical analysis." The method of logical analysis that the Viennese logical positivists had integrated into their scientific world-conception was mainly based upon Russell's notion of logical atomism, Whitehead and Russell's *Principia Mathematica* [1925], and Wittgenstein's *Tractatus Logico-Philosophicus (TLP)* [1922]. It was this method of logical analysis that essentially distinguished the Vienna Circle's version of positivism and empiricism from "the earlier version that was more biological-psychological in its orientation."

Logical analysis was presumed by the logical positivists to facilitate their collective efforts to achieve the goal of unified science. This effort consisted in the endeavor "to link and harmonize the achievements of individual investigators in their various fields of science." To do so, however, they had to "search for a neutral system of formulae, for a symbolism freed from the slag of historical languages, and also search for a total system of concepts." Thus, to the logical positivists, achieving the goal of unified science could envision the creation of a neutral unified language of science; a language free from the imprecision and vagueness of the ordinary language; that is, a language with its own unique concepts and its own unique grammar or syntax. This language was none other than the new symbolic logic that had been recently worked out by Whitehead and Russell and employed by Wittgenstein in his *Tractatus*.

Thus, equipped with their empiricism and logical analysis and defining their task as clarification of scientific assertions, the logical positivists drew a "sharp boundary between two kinds of statements," the *scientific* and the *metaphysical*. Scientific statements are the ones whose meanings could be "determined by logical analysis or, more precisely, through reduction to the simplest statements about the empirically given" (Neurath 1973, 306-07). Metaphysical statements, on the other hand, "reveal themselves as empty of meaning if one takes them in the way that metaphysicians intend" (Neurath 1973, 307). For example, the statements "there is God" or "the primary basis of the world is the unconscious" are not considered false, but meaningless, by the logical positivists. "If a metaphysician or theologian wants to retain the usual medium of language, then he must himself realize and bring out clearly that he is giving not description but expression, not theory or communication of knowledge, but poetry or myth" (Neurath 1973, 307). Wittgenstein, echoing Neurath, says: "What we cannot speak about we must pass over in silence" (Wittgenstein [1922] 1988, 74).

Positivism's Metatheory. The history of modern Western epistemology, in a sense, may be characterized as consisting of two opposing perspectives: rationalism and empiricism. A third category may be added which would consist of the philosophical attempts (Kant, Hegel) at reconciling the two. The two polar opposite representatives of rationalism and empiricism are considered to be Descartes (1596-1650) and Hume (1711-1776), respectively. As we saw above, the main tension between these two theories of knowledge, revolves around the argument that whether demonstrable (apodictic) knowledge is generated by the human intellect (reason) or the human senses (experience). In rationalism the products of reason are believed to be certain, and the products of experience, untrustworthy. In empiricism, it is just the other way around. For example, Descartes not only considered intuition and deduction as two fundamental operations of the mind, but they were also capable of eliminating any doubts; hence, arriving at an indubitable truth of his existence a priori and solely through thinking. On the other hand, Hume characterized Descartes's position as "dogmatic rationalism," and asserted that the limits of human reason are very narrow and that the alleged power of the mind to deduce and infer the necessary connections among things was merely based upon habit. Thus, it is clear that the two epistemological traditions of rationalism and empiricism are incommensurable.

If the assumption that every epistemology presupposes an ontology is correct, then, the incommensurability of these two conceptions of epistemology implies that their corresponding conceptions of reality (i.e., their ontologies) are *ipso facto* incommensurable. Hence, the metatheory of any philosophical or scientific paradigm that contains these two incommensurable pairs, would be certainly untenable. This is what I want to demonstrate with regard to the positivist metatheory. If this is successfully demonstrated, then positivism, as the philosophical paradigm undergirding any scientific discipline, must be discarded.

In order to demonstrate the internal contradiction within the positivist metatheory and also to elucidate many of the problems that positivism has encountered during its lifespan, I must present the empiricist and rationalist metatheories in turn. Before doing so, I should mention the important fact that the Viennese positivists were indeed conscious of their empiricist metatheory and in fact in their manifesto they had clearly acknowledged their debt to Hume and other radical empiricists, such as Mach and Avenarius. We cannot say the same thing about their rationalism however. The logic, that the positivists employed in conjunction with their empiricism, is something I will identify as "radical rationalism." This was considered by them as a method or a logical tool of analysis. Nonetheless, in employing that tool, the positivists were smuggling into their analyses certain ontological assumptions and epistemological criteria of which they were apparently unaware. It is the combination of these rationalist assumptions and criteria with those of the empiricism that, I submit, is responsible for the ultimate untenability of the positivist paradigm.

In his *An Enquiry Concerning Human Understanding* [1758], Hume divides "all the perceptions of the mind" into two classes: "ideas" and "impressions." Impressions are all of those perceptions that we receive through our senses. Ideas are of two kinds: simple ideas and complex. Simple ideas are "copies from a precedent feeling or sentiment." Complex ideas are created out of simple ideas by our imagination. Hume maintains that since all of our ideas, even the most complex and compound ones, are ultimately derived from our senses, "we can reasonably hope to remove all disputes, which may arise, concerning their nature and reality" by asking the question that from what impressions the idea in question has derived. For Hume it is this manner of linking the idea to its corresponding impression which determines a proposition's meaning, and truth or falsity.

Hume, furthermore, maintains that all the objects of study are divided into two kinds: relations of ideas and/or matters of fact. The first kind includes geometry, algebra, and arithmetic. The characteristic of these sciences is that the truth of their propositions is intuitively or demonstratively ascertained by the "mere operation of thought, without dependence on what is anywhere existent in the universe."

Matters of fact, on the other hand, are not amenable to the same manner of ascertainment. While the counter-proposition to a true proposition of the aforementioned mathematico-deductive sciences creates a contradiction (a contradiction which would make the counter-proposition false), a counter-proposition to a factual proposition would be possible.

Extending his argument of matters of fact, Hume states: "All reasoning concerning matters of fact seems to be founded on the relations of Cause and Effects." Hume emphasizes that the knowledge of the relations between cause and effect does not arise from reasoning; it arises from experience. It is our experience of "constantly conjoined" particular objects that lead us to infer that one is the cause of the other. If we ask what this inference is based upon, Hume's emphatic answer is: custom or habit. He says, "Without the influence of custom, we should be entirely ignorant of every matter of fact, beyond what is immediately present to the memory and senses." Our experience of a constant conjunction of two events, according to Hume, creates a habit in us to expect one event upon observation of the other. This habit of observing the two events together leads us to a supposition "that there is some connexion between them; some power on the one, by which it infallibly produces the other, and operates with the greatest certainty and strongest necessity." Hence, our belief in a necessary and internal connection between cause and effect, and also in the fact that it is the power inherent in the cause which produces the effect, do not have any foundation in reality; they are figments of our imagination that are formed by our habit. Thus, according to Hume, there is no necessary connection between the objects of reality; what there could be is uniformities or regularities in the appearance of conjoined objects:

> Our ideas, therefore, of necessity and causation arise entirely from the uniformity, observable in the

operations of nature; where similar objects are constantly conjoined together, and the mind is determined by custom to infer the one from the appearance of the other. These two circumstances form the whole of that necessity, which we ascribe to matter. Beyond the constant conjunction of similar objects, and the consequent inference from one to the other, we have no notion of any necessity, or connexion. (Hume 1758, 329)

Now, let me summarize the metatheory (i.e., ontology and epistemology) of Humean empiricism. Reality, according to Hume, consists of separate objects with no internal relations among them. Epistemologically, Hume maintains that these objects are such that their powers, principles of operation, and essences are secrets to us; that is to say, they are unknowable. What are knowable to us are the "superficial qualities of the objects;" the qualities that impressing upon our senses, give us impressions of these objects. What this means is that the possible source of our knowledge is not the object per se, but the appearance of the object. Thus, the point of departure for production of knowledge of empirical reality is the *phenomenal*, our sense data, our experience. Our knowledge of the empirical world, then, consists according to Hume, in the formulation of propositions (i.e., statements) about the constant conjunction of our two impressions, one supposedly of the object *A*, and the other of the object *B*. The epistemological criterion, that is, the criterion which enables us to examine the truth or falsity of the uniformity expressed within the proposition, is the extent to which the proposition corresponds to reality (the reality captured by our senses), i.e. the photocopy or correspondence theory of truth.

A few points should be made clear in passing about the Humean metatheory (I will develop these points later). First, as we saw, our individual understanding of external reality is mediated by our individual impressions. Thus, in order for us to be sure that we are talking about our shared understanding of the same object, we must assume that our individual impressions are not private. That is to say, we must assume that when we observe an object we all "see" the same thing (i.e., we form the same impressions). Second, Hume denies causality, seeing instead a regularity in the constant conjunction of two events. Since Hume denies the existence of internal relations among objects or events, allowing only for the contingent external relations, the question of why two events constantly happen to be seen together, cannot even be raised, let alone answered. Third, given the contingent nature of the objects of Humean ontology, the truth of the empirical propositions cannot be certain. Hume, we should remember, reserves the apodictic truth for the propositions concerning the relations of ideas.

Next I shall turn to the logical positivist notion of "logical analysis." In the preceding pages I said that the reason for the untenability of positivism was its combination of two contradictory metatheories of rationalism and empiricism. The Viennese positivists took Humean empiricist metatheory as a given, and attempted to use symbolic logic as a tool for the analysis and clarification of the scientific discourse (i.e., theories, hypotheses, statements of methodology, etc.). Being interested in scientific discourse and having had already separated scientific from metaphysical statements, the logical positivists attempted to create a language of science which would enable them to analyze scientific statements. This language would primarily consist of two classes of propositions (or statements) and syntax. The two classes of propositions, which would be exhaustive, were formal propositions and factual propositions. Formal propositions, similar to Humean propositions of relations of ideas, were those of logic and mathematics; these propositions are true apriori. Factual propositions are those that are empirically verifiable. The syntax of this language was none other than the modern symbolic logic that was worked out by Russell and had been used by Wittgenstein (a former student of Russell) in his *Tractatus* (Ayer 1959, 10-11). It is precisely this logical syntax, I will argue, that is the locus of tension and contradiction within logical positivism; it is this syntax that smuggles in a radical form of rationalism; and, finally, it is within this syntax that empiricism and rationalism are unjustifiably fused. Let me elaborate on these points in the following order: the rationalism of mathematical logic; the ontological assumption of this rationalism; and the source of the contradiction.

We saw above that the rationalist epistemology, in contradistinction to that of empiricism, emphasizes the centrality of reason in understanding and generating knowledge. In rationalism generally, and in the Cartesian tradition specifically, the power of reason consists in its innate ability to operate upon thought objects methodically, sorting out different propositions, reaching a conclusion that is based upon conceptual necessity. In the mathematical logic and also in symbolic logic that the Viennese positivists employed, conceptual necessity is transformed into a "logical necessity." Based upon the rules of this logic, complex propositions are created out of simple (or elementary) factual propositions; or simple propositions were derived from complex propositions. Stating the significance of symbolic logic, Carnap says, this logic . . .

> . . . consists in the clarification of the statements of empirical science; more specifically, in the decomposition of statements into their parts (concepts), the step by step reduction of concepts to more fundamental concepts and of statements to more fundamental statements. . . . By employing symbolism in logic, inferences acquire a rigor which is otherwise

unobtainable. Inferences are made by means of arithmetical operations on formulae analogous to calculations.... To be sure, material [i.e., the content] considerations guide the course of deduction, but they do not enter into the deduction itself. (Carnap 1959, 136)

What is the epistemological criterion of rationalism? As we mentioned above, for rationalists' truth consists in deductive coherence; That is to say, a theoretical system is true if its component statements, support each other and constitute a single coherent totality. In this totality, every theoretical proposition is considered true by virtue of being a component of the coherent system. In the logic that the Viennese positivists employed, the coherentism of the rationalists was radicalized into logical necessity. In other words, since the propositions are derived from one another, they are true by definition—they are apodictically (even if also trivially) true. Thus, in the view of logical positivism, a theory is a logical structure; to use Wittgenstein's expression, it is a "logical scaffold."

If theory is a totality of logically connected statements, and if theory is also a representation, or as Wittgenstein believed a "picture" of reality, then, what should the reality be like in order for us to be justified in holding up this logical picture? Simply put, what are the ontological assumptions that this rationalism of the logical positivists presupposes? The answer to this question is: The reality that we come to encounter must also be a pre-structured logical totality. What about the furniture of this reality? Well, the furniture of this reality cannot consist of the separate and unconnected objects; that is, our picture of this reality "shows" us that the objects of this reality are internally connected. This conception of reality, as we now see very clearly, is diametrically opposed to the Humean conception of reality, which logical positivists had professedly adopted as their ontology. Now, I shall illustrate the rationalism of the logical positivists by reviewing the "ideal language" that Wittgenstein attempted to create.

Bertrand Russel's "Introduction" to Wittgenstein's *Tractatus*, praises the "breadth and scope and profundity" of the *Tractatus*. He states that the work deserves "to be considered an important event in the philosophical world." Russell also states that in this work, Wittgenstein is "concerned with the conditions which would have to be fulfilled by a logically perfect language . . . ." (Russell [1922] in Wittgenstein 1988, ix). In this work, it should be mentioned, Wittgenstein employs both the logic of the *Principia* and the notions of "atomic" and "molecular" statements that Russell had introduced in his "logical atomism." Now let's take a brief look at Wittgenstein's conception of the ideal scientific language that illustrates the contradiction that I was talking about.

According to the *Tractatus*: The world is the full collection [Gesamtheit] of the facts. These facts are considered *atomic* facts because they are held to be *ontologically* independent of one another. We may make *logical* maps of these facts however. Only in their logical form do they form a *real* picture of this world. A proposition about a complex set of affairs stands in internal relation to the proposition about its constituent parts. The totality of these propositions is the language of logic. Logical research means the investigation of all deductive, inductive, and mathematical regularity. Outside logic all is accident according to the *Tractatus*. In the *TLP* the necessity for one thing to happen because another has happened does not exist. As there is only logical necessity, so there is only a logical impossibility.

The preceding paragraph clearly demonstrates the internal contradictions of the scientific language that the logical positivists were intent to create. It also shows that science starts with a number of atomic propositions (these were also called "protocol statements," "elementary statements," "basic statements," "observational statements," etc.). When these are true, then compound propositions are arrived at via logical derivation. These compound or general statements become the scientific hypotheses about the world that would be subjected to empirical tests. This method of arriving at universal propositions through observational statements is called inductivism, which has been subject to profound criticism (e.g., Popper 1959). Some logical positivists have even denied that their method was inductive (e.g., Ayer 1936). Regardless of whether, in the positivist view, science starts from the empirical observation and logically arrives at the universal scientific theories, or, as latter-day positivists maintained, science starts with a theory and attempts to test the hypotheses derived from the theory by observation, still their paradigm's metatheory is contradictory.

If my argument is correct, then positivism cannot be a tenable philosophical paradigm. What becomes also untenable is similar employment of mathematical logic in social sciences generally, and in sociology and economics more specifically. The untenability of the positivist paradigm, then, is located at its core; namely, its metatheory. Its metatheory consists of a combination of two contradictory conceptions of epistemology (correspondence and coherence) and ontology (i.e., reality as consisting of discrete, granular, atomic, unconnected objects and reality as an internally coherent totality). I believe that it is this contradictory metatheory that is both a source of numerous problems for the positivist paradigm, and is a framework within which these problems could not be satisfactorily solved. I also believe that my critique of positivism will provide a framework within which other criticisms of positivism can be meaningfully grounded.

Now, I shall examine other components of the positivist paradigm (i.e., the theoretical, methodological, and empirical/phenomenal components). In examining these components, it should be mentioned that I will attempt to illustrate the problems that were generated within these components by the problematic positivist metatheory. I will start with the empirical/phenomenal component.

The empirical/phenomenal or surface level within every paradigm is the gateway to the ontological realm. It is always the paradigm in question that determines whether there is a realm beyond the gate; whether the two realms, connected by the gate, are separate or the two are actually one continuous realm with the gate standing as a milestone; and whether or not the realm beyond the gate is knowable. The initial adoption of the Humean ontology forced the logical positivists to stop at the gate, so to speak. That is to say, by asserting that the real is comprised by our impressions of reality (phenomenalism), they collapsed the reality (the ontological level) to our perception of reality (the phenomenal level). This phenomenalism, which posited a flat reality with no ontological depth, however, gave rise to the problem of solipsism: a problem that if the referents of our propositions are our own private impressions, then how can we ascertain that we are talking about the same phenomena when we are engaged in a shared communication. In other words, the phenomenalism of the logical positivists made intersubjective communication (and verification of the scientific propositions) problematic at best. To remedy this problem, some of the positivists suggested to replace the phenomenalism with physicalism, a thesis which would posit the actual existence of physical objects. Physicalism, its proponents argued, not only would provide our impressions with empirical referents, it would also make the intersubjective communication among us possible. The logical positivists extended their notion of physicalism to also include such social scientific disciplines as psychology (Carnap 1959, 165-98) and sociology (Neurath 1973, 319-421). While the introduction of physicalism made the intersubjective communication possible, it did not solve the problems involved in the verification of theories.

Now we turn to the theoretical component of the positivist paradigm. Theories, as we saw above, are an important part of scientific practice in every discipline. The importance of theories for science derives from the fact that they are the means by which science explains the empirical events. It is important to note that as long as a theory remains untested, it is only a knowledge claim; that is, no knowledge has been generated. But once a theory is confirmed, we can say that the event in question has been successfully explained, and we call the explanation knowledge. Thus, theory and explanation in science are directly related.

For the positivists scientific theories consisted of a set of universal statements. Initially, these statements were universal generalizations based upon empirical observation and contained observational terms. Later on, theoretical terms were introduced by definition, and universal laws were formulated by means of theoretical (non-observational) terms (Suppe 1977, 11). The introduction of abstract theoretical terms into explanations becomes necessary because *science includes innumerable non-observational entities that preclude the use of exclusively observational terms in formulation of theories* (e.g., mass, electron, magnetic field, democracy, social class, intelligence, etc.). Given the positivist metatheory, the status of theoretical terms and verification of theories containing theoretical terms became immediately problematic. Let us take a look at the ways in which positivists dealt with this problem.

We saw that the positivist ontology initially posits the surface phenomena as constituting reality, and the positivist epistemology asserts a correspondence of a proposition to the reality so defined as the criterion of its factuality. Initially, the logical positivists considered the theoretical terms as abbreviations or short-hand designations of the phenomenal or observational descriptions. Thus, the meaning of theoretical concepts would be clarified by explicit definition in terms of the phenomenal description. Since logical positivists expressed laws as the relation among theoretical concepts mathematically, they introduced certain rules, called correspondence rules, which would "translate" a combination of observational terms into theoretical concepts. The correspondence rules, therefore, would function as the explicit determinants for the theoretical terms. A version of this, operational definition, was introduced by Percy Bridgman (1927). According to Bridgman: "In general, we mean by any concept nothing more than a set of operations; *the concept is synonymous with the corresponding set of operations*" (Bridgman 1991, 59, emphasis original). All of these elements (i.e., explicit definitions, correspondence rules, and operational definitions) constitute the central logical positivist doctrine of the *verification* theory of meaning: the meaning of a term is constituted by its method of verification. Any concept or proposition that cannot be verified in this manner is rejected as *metaphysical*.

The category of theoretical concepts creates an insurmountable problem for positivism. For, on the one hand, as we saw, scientific laws, as ostensibly universal statements which must hold true without restriction in their application to any time and space, cannot be conceived of without abstract theoretical concepts; on the other hand, theoretical concepts cannot be introduced by fiat; that is, they cannot be introduced if the ontology of the paradigm in question does not consider interrelationships among facts as facts to be real. We have seen that the positivist ontology further cannot accommodate the existence of socio-structural entities which do not lend themselves immediately to our senses. There are two choices for the positivists: If we take the theoretical concepts as an aggregation of sense-data, or to take the latter to which the theoretical concepts are "made" to correspond by the correspondence rules, then, there would be in effect no significant difference between the observational terms and theoretical concepts. Or, if we treat the abstract theoretical terms, which are not observable, as not being synonymous with observational terms, then, what we are doing is that we are positing a layer of reality that underlies that of the empirical, and of which the empirical is only a manifestation.

The result is clear: the positivist distinction between theoretical concepts and observational terms is untenable, and the Humean ontology upon which positivism is based must be abandoned. For both of these reasons the positivist paradigm itself becomes untenable. It is interesting to note that one of the prominent contributors to positivism, Carl Hempel, in one of his latter books (1966), moves toward a different ontology which is diametrically opposed to that of Hume.

> Theories seek to explain those regularities and, generally, to afford a deeper and more accurate understanding of the phenomena in question. To this end, a theory construes those phenomena as manifestations of entities and processes that lie behind or beneath them, as it were. These are assumed to be governed by characteristic theoretical laws, or theoretical principles, by means of which the theory then explains the empirical uniformities . . . . (Hempel 1966, 70)

> We have noted, however, that if science were thus to limit itself to the study of observable phenomena, it would hardly be able to formulate any precise and general explanatory laws at all, whereas

quantitatively precise and comprehensive explanatory principles can be formulated in terms of underlying entities such as molecules, atoms, and subatomic particles. (Hempel 1966, 81)

The positivist problem of verifying the meanings of theoretical concepts is related to the problem of conclusive verification of scientific theories. The positivists' standard method of testing scientific theories is referred to as the "hypothetico-deductive" method. According to this method, a scientific theory is never tested or verified directly; instead, a hypothesis is deduced from it and then the hypothesis is subjected to the empirical test. Thus, potentially innumerable hypotheses (instances) could be deduced from a theory and the tests of the instances would determine whether the theory is true or false. Although initially the positivists had maintained that scientific theories could be conclusively verified by means of observation, it became obvious that no finite amount of observation (because that is all we can have) can conclusively verify a theory. Thus, Carnap (1936) suggested that verification should be replaced with the notion of "gradually increasing confirmation." The notion of a second degree of confirmation not only liberalized (or, more precisely, discarded) the apodictic notion of truth in the positivists' ideal of the conclusive verification of theories, but it also ran into a problem of its own. The main problem with the degree of confirmation was that it could only express the degree of empirical support for the hypothesis; it could not determine its truth or falsity. To remedy this problem, Popper (1959), criticizing induction upon which both notions of verification and confirmation were based, introduced his method of falsification. Popper argued that observations should be used, not to verify or confirm the hypotheses, but to falsify them.

Conclusion. The rationale of my critique has run as follows: every scientific paradigm is undergirded by an abstract philosophical foundation. One important precondition for the development and maturity of every scientific discipline, I believe, is the extent to which the discipline is conscious of the philosophical foundation upon which it is based. It is the underlying philosophical foundation that provides the skeletal support for the scientific discipline in question. If there is a difference between philosophy and science, it is that former provides a foundation upon which many disciplines may be based, the latter may be specific to one discipline. It is the task of the practitioners in one discipline to adapt the general philosophical foundation to their own disciplinary specifications. A critical examination of crisis in a discipline like economics or sociology has two options to follow: 1) critically evaluate the existing disciplinary paradigm(s); or, 2) critically evaluate the underlying philosophical foundations. One might also do both 1 and 2. The real option, in my view, is this latter one, and is what I have attempted in this essay. The first option is not sufficient in itself: it is possible for the underlying philosophical paradigm to be correct, but the discipline's adaptation of it to be incorrect. The second option is necessary because if the foundation is found untenable, then it must be abandoned. The abandonment of the untenable philosophical foundation may make possible the emancipation of not just one, but many, scientific disciplines that were based upon the insupportable paradigm. Finally, the third option becomes relevant when the manifest crisis has occurred in a disciplines such as sociology and heterodox economics with multiple scientific paradigms. It should be mentioned that the second option, namely, the philosophical evaluation of the philosophical paradigms, should be the task of the philosophers of science. What this means is that the philosophers of science should act as the philosophers *for* science by developing certain analytical tools which would enable them not only to develop philosophical paradigms for sciences, but also to critically evaluate the suitability of a given philosophical paradigm for both the social and the natural sciences. The Structure of Scientific Practice, as presented in this essay, is an example of the analytical tools that I have in mind.

Thus, my answer to the question whether there is a future for heterodox economics is that obviously there could be if the first definition of pluralism is adopted and its requirements are addressed. If, as a field, it aspires to be a genuine social science, i.e. to generate an integrated knowledge of the economic activities and institutions and to present itself as a viable alternative to the neoclassical economics, the following steps would be my recommendations for further research and writing in heterodox economics:

1. Develop a philosophical reflexivity; that is, the heterodox economists should be aware of the philosophical presuppositions of their scientific practice of production of knowledge. They should, furthermore, realize that they cannot reject the orthodox economics and at the same time use in their own scientific practice the same philosophical principles upon which the orthodoxy is based.

2. Start the critique of the neoclassical economics with a critique of the positivist/empiricist philosophy within which the latter is grounded.

3. Realize that the anti-orthodox position of the heterodoxy puts the latter within the post-positivist phase of the philosophy of science. This position forces the heterodox economist to address #4 below.

4. Resolve the post-positivist problem of relativism.

5. Make the practice of heterodox economics an interdisciplinary one. This would require collaboration with the other disciplines of the social sciences to develop a transdisciplinary social ontology.

If heterodox economics is able to undertake these steps successfully, it may more fully and adequately cultivate its conception of science.

Bibliography

Ayer, A.J. [1936] 1952. *Language, Truth, and Logic.* Mineola, NY: Dover Publications.
⎯⎯⎯⎯. 1959. *Logical Positivism*. Glencoe, IL: The Free Press.
Bridgman, Percy. [1927] 1991. "The Operational Character of Scientific Concepts" in *The Philosophy of Science*, Richard Boyd, Philip Gasper, and J.D. Trout. Cambridge: The MIT Press.
Carnap, Rudolf. 1959. "The Old and the New Logic," in A.J. Ayer, *Logical Positivism*. Glencoe, IL; The Free Press.
Hempel, Carl. 1966. *Philosophy of Natural Science*. Upper Saddle River, NJ: Prentice-Hall.
Hume, David. 1758. *An Enquiry Concerning the Nature of Human Understanding*. London: A Millar.
Kuhn, Thomas S. 1970. *The Structure of Scientific Revolutions*. Chicago: University of Chicago Press.
Neurath, Otto. 1973. *Empiricism and Sociology*. Dordrecht: Riedel.
Popper, Karl. 1959. *The Logic of Scientific Discovery*. New York and London: Routledge.

Ritzer, George. 1980. *Sociology: A Multi-Paradigm Science.* Boston: Allyn and Bacon.

Suppe, Frederick. 1977. *The Structure of Scientific Theories.* Champaign-Urbana: The University of Illinois Press.

Thomas, David. 1979. *Naturalism and Social Science.* Cambridge: Cambridge University Press.

Wittgenstein, Ludwig. [1922] 1988. *Tractatus Logico-Philosophicus.* New York and London: Routledge.

CURTIS V. SMITH
Chapter Three

Rival Philosophies of Science and the Debates over the Constitution of Society

This essay will introduce, compare, and critique what I take as three rival philosophies of science, namely positivism, hermeneutics, and critical realism. I shall also examine debates about the constitution of society in terms of methodological individualism, methodological collectivism, and agency/structure. I will then take up a discussion of my perspective on the work of Morteza Ardebili, inasmuch as he has developed what I consider to be a viable method for evaluating these three competing philosophies. His heuristic is called the Structure of Scientific Practice (SSP).

Let me begin with some preliminary remarks on philosophy, which is often held to be composed essentially of ontological questions and epistemological questions. *Ontology* involves a theory of being, but *being* may be defined in various ways. The positivist ontology classically asserts that *to be is to be perceived* ("esse est percipi" Berkeley, Hume). The hermeneutic ontology contends that *to be is to be meaningful*. The critical realist ontology holds that *to be is to be able to do*, i.e. the real brings about material consequences. *Epistemology* concerns the nature and grounds of knowledge, such that what we claim to be the case is indeed the case. It deals with understanding the processes by which we can gain a certain degree of confidence about statements made about reality. The positivist epistemology is concerned with facts and how precisely they may validate or invalidate hypotheses about what is.[1] Hermeneutic epistemology offers a coherence theory of truth; if an interpretation is correct, it coheres with the larger universe of meaning. The critical realist epistemology is still debated, but most often it is considered a pragmatic theory of truth, or correspondence theory of truth, while some argue for a convergence of correspondence, coherence, and pragmatics.

An awareness that experience is theory-laden is taken as the one of the key elements of a post-positivist critique of the (positivist) notion that we all observe objects or events in the same way. There are, however, many instances where individuals look consciously at things from different perspectives. Post-positivism argues that how we interpret what we see is theoretically mediated. In fact, humans fail to have immediate access to understand, interpret, and explain what we see. Our understanding is always mediated by a set of concepts and theories. The post-positivist assertions that observation is theory-laden, and more broadly that communities of scientists within each paradigm have their own conception of reality, have led to a dangerous internal relativism. The best example of this surfaces with a few contrarian scientists who resist the anthropomorphic explanation for climate change. If knowledge generated in each paradigm is based on different criteria, and these paradigms are incommensurate, how can it be possible that everyone's knowledge is valid only for its own community of

---

[1] In this essay the positivist paradigm will refer to the logical empiricism, which dominated the philosophy of science from 1932-1962. The most influential authors of this period were Popper, Hempel, Oppenheim, Lakatos, and Hayek in social science.

scholars?[2]

Hermeneutical knowledge is commonly linked with social science since it is not based on a closed system or independent reality as is the more analytic "pure science" positivist paradigm. It occurs in an open system and its interpretative product is based upon previous interpretations. The hermeneutic circle takes into account prejudgments that comprise personal experiences, language, and ideological conceptions.[3] Charles Taylor asserts that we can intersubjectively communicate and share a universe of meaning; the empirical surface may be thin, but hermeneutics is thick and descriptive.[4] The main shortcoming of hermeneutics is that in order for something to be understood, reality is reduced to our meaning, and our language. Agreement on what something is does not mean it is actually what we think it is, especially if opposing groups have opposing understandings of the same social phenomenon. Its most important ontological mistake is that it does not give weight to actual events in reducing them to meaning.

The hermeneutic paradigm is idealist philosophically since society and reality are created in the mind. In trying to come up with correct interpretations, the hermeneutic philosophy loses its ability to explain transformation of meaning over time. Being is reduced to meaning without

---

[2] Margaret Archer, Roy Bhaskar, Alan Collier, Tony Lawson, and Alan Norrie (eds.), *Critical Realism: Essential Readings* (New York: Routledge, 1998) p. x.

[3] Berth Danermark, Mats Ekström, Liselotte Jakobsen, and Jan Ch. Karlsson, *Explaining Society: Critical Realism in the Social Sciences* (New York: Routledge, 2002) pp. 159, 160.

[4] Charles Taylor, "Interpretation and the Sciences of Man," *Philosophy and the Human Sciences: Philosophical Papers 2*. (New York: Cambridge University Press, 1985) p. 35.

addressing the conditions for changes in meaning, such as questions of power and structure. For example, if within a certain cultural norm you acquire also some quality regarded as legitimate outside the paradigmatic interpretation of that norm, you would be discredited. Finally, hermeneutics emphasizes coherence between meaning and interpretation, but theoretically considers only the realm of meaningful events as reality. Hermeneutic social theory is anthropocentric, based upon understanding relations between individuals in a social context. It offers coherence between meaning and reality, but also is open to the charge of epistemological and ontological relativism. Relativism raises serious questions about the legitimacy of science.

British philosopher, Roy Bhaskar, posited a view of science as primarily a concrete, practical, social activity aimed at influencing, transforming, improving, modifying, or manipulating the reality of which it is a part.[5] His critical realism challenges relativism and supports a qualified thesis of naturalism where social structures, unlike natural structures, are activity dependent, concept dependent, and geo-historically specific.[6] The philosophical ontology of critical realism finds that something is real if it can bring about material consequences. Its epistemology favors the production of knowledge structurally homologous to production of things requiring raw materials, means of production, and human labor.

Bhaskar may be regarded as the most influential scientist to provide critical realism with a coherent philosophical language. He inverts Kant's transcendental idealism, where certain categories are innate as to the way

---

[5] Danermark et. al., op. cit., p. 24
[6] William Outhwaite, "Realism in Social Science" in *Critical Realism: Essential Readings,* op. cit., p. 288

humans understand the world, and posits a transcendental *realism*, which implies the basic preconditions for our knowledge of reality are to be found in this reality independent of our seeking knowledge.[7] In other words, reality exists independently of us and can be different from our conception of it. With critical realism, Bhaskar posits a retroductive argument: in order for something to be visibly real it must have parallel invisible ontological characteristics. The core of critical realism consists of switching from epistemology to ontology within philosophy, and within ontology, a switch from events to generative mechanisms.[8]

Specific cases favoring the emancipatory capabilities of critical realism were developed by Margaret Archer, who writes:

> Social reality is unlike any other because of its human constitution. It is different from natural reality whose defining feature is self-subsistence: for its existence does not depend upon us, a fact which is not compromised by our human ability to intervene in the world of nature and change it. . . The nascent "social science" had to confront this entity, society, and deal conceptually with its three unique characteristics.[9]

The unique characteristics of society, as stated in the above paragraph by Margaret Archer, take the analysis a step further and get to the heart of the problem in sociology: understanding the relationship between individual and society. As human agents we are free and constrained at the

---

[7] Danermark, et. al., op. cit. p. 5.
[8] Ibid.
[9] Margaret S. Archer, *Realist Social Theory: The Morphogenetic Approach* (New York: Cambridge University Press, 1995) p. 1.

same time by society as a structure.[10] Our adequacy to theorize about society depends on our ability to recognize and reconcile these two aspects. How we see a social phenomenon not only determines what we think about the event, but also the way we theorize and develop models for elucidating knowledge. The lens selected to view the world determines how we reproduce, elaborate, or transfer ideas to the next generation. In this way every scholar has a bias that they bring to the classroom and to their research.

Critical realism, as the newest form of scientific method, is being used by scholars in the philosophy of social science, ethics, politics, film, literature, and the history of philosophy. It should not be understood as having claims about the nature of *absolute* reality, but rather it is critical of the nature of *actual* reality and of our understanding of social and natural reality. Critical realism holds promise because unlike natural science, social science is value-charged, thus it may challenge material interest groups, and is suspect in its ability to bring useful knowledge to the world.[11] It has been said the most powerful reason for utilizing critical realism is to acquire a framework for rational discussion of ontological questions.[12] The critical realist philosophy abandons the observation and the covering law model of explanation and replaces it with a complex network of theory and observational statements representing generative mechanisms.[13] Critical realists attempt to reconcile ontological realism, epistemology, relativism and judgmental rationality.[14]

---

[10] Ibid., p. 2
[11] Danermark, et. al., op. cit., p. 38
[12] Outhwaite, op. cit., p. 294.
[13] Ibid., p. 292.
[14] Danermark, et. al., op.cit., p. 10

Bhaskar's transcendental realist philosophy generated the following three stratified domains: the *empirical*, with experiential events, direct data, and facts; the *actual*, where events happen regardless of experience; and the *real*, where structures with causal powers and liabilities produce mechanisms that explain events in the actual world.[15] Social phenomena emerge from the deeply underlying real structures, become actual, and then empirical. Positivist and hermeneutical understandings of these social phenomena work in the opposite direction creating an epistemic fallacy. Critical realism looks for deep dimensions where generative mechanisms are to be found.

Natural or social science for the critical realist has two dimensions, which are referred to as the central paradox of science: the *intransitive* and *transitive* dimensions.[16] The intransitive dimension is the underlying structure of reality, which can be used to explain something of known structure. This operates independently of our knowledge, independently of any person's perceptions. The structures and arrangements of society constitute the intransitive objects of social science.[17] The transitive dimension involves our perception of reality, is epistemological, open to socio-historical change, consists of explanatory theory, scientific theory, conditions of conceptualization, ideas, notions of concepts of other interpretations, and is activity dependent.[18]

Debates on the Constitution of Society. If the nature of the constitution of society has something to do with beliefs, it is also necessary to comprehend the social and material

---

[15] Ibid., p. 20.
[16] Ibid., pp. 22, 23.
[17] Ibid., p. 35.
[18] Ibid., p. 35, 36.

preconditions for generating knowledge. The constitution of society is generally conceptualized in three distinct ways. The first consists of seeing society as a series of independent atomistic events with no necessary relations.[19] This conception of social reality in the West reflects the dominant ideology of rugged individualism and is in close alliance with the positivist paradigm. The second view is also framed by the positivist paradigm: to conceptualize society as a group of individuals that share a common culture.[20] Third, society can be conceived as an ensemble of relations where there is a structure with individual agents obligated to interact with a level of pre-determined behavior.[21] Margaret Archer's structure/agency model offers the latest most detailed expression of this concept within the critical realist paradigm, as I shall elaborate this below.

Today, positivism is the dominant paradigm for studying sociology, the physical and biological sciences, political science, and economics. While positivism works effectively to accumulate facts linearly, when it eliminates "the metaphysical," it sacrifices the ability to know what triggers an event, and what the world must be like in order for that event to have occurred. This is not to necessarily presuppose theological or religious causation, but, in contrast to Humean empiricism, which denies the causal nexus, legitimate scientific knowing *does* necessitate locating causal responsibility for an event: causal mechanisms must be theorized.

The positivist paradigm fails at internal consistency

---

[19] Watkins, J. W. N., "Ideal Types and Historical Explanation" in John O'Neil ed., *Modes of Individualism and Collectivism* (London: Heinemann, 1973).
[20] Taylor, op. cit.
[21] Archer, op. cit., p. 1.

when positivist scientific theory asserts there are no necessary relations between objects or events. When its atomistic ontology does not look at real, yet intangible ("metaphysical"), components, it reduces the reality of the positivist paradigm to the empirical. If reality is constituted by atomistic events without relations among them, then relations are exclusively external and contingent as opposed to internal and interconnected. In other words, there are no necessary internal relations, only external contingencies.

Methodological individualism was developed out of the Humean positivist philosophical ontology. This is the notion that theories must be constructed and analyzed in terms of individuals, "of their attitudes, expectations, relations, etc."[22] These actions must be explained by reference to atomistic intentional states or personal attitudes that motivate individual actors. Methodological individualism holds that if you want to generate knowledge about any phenomenon in society you must understand society as comprised of persons principally acting as individuals. Watkins adds critically that the positivist conception of social reality erroneously holds that "no social tendency exists which could not be altered if the individuals concerned both wanted to alter it and possessed the appropriate information."[23]

Maurice Mandelbaum effectively challenged methodological individualism with his advocacy of methodological collectivism in the late 1950s. His contention was that "the actual behavior of specific individuals towards one another is unintelligible unless one views their behavior in terms of their status and roles, and the concepts of status and roles are devoid of meaning unless one interprets them in

---

[22] Popper, Karl, R. *The Poverty of Historicism* (London: Routledge, 1961) p. 72.
[23] Ibid., p. 169.

terms of organization of the society to which the individuals belong."[24] He provided a now classic example of the irreducibility of social action to methodological individualism by describing the context of actual behavior of someone making a withdrawal at the bank and their interaction with the teller. The only way this behavior can be explained is for the rudiments of banking to be understood using concepts that refer to aspects of societal institutions. Mendelbaum posits how parts of society are not individual human beings rather they are specific institutions and other forms of societal organization.[25] He concludes that "We can do no better than to hold to the view that there are societal facts which exercise external constraints over individuals no less than there are facts concerning individual volition which often comes into conflict with these constraints."[26] From Mendelbaum it is clear that methodological individualism is not a valid theory of the constitution of society.

Now let us return to Margaret Archer who reminds us that it is social reality that determines how its explanation is approached. Social ontology serves as a regulator concerning the explanatory methodology because it conceptualizes social reality in a certain way, thus setting the identification of what there is to explain and ruling out explanation about entities or properties that are deemed non-existent.[27] Archer posits that empiricism causes problems for methodological individualism and methodological collectivism because of its ties to Humeian notions that are averse to causality, and the failure of supporting scholars to revise these two original conceptions of reality. She concludes that individuals do not restrict

---

[24] Maurice Mandelbaum, "Societal Facts," *British Journal of Philosophy*, 1957, p. 224
[25] Ibid., p. 231.
[26] Ibid., p. 234
[27] Archer, op.cit., p. 17.

themselves to sense-data because they conceptualize the world in terms of group properties like elections, interest rates, theories, and beliefs which are not simply empirical.[28]

Archer contends that facts about individuals are not any easier to understand than is social organization. The commitment to social atomism, where important things about people are identified independently of social context, creates a descriptive and explanatory problem by precluding *a priori* the possibility of human disposition being the dependent variable in historic explanation.[29] Archer characterizes methodological individualism as an attempt to understand the constitution of society as an aggregate of individuals whose actions can only be explained by a process of dis-aggregation and reduction.[30] Archer emphasizes that social structure is not passive; it is fully capable of conditioning individuals. Archer also criticizes methodological collectivism as denying the role individual human beings have in making up society. In other words, a conflation of structure and agent takes place, which poses severe problems methodologically, since it does not consider it possible to distinguish independently operating individuals possessing autonomous powers.[31]

In the 1980s it was Anthony Giddens who introduced the theory of structuration in *The Constitution of Society*. This was intended to unify methodological individualism and methodological collectivism. Structuration theory is based on a reciprocal interrelationship where structures shape people's practices and those practices in turn constitute and reproduce

---

[28] Ibid., p. 29.
[29] Ibid., p. 35.
[30] Ibid., p. 4.
[31] Danermark, op. cit., p. 179.

structures.³² Giddens thus worked with a totally different concept of structure as rules and resources became recursively implicated in social reproduction. That is, the activities of humans reproduce the conditions that make the activities possible. Giddens ultimately concedes that if social systems do not have structure, they nonetheless exhibit structural properties or principles. Archer criticizes Giddens use of structure and agency as a type of centralized conflation, she terms it *elisionism*, where the duality of individual and society is replaced with a mutualistic societal foundation.³³

Archer proposes a realist social theory in order to move out of this conflation and replaces it with a stratified social reality in which structure, culture and agency all possess emergent social properties and develop relational powers generated out of contingent combinations.³⁴ Her social realism is based upon the guiding methodological principle according to which the properties and powers of agents causally intertwine with structure.³⁵ Crucial emphasis is placed on whether the interplay is constraining or enabling between strata in order to develop causal powers. Archer's social theory transcends Watkins and Mandelbaum, finds much support in Bhaskar, and furnishes internal consistency within ontology, theory, and new methodology. Although still open to debate, Archer arrives at a three-stage epistemology using correspondence, coherence, and pragmatism. That is, knowledge must cohere and correspond with an already existing body of knowledge of the intransitive realm.

---

³² William H. Sewell, "A Theory of Structure: Duality, Agency, and Transformation," *American Journal of Sociology* 98; 1: 1-29, 1992. p. 4.
³³ Margaret S. Archer, *Realist Social Theory: The Morphogenetic Approach*. New York: Cambridge University Press, 1995. p. 60
³⁴ Ibid., p. 193
³⁵ Ibid., p. 15

The Structure of Scientific Practice. If the nature of science changes when we change paradigms, then we cannot consider the history of science, its continuity or discontinuity. If the nature of science does not change when we change paradigms, then we must ask, "What is science?" or to put another way, "What is scientific practice?" In order to better understand the constitution of society, and how it is important for social theorizing, Morteza Ardebili suggests we consider his account of the Structure of Scientific Practice (SSP) as an analytical tool. Ardebili argues that "while it may be a peaceful coexistence, where people agree to disagree, the specter of relativism is clear." Utilizing the SSP offers a way out of a relativist indictment of science and alleviates the confusion that has developed in the wake of so-called Kuhnian relativism.

For Ardebili, the argument is not to negate the ability of the three paradigms to be scientific, but to raise the question: what are the conditions of possibility and intelligibility for the production of knowledge? Two necessary dimensions of science are firstly the practical or actual, and secondly the theoretical or conceptual. It is the theoretical dimension that makes science intelligible.

Ardebili's critical contribution, the SSP, consists of a philosophical strategy composed of six layered categories of analysis: at the uppermost layer, empirical observation, methodology, and theoretical practice; below them on the next layer, epistemology and social ontology; and at the base layer, philosophical ontology. It is the philosophical ontology, or conception of the real, that constitutes our ultimate theoretical level. These six categories of scientific practice examine the preconditions for science in any paradigm. The conceptual categories are highly interrelated, stable, and inherent in all scientific conceptions. Their substantive content determines the intelligibility of science. As science is grounded in social reality, social ontology determines the object of study, and with epistemology guides investigational practice. Combining the object of study with scientific theories determines the methodology, type of data, and type of instruments used. Using the SSP we can undertake an internal critique to discern inconsistencies in any paradigm and thereby discover which paradigm has the most adequate philosophical ontology.

Ardebili contends that all three paradigms, positivism, hermeneutics, and critical realism, are important in generating scientific knowledge and point to the necessary conditions of intelligibility for science. However, the SSP reveals that the positivist paradigm has a core internal inconsistency by virtue of its Humeian ontology coupled with Cartesian epistemology, and cannot, therefore, be of full use in the production of knowledge about social reality. Hermeneutics transcends some of the problems of positivism and leads to new ways of thinking about the realm of meanings, with its thick description, interpretation, culture, and linguistics. Hermeneutics, however, leads to linguistic and conceptual fallacies. If reality is reduced to our meaning of it, and society can change, then as long as our conception of it has not changed, there is supposedly no change in society. The SSP also reveals a critical realist failure to differentiate a type of methodology that unifies both social and natural science, and formulate a way to critique practical social theory.

A major criticism of critical realism is that it is has not resolved the methodological debate for a unifying methodology in the social and natural sciences. The SSP resolves this problem by differentiating a pluralistic technical methodology from a unitary naturalistic methodology. The SSP presupposes that every theory of science must be able to explain its own emergence: It must be general enough to account for hermeneutics and positivism, yet specific enough to account for knowledge from religion. Thus the SSP acknowledges the core of critical realism that reality is separate from our conception of it in the intransitive, adds a hermeneutic that operates in the transitive by including antecedent knowledge while concomitantly transcending the view that "to be is to be meaningful" and shifting toward "to be is to exhibit causal material consequences." In this way the SSP's revised critical realism sustains the hermeneutic advance over positivism, that perception is conceptually mediated. Critical realism of this sort ultimately rejects the 'either-or' approach of theoretical versus empirical, or positivist versus hermeneutic, or quantitative versus qualitative, and favors the 'both and' approach.

In conclusion, this discussion of rival theories of science and the debates about the constitution of social reality is fundamental to our enlightened engagement with social life. Individuals in society raise structures that confine them, and also build systems of thought that deny those structures. A revitalized pluralistic democracy, with protected dissent, can offer intelligent mediation between a society and the individual, knowledge and passion, clarity and obfuscation, hope and doubt. A democratic society depends upon the advancement of science, upon the affirmation it gives to the human ability to reason about objects outside the mind, while recognizing the social and ideological dimension of all knowledge. These rivalries and debates have arisen because human beings are driven by real generative mechanisms to chart their lives and to know.

Chapter Three: Curtis V. Smith

Morteza Ardebili
Chapter Four

Historical Materialism:
A Philosophical Examination

The main objective of this paper is to present Marx's theory of the transformation of the structure of societies over time, i.e. historical materialism,[1] by grounding it in his intellectual framework, or, in what I will call, his philosophical system. If his historical materialism is to be fully comprehended, an understanding of the philosophical dimensions of this system is necessary.

An adequate philosophical analysis of Marx's system requires consideration of three functionally interrelated elements, which need to be understood as organic unity. The

---

[1] Marx himself never called his theory "historical materialism." He called it "historico-philosophical theory" (see Marx's reply to Mikhailovsky [1877], reprinted partly in McLelland (1971, 135-36). In his letter to Kugelmann [1868], Marx states that he is "a materialist" (see McLellend 1971, 135). Despite this, Marxist scholars have used the following expressions to denote what Marx meant by "historico-philosophical theory:" historical materialism; theory of history; philosophy of history; conception of history, etc. My preference is "historical materialism," and I will employ it in my paper to mean what Marx meant by "historico-philosophical theory."

three major elements are: 1) the *metatheoretical* (this itself is divided into *ontology* and *epistemology*); 2) the *methodological*; and, 3) the *theoretical*.

It must be clear from the outset of this essay that its aim is a *critical philosophical* examination and clarification of Marx's historical materialism, rather than any kind of partisan affirmation or denunciation of Marx's ostensible politics. Marx's system was intended to be a *scientific* one, and may well be evaluated utilizing the heuristic perspective I developed in Chapter 2, above, the Structure of Scientific Practice.

Marx's general problematic is how to understand the overall dynamism of historical societies. This is a macro-level sociological problematic to which Marx sought a social scientific answer. I will deal with the nature of his answer in this essay, but first the general problematic should be presented.

In the following passage from Marx note the words *science* and *men*:

> We know only a single science, the science of history. One can look at history from two sides and divide it into the history of nature and the history of men. The two sides are, however, inseparable; the history of nature and the history of men are dependent on each other so long as men exist. The history of nature, called natural science, does not concern us here; but we will have to examine the history of men, since almost the whole ideology amounts either to a distorted conception of this history or to a complete abstraction from it. (Marx, [*The German Ideology* 1845] 1976, 28-29).

Marx's Metatheory. Despite the fact that we find no independent treatment of ontological problems in Marx's corpus, it is, nevertheless, believed that not only was he concerned with the ontological questions since his doctoral dissertation (on the ancient Greek philosophical materialists, Democritus and Leucippus), but his concrete statements are also "[i]n the last instance intended as direct statements about an existent, i.e. they are specifically ontological" (Lukács 1978, 1).

To grasp the importance of ontological questions for Marx, attention should be focused on his evaluation and critique of Feuerbach's contribution to German philosophy. Marx credited him for the turning point that he represented in the process of the dissolution of Hegelian philosophy. This turning point, the so-called Feuerbachian "transformation," was of tremendous ontological significance for Marx. This ontological transformation was what Marx recognized as the very first step in criticizing the speculative philosophy of Hegel. According to Marx scholar, Dirk J. Struik, Marx was particularly aware of Feuerbach's materialist philosophical revolution:

> Feuerbach asserted that the search for truth, in particular for truth in religion, must lead beyond Hegel's abstract "Absolute" to man himself in his relation to nature. But when man is the starting point, then *religion as well as theology is a product of man*, is a reflection of man's state. Using in part Hegel's terminology, he explained how man by the "externalization" of his essential properties of his properties *not as an individual but as a species* (Gattungseigenschaften), creates God and makes Him the Creator of this world. By this externalization God, alien to man, is placed between man as a species and man as an individual entity. Religion is a form of

alienation of man from himself, a self-alienation which destroys his appropriate fulfillment as a "species being" (Gattungswesen) and lets it exist only as an illusion in an imaginary world of God and heaven. (Struik 1964, 16; emphases added)

The Feuerbachian philosophy, its materialist turning-point notwithstanding, ushered in an ontology which, due to certain limitations, Marx held had still to be transcended. It needed to be replaced with an explicitly social ontology.[2] To transcend the Feuerbachian limitations, which will be enumerated momentarily, the new social ontology had to be an ontology *socialized, historicized,* and *concretized*. This ontology is none other than Marx's social ontology.

Feuerbach's philosophy, insofar as it attempted to explain the material human condition, contained a number of defects. The concepts and categories of his ontology: "human," "essence," "human sensuous activity," "nature," etc., remained abstract, uncritical, and ontologically empty and obscure. They become such because, according to Marx, the Feuerbachian categories were "pure, unfalsified Hegelian categories," secularized. Through his critique of Feuerbach, Marx introduced his social ontology with its unique properties mentioned above.

The most remarkable shortcoming of Feuerbachian philosophy, according to Marx, was that it considered man as

---

[2] Social ontology is a branch of general ontology. While the latter is concerned with the question of "existence" in general; the former I take it to mean the specific realm of social existence. It is concerned with the nature, configuration, and historical development of the socially-formed categories that constitute the realm of social being as a whole.

an abstract entity by locating him outside of society in nature. This criticism by Marx should not be interpreted to the effect that nature does not occupy any place in his system. On the contrary, nature for Marx is a vital prerequisite for the existence of both man and society. Put in Marx's own words: "Man *lives* on nature—means that nature is his *body*, with which he must remain in continuous interchange if he is not to die" (Marx [1844] 1964, 112).

What is lacking in Feuerbach's philosophy, Marx believes, is a concept "society" articulated with the concept "nature." Feuerbach omits the former concept because he treats man in abstraction; i.e., in isolation. This abstraction, Marx argues, is a logical entailment of his resolving of the "essence of religion into the essence of man." But this must be rejected; for "the essence of man is no abstraction inherent in each single individual" (Marx and Engels [1845] 1974 "Theses on Feuerbach," 122). Men live in society, and the essence of man in its reality is "the ensemble of the social relations." Thus, not only does Feuerbach fail to see the essence of man in its sociality, but also he "does not see that the religious sentiment" is itself a social product, and that the abstract individual whom he analyzes belongs in reality to a particular form of society" (Marx and Engels [1845] 1974 "Theses on Feuerbach," 122).

Another logical entailment of this Feuerbachian abstraction, according to Marx, is the elimination of the historical quality of social being. In his sixth thesis on Feuerbach Marx formulates his criticism as follows:

> Feuerbach, who does not enter upon a criticism of this real essence is consequently compelled:
> 1. To abstract from the historical process and to define the religious sentiment as something by

itself and to presuppose an abstract—isolated—human individual.

2. Essence, therefore, can be comprehended only as "genus," as an internal, dumb, generality which *naturally* unites the many individuals only in a natural way. (Marx and Engels [1845] 1974, 122).

Having seen the social and historical properties of Marx's ontology, it should be pointed out that the complex realm of social existence, to Marx, is constituted by concrete social categories. But the genesis of social categories and their historical development, according to Marx, presupposes nature with which society constantly interacts through the medium of human labor. It is in the labor process indeed that the nature-imposed conditions of existence (i.e., natural determinations) are confronted for the purpose of production and reproduction of human life.

Labour, then, as the creator of use-values, as useful labour, is a condition of human existence which is independent of all forms of society; it is an eternal natural necessity which mediates the metabolism between man and nature. and therefore human life itself (Marx 1976, 133).

Labor, then, as an act of mediation, is the basic condition of existence, upon which all human life is dependent. But individual labor is an abstraction; it is "an absurdity." It is, to Marx, "as much of an absurdity as is the development of language without individuals living together and talking to each other" (Marx 1973, 84). There is, instead, *social* labor, or socio-historically specific modes of social laboring (i.e., production) whose specificity is determined by historically specific forms of society within which the production process is carried on:

> *Whenever* we speak of production, then, what is meant is *always* production at a definite stage of development—production by social individuals....
>
> All production is appropriation of nature on the part of an individual within and through a specific form of society (Marx, *Grundrisse* 1973, 85 and 87, emphasis added).

Thus production for society is as vital as labor for the individual human being: without production there can be no society. Hence, for Marx, from among the ontologically concrete categories of social being it is the category of production which has an *ontological primacy* over the other social categories. This is the essence of Marx's materialism.

The sociality of production (i.e., the economic category) simply means that production, as a mediating category between society and nature, becomes the site of *a double determination: natural and social.* While the social determination grows out of the natural determination, with the evolution of society this double determination constantly, but gradually, is transformed in favor of *social* determination until it becomes a single determination and purely social. Lukács has seen this very clearly:

> ... the essential tendency in the self-formation of social being consists precisely in that purely natural determinations are replaced by ontological mixtures of naturalness and sociality... and the purely social determinations develop further on this foundation. (Lukács 1978, 9)

Thus, in the social organization of production and reproduction the categories within the realm of social existence obtain a predominantly *social* character, going far beyond the level of mere *biological* maintenance. This means that in the concrete realm of social being, the social organization of production and reproduction, which in essence is an ontological "arrangement" of the social categories with a *definite structure* is, not limited to economic categories alone. This social organization is, rather, limited to an articulated combination of the *economic* and the *extra-economic* categories, which are in a dynamic process of dialectical interaction. The positions of these two sets of complexes of categories vis-à-vis each other within the structure of social existence is such that one is always considered as the *condition of existence* of the other: one cannot exist without the other. It should be pointed out that the constant development of the categories within the structure necessitates a structural *re-arrangement* of the categories at different historical conjunctures. This necessity for a restructuration is a significant symptom of a crisis in the realm of social existence. These historical periods of re-arrangement, or of structural change, are of immense theoretical significance for Marx.

It should be mentioned at this point that the emergence of a necessity for a structural change is itself a structurally conditioned phenomenon. This means that the necessity for change (i.e., crisis) is produced by an uneven historical development of the social categories within the structure of the social totality. It would certainly be an achievement in the Marxist science of social formation if its underlying principles, or *deep structure*, if any, could be known. I will have some suggestions on this below in the section on theory.

The abstract language in which the discussion of Marxian ontology generally, and of his categories specifically, has been presented here should not create an impression that they exist independently of concretely existing human beings. The categories indeed are of forms of being, characteristics of the existence of humans together with their ensemble of concrete social relations. In other words, the dialectical development of the complexes of categories within the realm of social existence is undergirded by the social actions of real persons.

Marx sees the dialectic of social development, not as a series of stages in the development of the Idea, that is, as dialectic of thought, but rather as one generated by the actions of real, concretely existing individuals (Gould 1978, 28).

Epistemology. Every epistemological system has some implicit or explicit ontological assumptions. In this regard Marxian epistemology is no exception. It is a realist epistemology with its own unique social ontology as has been presented above. Since Marxian epistemology stands in contradistinction to the classical theories of knowledge, namely empiricism and rationalism, the analysis of the Marxian theory of knowledge requires a prior discussion of the classical epistemologies. Thus a very brief and schematic presentation of the basic ontological and epistemological postulates of the classical theories of knowledge needs to be given as the follows.

Empiricist theory of knowledge assumes an ontologically given social world which is independent of the knowing subject but it is accessible to him through sense experience. It further assumes that there are regularities in the experiential world whose existence could be established in thought inductively. Thus theory in empiricism is constructed by a set of empirical generalizations based on a systematic observation of facts. The knowledge produced is validated through its epistemological criterion of truth, which will be presented momentarily.

Close scrutiny of the empiricist epistemology shows that, first, the extension of the uncritical ontology of nature to include the complex realm of social existence results in a naive social ontology. Empiricism's implicit social ontology does not give any account whatsoever of the origin, development, transformation. etc., of the complexes of social categories constituting the world of being. Nor does it give us any criterion according to which we could put the social categories in some rank order of ontological significance. All it asserts is that the categories are knowable in their immediacy, that is, as they *appear* to the senses of the knowing subject. Hence, what is not immediately present is unknowable.

Since knowledge is produced by a systematic observation of facts and by empirical generalization and abstraction from the observed facts, the empiricist theory of knowledge, in effect, reduces epistemology to a naive ontology. In other words, it is a psychologistic theory of knowledge that asserts a determination of theory by practice.

Rationalist theory of knowledge assumes the same ontological perspective as the empiricist epistemology: a realm of existence which is independent of human consciousness. But the rationalists, believing in the primacy of reason over experience, argue that the experiential world is never given to us immediately. They further argue that concepts and theories mediate our understanding of the empirical world of existence. Concepts encode the empirical reality and theories put them in a *logical* order. To know reality one has to always start from theory. The rationalist assertion is that the logical structure of theory is analogous to the structure of that part of reality with which the theory is concerned. Thus, knowing the reality becomes synonymous with an understanding of the concepts, together with their logical relationship within the structure of the theory. Hence the rationalist epistemology becomes a logistic epistemology which reduces ontology to epistemology; or, rather, to logic. Put differently, this logistic theory of knowledge implies a determination of practice by theory; since the realm of ontological immediacy is not of intrinsic epistemological value.

Contrary to the classical theories of knowledge, in Marxian epistemology the separate spheres of theory, ontology, methodology, etc., are not reducible to one another. Marxian epistemology is an epistemology, which transcends both empiricism and rationalism, while incorporating some valid elements of both. Marx's criticism of naive empiricism is reflected in his criticism of those economists whom he called vulgar:

> There it will be seen what the philistine's and vulgar economist's *way of looking at things* stem from, namely, from the fact that it is only the direct *form of manifestation* of relations that is reflected in their brains and not their *inner connection*. Incidentally, if the latter were the case, what need would there be of *science*? (Letter from Marx to Engels, 27 June 1867, noted in Marx 1976, 19)

Marx rejected rationalism and its idealist form in Hegel. In his 1844 "Critique of the Hegelian Dialectic and Philosophy as a Whole" (Marx 1964, 170-193), Marx criticized Hegel on the basis of the latter's rationalist idealism. Commenting on "a double error in Hegel," he writes:

> The whole *history of the alienation process* and the whole *process of the retraction* of the alienation are therefore nothing but the *history of the production* of abstract (i.e., absolute) thought—of logical, speculative thought. (Marx [1844] 1964, 175)

And also for Hegel ". . . only mind is the true essence of man, and the true form of mind is thinking mind, the logical, speculative mind" (Marx [1944] 1964, 176).

Marx himself subscribed to an epistemological and ontological realism. Lovell (1980, 22) sums up such realism very clearly:

> It makes assertions about the nature of the real world, and these assertions have consequences for the manner in which that world may be known. . . . It does not identify the real with what can be experienced [i.e., the appearance], but as a multi-layered structure, consisting of entities and processes lying at different levels of that structure, including the surface level of the empirical world. The empirical world with which we are familiar is causally connected to ontological levels, and it is by virtue of these causal connections that we can use sense-data, experience and observation in constructing knowledge of the structure and processes of the real. These causal connections cannot themselves be understood through experience, because neither the underlying structures not the connection between these structures and the empirical world are themselves experienced. The connection can only be reconstructed in knowledge [i.e., in thought]. (Lovell 1980, 22, emphasis and insertions are mine)

The deepest ontological level in the Marxian system, which is causally connected with other structural levels, is only given mediately. This deep structure and the elements within this structure are given theoretically. The *theory* which allows us to know this deep ontological structure through the concrete categories of social existence is historical materialism, or what Marx called "historico-philosophical theory" (McLelland 1971, 136). This theory, as we will see in my section below on theory, is a trans-historical entity.

In the section on Marxian ontology I showed that for Marx the concrete categories constituting the realm of social being undergo a historical process of development and change. Furthermore, an understanding of these categories is possible only insofar as they are studied within the historically specific social structure that they constitute.

We also saw that the constant uneven development of the concrete social categories within their respective structure necessitates a re-arrangement of the categories (i.e., a restructuration) at different historical conjunctures. Thus, over history, we observe the emergence of a social structure; its development; its restructuration or transformation into a new structure, and so forth. In other words, over history we observe a series of different social structures; one adjacent to the next.

Now, while historical materialism asserts within its own theoretical immanence *the general conditions* under which the transformation of the structure of a social formation becomes possible, or even inevitable, it does not assert anything *a priori* concerning the onto-logic according to which the social categories develop and interact with one another. Marx called this onto-logic the *law of motion* which must be discovered separately for each historical social formation. In the three volumes of *Capital*, especially in the third one, Marx presents the laws of motion of the capitalist social formations.

Marxian epistemology has a clear linkage to its ontology, and neither is reducible to the other. This is a necessary precondition for the production of scientific knowledge. This linkage is provided by the Marxian methodology to which we will turn in the next section.

Before we end our discussion of the Marxian epistemology, however, we should note the nature and the place of the standard of validity in this epistemology. The classical theories of knowledge, as we saw, posit their criterion of validity within their epistemological immanence in *a priori* fashion. Furthermore, since the criterion of validity itself is considered to be trans-historical, once validated, the validity of the proposition is considered to be timeless. But the epistemological cost of retaining this criterion of validity to the classical theories of knowledge, as we saw, is almost unbearable. Contrary to the classical theories of knowledge, in Marxian epistemology, the theoretically produced knowledge (i.e., its propositions) must be validated with respect to the specific structure to which they existentially refer. Now, given the multiplicity of the social structures in history, the truth of a given proposition becomes socio-historically relative. This Marxian criterion of truth has raised the problem of relativism. Relativism is not a new concept; it is a dead-end alley with which every historicist system of thought has confronted: "if the statement of relativism is true, then its truth is only relative" (Benton 1977, 139).

Nonetheless I believe relativism is *not* a serious problem for Marxian epistemology. I suggest the following simple solutions to the problem: despite the fact that the truth of our knowledge of the historical social formations is relative, the relativism is transcended once we ground the relativity of the truth of our knowledge in a theory (i.e., historical materialism) which itself is trans-historical. This means that once we find out *why*, as a general rule, our knowledge of social formations located in different historical epochs is relative, then, the relativity of the truth of our knowledge ceases to remain so. An example borrowed from physical science may make this assertion clearer. Suppose that our knowledge of the behavior of a given gas at four different temperature ranges has been presented by four separate formulas. Given the fact that the truth or validity of each of these formulas is determined by the temperature range to which the given formula refers, we can say, then, that our knowledge of the four temperature ranges is but relative. This, I accept, is quite true. But under one condition this relativism is transcended: when we come up with a general formula (i.e., the kinetic theory of gases) which, dissolving the four formulas in itself, allows us to know why those formulas explained, the behavior of the given gas at four different temperature ranges, exactly the way they did.

Methodology. In the Marxian philosophical system, as I mentioned above, methodology is the linkage between the ontologically concrete reality and epistemology. We also saw that the concrete social reality, having an *independent* existence apart from thought, could be known only through a theoretical mediation. The central function of methodology, as was elaborated by Marx in the "Introduction" to the *Grundrisse* is to arrive at an understanding of the *concrete* social totality by means of *abstractions* (Marx, "The Method of Political Economy," *Grundrisse* 1973, 100). The point of departure is always an abstraction from our initial chaotic conception of a whole. Such an abstraction, it must be stressed, is an independently existing element within the social totality itself (the many quantatitative or qualitative characteristics of the population, for example, isolated and abstracted from the totality of relations and determinations within which the category in question is concretely located).

It becomes the task of scholarship, science, and theory to penetrate into the abstractly given elements of the totality going deeper and deeper, by means of further abstraction, and by peeling off the different layers until we arrive at "the simplest determinations." Once the simplest determinations are established in thought, the journey has to be retraced until we arrive back where we had started: the abstract totality. But the totality at which we arrive, is totally different from the first one; because in the second one is now a "rich totality of many determinations and relations" which may legitimately be called *real knowledge*. As Marx characterizes the process:

> The concrete is concrete because it is the concentration of many determinations, hence unity of the diverse. It appears in the process of thinking, therefore, as a process of concentration, as a result, not as a point of departure, even though it is the point of departure in reality and hence also the point of departure for observation and conception. Along the first path the full conception was evaporated to yield an abstract determination; along the second, the abstract determinations lead towards a reproduction of the concrete by way of thought. (Marx 1973, 101).

We must avoid, incidentally, confusing our theoretical knowledge of the concrete totality with the concrete totality itself which exists independently of our knowledge of it. Marx is very clear on this point:

> The totality as it appears in the head, as a totality of thoughts, is a product of a thinking head, which appropriates the world in the only way it can . . . . The real subject retains its autonomous existence outside the head just as before . . . . (Marx 1973, 101-102).

An important point must be made here. *The theory which penetrates into the concrete totality presented in thought is none other than historical materialism.* The theory, as we saw in Marx, penetrates so deeply that it finally reaches the "simplest determinations." We must note that a category links society to nature and contains both natural and social determinations in their simplest and most essential form. This category is the category of *labor*, more concretely, of *production*.

> Labour seems a quite simple category. The conception of labour *in this general form*—as labour as such—is also immeasurably old. Nevertheless, when it is economically conceived in this simplicity, "labour" is as modern a category as are the relations which create this simple *abstraction*. (Marx 1973, 103, emphases added).

These simplest determinations are all located, within a given structure, at the level, which we called the "deep-structure" of the social formation. This deep-structure has an ontological primacy over other categories within the realm of social existence. Hence we must now turn to a discussion of the central component of Marx's philosophical system: historical materialism.

Theory. Historical materialism, or historico-philosophical theory as Marx himself called it, occupies a prominent position in the Marxian philosophical system. Both Marx and Engels believed it to be a theory capable of producing real knowledge on which science could be erected. Engels, moreover, in the "Preface to the Third German Edition" of *The Eighteenth Brumaire of Louis Bonaparte*, goes so far as to compare its significance to the "law of the transformation of energy" in natural science. The most scientific characteristic of this theory, to which Marxists and non-Marxists alike have rarely paid an attention, is its trans-historicity or supra-historicity. The trans-historicity of a theory, assuming other conditions are present, elevates the theory to a scientific level on the one hand, but it also puts a heavy burden on the theory of explaining different phenomena falling within its alleged domain on the other. In this regard, historical materialism is no exception: it must be capable of explaining, by means of its concepts, their relationships, and definitions, etc. the transformation of structures into different social formations.

The most systematic and compact presentation of historical materialism can be found in Marx's famous "Preface" to *A Contribution to the Critique of Political Economy*:

> In the social production of their existence, men inevitably enter into definite relations, which are independent of their will, namely relations of production appropriate [i.e., corresponding] to a given stage in the development of their material forces of production. The *totality* of these *relations of production* constitutes the economic structure of society, the real foundation, on which arises a legal and political *superstructure* and to which correspond definite forms of social consciousness. The mode of production of material life conditions the general process of social, political and intellectual life. It is not the consciousness of men that determines their existence, but their social existence that determines their consciousness. At a certain stage of development, the *material productive forces* of society come into conflict with the existing relations of production or—this merely expresses the same thing in legal terms—with the *property relations* within the framework of which they have operated hitherto. From forms of development of the productive forces these relations turn into their fetters. Then begins an era of social revolution. The changes in the economic foundation lead sooner or later to the transformation of the whole immense superstructure. In studying such transformations it is always necessary to distinguish between the material transformation of the economic conditions of production, which can be determined with the precision of natural science, and

the legal, political, religious, artistic or philosophic—in short, ideological forms in which men become conscious of this *conflict and fight it out.* Just as one does not judge an individual by what he thinks about himself, so one cannot judge such a period of transformation by its consciousness, but, on the contrary, this consciousness *must be explained* from the contradictions of material life, from the conflict existing between the social forces of production and the relations of *production.* No social order is ever destroyed before all the productive forces for which it is sufficient [i.e., there is room in it] have been developed, and new superior [i.e., higher] relations of production never replace older ones before the material conditions for their existence have matured within the framework of the old society. Mankind thus inevitably sets itself only such tasks as it is able to solve, since closer examination will always show that the problem itself arises only when the material conditions for its solution are already present or at least in the course of formation. In broad outline, the Asiatic, ancient, feudal and modern bourgeois modes of production may be designated as epochs marking progress in the economic development of society. The bourgeois mode of production is the last antagonistic form of the social process of production—antagonistic not in the sense of individual antagonism but of an antagonism that emanates from the individuals' social conditions of existence—but the productive *forces developing within bourgeois* society create also the material conditions for a solution of this antagonism. The prehistory of human society accordingly closes with this social formation. (Marx 1970, 20-22, emphases and insertions added)

The "Preface" should be understood as a general and

theoretical presentation of Marx's theory of the transformation of the social formations. What distinguishes one social formation from another is, to Marx, their specific *modes of production*. The modes of production of social formations, it should be stressed, are not given to us immediately; they have to be determined theoretically. Such a theoretical determination of the modes of production involves an understanding of the concepts, definitions, postulates, etc. of the theory which purports such an undertaking. Before we begin an analysis of the concepts of the theory we should give a preliminary definition of the concept "mode of production."

The concept *mode of production* could be defined as the social relations of production and the corresponding social "form" of the constitution of the *material* forces of production. Indeed, one of the most remarkable reasons for the existence of the technological determinist mode of interpretation of Marx is the failure of those who subscribe to it to grasp the distinction that Marx makes between material forces of production and the *social form* within which they are constituted. Such erroneous technological determinist positions, with varying degrees of sophistication, are found specifically found in the work of the following authors: Cohen, 1978; Shaw, 1978, and McMurtry, 1978.[3] This mode of interpreting Marx has been one of the major reasons for social theorists to reject historical materialism as a viable social theory. Actually, one of the main objectives of this essay has been a formulation, in general terms, of an alternative interpretation of the historical materialism that would transcend the deficiencies of this misrepresentation of historical materialism. The main defects of such presentations, according to Levine and Wright (1980, 48), are the following:

---

[3] One of the main defects of the technological determinist mode of interpreting Marx is that the concept "reproduction" is never even mentioned; see specifically Cohen (1978) and Shaw (1978).

they accord the primacy to productive *forces* over production *relations* and over the legal and political superstructures; they imply a mechanistic politics, and a denial of class struggle.

It should be remembered that, as we saw in the previous section, every social formation, for Marx, is a concrete dynamic totality. This totality is analytically divided into two spheres of economic base (i.e., production) and an extra-economic super-structure (i.e. the sphere of societal reproduction). The economic base, Marx tells us, conditions the sphere of reproduction; and the sphere of reproduction transforms almost everything, including the economic base.

> The act of reproduction itself changes not only the objective conditions . . . , but the producers change with it, by the emergence of new qualities, by transforming and developing themselves in production, forming new powers and new conceptions, new modes of intercourse, new needs, and new speech. (Marx 1965, 93, emphasis added)

Thus, not only the two spheres of production and reproduction correspond to each other, they also interact and change one another. Marx also informs us that relations of production correspond to "a given stage in the development of their material forces of production." Now, if we construe "a given stage" as an "historical epoch," then we will acknowledge that every historical epoch has its own appropriate relations of production. Furthermore, given that at "a certain stage of development, the material productive forces of society come into conflict with the existing relations of production" and then "begins an era of social revolution," it would be *incorrect* to assume that a conflict between the forces and the relations of production always existed throughout the life of the social formation in question. Such an assumption would blind us to the importance of the relations of production for the development of both the material forces of production and the social formation as a whole up to the point of *crisis*.

Marx does not give us a list of the forces of production; but the material characteristics, or the basic classes, of these forces are given. In our discussion of Marx's social ontology we saw that every system of production is doubly determined: naturally and socially. Natural determination involves relations between the producers and nature which Marx terms the *labor process*. The labor process is regarded by Marx as a "process independently of any specific social formation" (1976, 283). This process represents a combination of the following elements: purposeful activity, that is work itself; the object on which that work is performed; and the instruments of that work (1976, 284).

I call the *combination* of these three elements the natural or material determination of every labor process. By such determination I mean that it is *impossible* to produce a material use-value of any kind without combining *all* three of the aforementioned elements.

Marx uses two different adjectives—*material* and *social* to describe the forces of production. It is the material forces of production whose "given stage [i.e., the historical epoch] of development" corresponds to the social relations of production. Toward the end of the lengthy text quoted from the "Preface" Marx employs the adjective *social* before productive forces: "from the existing conflict between the social productive forces and the relations of production . . . ."

What Marx was attempting to construct was a theory that would articulate the nature of the *social forces* within which the *material forces* of production develop over history.
The *social form* within which the material forces of

production develop includes *the mode of distribution* and the *class structure* of society. Depending upon different modes of distribution of the elements of production there could be different social forms, thus, different class structures. The concept "mode of production" can be defined as a *unity* of the class structure and its *corresponding social relations of production*.

The concept "social relations of production" theoretically speaking forms a unity with the concept "class structure." It should be mentioned at this point that both the class structure and the social relations of production of a society are socially determined. This social determination, as we saw, stems from the natural determination of production.

The totality of the social relations of production is an all-embracing entity. In their totality, the social relations of production constitute society; that is, they constitute both the economic base (i.e., production) and the extra economic superstructure (i.e., reproduction). The two spheres correspond in their constitution. The reproduction function of the superstructure throughout the life of the social formation has been underestimated to say the least.

Within the sphere of *reproduction* (i.e., the superstructure), *property relations* define the relations of production, distribution, and consumption, the relationships human beings enter into among themselves in the process of reproducing their human life. The property relations, within the superstructure, give rise to *the legal codification* of what may be termed ownership relations. Now the social relations of production and the class structure of society form a *unity* in the sense that both essentially involve the same thing: the distribution of the means of consumption.

The capitalist mode of production, for example, rests on the fact that the material conditions of production are in the hands of non-workers in the form of property in capital and land, while the masses are only owners of the personal condition of production, labor power. Once the ownership of the elements of production are so distributed, then the present-day distribution of the means of consumption follows.

If the material conditions of production were the co-operative property of the workers themselves, then this could likewise result in a different distribution of the means of consumption from the present one. The mode of distribution (i.e., who gets what and how much), in other words, is a product of the class structure of society.

> The structure of distribution is completely determined by the structure of production. Distribution is itself a product of production, not only in its object, in that only the results of production can be distributed, but also in its form, in that the specific kind of participation in production determines the specific forms of distribution, i.e., the pattern of participation in distribution. (Marx 1973, 95).

But both "the pattern of participation in distribution" and the mode of distribution must be guaranteed and constantly reproduced if society is to persist over time. This guarantee is provided by the laws of the society in question.

> *Distribution* steps between the procedures and the products, hence between production and consumption, to determine in accordance with social laws what the producer's share will be in the world of products. (Marx 1973, 94)

Thus, we observe that distribution is a link between the two spheres of production and reproduction. In order for the former sphere to function properly, the latter sphere must constantly reproduce its condition of existence. The essential condition of existence of the social production of a determinate social formation is that its class structure (i.e., the social form within which the material forces of production develop) must be constantly reproduced. Reproduction of the class structure of a class society means a constant political and ideological reproduction of the position of the dominant class vis-à-vis the subordinate classes in a given society. The ideological reproduction of the position of the ruling class in society is principally aimed at the reproduction of the historically specific social relations of production upon which the very existence of the ruling class depends.

> The ideas of the ruling class are in every epoch the ruling ideas, i.e., the class which is the ruling *material* force of society is at the same time its ruling *intellectual* force. ...The ruling ideas are nothing more than the ideal expression of the dominant material relationships, the dominant material relationships grasped as ideas. ...The individuals composing the ruling class possess among other things consciousness, and therefore think. ...(H)ence among other things rule also as thinkers, as producers of ideas, and regulate the production and distribution of the ideas of their age: thus their ideas are the ruling ideas of the epoch. (Marx and Engels 1974, 67).

The political reproduction of the position of the ruling class in the society, according to Marx, is mainly rendered by the state.

> Since the State is the form in which the individuals of a ruling class assert their common interests, and in which the whole civil society of an epoch is epitomized, it follows that the State mediates in the formation of all common institutions and that

the institutions receive a political form. Hence the illusion that law is based on the will, and indeed on the will divorced from its real basis—on *free* will. Similarly, justice is in its turn reduced to the actual laws. (Marx and Engels 1974, 80).

That the unity of the social relations of production and the class structure of the society is a necessary precondition for the development of the society has become clear to us. Now, were the development of the society to come to a halt, its structure would start to transform itself, the epoch of social revolution would begin; unity would slip into disunity. From this moment on every act or cycle of distribution, instead of contributing to the development of the society, contributes towards its disintegration—hence toward the transformation of the structure of the social formation as a whole.

The cause of this disunity, or this rupture if you will, between the class structure of the society and its corresponding social relations of production is considered by Marx to be rooted in emergent class struggles. Given the level of the development of the material forces of production and the needs that they have produced over time, class struggles will occur because it becomes impossible for the subordinate classes to survive within the existing class structure. Thus, while the development of the material forces of production as the fundamental determining factors rest at *the deep structure* of society, socio-economically speaking, the *class struggle* is considered by Marx, to be the determinant of social change.

The designation of the class struggle as the "motor" of social change, in the manner that we have done here following Marx, provides a theoretical-practical space for a consideration of one of the most important aspects of the historical materialism, namely, revolutionary political practice. The class struggle, from an epistemological standpoint, becomes a concrete point of departure for historical materialism to analyze the transformation of the structure of the social formation in question.

A class struggle or a social revolution, it should be pointed out, however, does not take place simply and suddenly. These are rather the products of an accumulated contradiction of the social reproduction process (both political and ideological) obstructing the proper reproduction of the existing class structure. Althusser has a similar idea of the class struggle which he terms "overdetermination."

The importance of the concept of overdetermination for the historical materialism is that it illustrates the mutually determining role of the economic base and the extra-economic superstructure. We are fully aware of the role of economic base in conditioning the super-structure. What is less well known is Marx's conception of the influence of other things on material production.

> Man himself is the basis of his material production, as of any other production that he carries on. All circumstances, therefore, which affect man, the *subject* of production, more or less modify all his functions and activities, and therefore too his functions and activities as the creator of material wealth . . . . In this respect it can in fact be shown that *all* human relations and functions, however and in whatever form they may appear, influence material production and have a more or less decisive influence upon it. (Marx 1963a, 288)

In conclusion, I have argued the following points: historical materialism, as a trans-historical theory, constitutes the theoretical element of Marx's philosophical system. Historical materialism asserts the following: the class structure of a social formation is the "form" within which the material forces of production develop; class struggle can explain social change; class struggle is an overdetermined phenomenon; there is a mutual determination between the base (i.e., production) and the superstructure (i.e., reproduction). There is a coherent philosophical system in Marx consisting of meta-theoretical, methodological, and theoretical elements. Marx's social ontology is one in which the categories of being are social, historical and concrete. In the Marxian social ontology the category of production has an ontological primacy over other categories. Marxian epistemology, transcending both empiricism and rationalism, asserts the irreducibility of reason and experience to one another. Despite the fact that, in Marx, history is periodized, our knowledge of different social formations, situated in different historical epochs, is not relative. Marxian epistemology, furthermore, strives towards knowledge of essence through the world of appearance. Essence always lies at the deep structure of the social formation that could be known only through a theoretical mediation. The Marxian methodology, adopting the concrete social totality as its point of departure, links ontology to epistemology in Marx's philosophical system. What I have proposed in Chapter 2 as the Structure of Scientific Practice has made it possible, I believe, for me to furnish a just assessment of the adequacy of Marx's historical materialism to capture theoretically the human material condition.

Bibliography

Althusser, Louis. 1969a. "Contradiction and Overdetermination," in *For Marx*. London: Allen Lane.
————. 1969b. "On the Materialist Dialectic," in *For Marx*. London: Allen Lane.
Benton, Ted. 1977. *Philosophical Foundations of the Three Sociologies*.

London: Routledge and Kegan Paul.
Cohen, G.A. 1978. *Karl Marx's Theory of History, A Defense.* Princeton, New Jersey: Princeton University Press.
Giddens, Anthony. 1971. *Capitalism and Modern Social Theory, An Analysis of the Writings of Marx, Durkheim and Max Weber.* London: Cambridge University Press.
Gould, Carol. 1978. *Marx's Social Ontology, Individuality and Community in Marx's Theory of Social Reality.* Cambridge, MA: The MIT Press.
Hindess, Barry and Hirst, Paul Q. 1975. *Pre-capitalist Modes of Production.* London: Routledge and Kegan Paul.
Levine, A. and Erik Olin Wright. 1980. "Rationality and Class Struggle," in *New Left Review*, Vol. 123, pp. 47-68.
Lovell, Terry. 1980. *Pictures of Reality, Aesthetics, Politics. Pleasure.* London: British Film Institute.
Lukács, Georg. 1978. *Marx's Basic Ontological Principles.* London: Merlin Press.
Marx, Karl. 1934. *The Eighteenth Brumaire of Louis Bonaparte.* Moscow: Progress Publishers.
_____. 1938. *Critique of the Gotha Programme.* New York: International Publishers.
_____. 1948. *The Civil War in France.* Moscow: Progress Publishers.
_____. 1962. *Capital* Vol. III. Moscow: Progress Publishers.
_____. 1963 *Early Writings*, T.B. Bottomore (ed.), New York: McGraw-Hill.
_____. 1963a *Theories of Surplus-Value*, Part I, Moscow: Progress Publishers.
_____. 1964. *The Economic and Philosophical Manuscripts of 1844*, Dirk J. Struik (ed.), New York: International Publishers.
_____. 1965. *Pre-Capitalist Economic Formations*, Eric L. Hobsbawm (ed.) New York: International Publishers.
_____. 1970. *A Contribution to the Critique of Political Economy.* Maurice Dobb (ed.). New York: International Publishers.
_____. 1973. *Grundrisse.* New York: Vintage Books.
_____. 1976. *Capital*, Vol. I. London: Penguin.
_____. 1978a. *Wage Labour and Capita.* Peking: Foreign Languages Press.
_____. 1978b. *The Poverty of Philosophy.* Peking: Foreign

Languages Press.

———. 1981. *Capital*, Vol. III. New York: Vintage Books.

Marx, Karl and Frederick Engels. 1956. *The Holy Family, or Critique of Critical Criticism.* (Moscow: Progress Publishers.

———. 1964. *The Communist Manifesto.* New York: Pocket Books.

Marx, Karl and Frederick Engels. [1845] 1974. *The German Ideology.* Edited by C.J. Arthur. New York: International Publishers.

———. [1845] 1976. *The German Ideology. Marx-Engels Collected Works* Vol. 5. Moscow: Progress Publishers.

McLelland, David. 1971. *The Thought of Karl Marx: An Introduction.* New York: Harper Torchbooks.

McMurtry, John. 1978. *The Structure of Marx's World View* (New Jersey: Princeton University Press).

Rader, Melvin. 1979. *Marx's Interpretation of History.* New York: Oxford University Press.

Shaw, William H. 1978. *Marx's Theory of History.* Palo Alto, CA: Stanford University Press.

Struik. Dirk. l964. "Introduction," in *The Economic and Philosophical Manuscripts of 1844.* New York: International Publications.

CHARLES REITZ
Chapter Five

Materialism and Dialectics:
Nature, History, Knowing

The Chemistry of Concepts and Perceptions: Philosophical problems of nearly every sort are today assuming the very form they took 2000 years ago—how can something emerge from its opposite, for example, the rational out of the unrational, the sensate out of the lifeless, the logical out of the non-logical, dispassionate observation out of ambitious striving, living for others out of egoism, truth out of error? Metaphysical philosophy made things easier for itself by denying the emergence of any of these things out of the others, and by presuming a magical origin for those aspects it deemed of higher value ... Historical philosophy on the other hand—which cannot at all be thought of as separate from the natural sciences and which is the very youngest of all philosophical methods—demonstrates in quite another fashion ... that there are no absolute contradictions, ... and that an error in reasoning stands behind any presumed categorical exclusion.

The Congenital Defect of Philosophy: ... A lack of historical sense is the congenital defect of philosophy.

—Friedrich Nietzsche, *Human, All Too Human* (1886)
Paragraphs 1 & 2 (my translation)

Nietzsche is the incendiary philosopher of moral transvaluation and liberation of mind; Marx the theorist of workforce transformation through critical human consciousness and communist revolution. Neither was a particularly avid adherent of Hegel's teleological spiritualism, but they certainly did admire the dialectical method refined and developed by him. Nietzsche appropriated from Hegel's historical and dialectical philosophy the notion of the world as an Heraclitian flux, primarily characterized by becoming rather than being. He repudiated as utopian any non-recognition of change, as he felt this inevitably formed the basis for religious metaphysics and nihilism. He proclaimed that god was dead, and also that liberated humanity could joyfully—and *scientifically*—begin to alter history. He traced a genealogy of morals, in which values underwent dialectical transformation—with feudal vices (like usury) becoming bourgeois virtues, and Christian "vulnerabilities" (sensuality, this-worldliness) becoming anti-Christian strengths. He thought that consciousness had a basis in biology, and his psychology noted that the soul could die even before the body. Nietzsche believed that ideological distortion was more than simple untruth: it was a definite form of socially necessary falsehood required by historical circumstances for the survival not only of a particular ruling group, but of the entire human species itself. Nietzsche also called for the supersession of masters and slaves through the training of a qualitatively higher type of human being. He thought to have found the motor force of social change in the antithesis between the Apollonian and Dionysian aspects of humankind.

Quite apart from this Nietzschean anti-metaphysics, Karl Marx sought also to trace-out modern contradictions in history. Time itself was understood by Marx and Engels as a property of matter in motion, and the "timeliness" of this or that particular form of class rule was thought to hinge upon developments in material relations of production. Thus certain Marxists, then and now, pointed to the historical necessity of socialized ownership ultimately catching-up with the fact of socialized production, and to the obsolescent character of free trade/free market economic relations, tending to make even the capitalist economy impossible and therefore living on borrowed time. They saw the whole weight of existing affairs as pushing toward a world-historical rebellion against the social abuses connected with production for profit instead of human need. They theorized the historical and material warrant for communist revolutionary practice, and the labor force as the only class with an historically-rooted future. Even when capitalism is classically described as digging its own grave, no Marxist today would disagree that it remains to be quite consciously buried.

In order to make a critical assessment of the nature of dialectical methodology today, I undertake in the following a foundational critique of philosophical perspectives on key trends in early natural scientific and social theory and the progressive emergence of dialectics within these theoretical developments. Current controversies within the Marxist frame, highlighting problems of epistemological reductionism and the theory of reflection, will thereafter be examined.

Natural History and Social History. The Renaissance marked the modern beginning of a unified theory of the material world. Science was attempting to eliminate the "meta" from metaphysics, and stress the "uni" in universe. Mind and humankind were starting to be understood as integral parts of nature. Comprehension, itself, was now thought to require broadly based scientific knowledge of the macrocosm, as well as humanistic expertise in such fields as art and anatomy. Indeed, the Renaissance recognition of the inherent interconnections linking different areas of theoretical endeavor and practical concern was the most remarkable event of all. The new cosmology emerging during the Renaissance was at odds with the older scholastic metaphysics interpreting its geocentric world. Copernicus opposed the narrow, common sense, reductionism of the Ptolemaic view of nature, as well as the mysticism of the Church, when he (re)asserted (1543) that the sun was the center of the universe. Everyone could empirically see that his theory was patently ridiculous—except to those who could follow his reasoned mediations.

The Renaissance demonstrated that knowledge could indeed develop over time, but not without struggle. The ex-monk turned scientist and philosopher, Giordano Bruno, was burned at the Inquisitors' stake (in 1600) for advocating a pantheistic doctrine of an infinite material universe governed by its own internal powers. Likewise, Galileo was persecuted for his 1638 defense of Copernicus in the *Dialogue on the Two Great World Systems.* His apocryphal drop of weights from the Leaning Tower of Pisa was in all likelihood a thought experiment. Rigorous scientific theorization, often at variance with common sense observations and theological views, was now being recognized as required for critical apprehension of obdurate, yet invisible, forces.

Francis Bacon undertook a complete re-examination of the sciences in 1605. His *Advancement of Learning* represents a theoretical excursion through the studies of medicine, psychology, politics, and philosophy, noting especially that each of these fields is inadequate taken separately. The *Advancement of Learning* also reveals an emergent methodological reflexivity in even Bacon's thought. In it he maintains that science cannot progress blindly: the true method of experience must light a theoretical lamp to illuminate the path to new experiments. In addition to all of this, Bacon saw also that "knowledge is power." There was a practical/political relationship between science and human life. Of course Bacon was primarily a precursor of empiricism and the inductive method, still one might further say that a latent "sociology of knowledge" in the *Novum Organum* leads him to critique religious, political, and social "idols" in the manner centuries later of Karl Mannheim, namely "freeing" the scientist from apriori value judgments.

In 1637, Descartes' defense of the Christian metaphysics appealed to mathematics and the method of "radical doubt" to obtain renewed legitimacy. His starting point (under the challenge of modern science) could no longer remain "the Absolute." Instead, it became the rather more modest and lonely "cogitative act" of the individual human mind. John Locke went well beyond Descartes in rejecting the "innate" origin of thought altogether, and positing an external source in experience. This was a decisive step toward establishing the interpenetration of thought and reality, in contradistinction to their supposed metaphysical separation. Newton highlighted the inherent relationality of matter in his "universal theory of gravitation" in 1687. And while his physics of action and reaction remained enmeshed in a mechanical materialism, it nonetheless aided progress toward a unitary and materialistic worldview.

With Kant, however, came the first decisive recognition that nature has a history (in a mundane, rather than mythological sense). Kant taught geography and the natural sciences, as well as philosophy, at the University of Königsberg, and his *Universal History of Nature and the Theory of the Heavens* (1755) hypothesized the emergence of the solar system out of a primordial gaseous mass, rather than from an exertion of a divine will. Through reference to the natural forces of attraction and repulsion, it furthermore relocated the sources of physical change from external to internal forms of causation. Because his teachings were contrary to scripture, Kant was officially intimidated by the Prussian government. Manfred Buhr writes that Kant stood "at the threshold of the dialectic." Having counterposed the idea of a natural history to the merely mechanical and classificatory description of the world, Kant certainly earned that designation.

Epistemologically speaking, Kant foundationally criticized both pure empiricism and pure reason. He emphasized the interdependence of observation and conceptualization, maintaining that: "Thoughts without content are empty and perception without concepts is blind."[1] Each needed the other in a dialectical fashion that remained totally beyond the (purely mathematical) grasp of Descartes, and was only hinted at (ahistorically) in Locke. Thus, the Kantian theory of knowledge superseded both rationalism and empiricism. It also conditions the Kantian treatment of the epistemological problems involved when "pure" reason is separated from sense experience. Kant viewed apriori reason (*Vernunft*) as a grave source of intellectual error leading to the misconceived paralogisms, antinomies, and ideals discussed in his chapter on dialectic. The Kantian epistemology, then, is dialectical: reason itself was insufficient as a source of knowledge. Instead, sensibility and the analytic categories of the understanding were mutually required to make valid judgments about phenomena. Kant sided with Locke in claiming that knowledge stems from experience, but added that human beings also possess a unique ability to understand, even if this ability is also empty taken solely by itself.

Kant's critique of rationalism and pure reason was directly extended by Hegel's chapter on "Historical and Mathematical Truth" in the Preface to the *Phenomenology* (1807). Here Hegel criticizes (Cartesian) mathematics as a

---

[1] Manfred Buhr, *Immanuel Kant* (Leipzig: Reclam, 1974) p. 124. See also Frederick Engels, *Anti-Dühring* (New York: International, 1970) p. 65: "The Kantian theory of the origin of all existing bodies from rotating nebular masses was the greatest advance made by astronomy since Copernicus. For the first time the conception that nature had no history in time began to be shaken."

faulty method of science and logic. Hegel considers pure mathematics to be abstract, unphilosophical, and defective in attaining real knowledge. He rejected schematization and formalism because he thought science without history and the dialectic was unable to comprehend either experience or truth. A static, micro-analysis was simply not suited to grasping the motion, process and integrity of any complex and changing object of knowledge. Hegel's thoroughly historical analysis of nature and thought exposed the epistemological limitations of both mathematics and classical physics in ultimately appreciating the concrete totality of any developing situation. Mechanical, fixed categories and abstract principles were viewed as reductions of real historical processes, valid only within strict parameters. Hegel's elaboration of the dialectic was thus conceived as a scientific counter-movement to the increasing specialization and fragmentation of knowledge positivistically understood. That this historical approach to knowledge was also *realistic*, allowed Hegel to surpass Kant's reserved skepticism and subjectivism, affirming the objectivity of philosophical truth as an increasingly refined consciousness of the transformations of being. Hegel wrote of the "...complete worldliness of consciousness...." in the Preface to the *Phenomenology*.[2]

The clear-cut contribution of epistemology from Plato to Kant had been the recognition that one sees not only with one's eyes, but also with one's "mind's eye." Marx was later to assert that this insight does not necessarily entail idealism, but rather more strictly, an appreciation of dialectics. For Hegel also "the sensuous" (i.e. perceptible) had to be transformed into the "sensible" (i.e. meaningful), and it was precisely a realistic, historical, and dialectical theory of knowledge that afforded the "richly intelligent perception" required by

---

[2] See Walter Kaufmann, *Hegel: Texts and Commentary* (Garden City: Anchor, 1966) pp. 54, 56.

science and philosophy. Hegel's *Science of Logic* (1812) noted that genuine knowledge must entail an appreciation for movement and history, rather than focus on the "dead bones" of an ahistorical conceptual scheme. The book's seminal theories on contradiction, i.e. the interrelationship of the abstract and the concrete, the unity and difference of opposites, the negation of the negation, and the transformation of quantity into quality, remain the cornerstones of a dialectical conception of knowledge. These relationships were seen as key to the transformation of unmediated perception and sensuousness into a fuller, mediated conscious and sensuous appreciation.

Supposition in accordance with the elements of dialectical thinking was not considered mere conjecture, but a proper aspect of philosophical and scientific inquiry. Relational, dialectical, thinking was considered necessary to capture the essential interconnectivity upon which all *developmental*, yet *realistic*, truth was to be based. Hegel's *Philosophy of History* (1805) had dealt even earlier with the "becoming of knowledge," and viewed consciousness as both temporal and social, i.e. limited by the level of civilization. His book traces not merely a chronicle of ideas, but their development from lower to higher. It also propounds Hegel's central theory, that reason governs the world.[3] For Hegel, the motive forces of history were spiritual in character. He

---

[3] These notions were criticized, yet rethought, refined, and preserved at a higher level, in the further development of Hegel's philosophy by Marx and Engels. See, for example, Frederick Engels, *Ludwig Feuerbach* (New York: International, 1974) p.10 on the dialectical and materialistic reading of Hegel's theory of the reality of the rational. "In 1789 the French monarchy had become so unreal, that is to say, it had been so robbed of all necessity, so non-rational, that it had to be destroyed by the Great Revolution—of which Hegel always speaks with the greatest enthusiasm."

continues as a philosophical idealist even though he put a long epistemological distance between himself and Kant, not to mention the abstract rationalistic dualism of Descartes.

In 1859, Charles Darwin also asserted the activity of matter per his theories of fortuitous genetic variation and organismic adaptation, not to mention his notion of the eventual evolution of the human mind. Even the categories of genus and species were no longer immutable, but inevitably subject to change. His contributions to science are however unthinkable without Hegel and the German natural scientist, Alexander Humboldt. Humboldt's *Personal Narrative* (1819-29) of travels to the Americas is cited in Darwin's *Voyage of the Beagle*, and Darwin's autobiography hails Humboldt's work as an inspiration to his own travels and research.[4] Humboldt emphasized that a descriptive study of plant life leads necessarily into a study of climatology, and this into a study of geography, etc., each reciprocally conditioning the other. Humboldt's subsequent encyclopedic description of physical nature, the *Kosmos*, contains such Hegelian statements on methodology as: "My prime motivation was my effort to grasp the phenomena of the material world in their internal and universal interconnection—to see nature as a living whole moved by internal forces." Further: "I was convinced early on through my dealings with highly gifted men of science that any grand and universal view of the world was empty speculation without a serious effort toward knowledge of the particular. The particulars in the natural sciences, however, are essentially quite capable of fructifying one another in a

---

[4] Frank Baron, "From Alexander von Humboldt to Charles Darwin: Evolution in Observation and Interpretation." Internet *Zeitschrift für Kulturwissenschaften*, 17. Nr. February 2010.
http://www.inst.at/trans/17Nr/7-8/7-8_baron17.htm

mutual way."[5]

Modern science and philosophy have emphasized humankind as a part of nature and thought as a social product. The Kantian and Hegelian dialectic, as well as that of Marx and Engels, stress the activity of the mind in processing sense data, and currently most psychological theories assume that internal mental structures in some way regulate thought and behavior. At the turn of the century Freud propounded a developmental, depth psychology involving conscious and unconscious personality structures, and featuring a dialectic of life and death instincts. Freud noted that psychological stress could produce socio-physiological tensions, and that social or bodily injury could do damage to the mind.[6] As Russell Jacoby has emphasized: "The critical edge of psychoanalysis is rooted in this dialectic; it exposes the sham of the autonomous and private bourgeois individual with the secret of its socio-sexual-biological substratum."[7]

Because of the general dialectical recognition that the world cannot be adequately known through infinitely compartmentalized or highly specialized studies, an inter-disciplinary approach to knowledge has increasingly been advocated. Natural history and social history emerged in the

---

[5] According to Bertell Ollman, *Alienation* (Cambridge: Cambridge University Press, 1976) p. 53, Marx wanted to dedicate his *Capital* to Darwin. See Alexander Humboldt, *Kosmos*, (Philadelphia: F.W. Thomas & Söhne, 1869, in German). Humboldt was no Marxist: he was part of the political reaction that persuaded the Prussian police to take measures against Marx even in Paris, this according to Otto Rühle, *Karl Marx* (New York: New Home Library, 1928) p. 77.
[6] See especially Jürgen Habermas on psychoanalysis in chapters 10, 11, and 12 of his *Knowledge and Human Interests* (Boston: Beacon Press, 1972).
[7] Russell Jacoby, "Negative Psychoanalysis and Marxism," *Telos*, Winter 1972, p. 5.

20th century as methodological guides that overcame the finality of mathematico-deductive logic, and indicated an unmistakable trend toward dialectification in the critical philosophy of nature, society, science, and culture.

One of the chief questions discussed in the international debate on dialectics is the problem of methodological reductionism and the correspondence theory of truth as they relate to critical theory.

The Reductionism Controversy within Marxism. There are those who assert that Marxism has broken down even before capitalism. They insist that Marxist theory no longer holds because contemporary historical developments have forced it to give so much ground that its positions are no longer defensible. The main problem with "orthodox" Marxism was considered to be its ostensible reductionism. The real world was just too complex to be understood in terms of a "vulgar materialism" or "economic determinism." Lukács's contribution (1924) to the emergent lexicon of critical theory included the terms "totality" and "reification."[8] These must be understood with special reference to the problem of epistemological reductionism: they attempt to grasp both the issue and its answer. To his mind, dialectics insists on the concrete unity of the whole. Without this, fetishized relationships between parts prevent thought from ever finding meaning. "Totality" is therefore seen as the (revolutionary) category that governs reality, while "reification" is a reductionist distortion that gives a rigid, unhistorical, and natural appearance to social institutions. According to Lukács these concepts are more germane to a Marxist analysis than even the primacy of economic forces in historical explanation. Marx (he contends) understood this in

---

[8] See István Mészáros, *Lukács's Concept of the Dialectic* (London; Merlin Press, 1972).

his analysis of the commodification and commercialization of human relationships in *Capital* and in his call for the abolition of the wages system. Engels, however, had lost sight of these dialectical ideas and committed a reductionist error when he claimed (in *Anti-Dühring*) that bourgeois experiment and industry could produce direct knowledge of "things in themselves." Lukács's chapter on reification admonishes Engels for thus unfortunately involving Marxist philosophy with the "mechanical" correspondence theory of knowledge. To this he opposes an Hegelian hermeneutic approach citing Dilthey and Weber (and Rickert and Simmel) with much more approval than Engels.

One year earlier (1923), Karl Korsch had also written that Marxists themselves were forgetting "the original meaning of the dialectical principle."[9] Korsch contended that this tendency to "abolish" philosophy had undeniably negative results for class struggle and defined a crisis in Marxist theory and practice. To his mind, ostensible revolutionaries were refusing to take theoretical issues seriously, treating bourgeois ideology especially as mere illusion, rather than as part of the reality yet to be overcome.

---

[9] Karl Korsch, *Marxism and Philosophy* (London: NLB, 1970) p. 33. Korsch was criticizing the theory and practice of the Bolshevik party and Lenin, its leader. Nonetheless it was precisely revolutionary activity that inspired Lenin's philosophical production. Thus he had already polemicized against economism and workerism in *What Is To Be Done?* (1902) where he explicitly noted there could be no revolutionary practice without revolutionary theory. Korsch's book was scathingly attacked by the Bolshevik party, and Korsh retaliated by rejecting Lenin and Stalin as "vulgar materialists." Sebastiano Timpanaro has negatively evaluated Korsch's philosophy as a "radicalism of the intelligensia rather than a doctrine of the revolutionary proletariat." This in Sebastiano Timpanaro, "Marxism and Idealism," *New Left Review*, May-June 1974, #85, p. 4

Korsch implied that a cavalier attitude toward epistemological questions was entirely bourgeois, and would never supersede in practice what it never got beyond in theory. Korsch foreshadowed Lukács on reification in also stating that "the major weakness of vulgar socialism is ... a naive realism ... the normal positivist science of bourgeois society" (Korsch, 76).

Like Lukács and Korsch, Horkheimer, Fromm, Adorno and Marcuse rejected the epistemological theory of correspondence. Each of them attempted a critical "revitalization" of classical communist theory by infusing their versions of Marxism with elements from Kant and Hegel, *Lebensphilosophie* and hermeneutics (via Nietzsche and Dilthey), as well as the findings of Freudian psychoanalysis.

Horkheimer's 1937 essay on "Traditional and Critical Theory" is a seminal piece in this regard. In it he emphasizes the social and historical function of science, rather than its abstract, empirical achievements. After the fashion of Husserl, Horkheimer distinguishes between "positive" fact and the "transcendental" reflexivity of theory, and at the same time establishes a connection between them both. This unity he claims is grounded in the rational "kernel" of the Kantian epistemology, which holds that reality is not immediately accessible, but rather miserably sunk in ideological obscurity.[10] Critical theory is opposed to naive realistic thinking whether of a common sense or scientific sort. It emphasizes the complicated social, historical and political mediations that necessarily intervene in "pure" science, traditionally conceived. This epistemological understanding Horkheimer also applied to the orthodox Marxist theoretician who supposedly:

---

[10] Max Horkheimer, "Traditional and Critical Theory," in *Critical Theory* (New York: Herder and Herder, 1972) p. 203.

is satisfied to proclaim with reverent admiration the creative strength of the proletariat and finds satisfaction in canonizing it. He fails to see that such an evasion of theoretical effort (which the passivity of his own thinking spares him) and of temporary opposition to the masses (which active theoretical effort on his part might force upon him) only makes the masses blinder and weaker than they need be. His own thinking should in fact be a critical, promotive factor in the development of the masses.[11]

Writing in the midst of the Nazi era, Horkheimer felt that the "weight of history" was not necessarily pushing the world toward socialism, but only into a new period of capitalist crisis and barbarism. Beyond that, nothing could be said with certainty. While the outcome of the war was still uncertain, Horkheimer and Adorno (in U.S. exile) attempted to come to grips with fascism. Their *Dialectic of Enlightenment* (1944) reinterprets the basic social contradictions disclosed by classical Marxism as manifestations of a tragic paradox having increasingly pessimistic implications. The war and fascism were no longer to be understood as Leninist examples of the consequences of specific inter-imperialist rivalries and the intensified forms of class oppression these require. Critical theory saw them instead as the result of an epochal degeneration, an epochal display of human degradation and social injustice essentially grounded in the reductionist character of bourgeois intellectualism, science, and education. Their disappointment at the passivity of their academic colleagues and others, who "made it easy for the barbarians everywhere by being so stupid,"[12] reinforced their conviction that even liberal cultural and political beliefs subjectively

---

[11] Ibid., p. 214.
[12] Max Horkheimer and Theodor W. Adorno, *Dialectic of Enlightenment* (New York: Herder and Herder, 1972) p. 209.

prevented any real opposition to Hitler from forming within Germany. As they considered traditional Marxist theory to have no explanation for this cruel turn of events, they undertook an hermeneutical[13] interpretation of the Odysseus myth and texts from DeSade and Nietzsche in search of a more meaningful understanding. They concluded that the all-pervading bourgeois spirit of the Enlightenment limits the thought patterns of the masses to authoritarian and calculative modes. Thought is considered to have become so restricted to matters of administration and organization that most people have lost their power to "hear the unheard of "[14] and to conceive a world different from that in which they live.

Herbert Marcuse had written on the problems of the dialectic during the 1930s, and warned that "it does not help to appeal to Marx, as long as the original meaning of the dialectic in Marx has not been grasped."[15] Also utilizing the concept "totality," he hoped to recapture an ostensibly truer Marxist understanding of the dialectic. This he sought to accomplish with explicit reference to Dilthey and Heidegger. Marcuse studied in Freiburg under the latter, and came to

---

[13] According to a leading German historiographer, Georg G. Iggers, "The hermeneutic form of historicism lent itself well to a critique of socialism because it rejected social analysis as a legitimate form of inquiry...." Also: "...a scholarly reply to Marxism had to be formulated. Meinecke and Weber represent diverse ends of a spectrum...yet their explanations were to be found in human consciousness." See especially, Georg G. Iggers, *New Directions in European Historiography* (Middletown, Conn: Wesleyan University Press, 1975) pp. 24, 84-85.

[14] Ibid., p. 34.

[15] Herbert Marcuse, "On the Problem of the Dialectic," *Telos*, Spring 1976, p. 19. See also, Herbert Marcuse, *Heideggarian Marxism*, Richard Wolin and John Abromeit [eds.] (Lincoln, NE University of Nebraska Press, 2005).

conclude that "not all being is dialectical."[16]

Where Hegel had erroneously "absolutized"[17] the dialectic, applying it to all things, Marxism, phenomenology, and hermeneutics limited its application to the "life-world" of the human being. This because "knowledge of one's own existence and a knowing (not cognitive) attitude belong to true historical being."[18]

By thus asserting that there is no dialectic in nature (apart from one's own life-world), Marcuse added a new twist to the anti-scientism argument: he implied that positivism is an appropriate method in the mathematical and physical sciences, although these studies were of no help in understanding the human condition. During the 1950s he would formulate a critical analysis of philosophy and politics in the U.S.S.R. in his *Soviet Marxism* (1957), and find untenable the classical Marxist theory of dialectical and historical materialism. Yet Marcuse also assesses the dialectical relation between the structure of thought and structure of reality as having a common denominator:

> According to Hegel the traditional distinction between thought and its object is 'abstract' and falsifies the real relation. Thought and its object have a common denominator, which, itself 'real,' constitutes the subject of thought as well as its object. This common denominator is the inherent structure and the *telos* of all being i.e. Reason.[19]

---

[16] Marcuse, op. cit., p. 22.
[17] Ibid., p. 21.
[18] Ibid., p. 22.
[19] Ibid.

This is a promising insight that Marcuse would subsequently extend in *One-Dimensional Man*'s chapter 8 on the historical reality of universals. The Popper-Adorno controversy, begun in 1961, was another elaboration of the critical Marxist polemic against positivism. According to Paul Lorenzen's *Hermeneutik und Dialektik* (Tübingen: J.C.S. Mohr, 1970), this debate can be traced back to Kant's critique of Descartes and abstract rationalism. Adorno is here defending a dialectical understanding of science[20] emphasizing its normative dimensions, against a positivistic reduction of reason. In a marked advance over views critical of science and technology published in 1944 in *Dialectic of Enlightenment*, Adorno here advocated a structural systems-analysis over logical atomism and empiricism. He saw social scientific knowledge as itself societal, dialectical thought as itself societal, consistent with Lukács's notion of the concrete totality.

In contrast (and with a certain irony) the early 1960s saw Louis Althusser publish a series of articles in a Soviet-aligned French communist journal. These were later collected into *For Marx* (1965). In them he concludes that a dialectical Marxist epistemology has in large measure yet to be constituted. He notes that Marx never wrote a *Dialectics* to do for philosophy what his *Capital* had done for political economy. He asks if we even know what we mean should we speak of a Marxist philosophy, and if a Marxist philosophy exists, does it have a right to? He then proceeds to formulate his own notes on the materialist dialectic. The first question he believes must be settled is the specific difference between the Marxist and Hegelian forms of the dialectic. Of course, Marx was a materialist and Hegel an idealist; these truths, however,

---

[20] In this regard see also David Frisby, "The Popper-Adorno Controversy: The Methodological Dispute in German Sociology," *Philosophy of Social Science* 2 (1972) 105-119.

pertain to the substance of the dialectic rather than to its structure. Althusser feels that the philosophical development of Marxism depends precisely upon this elaboration of the structural differences in the Hegelian and Marxist notions of contradiction. In his view, Hegel's concept of contradiction is oversimplified: it reduces "... *the totality*, the infinite diversity of an historically given society ... to a *simple internal principle*. ... [T]his reduction ... of *all* the elements that make up the concrete life of an historical epoch ... to *one* principle of internal unity ... [is]...abstract ideology."[21]

The very structure of Hegelian contradiction is seen to reflect the "mystical shell" of his philosophy. It has led naive Marxists to postulate "... the beautiful contradiction between Capital and Labor."[22] Althusser maintains that the Marxist theory of the dialectic cannot remain "the *exact mirror image of the Hegelian Dialectic*,"[23] for the capital/labor contradiction is never pure and simple. It is "... *always specified* by the historically concrete forms and circumstances *in which it is exercised*."[24] The apparently simple contradiction is always actually "overdetermined." It is ultra-specified.

Althusser thus adds another dimension to the questions raised by Korsch and Lukács into the origins of orthodox Marxist reductionism, but his main target is *Hegelian positivism*. This term may not be so very paradoxical if it is related to a text from Marx's 1844 Paris manuscripts (which Althusser fails to mention although he devotes a section of *For Marx* to a specific consideration of them). See especially Marx's essay entitled "Critique of Hegel's Dialectic and

---

[21] Louis Althusser, *For Marx* (New York: Vintage, 1970) p. 103. Emphasis in original.
[22] Ibid., p. 104.
[23] Ibid.
[24] Ibid., p. 106.

General Philosophy," where he refers to the "dialectic of Feuerbach" that has demolished Hegelian philosophy.[25] Marx considers that Feuerbach had already discovered that:

> despite its thoroughly negative and critical appearance, and despite the genuine criticism which it contains ... there is already in the *Phenomenology*, as a germ, as a potentiality and a secret, the uncritical positivism and uncritical idealism of Hegel's later works—the philosophic dissolution and restoration of the existing empirical world.[26]

In this selection Marx agrees that a reductionism is present in Hegel, yet this is not conceived in terms of the dialectic's form, but rather Hegel's reconciliation with the established social order.

A critique of positivism is the main theme of Jürgen Habermas's *Knowledge and Human Interests* (1968). To his way of thinking, positivism cuts off epistemological inquiry into the conditions of possible knowledge and the explication of meaning. This, he claims, leads to a scientistic understanding of science void of methodological self-reflection. In his estimation, philosophy becomes scientistic if it renounces epistemological reference to the knowing subject and thus loses itself in naive realism and objectivism. Like Heidegger, and others in the hermeneutic tradition, Habermas is concerned that positivism "does not think." Instead it "represses" the reflexive theories of the limits of knowledge (from Kant to Hegel and Marx), and monopolizes the philosophy of science. Habermas points to Charles Sanders Peirce and William Dilthey as philosophers occupied early on with transcending the positivistic conception of science

---

[25] Karl Marx, *Early Writings* (New York: McGraw-Hill, 1964) p. 197.
[26] Ibid., p. 201.

through their pragmatic and hermeneutic theories of meaning. They, along with Kant, had an awareness of knowledge being rooted in subjective interest. Freudian psychoanalysis, as an interpretation of symbols and dreams after the hermeneutic model, also opened up an understanding of knowledge that positivism had closed-off. Little, if anything, in consciousness was a pure, unmediated, reflection of the external world. Much in fact could only be known "from within."

Habermas criticizes vulgarized Marxism for eliminating reflection as a motive force in history and replacing it with a scientistic conception of economic determinism. He supposes that traditional Marxist theory views its historical claims in exactly the same manner as the empirical findings of the natural sciences. Thus a positivist "atrophy" of knowledge has rendered it lifeless. The crisis in Marxist theory can only be overcome if it is recognized that critique must represent the dialectical unity of knowledge and interest, not merely the blind and destructive practice or unreflective accommodationism that are said to be the dual aspects of an unmediated Marxist approach to knowledge.

The problem of science and Marxist theory with particular regard to the nature of dialectical contradiction has been elaborated by Lucio Colletti. Approaching the problem from a different angle than Althusser, both men nonetheless substitute a philosophical pluralism for what they perceive as a reductionism in Marxist methodology. Colletti's line of argument is quite distinct from Althusser, yet there are underlying similarities. Both criticize the classical Marxist understanding of contradiction, and both believe that the dialectic is most appropriately applied to thought.

Colletti begins by emphasizing that the Marxist conception of contradiction includes a supposition of the inherent structural unity of opposites. Each aspect of a dialectical contradiction is regarded as necessarily related to its antithesis. Over against this notion, Colletti introduces the idea of "real opposition," as denoting opposition "without contradiction."[27]

In his estimation, material entities *may* be opposed to one another as *contraries* but *never* as aspects of a *contradiction*. "Contradiction" requires that both of its components be the *negativity* of the other, yet material things, objects, and factual data are in each case *real* and *positive*. Should they in some way conflict with one another, they do so as contraries, not contradictories. This is because "Each of the opposites is real and positive. Each subsists for itself ... each had no need to be referred to the other...."[28] According to Colletti, Marx was aware of this, even if Engels was not. He cites a statement from Marx to the effect that real opposites are not mediated and have no need of mediation, and implies that Marx would have found Engels's *Dialectics of Nature* quite illegitimate. He claims that *Capital* operates within the framework of "real opposition," rather than dialectical contradiction, and is therefore valid as a positivistic analysis of capitalism and economic crisis.

In Colletti's view Marxism is thus valid as a science of society, however the unMarxist (Hegelian) theory of dialectical contradiction in the real world must be dismissed as philosophical speculation. Dialectics has relevance only to the realm of *ideas*, where one may quite correctly speak of contradictory thoughts each being unintelligible without reference to the other. A dialectical *materialism* is therefore ill-conceived and useless. "Diamat gave us everything it could,

---

[27] Lucio Colletti, "Marxism and the Dialectic," *New Left Review* # 93 Sept-Oct. 1975, p. 3.
[28] Ibid., p. 6.

with Lysenko."[29] It is "that 'philosophical romance' to which Marxism has been reduced."[30] One recalls here Althusser's disparaging remark about the "beautiful" and "oversimplified" contradiction between capital and labor. Like Hobbes and the classical political economists, Colletti views worldly social conflict in terms of an abstract competition among essentially disparate elements. In so doing he denies that profits necessarily require unpaid surplus labor, and intimates that wage-labor and capital are but unmediated positive realities. Colletti's distinction in the present discussion derives from his advocacy of more positivism and less dialectic in Marxist theory. Paradoxically, he fully agrees with the critical Marxists who view the Marxist orthodoxy as a branch of undialectical empiricism.

Stanley Moore also agrees with Colletti that Marx adopted a valid, realist epistemology in opposition to Hegel. Moore sees *The Holy Family* and *The Poverty of Philosophy*, especially, as materialist in the traditional, anti-Hegelian and undialectical sense. When, however, in *Capital*, Marx uses the findings of Hegel's *Logic* in an affirmative fashion, Moore claims that Marx must be turned against himself. *Capital* merely encases "an irrational kernel of Dialectic within the rational hull of materialism."[31] Moore sees Marx's attempt to *dialectify* materialism as mistaken. A valid materialism, in his estimation, needs no "dialectical" distinctions between "appearance" and "essence," nor a doctrine of "internal relations." Moore's affinity to the neo-positivism of Colletti is certainly apparent.

---

[29] Ibid., p. 13.
[30] Ibid., p.18.
[31] Stanley Moore, "Marx and the Origin of Dialectical Materialism," *Inquiry* 14, 4, Winter 1971, p. 426.

A Critical Response to the Charge of Reductionism. Such have been the arguments in critical Marxist circles on one side of the debate surrounding the questions of science and dialectics, the theory of reflection, and the issue of reification/reductionism in Marxist method. A defense of the "traditional" Marxist position might be begun citing U.S. historian, William Appleman Williams:

> Marx talked about capitalism over a period of at least five centuries, whereas his critics dismiss him as hopelessly wrong on the evidence of less than one. For that matter, most Americans who dispense with him as being irrelevant base their arguments on the events of an infinitesimal period between 1941 and 1955. . . . Marx's foreshortened sense of time did have the effect of distorting some of his specific projections and predictions. But it seems fair to point out that the problem of understanding and being right about time is a difficulty that plagues all historians and social scientists. . . . Those who dismiss Marx have not met this challenge more effectively than he did.[32]

Williams stresses that the historical developments of Western capitalism in no way prove the "official myth"[33] that Marx was wrong about the revolutionary role of the proletariat. He feels that Keynesian economics have but temporarily "stalemated" the internal forces Marx cited as inevitably driving capitalism to its own destruction. In modern, "cybernated" production Williams sees yet another development adding its weight to the need for socialized ownership. He implies that the critical Marxists (of, say, a

---

[32] William Appleman Williams, "Karl Marx's Challenge to America," in his *History As a Way of Learning* (New York: New Viewpoints, 1973) p. 349.
[33] Ibid., p. 363.

Marcusean stripe) are as much short-sighted and empirical as they are ahistorical and audacious. His essay also emphasizes that Marxism is not now, and never has been, a form of economic determinism. Those who claim Marx made man into a machine have either never read him, or are engaging in deliberate falsification. As much of Marx's work was directly concerned with a critique of ideology, those who also claim he ignored ideas (and their impact in perceiving reality) are quite obviously wrong.

In 1897 another historian, Georg Plekhanov, composed two extremely important essays on historical materialism. As he himself had been confronted by those who summarily dismissed Marxism as a mechanical, economic determinism, his piece "On the Materialist Conception of History" charges those who fulminate against Marxism for supposedly attaching exaggerated importance to economic factors of being backward in theory. Such critics take that approach precisely "because the arguments of the late lamented economic materialists are easier to refute than the arguments of the dialectical materialists."[34]   Writing well before Lukács, he furthermore maintained: "Historical science cannot limit itself to the mere anatomy of society; it embraces the *totality of phenomena* that are *directly* or *indirectly* determined by social economics including the work of the imagination."[35] Historical materialism clearly was not a fatalistic determinism, in his estimation, and anti-Marxist ideology had to be *actively combatted* by Marxist intellectuals and dialecticians.

Plekhanov's 1897 "Role of the Individual in History" likewise critiqued the notion that Marxism is a nameless and impersonal determinism. This pejorative and "quietistic" view

---

[34] Georg Plekhanov, "The Materialist Conception of History," in *Essays in Historical Materialism* (New York: International, 1940) p. 20.
[35] Ibid., p. 24. (Emphasis in original.)

of Marxism is simply absurd, he asserts, in view of the conscious, party activism required of those persons interested not only in interpreting the world but also in changing it. Neither does this view admit that a materialist perspective on history can theoretically understand the oftentimes monumental contributions of individuals. Anticipating the elaborations of Mao Zedong on the dialectic in *On Contradiction* (1937), Plekhanov highlights the interrelationship of social framework and personal initiative in the making of history. Indeed, as Mao would later stress, the internal (personal and political) weaknesses and strengths of leading individuals are often enough the basis for practical-historical success or failure. External contradictions may only evoke what is internally possible.

Critical Marxism's rapprochement with hermeneutics, phenomenology, and psychoanalysis, as with Kant and Hegel, is vigorously attacked by Italian Marxist, Sabastiano Timpanaro. He has quite bluntly written in a 1974 essay that:

> Perhaps the sole characteristic common to all varieties of Western Marxism is, with very few exceptions, their concern to defend themselves against the accusation of materialism. Gramscian or Togliattian Marxists, Hegelian-Existentialist Marxists, Neo-Positivistic Marxists, Freudian or Structuralist Marxists, despite profound dissentions which otherwise divide them, are at one in rejecting all suspicion of collusion with "vulgar" or "mechanical" materialism, and they do so with such zeal as to cast out, together with mechanicalism or vulgarity, materialism *tout court*.[36]

---

[36] Sabastiano Timpanaro, "Marxism and Idealism," *New Left Review* #85, May-June 1974, p. 3.

Noting the objective predominance of idealism in bourgeois culture (it having undergone a twentieth century rebirth per Husserl, Dilthey, Weber, etc.), Timpanaro considers it philosophically strange that anyone should believe vulgar materialism to exert any sort of significant influence in the West. He asserts that critical Marxism much more likely wants to demonstrate in traditionally academic fashion that it is not "crude." He feels that this "self-purification" of Marxism typically devalues Engels because Engels "dragged Marxism down" from its "true philosophical heights" associating it with science and common sense. He rejects the critical Marxist *reduction of philosophy to methodology or theory of knowledge,* and articulates the need for a philosophy that is a broader vision of the world, i.e. one that would view *nature* (and not merely knowledge) as historical, and *history* (and not merely science) as material. "What is needed is an ideological confrontation between Marxism and these ['critical'] tendencies, an antagonistic and not merely receptive stance . . . a critique of their anti-materialism."[37]

In this regard, Lukács's early works, *The Soul and the Forms* (1910), *Aesthetic Culture* (1913), and the *Theory of the Novel* (1916) were explicitly idealist according to I. Mészáros' *Lukács's Concept of the Dialectic*.[38] Althusser claimed that dialectics worked on ideas and generalities—not on matter, in *For Marx*.[39] Moore felt the dialectic was incompatible with materialism, just as Marcuse, Heidegger, Dilthey and Husserl claimed it did not apply to nature. Korsch, Lukács and Horkheimer argued dialectically against reification in science. They polemicized more diligently against "calculative rationalization" and the "Enlightenment," however, than against the particular practico-realities of monopoly

---

[37] Ibid., p. 22.
[38] Mészáros , op. cit., p. 34.
[39] Althusser, op. cit., pp. 184, 190.

capitalism, or for any socio-political alternative.

Like Williams, one might conclude that critical Marxism perpetuates the "official myth" of Marx simply being wrong. Like Plekhanov, one might say that its theoretical innovations exhibit a painful lack of insight for the fallacy of Marxism being an economic determinism. And like Timpanaro, one might expose its hostility towards a Marxist materialism: when Marx is to be praised, he is read like Hegel or Kant or Plato; when he is to be damned, he is read like Machiavelli or Locke.

Marx himself had heaped scorn upon the "divine dialectic" that actually represented the positivist side of Hegel, justifying all that exists even after having negated it. Similarly, Gramsci in the *Prison Notebooks* derides as bourgeois imposters those "in verbal revolt against all that exists [but] accepting it after all."[40]

Classical Marxism's dialectics of nature combatted positivism as the "science" of nature or society. It was inspired by the rational kernel of the Hegelian system which saw both thought *and the world* as having an historical mode of existence. Thus, Lenin spoke of the "evolution of a stone," and of the "dialectics of things themselves, of Nature itself, of the course of events itself," in his 1914 "Conspectus on Hegel's Logic."[41] A briefer essay, "On the Question of Dialectics," (1915) also strictly differentiated between mechanistic materialism and dialectical materialism. With specific regard to the correspondence theory of truth, he contrasted the "immeasurably rich content" of dialectical philosophy

---

[40] Antonio Gramsci, *Prison Notebooks* (New York: International, 1976) p. 369.
[41] V. I. Lenin, *Philosophical Notebooks* (Moscow: Progress, 1972) p. 111.

compared to the starkness of "metaphysical" materialism: "the fundamental *misfortune* of which is its inability to apply dialectics to the *Bildertheorie* [theory of reflection], to the process and development of knowledge."[42] Lenin, then, was explicitly critical of Locke's theory of epistemological inscription. He did not "uncritically" hold knowledge to be an unmediated reflection of the real, even if there was an undeniable agreement between thought and its object. In addition to his epistemological studies, Lenin also contributed a genuinely new dimension to Marxist philosophy with his research into inter-imperialist rivalries and the political supersession of the bourgeois state. His *What Is To Be Done?* asserted, well before Lukács and Korsch, that there could be no revolutionary practice without revolutionary theory, and the events of October 1917 demonstrated his commitment to changing the world as well as understanding it.

Engels' *Dialectics of Nature* contends that nature is in motion and that science can discover and influence the contradictory structural relationships within this motion:

> The world is not to be comprehended as a complex of ready-made things but as a complex of processes, in which the things apparently stable no less than their mind images in our heads, the concepts, go through uninterrupted change of coming into being and passing away, in which in spite of all seeming accidentality and all temporary retro-gression, a progressive element asserts itself in the end . . . .[43]

---

[42] Ibid., p. 362.
[43] Engels in James Lawler, "Heidegger's Theory of Metaphysics and Dialectics," *Philosophy and Phenomenological Research*, V. 35, N. 3, March 1975, p. 364.

Mao Zedong also elaborated the Marxist theory of the dialectic in addition to leading, militarily, a protracted socialist revolution. His 1937 tracts, *On Practice* and *On Contradiction* are of especial epistemological importance. The former work gives a materialist turn to the Kantian thesis that thoughts without content are empty, perception without concepts, blind.

> Our practice proves that what is perceived cannot at once be comprehended and that only what is comprehended can be more deeply perceived. Perception only solves the problem of phenomena; theory alone can solve the problem of essence. . . . [T]he proletariat was only in the perceptual stage of cognition in the first period of its practice, the period of machine-smashing and spontaneous struggle; it knew only some aspects of the external relations of the phenomena of capitalism. . . but when it reached the second stage of its practice . . . the proletariat was able to comprehend the essence of capitalist society, the relations of exploitation between social classes and its own historical task.[44]

Mao repeatedly utilizes the notion of "totality" to designate the unified whole of internal relations grasped as knowledge develops from the shallower to the deeper. He nevertheless retains a "correspondence" or "agreement" thesis, and reinforces Engels when he claims that knowledge is objectively verified when it can anticipate the results of social (productive) practice. Every time we make a cup of tea we know something of the essence of the leaf.

---

[44] Mao Zedong [Mao Tse Tung], *Four Essays on Philosophy* (Peking: Foreign Languages Press, 1968) pp. 6-9.

His piece, *On Contradiction*, stresses the structural distinctions between internal and external forms of dialectical opposition. Internal to every single material entity is its own complex set of particular contradictions. These inherent tensions are the fundamental cause of its entire development. Matter itself is, thus, essentially active not passive. It changes over time, due to its own internal contradictions. A thing's interrelations and interactions with other things external to it are but secondary causes in its development. The pressure of external influences only becomes operative through the internal contradictions which are the basis for all motion. To use Mao's example: an egg when properly warmed may develop into a chick, a stone that is incubated forever will never do so. Likewise, internal social contradictions are the basis of historical transformations, and external forces are ultimately only operative as a function of them. Political action must thus have an historical and material warrant if it is to succeed in practice.

Dialectics in the Bio-Ecological Domain. During the 1920s and 1930s dialectification was much debated within the Soviet studies of biology and physiology. I. P. Pavlov's investigations into the inter-relationship of physiology and psychology stirred much internal discussion. His experiments demonstrated that mind and body do not function separately and independently. Through his work on conditioned reflexes, he established the fact that animal behavior was not innate, pre-determined or automatic, but was elicited from developments in environmental conditions. He concluded that the external environment is inseparably connected with the internal, and that the cerebral cortex mediated each stimulus and response. The influence of the nervous system in turn on metabolism and other vital functions (both physical and psychological) was also evident. Muscular activity and development influenced mental activity and development, and vice versa. Physiology was thus of epistemological importance. Where Nietzsche and Freud posited inborn, instinctual effects of life-interests on cognition, Pavlov stressed environmentally conditioned reflexes. He substituted the concept "cortico-visceral pathology" for the psychoanalytic term, "psycho-somatic disorder." The former expressed the dialectic, the latter merely a dualism. Timpanaro suggests Marxism may yet learn more from Pavlov than from Freud.[45]

I. V. Michurin and Trofim Lysenko stressed the dialectic in agriculture, even as Pavlov had done in medicine. Their studies of plant hybridization kept in mind the transitory character of everything and *in* everything, over against the view that things are final, absolute or sacred. They felt that plants and animals could acquire new characteristics under environmental influence, and furthermore (like Lamarck) that these acquired characteristics could be transmitted hereditarily. Michurin occupied himself primarily with "training" hybrids to grow in purposeful directions. He "acclimatized" certain varieties of fruit and wheat, that is, "trained" them to grow under severe geological and climatological conditions that would have otherwise killed them. Michurin held that the character of a hybrid variety of fruit or wheat began to develop in the first days of seedling growth. During this period, its nature was plastic or "destabilized." Utilizing proper methods of cultivation and acclimatization, seedlings of spring wheat could be transformed into a heartier species of winter wheat; winter wheat could likewise undergo mutation into varieties capable of cultivation in Siberia. Michurin was so taken by his findings that he spoke of "renovating the earth" through "creative evolution."[46]

---

[45] Timpanaro, op. cit., p. 22.
[46] I. V. Michurin, *Selected Works* (Moscow: Foreign Languages Publishing House, 1949) pp. xvi, xviii.

Trofim Lysenko labored his entire professional life to build upon Michurinism, and to formulate a comprehensive and dialectical theory of inheritance; this, in contradistinction to the "scholastic" views then reigning in the field of genetics. Mendelism-Morganism claimed that the hereditary substance was independent of the rest of the living body and its conditions of life. The chromosomes were thought to be found only in the germ plasm itself, and these cells were thought to be physiologically independent of an organism's other tissues or life processes. Mendelism-Morganism denied that germ plasm could develop from normal "vegetative" tissue. Thus an organism stood divided into "the mortal body and the immortal hereditary substance."[47]

In Lysenko's estimation as early as 1953 "every particle of a living body contains heredity"[48] not just the gametes. Developments in cloning (reproduction from any cell) bear further testimony to this. Lysenko claimed that the Michurinists had repeatedly succeeded in transmuting a 28-chromosomed variety of spring wheat into a 42-chromosomed variety of winter wheat through acclimatization. Thus its new sturdier qualities were incorporated into its hereditary make-up.[49] "Lysenkoism" has been received with unreserved hostility and scorn by many scientists in the West. The Thirties in the USA (it will be remembered) saw the greatest economic depression in its history. At a time when one third of this nation went "ill-housed, ill-clad and ill-nourished (FDR)," and California fruit-growers were dousing their crops with kerosene, the Soviet Union was experimenting in extending its assortment of fruit and wheat into its northern climes. Soviet industrialization also provided a job and an income for every

---

[47] Trofim Lysenko, *The Situation in Biological Science* (Moscow: Foreign Languages Publishing House, 1953) p. 3.
[48] Ibid., p. 58.
[49] Ibid., p. 50.

Soviet worker in an economy on the upswing. In the USA a racist eugenics movement was also astir, per Terman and Yerkes and the Kelloggs of Battle Creek, not to mention the fundamentalist opposition to Darwinism and evolution represented by the Scopes "monkey" trial (1925) in Tennessee. Lysenko cannot be accused of a metaphysical or mechanical reductionism in method. The fulminations against him may yet signal another instance of backwardness in theory.[50]

On the other hand in the U.S., the internationally renowned Sand County Wisconsin naturalist, Aldo Leopold, developed an ecological/dialectical interpretation of nature and history and proposed what he called "The Land Ethic." *Nature was considered to be a community to which humanity belongs.* The sun and the earth are fountains of energy flowing through waters, soils, plants, and animals. Ecological science discloses "the tendency of interdependent individuals or groups to evolve modes of cooperation. . . . All ethics so far evolved rest upon a single premise: that the individual is a member of a community of interdependent parts."[51]

Leopold's ecological perspective "discards at the outset the fallacious notion that the wild community is one thing, the human community another."[52]

The culture of primitive peoples is often based

---

[50] See also the column "Matter" by Carl Zimmer which discusses research that claims to show that and how male human gametes transmit experience, "Changing Up What's Passed Down," *The New York Times*, December 8, 2015, D3.

[51] Aldo Leopold, *The Sand County Almanac* (New York: Oxford University Press, [1949] 1966) pp. 218-219.

[52] Aldo Leopold, "The Role of Wildlife in Liberal Education [1942]" in *The River of the Mother of God and Other Essays by Aldo Leopold*, Edited by Susan L. Flader and J. Baird Callicott (Madison, WI: University of Wisconsin Press, 1991) p. 303.

on wildlife. Thus the plains Indian not only ate buffalo, but buffalo largely determined his architecture, dress, language, arts, and religion.[53]

Ultimately Leopold comes to replace the term "wildlife" with the term "land," because he sees the former is inextricably bound to the latter. He likewise argues that "for the purposes of a liberal education ecology is superior to evolution as a window through which to view the world."[54]

Materialism and Dialectics in Science and Philosophy. Irene Brennan is a British communist and professor of philosophy who argues that the concept of reflection is essential to a materialist analysis, and that "all the crucial debates about a Marxist theory of truth have centered on an analysis of the concept of reflection."[55] She extends Timpanaro's evaluation of critical Marxism highlighting its tendency toward hermeneutical subjectivism as well as toward anti-materialism. Marxism, she explains, cannot content itself with "understanding" the "meaning" of various "interpretations" of "phenomena" while at the same time disregarding questions of objective truth and falsity. A "dialectics" restricted to realms of human relevance and experience is trapped within unrealistic and utopian boundaries. The world has a much broader horizon: one the working class cannot afford to ignore. To make no statements about the world as it is, but only as it seems to us, means adopting the reactionary side of the Kantian philosophy: its epistemological agnosticism. This, as Lenin pointed out in *Materialism and Empirio-Criticism*, opens the door to religion and metaphysics, or the "divine dialectic" that ultimately

---

[53] Leopold, *Almanac*, op. cit., 195.
[54] Leopold, ". . . Liberal Education," op. cit., p. 305.
[55] Irene Brennan, "The Concept of Reflection," *Marxism Today*, April 1974, p. 120.

sanctifies immediate knowledge and excludes the most important conclusions of mediated reflectivity: the existence of an objective world prior to our sensation of it.

Brennan underscores *Lenin's adaptation* of the theory of correspondence. Lenin was aware that *material* entities were in no way merely inert metaphysical beings pursuing an unchanging, mathematical mode of existence. Rather, they were historical in their very nature. His use of the epistemological theory of reflection was therefore entirely distinct from the use made of it by ahistorical materialists. Nevertheless, Lenin contends that direct knowledge of change is possible. This undergirds his principled defense of "naive realism" and historical materialism—both of which stress the interdependence of intelligence and sensuous practical activity—against the agnostic reservations of the neo-Kantians.

J. D. House definitively demonstrated that positivism, from the classical Marxist point of view, has always been "bad science"[56] and that it is simply wrong to assume that positivism properly describes the modern methodologies in the natural sciences. Current forms of scientific theorizing are much more complicated than the simple inductive or deductive methods allow. A merely descriptive method, void of theoretical generalization, has long since lost its place in the actual practice of scientific circles, even if only classical Marxism has succeeded in articulating a well-developed, counter-positivist philosophy of science.

Albert E. Blumberg has cited philosopher of science, Hans Freistadt, as entertaining a friendly interpretation of dialectical materialism: "contrary to allegations occasionally made, dialectical materialism is a serious, consistent, and in

---

[56] J. D. House, "A Note on Positivism," the *Insurgent Sociologist*, IV, #2, Winter 1976, p. 94.

my opinion correct philosophy of science and not a dogma imposed by politicians which no scholar worthy of the name can even discuss . . . ."[57] Furthermore, Blumberg emphasizes that Freistadt consistently treats dialectics from a materialist standpoint which renders it that much more intelligible to the typical scientist who is accustomed to working from a materialist point of view.

Dialectics has emerged as the science of working with relationships, particularly those that are changing and contradictory, as found in the realms of nature, society and thought. As a science, it is an especially conscious and active human enterprise, whose general theory has developed over time from shallower to deeper through the reflective processes involved in sociocultural and economic practice. Dialectics thus represents an acquired skill—studied, utilized, and refined over generations—that renders humankind increasingly able to master its protracted struggle to understand, transform, and perfect reality.

The development of dialectical philosophy has progressed historically though not without serious debates and controversy, setbacks and irrelevancies. Dialectics can be said to be a philosophical procedure that distinguishes itself from rival methods precisely in so far as it formulates its questions in ways other approaches cannot. It does this characteristically by addressing itself to what it deems the necessary interpenetration of abstract and concrete aspects of any knowledge claim, value judgment or facet of material reality.

Some will argue that 20th century science *denies* dialectics. The biggest, most powerful general ideas are

---

[57] Albert E. Blumberg, "Science and Dialectics; A Preface to a Re-examination," *Science and Society*, Fall 1958, p. 306.

ostensibly those of thermodynamics, especial the law of entropy, astrophysics, and quantum mechanics. Do these bodies of knowledge ultimately have no need for an account of a causal dynamism internal to, as well as external to, domains of matter/energy, time, and change?[58] Contemporary creationists cite the second law of thermodynamics to deny evolution: the clockwork universe has been wound up by its designer, but is now winding down. Engels is [incorrectly] said to have denied the second law of thermodynamics, and he is thus thought to have denied the most contemporary general explanation of systems of matter/energy. Foster and Burkett (2008) show through textual analysis that Engels criticized not the entropy law itself but its extrapolation into an hypothesis of the "heat death theory of the universe...."[59] Gravitation, electro-magnetism, ecological inter-dependence, rotational and reflectional symmetry in nature, seem nonetheless amenable to the use of the term "dialectic." Its use would signify a philosophical conclusion as to the validity-in-principle of an essential "unity-in-difference" binding partiality to totality in the history of nature. From there we find consciousness distinguished from being, yet emergent from it; entities

---

[58] Before anyone gets too carried away with the supposedly non-dialectical or anti-dialectical qualities of science in the late 20th century, we must recall the influence of political interests that inevitably also condition what is called science. Consider what has been called science in the "controversy" over global warming, what has been called science by the tobacco industry, the asbestos industry, the beef industry, the sugar industry, etc.

[59] See especially John Bellamy Foster and Paul Burkett, "Classical Marxism and the Second Law of Thermodynamics: Marx/Engels, the Heat Death of the Universe Hypothesis, and the Origins of Ecological Economics," *Organization & Environment* 21-1 March 2008, pp. 3-37.

distinguished from entities, yet derived from primordial substance. Being or substance is itself regarded as dynamic and historical in character, and fundamentally capable of self-development.

If any theory is to know the world in its movement and integrity, it must both preserve and cancel certain aspects of the predominantly static methods of traditional mathematics and rationalism, and assimilate them on a higher level consistent with the basic dynamics of natural history and socio-intellectual history as modern philosophy has come to disclose them. The kinetic involved in these processes has been variously conceived, but with a telling emphasis on the driving force of internal tensions, i.e. between sustainability and over accumulation, base and superstructure, potentialities repressed by the actual, essence and appearance, etc.

Utilizing insights from Heraclitus to Kant, Hegel, Marx, Nietzsche, Freud and others, I have presented the preceding remarks in order to more fully comprehend various contemporary expressions of dialectical thought. I hope they may serve as a philosophical recapitulation of the dialectic's most significant modern sources and most noteworthy theoretical modes, and that they may make some sense as an introduction to the subject. Naturally they do not begin to exhaust it.

Marxism, phenomenology, existentialism, critical theory, etc., all have made contributions to dialectical philosophy in widely divergent ways. In the person of Marcuse, for example, one finds a Freudian-Heideggerian-Nietzschean critical Marxist, who also knows his Hegel. The validity of each strain of dialectical thought must be determined on its own practical and historical merits and demerits with regard to material conditions. A modern trend toward *materialism and dialectics in science and philosophy* seems indisputable. Its general direction is clear. The current elevation of materialism and dialectics in the study of natural science and social science is a process which has real historical and material roots and many modern proponents. This says something about the nature of the universe, social systems, and human consciousness as we are increasingly getting to know them. Should materialism and dialectics not belong exclusively to any particular "school," they underwrite nonetheless humanity's authentic search for science and philosophy as such.

Chapter Five: Charles Reitz

CHARLES REITZ
Chapter Six

The Labor Theory of Ethics and Commonwealth

This chapter utilizes a dialectical and materialist perspective to develop its understanding of an ethical core common to the wisdom traditions of the world's major religions as well as non-theistic humanist philosophy. An alternative to moral relativism and moral contingency is offered. Through an examination of the essentially economic features of the human condition and the history of our species as socially active human beings, I have sought the pivotal criteria of conscience that can ascertain the concrete unity-within-multiplicity, i.e. the common goods, undergirding the evaluation of moral practice. These are theorized as emerging from our sensuous practical activities, our subsistence strategies, and our earliest forms of communal labor in egalitarian partnership societies.

Our humanist ethical sensibilities arise within the fundamentally social and economic dimensions of our being. The theoretical starting point for this study is a critical examination of two of Herbert Marcuse's earliest essays, "On the Philosophical Foundation of the Concept of Labor in Economics" and "New Sources on Historical Materialism."[1]

---

[1] Republished by Richard Wolin and John Abromeit (eds), *Heideggerian Marxism* (Lincoln: University of Nebraska Press, 2005).

My engagement with Marcuse's philosophy is intended to liberate *the critical* in his critical theory. In this essay I educe a "new" Marcuse. This means I am pursuing here and now an appreciation of Marcuse's theoretical strengths above and beyond the weaknesses I have discussed in this volume and elsewhere (Reitz 2000). My dialectical approach will arrive at the historical materialist perspective latent in his early writings which are customarily noted as having predominately Heideggerian and phenomenological qualities and methods. I will emphasize his underappreciated understanding of the power of *sensuous living labor* to liberate itself from commodification and exploitation in order to make commonwealth the human condition.[2]

---

[2] *Sensuous living labor* is my term for the elemental form of the human material condition that I find theorized within in the social philosophies of Marx and Marcuse. The details will be developed as this chapter unfolds. It is not to be reduced to any form of classcircumstance. Sensuous living labor is the substrate of our being as humans. It is the foundation of our affective and intellectual capacities (and vulnerabilities), bio-ecologically developed within history. As a species we have endured because of our sensuous appreciation of our emergent powers: the power to subsist cooperatively; to create, communicate, and care communally within what Marx called a *Gemeinwesen* (see page 355 below), that I call a *commonwealth*. Our earliest proverbs, fables, and riddles teach the survival power of partnership and cooperation and the categorical ethical advantages empathy, reciprocity, hospitality, and respect for the good in common. Humanity experiences the satisfactions / dissatisfactions derived from our bio-ecologically generated economic, aesthetic, intellectual, and moral standards gravitating toward the humanism of a communally laboring commonwealth. Having brought into being these universalizable value criteria, our cultural, political, and emotional conditions can be characterized *critically* as authentic (when consistent with the *fullest potentials* of our species being. i.e what Marx called our *Gattungswesen*) or as alienated (when social power structurally distorts or denies humanity such authenticity).

Marcuse has been perhaps most famously noted for his contention that labor, narcotized and anaesthetized by consumerism and in collusion with business priorities, lacks a critical appreciation of the potential of a philosophy of labor to transcend existing society. "Under the conditions of a rising standard of living, non-conformity with the system appears to be socially useless, and the more so when it entails tangible economic and political disadvantages and threatens the smooth operation of the whole" (Marcuse 1964, 2).

Given capitalism's tendency toward periodic crisis, Marcuse certainly understood that this "smooth operation of the whole" is *not*, however, a permanent condition. In spite of dominant state of system-stability, regular episodes of economic collapse disclose that: "...forces and tendencies exist which may break this containment and explode the society" (Marcuse 1964, xv).

Marcuse's analysis of the alienation and commodfication of labor acknowledges the power of the workforce to enact and lead social change. His assessment undergirds a theory of labor humanism aiming at the dis-alienation of our essentially sensuous and creative practical and productive activities. Public ownership of socially produced wealth is *the* revolutionary starting point[3] for labor that can transform the contemporary human condition and re-create the labor process to reflect fully our human potential. I stress in addition that incomes must be de-linked from private property ownership and reconnected to human needs, public

---

[3] Marcuse's *Soviet Marxism* makes it clear that neither socialization nor nationalization of productive property, in and of itself, will preclude alienation (Reitz 2000, 165). Nonetheless he recognizes that public ownership of socially produced wealth is a necessary, if not sufficient, condition and starting point.

work,[4] and *public wealth*.

According to Marcuse, socialism in it most *radical* sense is more than a theory of democratic government. It is a philosophy of authentically human existence and the fulfillment of both human needs and the political promise of our human nature, where creative freedom provides the foundation for satisfaction in all of our works. Marcuse and Marx asserted *a radically materialist conception of the essence of socially active human beings*: seen from the outside, we are the ensemble of our social relations; seen from the inside, we are *sensuous living labor*. As I shall elaborate later in this chapter, this core sensuousness is tended by our empathic human capacity to care, a capacity more primordial than Heidegger's *Sorgestruktur* [ontological care structure], going back to the empathic "humanism" found in the behavior of primates (de Waal 2013). Humanistic sensibilities characterize the social core of our being, our sensuous practical activities, our subsistence strategies, our communal labor.

Douglas Kellner's (1973) essay with regard to *the concept of labor* in the development of Marcuse's thought is a remarkable exception to a general neglect of this material, and has been a key stimulus to my own commentary. During the 1930s and '40s Marcuse ([1933] 1973) elaborated an "ontology of labor"—a philosophy grounded in the human condition as living labor. This ontology of labor is said to have its source, not in Heidegger, but in Marx and Hegel themselves, and this

---

[4] "Public work" is a concept developed by Harry C. Boyte and Nancy N. Kari (1996) which I extend in a socialist manner. Public work aims at the public interest and the public good, work's larger civic purposes, not private accumulation. It is oriented toward meeting human needs, rather than market or commercial requirements. It is work become as Marx envisioned it: life's prime want and fulfillment.

is reprised in Marcuse's little-known last publication dealing with the nature of the "proletariat," and his final thoughts reinforce the labor humanist and commonwealth foundations of the critical philosophy that he shares with Marx: "The working class still is the 'ontological' antagonist of capital . . .." (Marcuse 1979).

Marcuse early on developed a critical study of work and social alienation looking at economic activity within the total complexity of other human activities and human existence in general. In his 1933 essay "On the Philosophical Foundation of the Concept of Labor in Economics" labor is seen as the key *activity* by which *humanity exteriorizes itself* and also *humanizes the world*. In addition to persons directly involved in production, others like politicians, artists, researchers, and clergy also *do work*, and in his estimation are members of the labor force. He contends that "labor is an ontological concept of human existence as such" (Marcuse [1933] 1973a, 11). We enhance our self-expression and flourishing through labor, and this can take many forms. Marcuse builds upon Hegel's theory of the laboring consciousness overcoming its alienated existence and attaining an emancipated perception of its authentic self (Marcuse [1930] 1976, 36). He tied this also to Marx's historical and dialectical theory of socialist revolution as having the *primary purpose* of the supersession of "capitalist commodity production" (Ibid., 38), and especially the deformation and commodification (i.e. alienation) of labor.

Marcuse likewise honors Marx's philosophical humanism as "The Foundation of Historical Materialism." In his essay having that title Marcuse ([1932] 1973b) emphasizes that Marx in the 1844 Manuscripts, as is now widely known, repeatedly identifies a genuine concept of communism with a humanist worldview, and that the alienation theory articulated there by Marx looks to the supersession of alienation through the actualization of the human essence (Marcuse [1932] 1973b, 7-8). Both Marcuse and Marx saw economics as a philosophy of human activity in which ". . . labor was seen as the living subject bringing all contradictions to a head and making socialism 'inevitable' . . . ." (Dunayevskaya 2012, 96).

I have indicated above that human beings are not only the ensemble of our social relations, we are sensuous living labor, a view I derive from Marx and Marcuse in the following manner. Marx's first thesis on Feuerbach reads: "The chief defect of all hitherto existing materialism—that of Feuerbach included—is that the thing, reality, sensuousness, is conceived only in the form of the *object or of contemplation*, but not as *sensuous human activity, practice*, not subjectively" (emphasis in original). Marx criticizes the lack of labor theory in the sensualism of Feuerbach, and Marcuse cites Marx in *Reason and Revolution* ([1941] 1960) on the centrality of *labor* to human existence:

Because he conceived human existence in terms of sense, Feuerbach disregarded this material function of labor altogether. 'Not satisfied with abstract thought, Feuerbach appeals to sense-perception [Anschauung]; but *he does not understand our sensuous nature as practical, human-sensuous activity.*' Labor transforms the natural conditions of human existence into social ones. By omitting the labor process from his philosophy of freedom, therefore, Feuerbach omitted the decisive factor through which nature might become the medium for freedom. (Marx in Marcuse [1941] 1960, 272, emphasis added)

Like Marx, Marcuse emphasized that labor must be seen as a central dimension of human life beyond its narrow confines within a commodified economy. They both understood human alienation as estranged labor: sensuous living labor's separation from: 1) its product, 2) the process of production, 3) other producers, and 4) from our species need for the gratification of our sensuous, intellectual, political and ethical faculties.

Marx's labor theory of culture is vividly expressed in *Capital* Volume 1, chapter 7, on the labor process. He connects his theory to that of Benjamin Franklin, whom he credits with defining humanity as a tool-making animal.

> As soon as the labor process has undergone the slightest development, it requires specially prepared instruments. Thus we find stone implements and weapons in the oldest caves. In the earliest period of human history, domesticated animals, i.e. animals that have undergone modification by means of labor, that have been bred specially, play the chief part as instruments of labor along with stones, wood, bones, and shells, which have also had work done on them. The use and construction of instruments of labor, although present in germ among certain species of animals, is characteristic of the specifically human labor process, and Franklin therefore defines man as a "tool-making animal. (Marx [1867] 1976, 286)

Marx also quite famously connected the human labor process with human insight into forms of the ideal, even an aesthetic ideal:

> A spider conducts operations which resemble those of the weaver, and a bee would put many an architect to shame by the construction of its honeycomb cells. But what distinguishes the worst architect from the best of bees is that the architect

builds the cell in his mind before he constructs it in wax. At the end of every labor process, a result emerges which had already been conceived by the worker at the beginning, hence already existed ideally. (Marx [1867] 1976, 284)

What Marx believed was true for all authentically free productive labor was also true for art—a point not lost on Marcuse who in 1969 would come to highlight the possibility of the aesthetic as a *gesellschaftliche Produktivkraft* (Marcuse 1969, 26, 45), *a social and productive force* (Reitz 2000, 113).

Marx and Marcuse saw *capital* as congealed labor or dead labor—*living labor* that had been objectified into productive equipment, the means and tools of production. Abraham Lincoln expressed the same view—consistent with Locke, Smith and Marx—of the relationship of labor to capital: "Labor is prior to, and independent of, capital. Capital is only the fruit of labor, and could never have existed if labor had not first existed. Labor is the superior of capital, and deserves much the higher consideration."[5]

Employing Rudolf Bahro's theory[6] of "surplus

---

[5] Lincoln's Annual Message to Congress, December 3, 1861 cited in Michael Parenti, *Democracy for the Few* (New York: St. Martin's Press, 1988) p. 10.

[6] Bahro held that even state functionaries in the U.S.S.R. or Eastern Bloc often did not fully identify with the apparatus of government or its political imperatives. There, system-thinking was easily undermined when social contradictions became politically heightened, and a surplus consciousness (*überschüssiges Bewußtsein*, literally "overflow" of consciousness) widely emerged (Bahro 1977a, 381). During the final stages of his own intellectual development, Marcuse believed Bahro's insight was immensely significant. Douglas Kellner concludes: "In effect, Bahro and Marcuse are arguing that critical consciousness and emancipatory

consciousness" (Bahro 1977a, 376ff; 1977b) Marcuse argues against his previous emphasis in *One Dimensional Man* (1964) on the system-integration of the consciousness of the workforce. In his estimation under the changed socio-economic conditions of 1977-78, a "counter-consciousness" (Marcuse 1979, 21) was already emerging that made it possible for the consciousness "of the underlying population [to be] penetrated by the inherent contradictions of capitalism" (1979, 21). This echoes his essays on labor humanism (1932) and the concept of labor in economics (1933) discussed above.

Zvi Tauber's 2013 essay on Marcuse's aesthetics of liberation focuses on an appreciation of the trans-historical dimension of art within its specific-historical content. He develops an understanding of the classic question of how the existence and consciousness of modern humans and the ancient Greeks, for example, can be interlinked such that we can recognize and enjoy the art of antiquity. Utilizing Hegel, Marx, and Marcuse as sources, Tauber highlights Hegel's view that the phenomena of human existence in their historical totality develop a sense of truth about the human condition that is trans-historical, general, and universal. He then explains how Hegel's historical analysis of the phenomena of human existence is translated by Marx into sociological language. The conscious expression of this sense of humanity's real social existence in great art, such as in Greek tragedy, is to be seen as both a disclosure of life's real possibilities and a denunciation of life's real limitations.

I would like to propose in a manner of my own, yet analogous to Tauber's treatment of art, that trans-historical

---

needs are being developed by the contradictions in the social conditions of advanced industrial society—capitalist and state socialist." (Kellner 1984, 308-09).

insights can also emerge from a *non-religious, demystifying reading of the history of ethical thought in the world's traditions of moral philosophy*. I understand ethics here as rooted in specific-historical realities and practices and at the same time as a negation of these realities raised to a higher, ideal level. The ideals are themselves *practical:* aiming at the transformation and pacification of everyday conflict. I contend they too can be understood in social and historical terms that can ground a materialist theory of ethics and commonwealth.

The feminist anthropologist Riane Eisler (1987) introduced the term "partnership power" to describe cultural patterns in which men and women have different roles, yet these are not unequal. Though Eisler studied early Minoan civilization, similar qualities of ethical and political partnership have been noted as characteristic of the gathering and hunting societies and other largely egalitarian social formations prior to agriculture in which all persons were more alike than different (Nolan and Lenski 2005). Solidarity and partnership power generally characterized human relationships, rather than what Eisler criticizes as the later appearance of dominator power.

Humanity's first explicitly ethical maxims emerged as the proverbs that in a general way regulated life in the earliest African partnership cultures. These cultures centered on the customary sense of empathy and principles of reciprocity and solidarity in communal life, team work, modesty and mutuality, and included the first formulations of the golden rule. Philosophy professor, Godwin Azenabor (2008, 234), of the University of Lagos has argued for the underlying identity of African proverbs and Kant's categorical imperative. Of course there could be conflict within and between tribes. Nonetheless, these proverbs constituted universalizable humanist, i.e. not narrowly tribal, teachings for the guidance of practical life, and can in no way to be confused with purely religious teachings. "The cotton thread says that it is only as a team that you can carry a stone." "Many hands make light work." "It takes a whole village to raise a child." Not gods, but communally laboring humanity can be seen as the source of ethics here. Today many observers consider African cultures to be notoriously religious, some also profoundly misogynistic. Yet the secular humanistic foundations of African moral philosophy are soundly attested to by scholars such as Kwame Gyekye (2010), Kwasi Wiredu (1991) and Alfred T. Kisubi (2015).

In ancient China, the Dao was regarded as the "way" of the world. Opposites interpenetrated and emerged out of the other in a dialectical manner (centuries before Hegel and Marx developed their elaborations of the notion). Understanding the interconnectedness of all things, the yin/yang dynamics of both nature and human life, was necessary for concrete thinking and itself a social product. "Lay plans for the accomplishment of the difficult before it becomes difficult; make something big by starting with it when small" (*Dao De Jing*, LXIII). Today information processing would call this methodology a form of enhanced decision-making through systems analysis. Daoism's dialectical naturalism and humanism taught harmony, balance, gentleness, and equanimity with regard to life's changes. It accepted significant social inequalities, yet was skeptical of official knowledge. Political authority was considered legitimate only if it assured the material well-being of the masses as the "mandate of heaven" required. Heaven was thus a metaphor for the satisfaction through politics of human needs. When the policies of the prevailing powers did not or could not meet the economic needs of the people, the people's rights of rebellion and overthrow were to be exercised (Mèng Zǐ [Mencius], in Chan 2012).

For Kong Fuzi (Confucius) "heaven's" mandate

regarding the welfare of the common people also defined the purpose of government. An early form of a labor theory of ethics and justice may also be extrapolated from his *Analects:* "The head of a state or noble family worries not about underpopulation but about uneven distribution .... where there is even distribution there is no such thing as poverty" (*Analects* XVI.1). Humanist principles of benevolence, mutual regard, fairness, and humility are elaborated as *ren* or "human-heartedness." This was illustrated through the Principle of the Measuring Square: if there are those behind you, treat them as you would have those *in front of you* treat you; if there are those below you, treat them as you would have those *above you* treat you. With regard to religious practices, Kong Fuzi advised: "[W]ork for the things the common people have a right to and keep one's distance from gods and spirits while showing them reverence" (*Analects* VI.22). If one does not know how to serve one's comrades, how can one presume to serve gods (*Analects* XI.12). Rites in ancient China were observed in virtually all human affairs. They clearly went well beyond religion, and were part of everyday etiquette. Kong Fuzi taught open-mindedness, even in religion, with regard to these rites: "The asking of questions is in itself the correct rite" (*Analects* III.15). The golden rule appears as the injunction: "Do not impose upon others what you yourself do not desire" (*Analects* XV.24).

Ancient humanism in each of the forms above, was *not* a philosophy of the natural and unmediated goodness of human beings, as in the Romanticism of Rousseau. It was a philosophy of the humanizing influence of parents and teachers, customs, culture, and laws within a conflictual societal context. Plato's dialectics were borrowed from Socrates and derived from the high level conversations, actually social debates, which could arrive at truth. Plato, as *political* educator in the *Republic,* furnishes us with his key cave allegory. Its first sentence raises the issue: to what extent have we become enlightened or unenlightened about our being? "Let me tell you in a parable about whether the mind of humans is educated or uneducated about human nature and the human condition" (Steph. VII, 514a). Plato understands the propensities of our sensuous living substance toward illusion, delusion, dishonor, and disgrace. At the same time his dialectical humanism stresses that to be enlightened/educated about our being and reality means we are capable of constructing from within ourselves rational knowledge addressing our uncertain general condition —resolving the appearance/reality conundrum in terms of an idea or model of the moral good to be pursued and obtained in our individual lives—including a "Platonic love" of learning, wisdom, the good society, and the good life. In sharp contrast to divine command theories of ethics and politics, which taught obedience to a supernatural protective authority above all else, Plato taught that critical thinking, rather than the unfathomable and arbitrary will of the gods, could determine right conduct.

Plato argued that conventional beliefs about the visible and intelligible worlds are subject to question, and if not examined, they often lead to a shallow, disillusioned life. Education should remove the chains of illusion. An education to ideals as criteria of judgment makes possible the realization of our dignity and our greatest (intellectual and political) satisfactions. Rational minds learn through dialogue and debate as well as through logical deduction (mathematical reasoning). Study and inquiry can disclose how the best possible human relations and human communities may be constituted. He theorizes that justice is the characteristic of the public work of the leaders of the ideal city/state insofar as this political entity is governed by equal numbers of men and women educated to the (conflicted) human condition, living communally, with intelligence moderating appetite and spirit, disinterested and detached from lust for property, power, fame, etc., devoutly acting in accordance (not with God's will, but) with principles we have deciphered as to what is substantively advantageous for the pacification of our conflicted species life.

Today we are aware of the African and Asian roots of Plato's view of the world (Bernal 1991): how the *Republic* and the *Meno*, especially, share with Egyptian, Indian, and Buddhist philosophies cultural notions of communal harmonization, transmigration of souls/reincarnation in a caste system, enlightenment and equanimity. Plato's *Republic* did not include the general public as participants at any level of government, unless they first met educational qualifications, and this reflected existing aristocratic practice. Thus, many have seen his particular political and educational recommendations as authoritarian and conservative. His guardians seem legitimated as elite human beings. Still, Meno was a common slave-boy fully able to comprehend the highest forms of mathematical reasoning following the guidance of Socrates, thus he was a potential leader as well.

Marcuse stresses the *practical and subversive* nature of Plato's philosophy: "[T]he authentic, basic demand of idealism is that this material world be transformed and improved by knowledge of the Ideas. Plato's answer to this demand is his program for a reorganization of society" ([1937] 1968, 91-92). Likewise, we need to comprehend the proto-humanistic elements embedded in other ancient wisdom traditions such as Judaism and Hinduism.

Judaism requires us to do well the labor that confronts us as a necessity, to make amends annually to those we may have offended or to whom we may owe a debt, and it also supplies dozens of proverbs for right conduct. So too its veneration of the exodus from oppression and escape from slavery (a political-economic denunciation and liberation ethic which also abides in Islam and Christianity).

Hinduism teaches the ideal and power of *Dharma*: that benevolence is to be engraved in human hearts, and people are to live such that they might become worthy of immortal bliss. The instrument of this ideal is the ostensible power of karma, the doctrine of reciprocity and the rise in the long run of the indestructible human species essence (Atman) within an individual to attain fulfillment, happiness, and nirvana. Only honest labor/action, consecrated by good will in work/struggle, detached from consequences, can lead to good fortune. A version of the golden rule rises once more in the *Mahabharata* in Dharma's famous questioning of Yudhishthira (in the "Virata"): "What is honesty?—That is to look and see every living creature as yourself, bearing your own will to live, and your own fear of death.....What is it that humanity calls good fortune?—That is the result of what they have done honestly" (Buck 1973, 121).

The doctrine of karma legitimates dramatic and devastating social inequality, and like the caste system itself, these features have been negated and superseded through struggle in modern India. The idea of karma may nevertheless be seen as a metaphor for the real social interconnectedness of the conditions facing newer generations as these have been impacted by the work, for better or worse, of older generations. This may also be seen as a token of the moral principle of reciprocity analogous to the Confucian doctrine of the Measuring Square. Nirmal Kumar Bose (1965) has stressed a view of Gandhi as a humanist and socialist, emphasizing his classic practice of *satyagraha*, the refusal to cooperate with unethical social conventions, and Gandhi's belief that honest labor undergirds a life worth living (Bose 1965, 90-91).

Buddhism, as a view of the world without gods,

pursues the cessation of human suffering. Gotama Siddhartha, its founder, taught that we might become enlightened as to the human condition. At its root, therefore, Buddhism is an ethics of humanism, expressed most concisely in its *Four Noble Truths* [Proverbs]: life is suffering; suffering has its cause(s); these causes can be overcome; act/work/live in that manner which relieves the suffering in oneself—and that of others (as does the socially activist figure of the Bodhisattva).

Buddha, Socrates, and Kong Fuzi preceded Aristotle by a full generation or more. Aristotle saw humanity as a political animal, the *zoon politikon,* and politics the master art in the proper fashioning of human life and human society. As Marcuse explains:

> The doctrine that all human knowledge is oriented toward practice belonged to the nucleus of ancient philosophy. It was Aristotle's view that the truths arrived at through knowledge should direct practice in daily life as in the arts and sciences. In the struggle for existence, men need the effort of knowledge, the search for truth, because what is good, beneficial, and right for them is not immediately evident. (Marcuse [1937] 1968, 88)

Aristotle theorized that our highest happiness derived from the actualization of our essentially human capacities, powers, and potentials: speech/thought; worthy conduct, integrity, character, and moderation by way of the golden mean. Our task was to become intellectually and politically accomplished. To this end one's upbringing, parenting, education, and the social structure supportive of these nurturing forces, were the most crucial factors. Aristotle's naturalism and humanism inquired into the ways and means by which our species might thrive and flourish. In economics and ethics, a chief vice was the boundless pursuit of property accumulation; a chief virtue, the pursuit of the well-being of the community (*Politics* Chapter IX).

Among the key social teachings of medieval Islam, Christianity, and Judaism were those that preserved essential elements of Aristotle's philosophy of moderation in economic pursuits (condemning excess and insufficiency, the charging of interest, etc.). Ibn Khaldun is said to have adapted Aristotle's political concept of humanity in the fourteenth century. His central notion of *asabiyyah* emphasized the sense of shared social purpose and solidarity making for community cohesion, and he developed a perspective on political economy rooted in the idea that all earnings derive from the value created through labor.

Bertrand Russell's essay, "Why I am Not a Christian," ([1927] 1967) treats Jesus as a non-divine, human teacher. In the Sermon on the Mount, once again, the golden rule holds an honored position. This and other precepts and proverbs, however, are attested to by Russell as, by and large, a reprise of earlier teachings of the Daoist master, Laozi, as well as Buddha and Socrates on humility, forgiveness, loving-kindness, and generosity to the poor.

In the modern epoch Kant is thought to have philosophized about benevolence, good will, and the golden rule most prodigiously. He transfigures these into the proverbial categorical imperative:

Never act except in such a way that your practice models what you would desire as the universal behavioral ideal. Against the notion of the supernatural origin of ethical standards, in his view *humanist* standards are the origin of everything that might be called truly sacred:[7]

> God is not a substance existing outside me, but merely a moral relation within me....The categorical imperative does not assume a substance issuing its commands from on high, conceived therefore as outside me, but is a commandment or a prohibition of my own reason.... The categorical imperative represents human duties as divine commandments not in the historical sense, as if [a divine being] had given commands to men, but in the sense that reason...has the power to command with the authority and in the guise of a divine person.... The Idea of such a being, before whom all bend the knee, etc. arises out of the categorical imperative, and not vice versa....[8]

Kant saw enlightenment as political education: individuals, having formerly consented to remain silent with regard to political judgment, could emerge from this self-inflicted disfranchisement by using their own intellectual faculties to weigh and evaluate circumstances free of the political guidance of the prevailing religious and governmental authorities. Enlightenment political education could gradually bring us closer to a constitution establishing world citizenship, which he saw as also indispensable for the

---

[7] Kant explicitly distinguishes the proverbial golden rule from *his* notion of the categorical imperative, elevating the ostensibly wholly rational origins of his imperative above the practical, proverbial origins of the former. This is bitterly ironic when seen in conjunction with his subsequent defense (ill-fitted to his Enlightenment aspirations) of the practice of religion as a legitimate intellectual foundation for a proof of god's existence.

[8] Immanuel Kant, *Posthumous papers*, cited in Will Durant, *The Story of Civilization*, Volume X, (New York: Simon and Schuster, 1967) p. 550.

maintenance of the global public's human rights and hence also world peace. Though there was no talk of rights in early forms of ethical thinking, there is today a common language of human rights epitomized in the UN Universal Declaration (1948).

In *Perpetual Peace* Kant argues the theoretical warrant for the emergence of a "universal cosmopolitan state" (Kant [1784] 1983, 38). He acknowledges in advance that this proposal will be met by ostensibly "*worldly-wise* statesmen" with smugness (Kant [1795] 1983, 107), and that they would deride and dismiss his political views as "mere theory." The "practical politician" would mock the human duty towards peace, and assert instead the "right" of the strong to make the weak obey them. "Nonetheless, … reason absolutely condemns war as a means of determining right and makes seeking the state of peace a matter of unmitigated duty…. A league of a special sort must therefore be established, one that we can call a *league of peace*… to end *all* wars forever" (Kant [1795] 1983, 116-17).

Hegel and Marx further developed the logic and strategy that undergirds today's commonwealth aspirations. Hegel taught that history is a way of learning, and he raised the contemporary philosophical issue of why humanity's social and intellectual life is still controlled by the powerful few rather than by the multitude. Hegel argued the social evolution of reason from lower to higher which would absorb and complete the limited and alienated products of an earlier form of culture and education, attaining thereby an advanced level of intelligence, art, and civilization. Hegel's theory proposed that dis-alienation had to be the *work* of the alienated elements themselves, educationally and politically. It remained for Marx's *labor theory of history* to buttress Hegel on alienation and to call attention to the appropriative and expropriative economic and political processes of the past and those which we continue to confront today in advanced capitalist modes, as well as the re-appropriation challenges of the global workforce. The tenth Feuerbach thesis tells us: "The standpoint of the old materialism is civil society; the standpoint of the new is human society, or social humanity." Marx replaces the bourgeois notion of civil society (which claims a spurious social status separate from the government and the economy) with the notion of social humanity as a governmental and economic power, i.e. human society as commonwealth.

My sketch here of some of the features of the world's practical wisdom traditions is consistent with Marx's philosophical materialism: "The mode of production of material life determines the general character of the social, political, and spiritual processes of life. It is not the consciousness of men that determines their being, but on the contrary, their social being determines their consciousness" (Marx [1859] 2009, 11). As we have seen, Marcuse emphasized that practical social problems gave rise dialectically to ideas subversive to the established reality. The source may be said to be within us insofar as *social customs of empathy and solidarity* find *instinctual* expression in the life-preserving force of Eros, longing for the pacification of the struggle for existence. The primatologist Frans de Waal (2013, 2009, 2006) has demonstrated convincingly how morality evolved, and has argued the emergence of an instinctual sense of empathy in certain primates and humans: "distress at the sight of another's pain is an impulse over which we exert little or no control; it grabs us instantaneously, like a reflex, with no time to weigh the pros and cons" (2006, 51).

Herbert Marcuse's 1969 *Essay on Liberation* with its consideration of "A Biological Foundation for Socialism?" actually presages de Waal's perspective. Human existence is seen as a function not only of one's ensemble of social relations, but also in terms of the gratification and/or the frustration of *our essential sensuousness*. This historical and material dynamic propels a *politics of labor ownership of wealth* as the liberation of the repressed political potential of the human species.

Thus, Richard Wolin and John Abromeit also remind us of Marcuse's discussion in *Essay on Liberation* of the biological and instinctual foundations of socialism:

> Prior to all ethical behavior in accordance with specific social standards, prior to all ideological expression, *morality is a disposition of the organism*, perhaps rooted in the erotic drive to counter aggressiveness, to create and preserve "ever greater unities of life." We would then have, this side of all "values," *an instinctual foundation for solidarity among human beings*—a solidarity which has been effectively repressed in line with the requirements of a class society but which now appears as a precondition for liberation.[9]

Marcuse's 1965 essay "Socialist Humanism?" argued that the prospects of a socialist humanist politics needed to be investigated once again. He criticized the ostensible humanism of the then-U.S.S.R., but not as this was usually done, i.e. rejecting it because its policies were implemented through violence and duress. Marcuse emphasized how the American and European imperialists likewise used their war machines to advocate human rights in foreign places, while on

---

[9] Marcuse in Richard Wolin and John Abromeit (eds), "Introduction" to their *Heideggerian Marxism* (Lincoln, NE: University of Nebraska Press, 2005) p. xxix.

the home front it simultaneously reduced and restricted these rights. In his estimation, Marxism stresses correctly that humanism can only be realized through the expropriation of the expropriators, the elimination of commodity exchange, the reduction of the work week, the transformation of the labor process itself, and the dismantling of the military industrial complex. Humanism can *begin*, however, Marcuse says, within the existing capitalist society itself if it becomes a vital need of human beings who stand ready to liberate humanity and revolutionize human relationships. This need must then come to direct economic and political praxis as a component of material culture.

In 1962, Marcuse similarly confronted a core humanist conundrum:

> Today the words "humanity" and "humanism" cause us some perplexity. Clearly something about them has not worked. It seems as though these ideas, these concepts, are of only antiquarian value, that humanism and humanity belong only to history. But what does that mean: that they belong only to history? If something happened just thirty years ago, that is history, and yet it conditions the present and will also affect our future. What we have learned during these thirty years that we had not earlier known, is this: *what human beings can be made to do. They can be made into inhuman beings.* (Marcuse in Reitz 2015)

Marcuse emphasized that "Marxism must risk defining freedom in such a way that people become conscious of and recognize it as something that is nowhere already in existence. And precisely because the so-called utopian possibilities are not at all utopian but rather the determinate socio-historical negation of what exists, a very real and very pragmatic opposition is required of us . . . ." (Marcuse 1970b, 69). A materialist interpretation of the humanist tradition demonstrates how labor-based opposition today can also express the "social force of a new general interest" (Marcuse 1970a, 90).

Che Guevara's famous statement on the ethos of Platonic love in the socialist revolutionary vanguard is also worth recollecting here:

> This vanguard was the catalyzing agent that created the subjective conditions necessary for victory. . . Every one of the fighters of the Sierra Maestra who reached an upper rank in the revolutionary forces has a record of outstanding deeds to his credit. They attained their rank on this basis . . . they competed for the heaviest responsibilities, for the greatest dangers, with no other satisfaction than fulfilling a duty. . . . At the risk of seeming ridiculous, let me say that the true revolutionary is guided by great feelings of love. It is impossible to think of a genuine revolutionary lacking this quality. Perhaps it is one of the great dramas of the leader that he must combine a passionate spirit with a cold intelligence and make painful decisions without flinching. Our vanguard revolutionaries must make an ideal of this love of the people, of the most sacred causes, and make it one and indivisible. . . . In these circumstances one must have a big dose of humanity, a big dose of a sense of justice and truth in order not to fall into dogmatic extremes, into cold scholasticism, into an isolation from the masses. We must strive every day so that this love of living humanity is transformed into actual deeds, into acts

that serve as examples, as a moving force.[10]

Of course Guevara understood that revolutionaries need and have friends, wives, families whom they love in the usual sense, and that it is *from* these relationships that a revolutionary love is forged.

Multiple modes of moral reasoning contend with socialist humanism and the labor theory of ethics. The latter, as humanism, negates divine command theory, yet absorbs and preserves character-based and duty-based approaches, as well as the social utilitarianism of Mill. The personal utility calculus of Bentham is regarded by Marx as a form of moral egoism consistent only with bourgeois philistinism, as was the theory that even private economic evils can contribute—through the magic of the market—to the public good. Max Stirner, Friedrich Nietzsche, and Ayn Rand fall into similar categories of egoist illegitimacy.

Aldo Leopold's ecological conception of land as a biotic system—to which we belong—led him to a logic of husbandry, love, and respect for nature in recreation—and production; the land is healthy if it has the capacity for self-renewal. Leoplold's "land ethic" enlarges the boundaries of the community concept to include soils, water, plants, animals, air. Humanity is not the conqueror of the land-community, but a citizen of what I would call a Green Commonwealth. Conservation and cooperation are the effects of an "ecological conscience"—

[E]thics, so far studied only by philosophers, is actually a process in ecological evolution. Its

---

[10] Che Guevara, "Man and Socialism Speech (1965)" retrieved February 20, 2013 from http://www.hey-che.com/man-socialism-speech-1965/

sequences may be described in ecological as well as in philosophical terms. An ethic, ecologically, is a limitation on freedom of action in the struggle for existence. An ethic, philosophically, is a differentiation of social from anti-social conduct. These are two definitions of one thing. The thing has its origin in the tendency of interdependent individuals or groups to evolve modes of cooperation . . . . cooperative mechanisms with an ethical content. (Leopold [1949] 1966, 217-218).

To Leopold, earth was awesome, earth was radical. His "Land Aesthetic" elaborates this view: "What is art? Only the drama of the land's workings."[11] Aside from humans, does any other living being on the face of the planet appreciate its beauty, its ethical promise?

Cognizant of the prevalence of malevolence and cruelty, conquest, unjust imprisonment, torture, starvation, that have continually destroyed and damaged human lives and the human promise throughout history, the *socialist humanist vision* of an egalitarian and partnership society (like that of Marcuse and Marx) with an economic foundation informed by ethics, may appear to be obsolete. How can this vision be defended against its usual rejection as impossibly utopian, at best good in theory, but of no practical political-economic value?

The dialectic of enlightenment as elaborated by Max Horkheimer and Theodor W. Adorno ([1944] 1972) profoundly undermined philosophical and political confidence in the trans-historical truths of high German art. Adorno, as is well known, questioned the very possibility of

---

[11] Ibid., p. 303.

poetry after Auschwitz. This is quite possibly what led Marcuse to endorse in 1967 Thomas Mann's call for the revocation of Beethoven's Ninth Symphony, which incorporated Schiller's "Ode to Joy" ["Alle Menschen werden Brüder"—"All human beings are becoming brothers" —Reitz]. Marcuse found this sublime art work to be an illusion that justified the "no longer justifiable" (Marcuse [1967] 1973, 66; Reitz 2000, 202). Are the values preserved in a humanist ethics also "bright shining lies," at best only abstract criteria of judgment, trans-historically insightful perhaps, yet impotent in terms of the formation of moral and political praxis? Must the categorical imperative and golden rule also be revoked? Or in some manner can they be considered to retain a significance on a par with the dignified, if tragically conflicted, view of humanity and world found in much profound and great art?

Marx's dialectics teaches us that groups can and do have contradictory material interests. Sometimes these are completely antagonistic, and the context will not allow a resolution of the conflict. Antagonism is certainly not a necessary feature of societies that are internally differentiated. How to live in society in ways that are just and sustainable is not self-evident, and this has been a trans-historical and critical challenge to human cultures.

Marx was aware, in an insight derived from Aristotle that the pursuit of private accumulation—beyond all bounds—was not compatible with the meaning of *oikonomia*, economics. *Oikonomia* referred to *the concrete considerations given to ensure the well-being or flourishing of the household, and by extension, the community.*

To use Ernest Manheim's ([1932] in Reitz 2016) terminology, today we know that the global regime of capital accumulation is "an economy which is not one" (A/1). How do we develop a transformative praxis that can produce a form of social organization that would allow us to say "Now THIS is an economy!" (A/3). Manheim tells us A/1 is to be understood as having a tendency to supersede itself [*sich aufzuheben*], it contains from the outset its own negation. It is part of a larger concrete unity of opposites (totality) to be understood and guided in its essential dynamism.

> Dialectics . . . is the method of construction of rational (and not rationalistic) concepts from being itself. The construction and systematization of concrete concepts is thus not derived from a creative intuition or phantasy—dialectics is a rational guide in the thinking of reality as a complete system . . . This reality is human existence in its individual, social, and historical details. (Manheim in Reitz 2016, 47)

Marcuse also asserts our "consciousness of a divided world in which 'that which is' falls short of and even denies 'that which can be'" (Marcuse 1964, 213). "Thus the [concrete] concept of beauty comprehends all the beauty not *yet* realized; the [concrete] concept of freedom all the liberty not *yet* attained" (Ibid., 214). Life and art are always troubled by conflicting conditions and forces. People [and conditions] are always contradictory; we are always "both better and worse than we are" (Simmons 1997). Yet *excellence* is the *telos* that directs praxis to transform the extant societal ground to its attainable sociological and historical potentials (even if these are temporarily arrested). Marcuse notes that the universal in Greek philosophy denotes "the most general as the highest, the first in 'excellence,' and therefore the real reality" (Marcuse 1964, 214).

According to Manheim's ([1932] 2016) fourfold perspective on the dialectic, a concrete logic is a matter of how *what is thought* is connected to *what is,* and *how* both social thought and *social being* change (or fail to change) for the better through negation of the negation:

    1. Positive and negative aspects of the contradictory social reality exist simultaneously.
    2. The negative aspects of this totality/system must be recognized and acknowledged. The obvious, though one-sided, positive benefits must be discounted as one-sided.
    3. Yet we must affirm the best within these positives while the negative aspects of experience must be rooted out.
    4. Finally, *critical praxis with its mediating and radical norm of excellence against alienation in labor, ethics, art, and politics* has the power to obviate the crucial negatives and liberate the arrested positives such that what is approaches its best condition.

    Over against the misanthropic and cynical conservatism—that asserts inborn human aggression, the right of the stronger to economic exploitation, and imperial manifest destiny, etc.—Marx, Marcuse and Manheim saw philosophical humanism *not* as politically powerless, but on the contrary: *practical* struggles for human dignity, respect, and empowerment have led to significant intercultural learning and social progress. The overarching aim of a humanist morality, in my view, is to offer an apt contribution to the project of human liberation and preservation; from the facts of crisis and suffering to discern their causes, eliminate their sources, alleviate the suffering, and stabilize a long term resolution—in order to establish human dignity and a commonwealth culture as the radical goals of the global socialist rising of, by, and for sensuous living labor.

    Today's intensifying levels of global economic oppression necessitate intellectual and political growth. The ethic of intercultural solidarity today is essential in terms of praxis if the human species is to go on living. The labor movement must be able to explain this praxis and the necessity of socialism and humanism. This is a matter of our very survival, as attested to by many writers but perhaps most vividly by Chris Hedges and Joe Sacco in *Days of Destruction, Days of Revolt*: "Corporate capitalism will, quite literally, kill us, as it has killed Native Americans, African Americans trapped in our internal colonies, in the inner cities, those left behind in the devastated coal fields, and those who live as serfs in our nation's produce fields" (Hedges and Sacco 2012, xii).

This dialectics of the concrete concept is the precondition for the fulfillment of our species being. Marcuse's perspective on the historical reality of universals is likewise essential for liberation. "The universal comprehends in one ides the possibilities which are realized, and at the same time arrested, in reality" (ODM, 210). "The substantive universal intends qualities which surpass all particular experience, but persist in the mind, not as a figment of the imagination nor as mere logical possibilities, but as the 'stuff' of which our world consists" (ODM, 213).

My contention (building upon Marx, Manheim and Marcuse) is that *an intercultural labor force humanism* is not only necessary but feasible: it is the instinctual and gravitational center holding social life together despite flare ups and explosions caused by the massive forces of careening corporate capitalism. The labor force can rely *only* upon itself and the world's commonwealth traditions to mobilize its fullest transformative power. Labor's humanism in this sense defines not only a revolutionary ethos like that described by Che Guevara, but the type of economic, social, and political structure that is needed for to provide human sustainability, justice, and peace.

The workforce is a resource with programmatic power. It is the creative force in the economy. *Everything depends on labor.* This realization stands at the heart of concrete, praxis-oriented philosophizing. Labor occurs in social relationships; it is a communal project of social beings to meet human needs and promote human flourishing. Because social labor is the source of all socially created wealth, *only the labor force, as a group, has a legitimate right to the ownership of this wealth.*

Radical activists/authors today are coming to realize also that: "the only way forward is a new arrangement, based on ones that have better served societies since the dawn of civilization" (Pettifor 2012, 24). These "new" arrangements are derived from the commonwealth practices that prevailed for the longest period in human history in ancient African (and subsequently other, e.g. Minoan) partnership societies, and which persist in the contemporary labor theory of ethics as outlined here. Just one indication of this advancing perspective is that of British ecological economist, Brian Davey, who suggests as a new socialist starting point "the philosophy, culture, and political economic ideas of a diversity of indigenous communities and tribes in the Andean region" (Davey 2012). These peoples were modeling a "solidarity economy" blending ecology and socialism after a long history of colonial oppression, racism, and sexism. The contemporary combination of socialism and ecological policy is likewise seen by others (Kozloff 2008; Bateman 2012; Sitrin 2012) as offering further examples in Spain, Argentina, Cuba, Venezuela, Bolivia, Brazil, and elsewhere.

In my view, a *commonwealth* arrangement of the economy would *hold and control resources publicly, eliminate rent-seeking and the for-profit financial industry as modes of privilege, distribute incomes without reference to individual productivity according to need and as equally as feasible, substantially reduce hours of labor, and make possible, through socialist general education privileging no single culture or language, the well-rounded scientific and multicultural development of the young.* Bertrand Russell proposes, only half sardonically, that labor is valuable not because work is intrinsically good, but because leisure is good. "A great deal of harm is being done in the modern world by belief in the virtuousness of *work* ... the road to happiness and prosperity lies in the organized diminution of work" (Russell 1965, 227). Of course Russell is referring to alienated labor. Nonetheless, as Marx and Marcuse also stress, a great deal of leisure in each person's life would be an irreplaceable resource for the free play of human energy and effort in one's own artistic or avocational projects, and must be an essential element of any new labor-humanist or commonwealth arrangement. Artwork *is* work, as Marx himself emphasized.

Commonwealth combines unity with multiplicity. If we say the human species is a multicultural species because humans have lived in a variety of geographical settings in various historical circumstances, we mean to acknowledge that a diversity of cultures has emerged. Certain of these cultures, as with the Anglo-American imperium, have displaced and dominated others. Traditionally Anglo-conformist higher education in the U.S., with its entrenched and discriminatory politics of race, gender, and class, typified *mono*cultural and exceptionalist assertions of superiority and concomitant internal hierarchies. Horkheimer and Adorno in *Dialectic of Enlightenment* subverted the claims of a similar kind of arrogant self-regard, demonstrating how Germany's ostensibly enlightened monoculture was historically compatible with genocidal chauvinism, predation, and war.

Marcuse's writing counterposed a critical and multi-dimensional philosophical perspective against the single-dimensional qualities and economic deformations of cultures that reproduce oppression and inequality. Through explicit attempts to overcome the dominant forms of monoculturalism and nationalistic exceptionalism, which only see differences as deficiencies, we can attain a deeper, more complete understanding and relationship to reality. In this sense, the reification and restriction of the consciousness of the labor force, identified as the central problematic or conundrum of Western Marxism since the writings of Lukács, preventing labor from comprehending its condition and acting to build beyond it, is receding in relevance in proportion to the advance of a more complete multicultural and *inter*cultural understanding of the human condition. What have been recognized as the civilizing forces of our age: the labor movement, civil rights movement, women's rights movement, the anti-war movement, the LGBT (lesbian, gay, bisexual, transgender) movement, and widespread ecological efforts, have educated the general population about alienation, oppression, power, and empowerment as they have engaged in creative struggles for egalitarian social change.

Marcuse saw this coming, and in his last essay on "The Reification of the Proletariat," wrote of a "counter-consciousness" emergent "among the dependent population (today about 90% of the total?), an awareness of the ever more blatant obsolescence of the established social division and organization of work" (Marcuse 1979, 21). This counter-consciousness included a consciousness of growing frustration, humiliation, and waste that is tending to become "a material force" (1979, 22).

In Marcuse's final book, *The Aesthetic Dimension*, he concluded that great works, even given their apparently illusory qualities, were always and permanently a manifestation of the struggle for liberation. Likewise, I argue here the enduring value of those particular aspects of the world's traditions in moral philosophy, i.e., those consistent with the labor theory of ethics and socialist humanism, as furnishing trans-historical, material and intellectual warrants for humanity's as yet unfinished project of liberation and actualization.

The labor theory of ethics grounds its commonwealth criteria of judgment in the real and enduring material possibilities that concretely encompass all of our engagement and action.

We have learned from the movements against racism and sexism in the United States that class relations do not wholly demarcate structures of dominator power. Racism, patriarchy, homophobia, and other forms of discrimination, disrespect, and inequality sorely inhibit our capacity for social- and self-actualization. Forms of persecution are multiplying amidst growing inequality. Reactionary forces reinforce bias of every sort in the hoary yet effective strategy of divide and conquer. While the general abolition of the wages-system is not absolutely *sufficient* to secure the conditions for each of us to become all that we are capable of being, *the alienation and exploitation of labor is the enabling material core that today requires dominant cultures to subjugate innocent minorities.*

Shortly before he died Marcuse posed the question of whether the ascendency of a neo-fascist regime in the U.S.A. can be prevented. Among the reasons why he asked this was his conviction that since at least 1972 the U.S. had entered a period of preemptive counterrevolution.

Certainly this tendency has only worsened after 9/11. Douglas Kellner (2003) elaborates this kind of conservative counterrevolution by citing foreign and domestic policy initiatives of the second Bush administration which wished to make "the global war on terror" the defining struggle of the era. Kellner re-named this policy Terror War because the key developments of the global war on terror are comprised of basically totalitarian components: bellicose nationalism and aggressive militarism, under the rubrics of "crusade" against enemy jihadists. Combating the "axis of evil" legitimated "preemptive strikes" and "regime change," as well as domestic police state powers under the U.S.A. Patriot Act and the National Security Agency. Kellner demonstrates, further, that these policies have propelled the U.S. into being itself a rogue state, a renewed imperialist power, and whose projection of military might continues to be oblivious of civilian casualties and war crimes.

Marcuse advises: "Today radical opposition can be considered only in a global framework" (Marcuse 1970a, 83). "All the material and intellectual forces which could be put to work for the realization of a free society are at hand. That they are not used for that purpose is to be attributed to the total mobilization of the existing society against its own potential for liberation" (Marcuse 1970b, 64).

Today's global capitalist crisis is a crucial opportunity for a new political beginning. The goal of building a universal human community on the foundation of universal human rights cannot be accomplished by a renewed call for education to emancipatory consciousness alone. We must acknowledge *the fundamental role of the labor process in the sustenance of the human community.* Even though this can be dehumanized and degraded, we have learned that it also has the irreplaceable power to build the commonwealth, past and future.

Our task is to "Look capitalism in the eye" and address its most sacred cows: We need to expropriate the expropriators; eliminate commodity exchange; reduce the work week; guarantee incomes to all; dismantle the military industrial complex. Under system duress, continuing allegiances to crumbling structures of power will be seen as fatally misguided, because they entail real material loss and suffering; they can and will swiftly shift. We need to replace capitalist self-destruction with intercultural labor force activism and humanism—to create laboring humanity's sovereign cosmopolitan commonwealth.

Bibliography

Amnesty International. 1998. *United States of America. Rights for All.* New York: Amnesty International U.S.A.

Azcárate, Manuel. 1978. "What is Eurocommunism," in G.R. Urban (ed). *Eurocommunism.* London: Maurice Temple Smith.

Azenabor, Godwin. 2008. *QUEST: An African Journal of Philosophy / Revue Africaine de Philosophie* XXI: 229-240.

Bernal, Martin. 1991. *Black Athena: The Afroasiatic Roots of Classical Civilization: The Fabrication of Ancient Greece 1785-1985.* New York: Random House.

Buck, William. 1973. *Mahabharata.* New York: New American Library.

Bose, Nirmal Kumar. 1965. "Gandhi: Humanist and Socialist" in Erich Fromm (ed). *Socialist Humanism.* Garden City, NY: Doubleday.

Chan, Peter, M. K. 2012. *The Six Patriarchs of Chinese Humanism.* Lulu.com
http://www.lulu.com/shop/peter-mk-chan/the-six-patriarchs-of-chinese-humanism/ebook/product-20158012.html

Daniel, Lloyd C. 2003. *Liberation Education.* Kansas City, Mo: New Democracy Press.

Davey, Brian. 2012. "Perhaps We Can Create a Society in which a Good Life is Possible," in Kalle Lasn (ed). *Meme Wars.* New York: Seven Stories Press.

Dean, Jodi. 2012. *The Communist Horizon.* London: Verso Press.

De Waal, Frans. 2013. *The Bonobo and the Atheist: In Search of Humanism among the Primates.* New York: W.W. Norton
_____. 2009. *The Age of Empathy.* New York: Random House.
_____. 2006. *Primates and Philosophers.* Princeton, NJ: Princeton University Press.
Dunayevskaya, Raya. 1965. "Marx's Humanism Today" in Erich Fromm (ed.). *Socialist Humanism.* Garden City, NY: Doubleday.
Eisler, Riane. 1987. *The Chalace and the Blade.* San Francisco: Harper.
Gyekye, Kwame. 2010. "African Ethics" in *The Stanford Encyclopedia of Philosophy* (Fall 2011 Edition), Edward N. Zalta (ed.), URL = <http://plato.stanford.edu/archives/fall2011/entries/african-ethics/>.
Habermas, Jürgen. 1981. *Philosophisch-politische Profile.* Frankfurt: Suhrkamp.
Horkheimer, Max and Theodor W. Adorno. [1944] 1972. *Dialectic of Enlightenment.* New York: Herder and Herder.
Kant, Immanuel. [1795] 1983. *Perpetual Peace and Other Essays.* Translated by Ted Humphrey with a dedication to Herbert Marcuse [!] Indianapolis, IN: Hackett Publishing.
Marcuse, Herbert. [1968] 2009. "Lecture on Education, Brooklyn College, 1968" in Douglas Kellner, Tyson Lewis, Clayton Pierce, K. Daniel Cho. 2009. *Marcuse's Challenge to Education.* Lanham, MD: Rowman & Littlefield.
_____. [1977] 2005a. "Thoughts on Judaism, Israel, etc." in Douglas Kellner (ed.) *Herbert Marcuse the New Left and the 1960s, Collected Papers of Herbert Marcuse, Volume III.* London and New York: Routledge.
_____. [1968] 2005b. "Marcuse Defines His New Left Line" in Douglas Kellner (ed.) *Herbert Marcuse the New Left and the 1960s, Collected Papers of Herbert Marcuse, Volume III.* London and New York: Routledge.
_____. 1979. "The Reification of the Proletariat," *Canadian Journal of Political and Social Theory / Revue canadienne de théorie politique et sociale,* Vol 3, No 1 (Winter/Hiver).
_____. [1955] 1974. *Eros and Civilization.* Boston: Beacon.

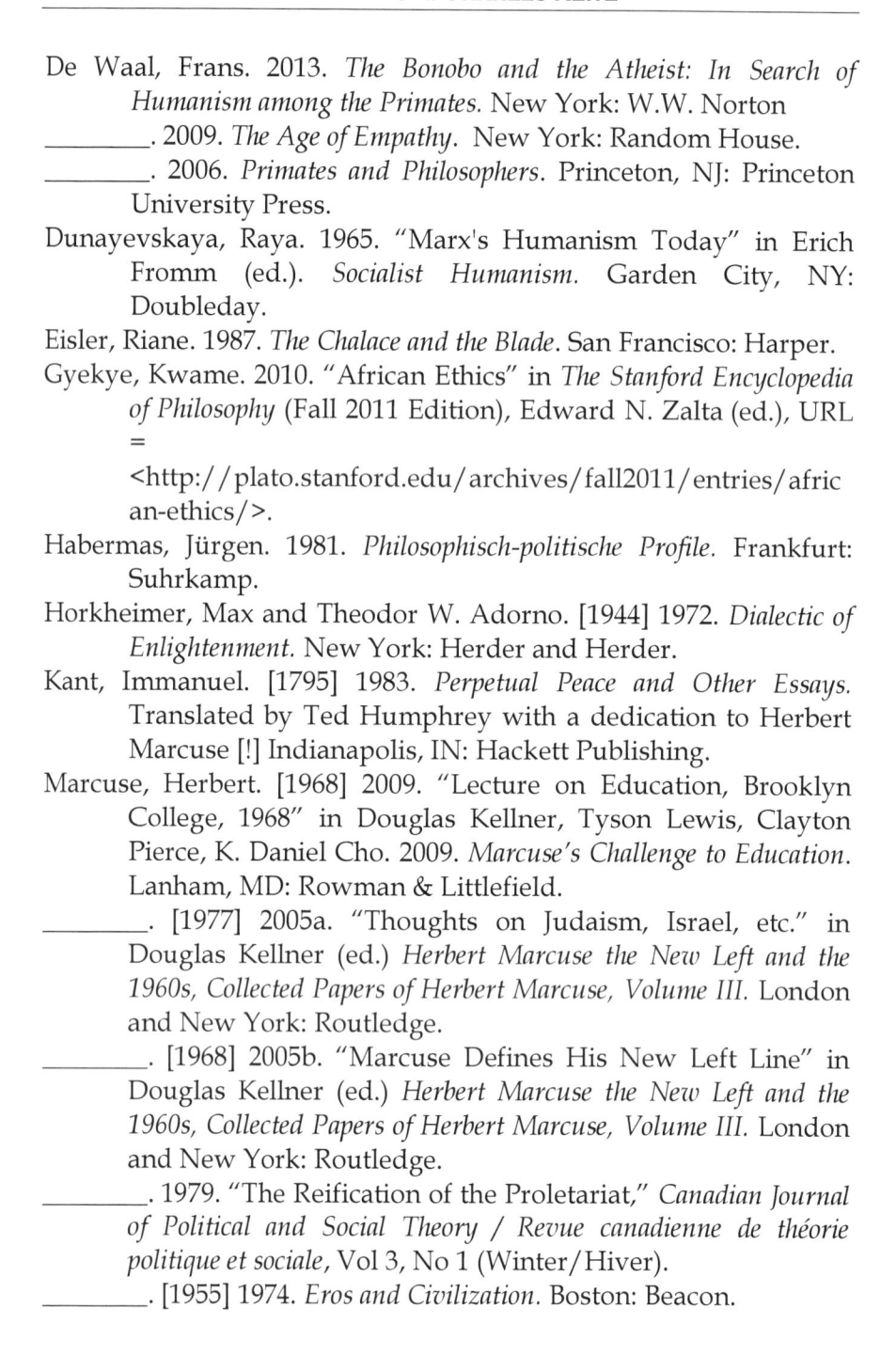

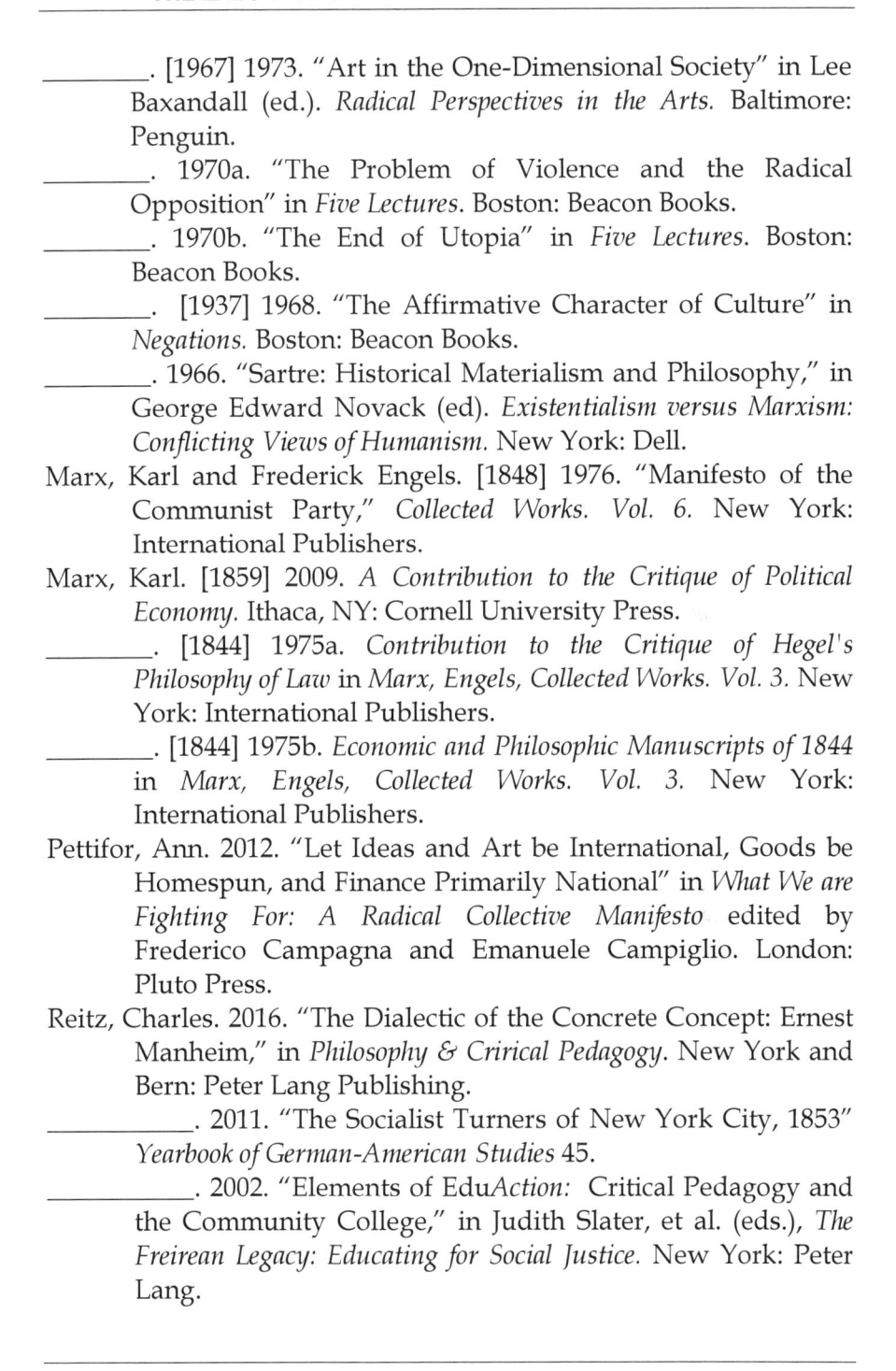

_____. [1967] 1973. "Art in the One-Dimensional Society" in Lee Baxandall (ed.). *Radical Perspectives in the Arts.* Baltimore: Penguin.

_____. 1970a. "The Problem of Violence and the Radical Opposition" in *Five Lectures.* Boston: Beacon Books.

_____. 1970b. "The End of Utopia" in *Five Lectures.* Boston: Beacon Books.

_____. [1937] 1968. "The Affirmative Character of Culture" in *Negations.* Boston: Beacon Books.

_____. 1966. "Sartre: Historical Materialism and Philosophy," in George Edward Novack (ed). *Existentialism versus Marxism: Conflicting Views of Humanism.* New York: Dell.

Marx, Karl and Frederick Engels. [1848] 1976. "Manifesto of the Communist Party," *Collected Works.* Vol. 6. New York: International Publishers.

Marx, Karl. [1859] 2009. *A Contribution to the Critique of Political Economy.* Ithaca, NY: Cornell University Press.

_____. [1844] 1975a. *Contribution to the Critique of Hegel's Philosophy of Law* in *Marx, Engels, Collected Works.* Vol. 3. New York: International Publishers.

_____. [1844] 1975b. *Economic and Philosophic Manuscripts of 1844* in *Marx, Engels, Collected Works.* Vol. 3. New York: International Publishers.

Pettifor, Ann. 2012. "Let Ideas and Art be International, Goods be Homespun, and Finance Primarily National" in *What We are Fighting For: A Radical Collective Manifesto* edited by Frederico Campagna and Emanuele Campiglio. London: Pluto Press.

Reitz, Charles. 2016. "The Dialectic of the Concrete Concept: Ernest Manheim," in *Philosophy & Crirical Pedagogy.* New York and Bern: Peter Lang Publishing.

_____. 2011. "The Socialist Turners of New York City, 1853" *Yearbook of German-American Studies* 45.

_____. 2002. "Elements of EduAction: Critical Pedagogy and the Community College," in Judith Slater, et al. (eds.), *The Freirean Legacy: Educating for Social Justice.* New York: Peter Lang.

_____. 2000. *Art, Alienation, and the Humanities. A Critical Engagement with Herbert Marcuse*. Albany: SUNY Press.

Russell, Bertrand. [1932] 1965. "In Praise of Idleness" in Erich Fromm (ed). *Socialist Humanism*. Garden City, NY: Doubleday.

Seymour, Richard. 2012. "Towards a New Model Commune," in *What We are Fighting For: A Radical Collective Manifesto* edited by Frederico Campagna and Emanuele Campiglio. London: Pluto Press.

Tauber, Zvi. 2012. "Herbert Marcuse on the Arab-Israeli Conflict: His Conversation with Moshe Dayan," *Telos* 158 (Spring).Whitehead, Fred and Verle Muher. 1992. *Freethought on the American Frontier*. Buffalo, NY: Prometheus Press.

Wiredu, Kwasi. 1991, "Morality and Religion in Akan Thought," in Norm R. Allen, Jr. *African-American Humanism*. Buffalo, NY: Prometheus Press.

Woolfson, Charles. 1982. *The Labor Theory of Culture: A Re-examination of Engels's Theory of Human Origins*. London: Routledge and Kagan Paul.

CHARLES REITZ
STEPHEN SPARTAN
Chapter Seven

The Political Economy of Predation and Counterrevolution

Corporate globalization is intensifying social inequality and cultural polarization worldwide. Increasing globalization correlates directly with growing inequality both within and between nations (Sernau, 2001, 52-55). This global polarization and growing immiseration have brought to an end what Herbert Marcuse (1964) theorized in *One-Dimensional Man* as the totally integrated and completely administered political universe of the liberal welfare/warfare state. Neoliberalism has replaced this "comfortable, smooth, democratic unfreedom" (Marcuse, 1964, 1) with something more openly vicious. Peter McLaren (1997, 2) and others call it predatory culture: "Predatory culture is the left-over detritus of bourgeois culture stripped of its arrogant pretense to civility and cultural lyricism and replaced by a stark obsession with power fed by the voraciousness of capitalism's global voyage." Michael Apple (2001, 18) describes it as "capitalism with the gloves off." David Korten (1995, 195) writes similarly of predatory finance: "The global economy is not, however, a healthy economy. In all too many instances it rewards *extractive* investors who do not create wealth, but simply extract and concentrate existing wealth. The extractive investor's gain is at the expense of other individuals or the society at large."

Marcuse, called this new stage *counterrevolution* (1972; 1987), and stressed the necessity of addressing anew the radical goals of socialism. We will elaborate these insights as this chapter unfolds. But first we need to look more deeply into the causes and consequences of capitalist inequality in its historical and political context. Douglas Dowd's *Inequality and the Global Economic Crisis* (2009) offers a systematic overview:

> Capitalism is, and must be, not only an economic but also a political and social system whose processes go well beyond production and trade for profit. . . . Britain was the first to seek and achieve the necessary depth and breadth of the processes *systemic* to capitalism: 1) expansion, 2) exploitation, and 3) oligarchic rule . . . . The interaction of capitalism's "imperatives" has inexorably produced intermittent crises and threats to its very survival, most destructively the socio-economic upheavals and wars of the twentieth century. (Dowd 2009, 11)

The imperative of exploitation is intensifying today through the "race to the bottom" as capitalism searches the globe for the lowest wage labor markets. Inequalities of income and wealth have been increasing over the last three decades in the United States, a tendency established well before the current economic fiasco in the banking and real estate industries. As we shall see, middle range households have lost the most. In large part this is the toll of capitalist globalization, while in November 2010 U.S. corporations reported their best quarter ever, after seven consecutive quarters at the highest rates of growth in history.[1] Clearly this rate could not endure, but following decades of labor speedup, the jobless recovery continues to facilitate enormous amounts of capital accumulation and the intensification of

---

[1] *The New York Times*, November 24, 2010, p. B-2.

poverty.[2] As reported front page by *The New York Times* March 4, 2013, "Recovery in the U.S. Lifting Profits, Not Adding Jobs; Wall Street is Buoyant." Its author, Nelson D. Schwartz, reports "the split between American workers and the companies that employ them is widening... 'So far in this recovery, corporations have captured an unusually high share of the income gains' said Ethan Harris, co-head of global economics at Bank of America Merrill Lynch."

The sharpest wealth declines in the U.S. have hit minority families. Hispanic households suffered asset losses of 66 percent between 2005 and 2009; wealth in Asian American households fell by 54 percent; African American households dropped 53percent.[3] During 2011, compensation to those in Wall Street's financial industry in total rose to near record

---

[2] ** See *The New York Times*, July 11, 2011, "Weak Results are Projected for Wall Street" p. B-1. However, by March 8, 2013 Wall Street was again flying high, with a nominal rise to pre-2007 levels, though still 10 percent below that when adjusted for inflation. See Floyd Norris, "A Long Way Back for Dow Industrials" *The New York Times*, March 8, 2013, p. B-3.

** See Monika Bauerlein and Clara Jeffery, "Speedup. All Work and No Pay," the cover story in *Mother Jones* July and August 2011, pp. 18-25. Also Ben Agger, *Speeding Up Fast Capitalism* (Boulder, CO: Paradigm Publishers 2004).

** See also "Companies Spend on Equipment, Not Workers," *The New York Times*, June 10, 2011, p. A-1.

** Sabrina Tavernise, "Poverty Reaches 52-Year Peak, Government Says," *The New York Times*, September 14, 2011, p. A-1.

[3] Sabrina Tavernise, "Recession Study Finds Hispanics Hit Hardest: Sharp Wealth Decline," *New York Times*, July 26, 2011, p. A-1. The impact of institutional relationships of racial inequality on wage-related income disparities has been classically demonstrated in the study by Michael Reich, *Racial Inequality* (Princeton: Princeton University Press, 1981). See also Sharon Smith, "Race, Class and 'Whiteness Theory'" *International Socialist Review*, Issue 46, March-April 2006.

levels, up 4 percent over 2010,[4] and in October 2012 Wells Fargo bank reported a jump of 22 percent in profits, JP Morgan 34 percent.[5]

A critical examination of these kinds of social dynamics is a vital part of radical pedagogy. Anyone who has grown up in the U.S.A. typically has little awareness of the nature of wealth or the pattern of its distribution in society. We also lack insight into the connection of income flows to relations of capitalist property ownership and the commodification of labor and life. A widely-used text, *Social Problems,* by Macionis (2012, 31) stands out admirably in its emphasis on the facts of the unequal distribution of wealth. Macionis utilizes the standard economic definition of wealth in terms of the value of the property to which one has title, minus debts. In the U.S.A. today, wealth distribution can be depicted on a vertical line representing all households in a declining order of property ownership, from top to bottom in quintiles as follows:

- 85 percent of the *total wealth* is held by the richest fifth of all households
- 11 percent by the second wealthiest fifth
- 4 percent by the middle fifth
- 1 percent by the second lowest fifth
- -1 percent by the poorest fifth of all households

When we first started teaching twenty-five years ago, the top quintile owned significantly less, 78 percent of the total

---

[4] Susanne Craig and Ben Protess, "A Bigger Paycheck On Wall St.," *The New York Times*, October 10, 2012, p. B-1.
[5] Ben Protess, "Wells Fargo Reports a 22 percent Jump in Profit," *The New York Times*, October 13, 2012, p. B-2; Jessica Silver-Greenberg, "Mortgage Lending Helps JP Morgan Profit Rise 34 percent," *The New York Times*, October 13, 2012, p. B-1.

wealth, and the poorest quintile owned a positive, albeit tiny, percentage (1 percent). The second richest quintile then had 15 percent of the wealth compared to its 11 percent share today.

This pattern of polarization has also transpired with regard to incomes, over time, such that today "income inequality has soared to the highest levels since the Great Depression."[6] "The increase in incomes of the top 1 percent from 2003 to 2005 exceeded total income of the poorest 20 percent of Americans. . . ." (U.S. Congressional Budget Office in Dowd 2009, 122). On top of this, in February 2013, Emmanuel Saez of the University of California, Berkeley, reports that during the current recovery the incomes of the top 1 percent rose 11.2 percent, while the incomes of the remaining 99 percent fell by 0.4 percent.[7] According to economist Saez and his colleague Thomas Piketty of the Paris School of Economics, the general pattern is this: *about half of all income the economy produces accrues to the top 10 percent of income earners.*[8]

If the facts of increasing economic inequality are largely undisputed, the same may not be said of their social significance. The prevailing views among economists and business utopians, represented in the writings of George Gilder (1993) for example, hold that these inequalities are natural and normal, a positive social good. They signify a ladder of opportunity, and meritocratically reward differences in talent, effort, intelligence, perseverance, etc. In their view, it is precisely the possibility of upward mobility that characterizes a democratic economy.

---

[6] Annie Lowrey, "Costs Seen in Income Inequality," *The New York Times*, October 17, 2012, p. B-1.
[7] Annie Lowrey, "Incomes Flat in Recovery, but not for the 1%," *The New York Times*, February 16, 2013, p. B-1.
[8] Ibid., p. B-4.

On the other hand, writers in economics like Dowd (2009) and Stiglitz (2012), in sociology like Macionis (2012, 37-39), and political philosophers like John Rawls (1971) characteristically emphasize the profoundly alienating, unequal, and *un*democratic impacts that such wealth and income maldistribution have on *life chances.* "Life chances" is a technical term in sociology used to indicate the relative access a household has to the society's economic resources: decent housing, health care, education, employment, etc. The greater the wealth in one's household, the greater one's life chances. The less wealth in one's household, the fewer the life chances. Life chances (as well as wealth and income) are today being transferred away from the vast majority of households and redistributed to the advantage of the wealthiest. Rawls (1971) has argued that departures from universal equality are in principle departures from social justice, and his views are persuasive in terms of social contract theory and a version of Kant's ethical universalism. One might frame an ingenious thought experiment utilizing his methodology and his concept of the "veil of ignorance" to demonstrate, through abstract logical analysis alone, the advantage (in terms of the sheer probability of enhancing one's life chances) of making the "blind" choice to be born in a perfectly equal society (where each population quintile owned 20 percent of wealth) rather than in one characterized by the stark lopsidedness in the distribution of wealth and life chances as in the U.S. today. In the latter, four out of five quintiles each owns substantially less than 20 percent; only the top quintile owns more. Nonetheless, the abstract philosophical (i.e. ahistorical and asociological) quality of Rawls's theory renders it oblivious to other issues, especially the important impacts of racial inequality. Arnold L. Farr, a contemporary Marcusean philosopher with deep appreciation for the work of Charles Mills, makes a trenchant critique of latent racism even in Rawls, liberal democracy's foremost political theoretician

(Farr 2009). Above and beyond Rawls, we shall indicate below the outlines of the socialist labor theory of commonwealth ownership and justice utilized by both Marx and Marcuse and which we contend has a greater material and sociological warrant.

Wealth [Capital] Accumulation and Workforce Remuneration. Seldom discussed among students (or among faculty) is the question of where wealth comes from or the nature of the relationship of wealth to labor. These issues were first formulated, and for many economists settled without controversy, in the classical economic theory of John Locke and Adam Smith. As is well known, they held that a person's labor is the real source of all wealth and property that one might have the right to call one's own. Locke emphasized the natural equality of human beings and that nature was given to humanity in common:

> Though the earth and all inferior creatures be common to all men, yet every man has a property in his own person; this nobody has any right to but himself. The labor of his body and the work of his hands we may say are properly his. Whatsoever, then, he removes out of the state that nature hath provided and left it in, he hath mixed his labor with, and joined to it something that is his own, and thereby makes it his property. –John Locke, 1690. *An Essay Concerning the True Original Extent and End of Civil Government*, Chapter V, Paragraph #27.

Similarly Adam Smith held:

> The produce of labor constitutes the natural recompense or wages of labor. In that state of things which preceded both the appropriation of land and the accumulation of stock, *the whole produce of labor*

belongs to the laborer.... In the arts and manufactures the greater part of the workmen stand in need of a master to advance them the materials of their work, and their wages and maintenance till it be completed. He shares the produce of their labor, or the value which it adds to the materials upon which it is bestowed; and in this share consists his profit. –Adam Smith, 1776. *Wealth of Nations,* Chapter VIII, Paragraphs 1, 2, and 8 (emphasis added).

Marx and Marcuse built upon Locke and Smith, but stressed that labor is a *social* process; that the value created through labor is most genuinely measured by socially necessary labor time; and its product rightfully *belongs* to the labor force as a *body*, not to individuals as such, i.e. grounding a theory of common ownership and justice, i.e. Common*Wealth*.

We can see how much current political discourse has devolved when we note here that even Abraham Lincoln emphasized that "Labor is prior to, and independent of, capital. Capital is only the fruit of labor, and could never have existed if labor had not first existed. Labor is the superior of capital, and deserves much the higher consideration." This foundational economic and political insight is from Lincoln's Annual Message to Congress, December 3, 1861, cited in Michael Parenti (1988, 10). Lincoln was aware of Marx's writing and ideas via the mediation of socialist Horace Greeley's *New York Tribune*,[9] which published articles under Marx's byline from 1852-1862 (Reitz 2009).

Marx and Marcuse encompassed the theories of Locke and Smith within a larger philosophy of labor. Where Locke

---

[9] See also John Nichols (2011) and Robin Blackburn (2011). Further, see Kevin B. Anderson (2010) and Charles Reitz (2009).

and Smith saw individual labor as the source of private property, in an atomistic (Robinsonian) manner, Marx recognized that all humans are born into a social context. Humanity's earliest *customs*, i.e. communal production, shared ownership, and solidarity assured that the needs of all were met, i.e. including those not directly involved in production like children, the disabled, and the elderly. This right of the commonwealth to govern itself, and humanity's earliest ethic of holding property in common, derive only secondarily from factual individual contributions to production; they are rooted primarily in our essentially shared species nature as humans, as empathic beings whose condition is that of *sensuous living labor*, a perspective discussed in detail in Reitz's previous chapter. Richard Leakey (1994, 60-63; Leakey and Lewin 1978) and Frans de Waal (2013, 2009) stress that the cultural context of cooperation and caring fostered interdependence and an awareness of the power of partnership. These customs and behaviors had the capacity to ensure survival. Subsistence needs were met with relatively little time spent in the collaborative acquisition of necessities (3-4 hours a day); thus the foundation was established for the fuller species life to flourish within the human community. This included the development of language as a derivative of the communal human condition (Leakey 1994, 124).

Communal labor sustained human life and human development. When commodified as it is today, labor's wealth-creating activity is no longer a good in itself. The overall "value" of the activity of the workforce, governed by capitalist property relations, is reduced to its aggregate payroll. The workforce is never fully remunerated for its contribution to the production process precisely because its contribution, when commodified through the labor market, *is reduced to the equivalent of the cost of labor force reproduction,* and the "surplus" is appropriated as property by powerful non-producers. Classical political economy (Ricardo, then Marx) called the downward pressures upon the "value" of commodified labor to drop to de-humanized levels of bare subsistence "the iron law of wages."

For these reasons we wish to argue, as Marcuse clearly saw, that there can be no rehumanization of society and social philosophy without the decommodification of labor. Douglas Kellner called Marcuse's notion of labor decommodification the *"liberation of labor"* (Kellner 1973, 3 emphasis in original). Rehumanization cannot be accomplished without a form of justice grounded in commonwealth ownership. Kellner (1973, 7) has importantly pointed out that by 1967 Marcuse clearly indicated "the qualitative difference between the free and unfree society is that of letting the realm of freedom appear within the realm of necessity—in labor and not only beyond labor" (Marcuse 1970, 63). Like Kellner, we (Reitz 2000, 64) have criticized the earlier Marcuse ([1933] 1973) who tended to overemphasize the activity of *play* as a countervailing force to the alienating attributes of work. But play, like art, can be seen as an extension of the essential activity of sensuous living labor, not as qualitatively distinguished from it. Richard Leakey (1994, 93) emphasizes tool-making as humanity's first industry, and that tools became works of art. The urge to produce depictions of animals and humans also seems to have been irresistible. Marcuse recognized this affinity of art with unalienated labor.

Labor Theory of Value / Critical Theory of Work. The labor theory of value, even in Locke and Smith, is rejected by most conventional economists who contend that labor is merely a cost of doing business, and that profit accrues from entrepreneurial skill, technological innovation, and risk-taking. These factors may increase profit in the short run in a sub-division of any given industry, where fractions of capital compete, yet in the long run the innovative production processes and reduced costs and payrolls become the new social average. What has meaning for an individual entrepreneur does not explain the aggregate picture. National income accounts, on the other hand, reveal the structural fundamentals of the value production process. These accounts are insightful and useful in Marxist terms in that they presuppose that labor in each firm (and by extension each branch of production) is paid for through payroll outlays from the total value that is added through the firm's value production process. A critical philosophical perspective demonstrates that labor has a reality and a capacity beyond its theoretical and practical confinement within its commodified form (i.e. a wage or salary). The fuller potential and power of labor, as recognized also by Locke and Smith, challenges the presumption that capital produces value, the view that profit *unilaterally* accrues as a reward for the contribution of the investor/employer. Labor provides the total value added in the production process. Profit is a *subtraction* from the value produced.

The Americanization of the world-wide economy aims at the overall reduction of payrolls on the global assembly line, no matter the greater levels of manufacturing employment in developing countries. The model we develop in this chapter[10] will illustrate the dynamics of wealth acquisition and accumulation and the generative mechanisms that are the origins of inequality (**Figure 1**). This will substantiate our thesis that inequality is not simply a matter of the gap between rich and poor, but of the structural

---

[10] Thanks also to Ken Stone, a radical labor activist and friend of long ago in Hamilton, Ontario, who helped me understand Marxist political economy in the 1970s. He has been involved in anti-racism, human rights, and anti-war activities over the years and is currently a member of the National Steering Committee of the Canadian Peace Alliance and was on the International Central Committee of the Global March to Jerusalem.

relationships in the economic arena between propertied and non-propertied segments of populations. Our model may serve as a small but necessary contribution to the advancement of a more economically informed critical theory of society and indicate how and why *property relations* must be addressed in order to root out recurring crises. **Figure 1** outlines the dynamics of this value *production* process in manufacturing, and discloses the fundamental *distributive* structures of the contemporary business economy: capital acquisition/accumulation and workforce remuneration. If labor creates all wealth, as John Locke and Adam Smith maintained, then labor creates all the value that is distributed as income to the labor force (wages and salaries) and to capital (rent, interest, dividends, and profit).

The social relations of production that organize society's productive forces to produce a surplus product are not merely modes of essential cooperation, they are also power and privilege relations. The power and privilege relations of a society will dominate the productive forces and essential work relations to ensure that total product be more than the minimum necessary product. We emphasize that incomes returned to capital and labor are *structurally determined*, i.e. conditioned primarily by societal, rather than individual, factors.

The *Statistical Abstract of the United States* includes data from the U.S. Department of Commerce and the Census Bureau. The methodology utilized to calculate the gross domestic product looks at the amount of *new wealth created, i.e. value added* through production in each firm and each industry. This is calculated by deducting the dollar costs of the *inputs* (supplies, raw materials, tools, fuel, electricity, etc.) from the dollar value of the *outputs*. Very importantly, these national income accounts—unlike the prevailing business utopian models--do *not* include the "cost" of labor among the *input* costs in the conception of the production process they utilize. Instead, they treat workforce remuneration as do Locke, Smith, and Marx, above,—as an income flow stemming from the *value production process* itself.

The following discussion of the origins and outcomes of income inequality in the manufacturing sector offers several insights that can be useful when considering other sectors of the U.S. and global economies, such as financial and information-based services. We recognize that the financial sector of the economy has been producing increasing shares of GDP: 2.8 percent in 1950, 4.8 percent in 1980, and 7.9 percent in 2007 according to the research of David Scharfstein and Robin Greenwood of Harvard Business School as reported by recently by Gretchen Morgenson.[11] Joseph E. Stiglitz also emphasizes that growth in the financial sector has contributed "powerfully to our society's current level of inequality," and this largely because it has "developed expertise in a wide variety of forms of rent-seeking" (Stiglitz, 2012, 36-37). Much more needs to be said about rent-seeking, and we shall do so in this chapter below. The analysis of manufacturing data that concerns of here, however, is absolutely necessary in order to build our critical theoretical foundation. This will allow us to clarify and distinguish our views on value production, as we do below, from those of some postmodern and neoliberal theorists who confuse an inflation of asset prices for production of value. As Morgenson points out,[12] income to money management firms, like mutual funds, hedge funds, and private equity concerns, increases when the *price* of assets that are overseen increases, even though the cost of providing financial services does not increase. This increased income does not derive from the

---

[11] Gretchen Morgenson, *The New York Times*, October 28, 1012, pp. B-1, B-6.
[12] Ibid.

creation of *value* but from an *extraction of wealth* from savers (like pension funds, and institutional investors) to the financial sector. Jodi Dean (2012, 136-54) describes in striking fashion the information and knowledge sector's most novel contemporary elaborations of exploitation and expropriation—including new labor forms that even *dispense* with wage payment (i.e. contests and prize competitions in which only a few are rewarded but all create viable products with their labor).

Our analysis seeks to draw out basic implications latent in standard economic data, and to arrive at certain significant findings that have been avoided in standard economics and business textbooks. In agreement with Marcuse's dialectical analysis, we see the global system of finance and commerce as no longer viable, plunging toward a dreadful reckoning with its own contradictions: attempting to reproduce its mode of privilege at the expense of the reproduction of the productive base (see also Greider 1997, 316).

Though the basics of value creation and the dynamics of capital acquisition and workforce remuneration are well known in critical Marxist circles, let us illustrate them here nonetheless with a simple hypothetical. In this example assume that you can buy for $50 a quilting kit containing everything you need (fabrics, thread, pins, needles, scissors, and design) to construct by hand an attractive quilt. After you assemble the kit, the finished quilt is an item you can really sell for $350. By the end of the production process, the materials in the kit have been transformed in economic value: there is $300 in *value added*. The factor that generated the added value is your labor. Since you bought the kit and built the quilt, you earned $300 through your productive activity. Assume also that you can get someone else to build a similar quilt from a $50 kit you already own. This person agrees to construct the quilt for $100. At the end of the work/production process under capitalist productive relations, you own the quilt, because you owned the kit and you hired another to work-up the materials. After again selling the quilt for $350 and paying your employee the $100 fee for the labor provided, you keep $200 of the $300 value added as your due, though you were not active in the actual production process yourself. In this case, the employee gets income from this activity because of his or her labor. You get income because of your ownership. In this sense business people traditionally speak of the ownership of *income-producing property*. We know it was not the *property* that produces income, rather it is the *property and power relationships* of the business system that allow owners of capital to appropriate income that it has not earned from wealth it has not created. Major firms in the garment industry operate according to the structural dynamics of this example with their labor force functioning as the employee above did, writ large. Whether at the macro or micro level, however, under this system, private ownership of capital is clearly not socially necessary for *value production*. The necessary component is *labor*. We must abstract from the particular qualities of the labor power of any individual person and instead focus on labor power at the average industry rate of productivity, what Marx called socially necessary labor time (see Raj Patel 2009, 66). A *critical* appreciation of work turns "right side 'round" the empiricist assertion that "job creators" are paying their employees, and demonstrates that employ*ees* are paying their employ*ers*. Our analysis of 2011 U.S. Census Bureau data undertaken below will demonstrate this. The power of the strike is to withhold these payments to propertied interests; the power of socialism is the reduction/elimination of them. In any society the labor force must produce a surplus of value/wealth to maintain infrastructure and provide for social goods such as health care, education, etc., over and above incomes to individuals. Marx's point is that *only the labor force as a social body* has a legitimate right to manage this surplus. When it does, the first condition for a humanist commonwealth has been met.

Critical political economy has developed a vocabulary (as Stephen Spartan elaborates in Chapter 7 below, deriving from Perry Anderson and Nicos Poulantzas) of "modes of base reproduction," "modes of surplus reproduction," the "reproduction of modes of privilege," and the "reproduction of modes of governance" — each of which involved a mode of productive labor. These will be helpful also in explaining our **Figure 1.**

The "Capital-Labor Split." Every dollar of the value added in U.S. manufacturing—for example in 2008, **$2,274,367 million**[13] (the most recent available figure)—was distributed into one of the two basic reproduction categories:

1) as income to the workforce—as *payroll* (wages and salaries)— **$607,447 million**; and

2) as income to owners and investors—as *profit, rent, dividends, and interest*— **$1,666,920 million**.

Something very like this disproportionate division of the added value between labor **(26.7 percent)** *and capital* **(73.3 percent)** *is structured by unequal property relations into the dynamics of reproduction in every sector of the economy and into the division of the Gross Domestic Product overall.* This is the root of capitalism's recurrent over-appropriation crises, to which we shall turn below.

---

[13] This and other figures from: Table 1006. Manufactures—Summary by Selected Industry, 2008. *Statistical Abstract of the United States: 2011*, p. 634.

Figure 1
Value Production and Distribution *as Income*:
The "Capital-Labor Split" Dynamics and Structure

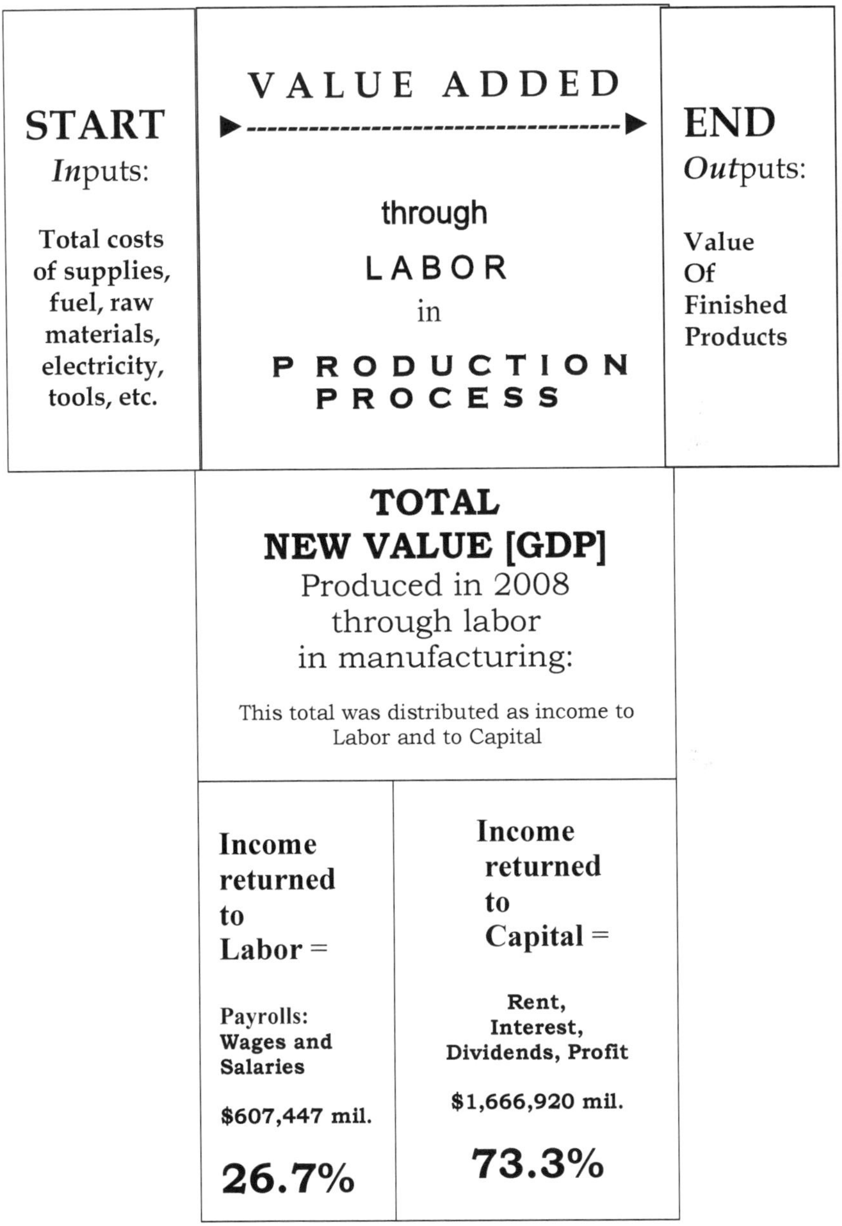

START *In*puts: Total costs of supplies, fuel, raw materials, electricity, tools, etc.	VALUE ADDED ▶--------------------------------▶ through **LABOR** in **PRODUCTION PROCESS**	END *Out*puts: Value Of Finished Products

TOTAL NEW VALUE [GDP]
Produced in 2008
through labor
in manufacturing:

This total was distributed as income to Labor and to Capital

Income returned to Labor = Payrolls: Wages and Salaries $607,447 mil. **26.7%**	**Income returned to Capital** = Rent, Interest, Dividends, Profit $1,666,920 mil. **73.3%**

Figure 1 depicts the three inextricably interconnected activities of production, distribution, and capital accumulation. It discloses how *a system of appropriation is embedded within the relationship of wage labor to capital* in the distribution process. As we have seen, the **GDP is completely distributed as income.** In the U.S. manufacturing sector in 2008 (not an untypical year) this meant that **73.3% of its contribution to GDP was returned to capital; 26.7% was returned to labor.** This model is derived from standard approaches to national income accounting, for example in McConnell and Brue (2005) and Parkin (2005). Our theoretical contribution here is to bridge the traditional macro-micro separations, which artificially and unnecessarily detach a macro discussion of national income from a micro consideration of income distribution in terms of wages, salaries, rents, profits, dividends and interest. **Figure 1** shows that income distribution fundamentally occurs in a structurally determined manner (contrary to the prevailing emphasis on the individual features of performance and remuneration).

Figure 2 presents empirical data from the *Statistical Abstract of the United States 2011* measuring wealth created (value added) in manufacturing. Looking at data, we see, for example, that in category 3152, *cut and sew apparel* (analogous to our quilt example), total value added (in millions) was *$7,385*. The payroll (in millions) was *$3,075*. Therefore the amount returned to capital (in millions) was *$4,310*. This latter figure is an amount equal to 100 percent of what was paid to the workforce *plus* an extra 40 percent. What is true in this sector of the economy holds true in every other branch even more dramatically. In category 3118, *bakeries and tortilla,* total value added (in millions) was *$34,108*, the payroll was *$9,442;* hence *$24,666* was returned to capital, more than double the amount returned to labor.

POLITICAL ECONOMY OF PREDATION AND COUNTERREVOLUTION

Figure 2
Value Added by Manufactures − Total Payroll = Income Returned to Capital

Table 1006. Manufactures—Summary by Selected Industry: 2008

[12,781.2 represents 12,781,200. Based on the Annual Survey of Manufactures; see Appendix III]

Industry based on shipments	2002 NAICS code [1]	All employees Number [2] (1,000)	Payroll Total (mil. dol.)	Payroll Per employee (dol.)	Production workers [2] (1,000)	Value added by manufactures [3] (mil. dol.)	Value of shipments [4] (mil. dol.)
Manufacturing, total	31–33	12,781.2	607,447	47,527	8,872.9	2,274,367	5,486,266
Food [5]	311	1,437.8	51,818	36,039	1,113.7	246,222	649,056
Grain and oil seed milling	3112	53.2	2,817	52,953	39.5	28,988	94,000
Sugar and confectionery products	3113	61.9	2,625	42,431	47.3	13,184	25,648
Fruit and vegetable preserving and specialty food	3114	167.7	6,232	37,161	138.5	28,045	63,187
Dairy products	3115	132.3	5,899	44,592	95.6	27,072	98,118
Animal slaughtering and processing	3116	505.7	15,217	30,094	438.9	50,828	169,925
Bakeries and tortilla	3118	271.6	9,442	34,760	172.8	34,108	58,701
Beverage and tobacco products	312	152.8	7,322	47,905	87.0	76,292	125,520
Beverage	3121	134.7	6,223	46,196	73.5	44,833	88,085
Textile mills	313	135.6	4,661	34,383	113.1	12,471	31,845
Textile product mills	314	136.3	4,151	30,455	104.9	11,540	26,530
Apparel	315	148.9	3,887	26,112	116.2	9,237	19,596
Cut and sew apparel	3152	118.5	3,075	25,951	92.2	7,385	15,608
Leather and allied products	316	31.7	994	31,361	23.9	2,619	5,411
Wood products [5]	321	461.8	15,619	33,834	365.5	34,577	88,004
Sawmills and wood preservation	3211	91.7	3,394	37,024	76.9	7,278	24,272
Paper	322	403.2	20,546	50,957	311.6	79,175	178,749
Pulp, paper, and paperboard mills	3221	117.8	7,794	66,142	93.6	40,476	82,923
Converted paper products	3222	285.4	12,752	44,687	218.0	38,700	95,826
Printing and related support activities	323	605.9	25,138	41,491	422.4	60,003	99,167
Petroleum and coal products	324	105.9	8,415	79,444	68.2	91,559	769,886
Chemical [5]	325	780.1	50,766	65,074	448.8	355,481	751,030
Basic chemical	3251	151.8	10,880	71,656	92.2	83,629	244,174
Pharmaceutical and medicine	3254	249.1	18,771	75,347	117.8	142,773	194,478
Soap, cleaning compound, and toilet preparation	3256	104.4	5,667	54,259	62.7	46,661	97,431
Plastics and rubber products	326	796.5	31,580	39,651	613.2	91,431	204,679
Plastics products	3261	651.8	25,299	38,815	499.7	76,503	167,423
Rubber product	3262	144.7	6,281	43,415	113.5	14,929	37,256
Nonmetallic mineral products	327	443.4	19,372	43,694	338.0	61,994	115,920
Glass and glass product	3272	93.9	4,227	45,042	74.0	12,562	23,197
Cement and concrete products	3273	213.6	9,106	42,637	161.8	29,774	57,779
Primary metal [5]	331	418.3	22,693	54,245	328.7	93,564	282,141
Iron and steel mills and ferroalloy	3311	109.3	7,668	70,150	87.4	43,036	126,332
Foundries	3315	144.0	6,435	44,689	116.3	15,492	31,842
Fabricated metal products [5]	332	1,572.7	69,231	44,021	1,153.4	188,072	358,363
Forging and stamping	3321	123.5	5,763	46,663	92.0	15,834	34,899
Architectural and structural metals	3323	408.5	17,253	42,239	293.1	44,878	94,980
Machine shops, turned product and screw, nut, and bolt	3327	398.5	17,748	44,537	298.5	39,941	64,064
Coating, engraving, heat treating, and allied activities	3328	136.0	5,360	39,403	104.0	16,432	27,740
Machinery [5]	333	1,127.4	57,212	50,749	726.1	168,153	356,954
Agriculture, construction, and mining machinery	3331	209.2	10,279	49,147	143.0	39,037	94,334
Industrial machinery	3332	127.6	7,648	59,919	67.6	18,703	35,612
Ventilation, heating, air conditioning, and commercial refrigeration equipment	3334	145.8	6,019	41,297	104.7	19,092	40,702
Metalworking machinery	3335	161.3	8,305	51,502	112.1	17,325	29,277
Computer and electronic products [5]	334	1,034.1	66,345	64,156	493.8	234,390	391,082
Computer and peripheral equipment	3341	92.6	5,908	63,792	34.7	38,727	68,110
Communications equipment	3342	132.8	8,961	67,481	53.9	30,504	53,865
Semiconductor and other electronic component	3344	371.6	20,486	55,123	227.9	71,258	116,809
Navigational, measuring, medical, and control instruments	3345	395.1	29,033	73,475	151.3	88,473	139,775
Electrical equipment, appliance, and component	335	411.9	19,036	46,226	285.3	61,975	131,759
Electrical equipment	3353	144.4	6,890	47,705	96.1	21,840	44,301
Transportation equipment [5]	336	1,474.4	82,532	55,976	1,018.6	252,187	666,807
Motor vehicle	3361	163.0	11,318	69,424	139.5	52,337	210,978
Motor vehicle body and trailer	3362	123.5	4,789	38,790	95.0	10,208	29,764
Motor vehicle parts	3363	523.7	24,771	47,297	391.6	62,812	174,646
Aerospace product and parts	3364	439.8	30,892	70,240	236.2	93,036	178,709
Ship and boat building	3366	149.0	6,857	46,016	103.1	16,665	30,430
Furniture and related products [5]	337	459.8	16,344	35,544	343.3	43,965	80,452
Miscellaneous [5]	339	642.9	29,782	46,322	397.1	99,460	153,200
Medical equipment and supplies	3391	313.7	16,151	51,491	188.3	60,424	84,029

[1] North American Industrial Classification System, 2002; see text, Section 15. [2] Includes employment and payroll at administrative offices and auxiliary units. All employees represents the average of production workers plus all other employees for the payroll period ended nearest the 12th of March. Production workers represent the average of the employment for the payroll periods ended nearest the 12th of March, May, August, and November. [3] Adjusted value added; takes into account (a) value added by merchandising operations (that is, difference between the sales value and cost of merchandise sold without further manufacture, processing, or assembly), plus (b) net change in finished goods and work-in-process inventories between beginning and end of year. [4] Includes extensive and unmeasurable duplication from shipments between establishments in the same industry classification. [5] Includes industries not shown separately.

Source: U.S. Census Bureau, Annual Survey of Manufactures, "Statistics for Industry Groups and Industries: 2008," June 2010, <http://www.census.gov/manufacturing/asm/index.html>.

634 Manufactures U.S. Census Bureau, Statistical Abstract of the United States: 2011

This analysis has examined incomes in the context of political and property relationships that are key to wealth accumulation, emphasizing how property relations account for the basic fact of the U.S. economy--the highly unequal distribution of incomes resulting from the patterns of workforce remuneration and the patterns of returns flowing to capital (via "income-producing wealth").

Intensifying Inequality and the Capital Valorization Crisis. Global economic polarization between those with immense property holdings versus the intensified immiseration of those without has led to the deepening crisis of finance capitalism that much of the world is currently witnessing. The 2008 economic debacle in the U.S. resulted in massive investment and job losses stemming directly from the institutional inability of the "world's strongest financial system" (The Financial Crisis Inquiry Commission 2011, xvi) to manage huge U.S. surpluses of capital without reckless speculation and massive waste of societal resources. The brutal consequences of this crisis are fairly well-known; its origins, however, are not. It was necessary therefore to impel the analysis *forward* with contemporary data, as we have done above, and *more deeply*, through to a critical understanding of the roots of capitalism's remuneration/reproduction dynamics and structure, summarized above in our model, **Figure 1.**

The global economy is increasingly one world supervised by global finance capital (Greider 1997). Finance capital derives its income from interest payments on massively extended credit (Greider 1997, 285-289). A governing system of, by, and for finance capital has emerged largely led by U.S. interests, yet it is unsustainable in its own terms.

Austerity budgeting is the preferred social policy of hegemonic U.S. and global financial interests today, and now the primary function of sovereign states is the enforcement of debt payments to Wall Street and its own debt service through structural adjustment policies and budgeting that shifts resources from social needs oriented programs to financial institutions. Keynesian strategies in support of the U.S. (or Greek or Portugese) labor force are no longer necessary in a political milieu where reactionary politicians will demand and liberal politicians will agree to direct government subsidies to finance capital.[14] Clearly the political terrain is contested, with recent major demonstrations and general strikes in Spain and Greece suppressed with police state tactics mid-September, and again in mid-November, 2012.

Predation within the economy has intensified with the emergence of "fast" capitalism—characterized by manic investing unhinged from reality in pursuit of market advantage in financial assets—described by Ben Agger (1989, 2004). Given deregulation, megamergers of financial institutions, globalized communications technologies facilitating instantaneous capital flows, reckless investment in the real economy (commercial and residential real estate) and synthetic product (unreal derivatives, etc.), huge accumulations of capital (Greider, 232) have been amassed at the pinnacle of the global economy (i.e. largely in the U.S.). The U.S. capital glut led to a condition where investment banks have had to devise ever more speculative strategies to realize profit given the super-abundance of wealth accumulated at the top. This is what we refer to as the over-

---

[14] See Raphael Minder, "Revolt raises pressure on Spanish government," *International Herald Tribune,* September 26, 2012, p. A-1; also Liz Alderman and Niki Kitsantonis, "Clashes erupt in Athens during anti-austerity strike," *International Herald Tribune,* September 27, 2012, p. A-3.

appropriation crisis or the crisis of capital valorization. Today the global capitalist system is hyperactive. It is erratic,[15] desperate, disintegrating, and self-destructive. We have just witnessed two typical scandals of desperate and self-destructive finance capital today: JP Morgan's enormous hedging designed to distort financial markets in their favor, and the Barclay's scandal of manipulation the Libor (London interbank offered rate) with knowledge of New York Fed regulators.[16]

Never content to receive less than maximal returns, capital is today as always hungry for valorization, seeking yields above average rates of profit. Yet the capital valorization process is currently in crisis. Prior to 2008 Wall Street institutions like American International Group (AIG), Bear Stearns, Citigroup, Countrywide Financial, Fannie Mae, Goldman Sachs, Lehman Brothers, Merrill Lynch, Moody's, and Wachovia had huge capital surpluses which they were frantic to valorize.

One strategy of some key financial institutions was to back massively real estate development trusts (REITs) to overbuild both commercial and residential properties. In order to reap big returns this business plan also required that banks recklessly issue enormous amounts of mortgage credit to commercial and residential buyers, even when these were

---

[15] Louise Story and Graham Bowlet, "Market Swings are Becoming the New Standard," *The New York Times* September 12, 2011, p. A-1: "…canny investors could profit from the big swings…."

[16] See Michael J. de la Merced and Ben Protess, "New York Fed Knew of False Barclays Reports on Rates," *The New York Times* July 14, 2012, p. A-1. Also, Jessica Silver-Greenberg, "New Fraud Inquiry as JP Morgan's Loss Mounts," *The New York Times* July 14, 2012, p. A-1. Further: "The Spreading Scourge of Corporate Corruption," *The New York Times* July 13, 2012, pp. B-1, B-5.

patently unqualified. Investment bankers then hedged their real estate investment bets by insuring themselves against commercial and residential mortgage client default through convoluted over-the-counter derivatives, credit default swaps.

Many financial institutions designed investment instruments consisting of bundles of the so-called subprime (in fact fraudulent) mortgages, had them triple-A rated by complicitous auditors,[17] "flipped" the lethal assets for a fee, and shunted them to those less astute (institutional investors, pension plans, credit unions, etc.) who would directly bear the loss.[18] Some investment banks then conducted credit default swaps such that they, not the parties who had been sold the assets, were the beneficiaries when the defective investment products inevitably crashed and burned. Taxpayers covered the insurers' liabilities (AIG was "too big to fail") so that Wall Street, whose reproduction as a mode of privilege within the current social formation is imperative, was guaranteed payment for its worthless investment instruments.

The strategic irrationality of this country's leading investment banking institutions arises from the systemic fetish characteristic of *finance* capital (as well as of *industrial* capital

---

[17] A separate, yet indicative, case against a ratings agency has recently made it to court. An Austrailian judge, Jayne Jagot, found that Standard and Poor's was liable for rating an investment instrument AAA in a manner "no reasonably competent ratings agency" would have. See Floyd Norris, "A Casino Strategy, Rated AAA," November 9, 2012, p. B-1.

[18] JPMorgan Chase and Credit Suisse recently settled for $417 million, government charges that they had packaged and sold troubled mortgage securities to investors, without admitting guilt. In 2010, Goldman Sachs settled a similar suit for $550 million. See Jessica Silver-Greenberg, "2 Banks to Settle Case for $417 Million," *The New York Times* November 17, 2012, p. B-1.

as emphasized by Marx in *Capital*.)[19] This is the obsession with an asset's ostensible price (as a marketable commodity) independent of its value as a function of socially necessary labor time or its use. The bubbles in asset prices in the dot.com area, telecommunications, as in commercial and residential real estate, resulted from finance capital's compulsion under penalty of extinction to seek the valorization of capital (profit acquisition/accumulation) through desperate bets on price fluctuations and volatile market values in speculative transactions independent of values as measured by real factors of production. A highly financialized economy, in which capital seeks valorization without employment, leads to the delusional (inflated, unreal) claims on wealth that are not sustainable. "Real estate values are up! The stock market is up!" These gains are "really there" only if the conditions that inflate these prices persist. Price fetishism confuses selling price growth with real value growth. Investment in U.S. Treasury bonds has also been a traditional haven for surplus capital. After the debt limit showdown of mid-summer 2011, investment ratings agencies like Standard & Poor's have downgraded U.S. bonds. This increases the U.S. government's costs of borrowing and also increases the returns on these investment instruments. From the bondholder/rentier perspective, awash in wealth and wishing to maximize revenues, a bounce in the premiums the U.S. government can be made to pay on its borrowed funds is a desirable prospect.[20] Similarly, changes to the U.S. tax code favorable to

---

[19] On the commodity fetish, see Karl Marx (1968, 85-98). Capitalist relations involve a paradoxical inversion: "… sachliche Verhältnisse der Personen und gesellschaftliche Verhältnisse der Sachen.…" Human beings are valued only as matters of business, and only matters of business are seen as having human value.

[20] Binyamin Appelbaum, "Taking a Closer Look At a Downgrade's Result: Treasuries Likely to Still Appeal to Investors," *The New York Times* July 31, 2011, p. A-13.

the biggest corporations and the super-rich have not only relieved them of a significant tax burden: monies spared from taxation in this manner may instead be loaned back to the U.S. Treasury, earning interest, thus providing wealthy individuals and large corporations a positive rather than a negative income flow.

Neoliberal and neoconservative politicies today serve what William Greider (1997, 285-289) has termed "The Rentiers' Regime." Joseph E. Stiglitz (2012) has also linked "rent seeking" to his understanding of the world's "1 Percent Problem." In light of Stephan Spartan's analytical categories developed in the next chapter on the overaccumulation and reproduction crises in ancient Rome, rent-seeking may also be seen as a mode of privileged accumulation and surplus over-appropriation.

The term "rent" was originally used to describe the returns to land, since the owner of land receives these payments by virtue of his ownership and not because of anything he *does*. This stands in contrast to the situation of workers, for example, whose wages are compensation for the *effort* they provide. The term "rent" was then extended to include monopoly profits, or monopoly rents, the income one receives simply from control of a monopoly. Eventually the term was expanded still further to include the returns on similar ownership claims. (Stiglitz 2012, 39)

Marcuse understood what subsequent writers called neoliberal and rentier politics as preemptive counterrevolution. Today this entails: the police-state U.S.A. Patriot Act, Global Terror Wars, a "money-is-speech" Supreme Court, and intensifying political economic inequalities. We can see how the neoliberal business utopian model is incapable of liberating humanity because it requires humanity to remain dependent on commodities, markets, and the financial and investment priorities of those who monopolize the capital accumulation process and speculate on the temporary price-fluctuations of assets. Commodity-dependency is the foundation of unfreedom in contemporary societies.

Importantly, this dependency on commodities, markets, and finance, is not inevitable. Realigning the social order to conform with the highest potentials of our economy, technology, and human nature requires the de-commodification of certain economic minimums: health care, child care, education, food, transportation, housing,—and work, through a guaranteed income. These are pre-revolutionary, *transitional* goals. *Revolutionary* goals envisage a more encompassing view of liberation and human flourishing: the passage from wages and salaries to public work in the public interest—public work for a commonwealth of freedom, with work as life's prime want. "Commonwealth of freedom" is a concept developed by Boyte and Kari (1996) which we extend in the direction of Marcuse's radical goals of socialism. We sharply distinguish our analysis from the reputedly radical commentators Hardt and Negri (2009, 2000), whose critique of the Marxist tradition displaces the foundational philosophies of labor humanism and socialism with Foucaultean biopolitical categories and a Wittgensteinean philosophy of language that re-configures notions of the commons in immaterial directions.

The vision of re-humanized social action and social ownership developed in this chapter is an extension and refinement of classical philosophical sources: Aristotle on human beings as the *zoon politikon*: social beings with politics as the key art to the good life; Buddha and Aquinas on good works and relief of suffering; Kant on cosmopolitan humanism; Marx on communism as the actualization of human species potential [Gattungswesen]. It is a mature philosophy of human freedom and fulfillment grounded in human capacities as sensuous living labor. We pursue here also Marcuse's recommendations on ending the material bases of domination, reshaping the productive forces in accordance with aesthetic form, and the free development of human needs and faculties toward peace and gratification. Authentic freedom is ours when we, as sensuous living labor, grasp intellectually and hold politically the resources that we have produced and which can be possessed by all within a de-commodified and re-humanized world.

As Marcuse recognizes, the abolition of commodified labor is impossible under capitalism. Hence a critical liberal arts education that helps humanity accomplish its own humanization is inherently limited by the affirmative character of culture (i.e. its tendency to reproduce established inequalities), and is institutionally obstructed today. The Marxist conceptions of *wage-labor* and *commodity fetishism* are the key analytical criteria that measure the underlying dehumanization and commercialization of education and life itself under capitalism. Abolition of these phenomena will be the hallmark of humanist advancement in society and culture.

This society is fully capable of abundance as Marcuse recognized in *One-Dimensional Man,* yet the material foundation for the persistence of economic want and political unfreedom is *commodity-dependency*. Work, as the most crucial of all human activities, by which humanity has developed to its present stage of civilization, can be and should be a source of human satisfaction. Under capitalism it is reduced to a mere means for the receipt of wages. Sensuous living laborers are reduced to being mere containers for the only commodity they can bring to the system of commodity exchange, their ability to work. Necessities of life are available to the public exclusively as commodities through market mechanisms based upon ability to pay.

Commodified existence is not natural; it is contrived. Significant portions of commodified social life need to be rethought and reconstructed. We need to articulate a common-ground political platform that can unify progressive forces to reclaim our common humanity. See the last chapter in this volume. We raise questions there about the kind of world we want to live in, and discuss *Charter 2000* as a broad, unifying, coherent draft program. It proposes a set of universal desirable outcomes envisioning a democratic society with sustainable abundance.

Consistent with Marcuse's obstinate utopianism ([1937] 1968, 143), we must hammer out what we really desire. What are the most intelligent/wisest uses of labor? We emphasize here the transformation of commodified human labor into *public* work, i.e. work that aims at the public good rather than private accumulation (Boyte and Kari 1996), and how this would undergird progressive political advance. Work in the public interest in the public sector expands areas of the economy traditionally considered the public domain, the public sphere, the commonwealth: social needs oriented projects like libraries, parks, utilities, the media, telephone service, postal service, transportation, social services.

The decommodification of services in these areas, along with a policy ensuring a guaranteed minimum income, would supply a socialist alternative its fundamental economic viability. So too the decommodification of health care, housing, and education. Already we see that areas within the field of information technology are pregnant with the possibility of decommodification: public-domain software and shareware on the internet, market-free access to Skype, etc.

The demand for decommodification sets Marcuse's analysis—and ours—distinctly apart from a *liberal* call for a "politics of recognition" (Taylor 1994; Honneth 1994, 2005) that features *attitudinal* and/or minimal *redistributive* remedies (Fraser and Honneth 2003). While recognition and redistribution are certainly needed, they are not sufficient. The slogan "tax the rich," while helpful in *liberal* terms, misses the *revolutionary socialist* point that the cure for today's harsh distributional inequalities lies in new relationships of common ownership that restructure the very processes of value creation, production, income and wealth distribution, exchange, and consumption.

No non-socialist theory of society or education has any profound quarrel with wage labor or the general system of commodity dependency. Marx admonishes workers: "...instead of the *conservative* motto 'A fair day's wage for a fair day's work!' they should inscribe on their banner the *revolutionary* watchword, 'Abolition of the wages-system!'" (Marx [1865] 1965, emphasis in original). We have reiterated above how Marx clarified capitalist society's obsession with production for profit rather than human need. This is its structurally generated fetish/addiction to production for commodity exchange rather than for use-values. Production for *use* rather than *exchange* would optimize living conditions within the social formation as a whole. Capitalist productive relations are driving global labor to its knees. Only the abolition of wage labor and commodity fetishism in the economy can restore satisfaction and dignity to an uncommodified labor process.

Like Hegel and Marx, Marcuse understood that a subaltern, serving consciousness becomes aware through labor of its own dependency and unmet human needs. Ultimately, it learns also that those it serves are not absolutely independent and free, but rather dependent on it, labor. This reality is a key source of labor's own political education, and the foundation of its philosophy of possibility and hope. The frustration of *our essential sensuous practical activity, labor*, will ultimately propel a *politics of labor ownership of wealth* as the liberation of the repressed political potential of the human species. In the dominator systems that characterize global cultures today, not even the oppressors or their children are capable of coming to self-knowledge strictly through the agency of those educational forces committed institutionally to the reproduction of an oppressive social division of labor. Only through the practical and intellectual opposition to the reproduction patterns of domination can any theorist emancipate himself or herself from even the most consoling mystifications of oppressor systems. And only thus does practice or theory become critical.

We have learned from the movements against racism and sexism that class relations do not wholly demarcate structures of dominator power. Racism, patriarchy, homophobia, and other forms of discrimination, disrespect, and inequality sorely inhibit our powers of actualization. Reactionary forces reinforce bias of every sort in the hoary yet effective strategy of divide and conquer. While the general abolition of the wages-system is not absolutely *sufficient* to secure the conditions for each of us to become all that we are capable of being, *the alienation and exploitation of labor is the enabling material core that today requires the dominant culture to target innocent minorities as scapegoats.*[21] Radical social science must empower general education students (i.e. the labor force in a multicultural society) intellectually, politically, and culturally to end these abuses.

Labor's key challenge today is re-thinking economics, building a theory and a practice for a humane world system.

---

[21] See Steven Greenhouse and Steven Yaccino, "Fight Over Immigrant Firings, Strikers Say Pizza Factory Cracked Down to Prevent Union from Organizing," *The New York Times* July 28, 2012, p. B -1.

We stress here also the important role of theory in scholarly research, explanation, social science. The business mind—the logic of marginal advantage within a market society that ostensibly accomplishes widespread prosperity—has been confronted here with the its own contradictions: dehumanized production, an overworked and underpaid labor force, increasing impoverishment. We emphasize the power of the labor movement not only as a source of class contestation over the distribution of the economic value that it has produced, but also as a source of learning and advances in theory and social organization. Labor's traditional values have built the common good, and revolutionary critical pedagogy begins with labor's untold story (see also Boyer and Morais [1955] 1997). Economic processes today divest us from our own creative work, yet these also form the sources of our future social power. We have recast the discussion of dehumanization and rehumanization in terms of the commodification and decommodification of sensuous living labor. We have thus attempted to furnish the beginnings of a more comprehensive critical social theory stressing the centrality of labor in the economy. Critical philosophy and radical pedagogy must theorize the origins and outcomes of economic and cultural oppression, and be engaged politically with the labor force to end them. This is the logic and manifesto that can liberate the fuller potential of any critical theory of society. As Peter McLaren has emphasized (2015b) critical theory must come to inform the full curriculum, such that its new norms of understanding and justice may enable us to build from within the realities of the present the partnership organizations of the future that will make possible new ways of holding resources and real opportunities for all persons to reclaim the full social power of labor, leadership, and learning.

We have extended some of the most radical components of Marcuse's critical social analysis, and augmented these with our own contributions—primarily through our interpretation and modeling of fact-based observations drawn from the national income accounts and also our work in critical pedagogy, labor education, and in the multicultural education reform movement. We have furnished material for curriculum components that may elicit freshened perceptions of the basic workings of the U.S. economy as well as challenge established patterns of education. Such perceptions can help generate a "new sensibility" (Marcuse 1969) with regard to the origins of social inequality, the irrationality and destructive nature of current patterns in the distribution of income and wealth, and the real possibility of a more humane, just, and abundant future. This new sensibility is a "refusal of the actual" (Marcuse 1969, 34), a form of consciousness in which science, technology, and art are released from service to exploitation and mobilized for a new vision of socialism (Marcuse 1969, 23, 26).

The analytical innovations presented here can be regarded as Marcusean insofar as they embody a form of the "Great Refusal" and disclose truths about our human condition and our human potential that are absent from established patterns of academic and political of discourse. We have attempted to do this in our discussions of the intensifying inequalities in the social distribution of income and wealth, rival interpretations of the meaning of inequality, the implications of the labor theory of value for wealth accumulation, ownership, and justice, and finally, the 2008 financial crisis in the U.S. Of special significance, we feel, is our model of workforce remuneration and capital accumulation. A depth-dimensional understanding of these dynamics undergirds our entire approach to revolutionary politics, pedagogy, and praxis.

Bibliography

Agger, Ben. 2004. *Speeding Up Fast Capitalism: Cultures, Jobs, Families, Schools, Bodies.* Boulder, CO: Paradigm Publishers.

_____. 1989. *Fast Capitalism.* Urbana, IL: University of Illinois Press.

Anderson, Kevin B. 2010. "Race, Class, and Slavery: The Civil War as Second American Revolution" Chapter 3 in *Marx at the Margins.* Chicago: University of Chicago Press.

Apple, Michael W. 2001. *Educating the 'Right' Way: Markets, Standards, God and Inequality.* New York & London: RoutledgeFalmer.

Blackburn, Robin. 2011. *An Unfinished Revolution: Karl Marx and Abraham Lincoln.* London and New York: Verso Press.

Boyer, Richard O. and Herbert M. Morais. [1955] 1997. *Labor's Untold Story.* United Electrical Radio & Machine Workers of America.

Boyte, Harry C. and Nancy Kari. 1996. *Building America: The Democratic Promise of Public Work.* Philadelphia: Temple University Press.

Dean, Jodi. 2012. *The Communist Horizon.* London: Verso.

De Waal, Frans. 2013. *The Bonobo and the Atheist: In Search of Humanism Among the Primates.* New York: W. W. Norton.

_____. 2009. *The Age of Empathy.* New York: Three Rivers Press.

Dowd, Douglas. 2009. *Inequality and the Global Economic Crisis.* London: Pluto Press.

_____. 2004. *Capitalism and Its Economics.* London: Pluto Press.

_____. 1997. *Blues for America.* New York: Monthly Review Press.

Farr, Arnold L. 2009. *Critical Theory and Democratic Vision: Herbert Marcuse and Recent Liberation Philosophies.* Lanham, MD: Lexington Books.

Financial Crisis Inquiry Commission, The. 2011. *The Financial Crisis Inquiry Report: Final Report of the National Commission on the Causes of the Financial and Economic Crisis in the United States.* New York: Public Affairs.

Fraser, Nancy and Axel Honneth. 2003. *Umverteilung oder Anerkennung?* Frankfurt a. M.: Suhrkamp.

Gilder, George. 1993. *Wealth and Poverty.* Oakland, CA: ICS Press.

Greider, William. 1997. *One World, Ready or Not.* New York: Simon & Schuster.
Hardt, Michael and Antonio Negri. 2009. *Commonwealth.* Cambridge: Harvard University Press.
_____. 2000. *Empire.* Cambridge: Harvard University Press.
Honneth, Axel. 2005. *Verdinglichung.* Frankfurt a. M.: Suhrkamp.
_____. 1994. *Kampf um Anerkennung.* Frankfurt a. M.: Suhrkamp.
Kellner, Douglas. 1973. "Introduction to 'On the Philosophical Foundation of the Concept of Labor,'" *Telos,* No. 16, Summer.
Korten, David C. 1995. *When Corporations Rule the World.* West Hartford, CT: Kumarian Press.
Leakey, Richard. 1994. *The Origin of Humankind.* New York: Basic Books.
Leakey, Richard and Roger Lewin. 1978. *People of the Lake.* Garden City, NY: Anchor/Doubleday.
Macionis, John C. 2012. *Social Problems .* Upper Saddle River, NJ: Pearson/Prentice Hall.
Marcuse, Herbert. [1974] 1987. *Zeit-Messungen.* In *Herbert Marcuse Schriften 9.* Frankfurt: Suhrkamp.
_____. [1933] 1973. "On the Philosophical Foundation of the Concept of Labor in Economics," *Telos,* No. 16, Summer 1973.
_____. 1972. Counterrevolution and Revolt. Boston: Beacon.
_____. 1970. "The End of Utopia," in his *Five Lectures.* Boston: Beacon.
_____. 1969. *An Essay On Liberation.* Boston: Beacon.
_____. [1937] 1968. "Philosophy and Critical Theory," in *Negations, Essays in Critical Theory.* Boston: Beacon.
_____. 1964. *One-Dimensional Man: Studies in the Ideology of Advanced Industrial Society.* Boston: Beacon.
Marx, Karl. [1867] 1968. *Das Kapital* Erster Band in *Marx-Engels Werke* Band 23. Berlin, East: Dietz Verlag.
_____. [1865] 1965. *Wages, Price, and Profit.* Beijing: Foreign Languages Press.
McConnell, Campbell R. and Stanley L. Brue. 2005. *Economics: Principles, Problems, and Policies.* Boston: McGraw-Hill.

McLaren, Peter. 2015a. *Pedagogy of Insurrection.* New York and Bern: Peter Lang Publishing.

_____. 2015b. "Revolutionary Critical Pedagogy for a Socialist Society," in Crisis and Commonwealth, Charles Reitz, editor. Lanham, MD: Lexington Books.

_____. 1997. *Revolutionary Multiculturalism: Pedagogies of Dissent for the New Millennium.* Boulder: Westview Press, HarperCollins.

Nichols, John. 2011. "Reading Marx with Abraham Lincoln" Chapter 3 in *The "S" Word: A Short History of an American Tradition.* London and New York: Verso.

Parkin, Michael. 2005. *Economics.* Boston: Pearson Addison Wesley.

Parenti, Michael. 1988. *Democracy for the Few.* New York: St. Martin's.

Patel, Raj. 2009. *The Value of Nothing.* New York: A Picador Book of St. Martin's Press.

Rawls, John. 1971. *A Theory of Justice.* Cambridge, MA: Harvard University Press.

Reitz, Charles. 2009. "Horace Greeley, Karl Marx, and German 48ers: Anti-Racism in the Kansas Free State Struggle, 1854-64," *Marx-Engels Jahrbuch 2008.* Berlin: Akademie Verlag.

_____. 2000. *Art, Alienation, and the Humanities. A Critical Engagement with Herbert Marcuse.* Albany: SUNY Press.

_____. 1976. "A Critical Outline of the Political Philosophy of Social Reconstructionism," *Cutting-Edge, Journal of the Society for Educational Reconstruction,* 7:4 (Summer).

Sernau, Scott. 2001. *Worlds Apart: Social Inequalities in a New Century.* Thousand Oaks, CA: Pine Forge Press.

Stiglitz, Joseph E. 2012. *The Price of Inequality.* New York: W. W. Norton.

Taylor, Charles. 1994. "The Politics of Recognition," in *Multiculturalism* edited by Amy Gutman. Princeton, NJ: Princeton University Press.

U.S. Census Bureau. 2011. *Statistical Abstract of the United States.* http://www.census.gov/prod/2011pubs/11statab/manufact.pdf (retrieved June 11, 2011).

Chapter Seven: Charles Reitz and Stephen Spartan

Stephen Spartan
Chapter Eight

Surplus Over-Appropriation and the Reproduction Crisis of the Roman Empire

Over recent decades the incomes, wealth, and powers of the most parasitic elements of the U.S. economy and military have grown excessively relative to the system's total output. Meanwhile, components of the system's productive forces (e.g. infrastructure, labor force skills, the global ecosystem) are being "under reproduced." All of the chapters in Part Three of this book on "Critical Political Economy and Praxis" address various aspects of the Anglo-American world system's malignant nature. This chapter is not *directly* concerned with present developments, except to warn that excessive growth of parasitic privilege and excessive military funding will eventuate in ill-consequences.

This essay utilizes and revises basic materialist concepts (e.g. social formations, mode of production, surplus product, state) to explicate a specific historical consequence of "surplus over-appropriation" — the reproduction crisis of the Roman Empire.

Critical Political Economy.

Social formation is a Marxist concept similar to the functionalist notions of "society" or "socio-cultural system."

Perry Anderson defines a social formation in the following way in his own analytical writing:

> Throughout this text, the term "social formation" will generally be preferred to that of "society." In Marxist usage, the purport of the concept of social formation is precisely to underline the plurality and heterogeneity of possible modes of production within any given historical and social totality. Uncritical repetition of the term "society" conversely, all too often conveys the assumption of the inherent unity of economy, polity, or culture within an historical ensemble, when in fact that simple unity and identity does not exist. Social formations, unless specified otherwise, are thus here always concrete combinations of different modes of production, organized under the dominance of one of them. For this distinction, see Nicos Poulantzas, *Pouvour, Politique, et Classes Sociales,* Paris 1968, pp. 10-12. Having made this clear, it would be pedantry to avoid the term "society" altogether, and no attempt will be made to do so here. (Anderson 1978, 22)

The notable point of this discussion is its stress on the coexistence of heterogenous modes of production within a formation. This implies that tensions may exist between modes which affect the structure and function of the formation. The specific form of the society is the result of the combined necessities and possibilities of several distinct modes of production, each with unique reproduction imperatives. The mode of production which dominates the forces of production essential to other modes is the "dominant mode of production" (Anderson 1978, 22).

A *mode of production* is a structured organization of productive forces that coordinates the conversion of inputs (productive resources) into outputs (products). The productive forces are labor power, the instruments of labor, and the materials worked upon. The latter two constitute means of production (Shaw 1978, 10). Labor without means and (it goes without saying) means without labor are not productive. Thus, means and labor are inseparable complementary components of production that must be brought together in order for production to occur. Consequently, social production requires a structuring of productive activity, a *mode of cooperation,* to mobilize and blend the specific production inputs necessary for specific production. Marx stressed the necessity of organizing the productive forces in his discussion of cooperation in *Capital, Volume 1,* Chapter 13.

> All directly social or communal labour on a large scale requires, to a greater or a lesser degree, a directing authority, in order to secure the harmonious co-operation of the activities of individuals, and to perform the general functions that have their origins in the motion of total productive organisms, as distinguished from the motion of its separate organs. (Marx, [1867] 1976, 448).

A mode of production thus involves various *social relations of production,* some of which are essential to the production process and others of which are surplus. This distinction between essential and surplus relations of production will be utilized in various ways throughout the analysis which follows. It can also be considered similar to Shaw's (1978, 28-47) distinction between work relations and ownership relations. The forces of production and the mode of essential cooperation together constitute the *productive base.* That portion of the total product necessary to reproduce the productive base can be labeled *necessary product.* The social relations of production that generate necessary product is the *mode of necessary production,* which is also the mode of essential cooperation. The social relations of distribution that direct necessary product back to the simple reproduction of the productive base constitute the *mode of base reproduction.* If the production process of a society generates a total product flow greater than the necessary product, a *surplus product* is available.

The social relations of production that organize society's productive forces to produce a surplus product can be labeled the *mode of surplus production,* i.e. mode of surplus cooperation. The social relations of distribution (or appropriation) that ensure the continued extraction of surplus product from the base can be seen as the *mode of surplus reproduction.* The modes of surplus production and reproduction are *surplus relations* vis à vis the simple reproduction of the productive base. Thus the social relations of production are not merely modes of necessary production and distribution, they are also the modes of surplus production and distribution. Likewise, the social relations of production are not merely modes of essential cooperation, they are also power and privilege relations. The power and privilege relations of a society will dominate the productive forces and essential work relations to ensure that total product be more than the minimum necessary product.

Marx analyzed in depth only the reproduction dynamics of the capitalist mode of production in the abstract, but he also reflected on pre-capitalist social formations. Marx noted that pre-capitalist social formations differ from capitalism primarily in the limited manner that markets and money (generalized commodity exchange) served as mechanisms of productive forces mobilization, ruling class domination, and working class dependence. Capitalism is unique in its organization of production and distribution on a large scale by "non-coercive" means of control; that is by general social dependency on markets (commodity exchange) and money (capital) as forms of reproductive resource distribution. Obviously capitalism also utilizes force and coercion, but the point here is the degree of control by generalized commodity dependency and the fetishism it engenders (see Marx [1867] 1976, Chapter 1, Section 4, 163-177).

In those pre-capitalist social formations organized to generate surplus product, dominance and dependency were more obvious and non-fetishized. "[D]irect relations of dominance and servitude" (Marx [1867] 1976, 452) were the mode of productive coordination and surplus appropriation. Thus in surplus producing pre-capitalist formations, the state and ideology, rather than commodity dependency, reproduced the mode of surplus.

Following Marx, Lenin stressed that the state is the coercive instrument of ruling class domination, serving the purpose of defending the existent modes of surplus production and distribution. It is obvious that owner elites and the state have a common interest in the reproduction of the mode of surplus because both are reproduced by surplus product. But this common necessity to command surplus product may under certain circumstances generate tensions between elites and the state. This tension could exist even if it is not consciously recognized by the social actors involved. Both owner elites and states subsist on surplus product, yet they have distinct reproduction priorities. Hence we must distinguish between surplus product to reproduce elites and surplus product to reproduce the state. The *mode of privilege* (ownership relations) must be distinguished from the *mode of governance* (the state).

The mode of privilege can be understood as the relations of surplus production and distribution that reproduce non-productive elites who appropriate part of surplus product by virtue of ownership power, social customs, or other ideological means, but do not contribute directly or indirectly to the essential management of the productive forces. The mode of governance can be defined as the relations of surplus production and distribution that reproduce quasi-productive elites who appropriate part of surplus product, but do contribute indirectly to the essential management of the productive forces. The mode of governance is an administrative structure which supplies vital organizational services, such as social peace, and common infrastructure, such as roads, water supply, etc. The mode of governance is a more general and abstract concept than state, and is applicable to any social formation, whereas the state is a legal-rational mode of governance developed to administer complex societies.

A state is a type of governance mode, but is not just a rational administrative structure functional to the productive base; it is also a structure of legitimate force that enforces unequal access to social power and wealth. Thus the modes of privilege and governance might not be empirically distinguishable in every social formation; indeed in many social formations the mode of privilege and mode of governance are synonymous. They can be defined, however, as distinct reproduction imperatives. The differentiation of mode of privilege and mode of governance is necessary because the reproduction imperatives of elite owners may be distinct from the reproduction imperatives of the state.

Following this line of argument, complex social formations are not just "concrete combinations of different modes of production organized under the dominance of one of them" (Anderson 1978, 22), but are also concrete combination of different *re*production imperatives organized under the dominance of one of them. I treat the *state* as a *mode* *of reproduction* of a social formation that must coordinate tensions between the different levels of a formation. I also propose re-conceiving the state as a "state formation" analogous to Anderson's description of social formation, discussed above, replacing terms in the Anderson quotation above as follows: "social formation" with "*state* formation" and "production" with "*re*production"—

> [T]he term "*state formation*" will generally be preferred to that of "*state*". . . . [T]he purport of the concept of *state formation* is precisely to underline the plurality and heterogeneity of possible modes of *reproduction* within any given historical and *state* totality. Uncritical repetition of the term "state" conversely, all too often conveys the assumption of the inherent unity of *reproduction behavior* within an historical ensemble, when in fact that simple unity and identity does not exist. *State formations*, unless specified otherwise, are thus here always concrete combinations of different modes of *reproduction*, organized under the dominance of one of them. . . Having made this clear, it would be pedantry to avoid the term "state" altogether, and no attempt will be made to do so here.

We would expect that reproduction of the productive base must be the dominant reproduction imperative or any social formation, for ultimately the mode of privilege and the mode of governance cannot be reproduced unless the productive base, which provides surplus product, is reproduced. Thus, in the abstract, it could be argued that the mode of base reproduction is ultimately dominant, to the extent that it is essential to the reproduction of the two surplus modes and the social formation in general. In the concrete, however, there are significant illustrations of a given productive base failing to be reproduced, though the modes of privilege and/or governance did reproduce, if in a somewhat altered form. The evolution of English feudal aristocrats into wool export capitalists, co-terminously (via enclosure measures) with the destruction of English peasant-serf agriculture is only one famous illustration of the reproduction of a mode of privilege without the reproduction of its initial productive base.

Furthermore, there are also illustrations of elites and/or states over-appropriating surplus product, i.e., the mode of surplus reproduction dominates at the expense of the mode of base reproduction. In such circumstances, either the base must be radically altered (i.e. industrial revolution) to expand total product, or the modes of surplus must reduce their over-appropriation to stable limits. If neither of these adjustments are immediately made, the base will not be reproduced and thus total product will fall, requiring even greater readjustment of product distribution if the formation is to survive. As total product falls relative to base and surplus reproduction requirements, the formation will experience extreme reproduction contradictions. If the state does not impose compensating limits on privileged appropriation of surplus product, either the state must reduce its appropriation proportionately or the productive base (and total product) will progressively wither, eventually carrying with it the social formation in general. An extreme reproduction contradiction of this kind (i.e., a surplus over-appropriation crisis) is an excellent opportunity to examine the nature of the state.

Evolution of the Over-Appropriation Crisis of the Roman Empire. The Roman Empire achieved a level of political-economic integration that was the culminating feature of ancient civilization. Contradictions inherited from its Republican foundation remained unresolved however. Of particular importance was the Western Empire's inability to achieve a monarchical centralization of power free from the dominance of an aristocratic mode of privilege. My account here will draw substantially upon classical studies of the period by Antonio (1979), Boak and Sinnigen (1965), Boren (1977), Diehl 1957, Jones (1966), Rostovtzeff (1957), Runciman (1956), Starr (1973), and Walbank (1969).

During the expansionary period of the Roman Republic, the mode of privilege was not entirely parasitic, but instead could be treated as a mode of productive governance, i.e. as a system of social power that expanded the productive forces of the formation in general. The productive base of the social formation was expanded primarily by successful warfare and a unique ability to assimilate other Latin tribes, Etruscans, Samnites, Magna Graecia, and others into a unified Italian heartland (see Boren 1977, 31-41; Starr 1973, 21). The successful wars with Carthage, the annexation of the Hellenistic states, and the conquest of Gaul resulted in a further immense expansion of the land and labor resources of the Roman social formation (see Anderson 1978. 60-62; Boak and Sinnigen 1965, Chapters 8 through 10).

The aristocratic mode of privilege and governance of the early Republic was inevitably incapable of administering this vast domain; thus a new mode of governance was essential if this expanded base was to be retained and reproduced.

> The Republic had won Rome its empire: it was rendered anachronistic by its own victories. The oligarchy of a single city could not hold the Mediterranean together in a unitary polity—it had been outgrown by the very scale of its success . . . . [T]he self-protective immobilism and haphazard misgovernment of the Roman nobility in the conduct of its rule over the provinces rendered it increasingly unfit to manage a cosmopolitan empire. . . . . A stable,

universal monarchy emerged from Actium, because it alone could transcend the narrow municipalism of the senatorial oligarchy in Rome. (Anderson 1978, 67-70).

The contradiction between the complexities of administering an expanded productive base on the one hand, and the efficiency limitations of an aristocratic republic on the other, could be resolved in only one of two ways: either a reduction of the expanded base or the development of a new mode of governance, i.e. a bureaucratic state.

The development of the imperial bureaucratic state as the mode of governance was essential to reproduce the expanded production base and the expanded mode of privilege resulting from the conquest and integration of formerly exogenous forces of production. The expansion of the empire brought new potential forces of production within control of the Roman mode of privilege, but it also required the development of a new mode of governance to realize the potentially higher surplus product of these enhanced forces. The imperial bureaucratic mode of governance was the by-product of the uneven and combined development of expanded forces of production and the increased reproduction necessities of an expanded mode of surplus. Thus, from its inception the bureaucratic imperial state was faced with three reproduction imperatives. It had to reproduce an expanded production base; it had to reproduce the expanded (end ever-expanding) mode of privilege; and it had to reproduce the expanded (end ever-expanding) mode of governance, i.e. reproduce itself.

The assassination of Julius Caesar reflected a conflict between the traditional Republican (aristocratic) mode of privilege and an evolving imperial bureaucratic mode of governance. Augustus won the civil wars following the aristocracy's assassination of Julius Caesar, but Augustus did not attempt to uproot the traditional mode of privilege, instead he established a new imperial mode of governance overlaid on the republican aristocratic mode (see Boak and Sinnigen 1965, 146-56). This new state formation was a compromise between an expanded traditional mode of privilege and a new centralized mode of governance which allowed the aristocracy to maintain control over the Senate and thus ensure its legal right to surplus (Rostovtzeff 1966, 46-47; Boren 1977, 155). According to Anderson:

> [W]hile the Senate as an institution became a stately shell of its former self, the senatorial order itself—now purged and renovated by the reforms of the Principate—continued to be the ruling class of the Empire, largely dominating the imperial state machine even after equestran appointments became normal to a wider range of positions within it . . . . The possessing classes continued to be juridically guaranteed in their property by the precepts established in the Republic. (Anderson 1978, 73-74.)

During the expansionary phase, pillage from conquest was a direct source of surplus product that financed significant expanded reproduction of both the mode of privilege and mode of governance. For example,

> [T]he spoils of war with Macedonia brought such an enormous booty into the Roman treasury that after 167 [BCE], the war tax on property . . . ceased to be levied. The income of the empire enabled the government to relieve Roman citizens of all direct taxation (Boak and Sinnigen 1965, 134).

Conquest also expanded the productive base of the society by bringing new lands and a new labor force under the dominance of the Roman mode of surplus. The conquest phase of Roman history vastly expanded the quantity of productive forces and consequently total product, but it also allowed and required an expansion of the mode of surplus.

As conquest ceased, direct pillage and incorporation of new lands and labor also ceases, effectively ending expanded reproduction of the productive base. Max Weber argued that the end of Roman expansion was ". . . the turning point in the development of ancient civilization." He dated this to "the battle in the Forest of Teutoburg" which encouraged "the suspension of offensive warfare on the Rhine" (Weber 1950, 346-47). The end of conquest manifested the contradictions of the slave mode of production and exposed the fragile urban-rural balance of Roman commodity production (Anderson 1978, 76-82). The end of conquest also effectively ended the considerable inflow of direct pillage to which Rome had grown accustomed. Henceforth, the expanding modes of privilege and governance both had to be reproduced from the same limited productive base. This was the beginning of a contradiction of reproduction imperatives within the mode of surplus due to (and intensifying) a surplus over-appropriation crisis. The mode of governance was particularly dislocated by the end of expansion because conquest had always provided a significant source of state revenues; thus, the end of conquest forced the state to finance its expanded reproduction exclusively from indigenous surpluses. This however was a fragile base due to the large and growing mode of privilege the limited productive base was already supporting. The output of a productive base is limited by the growth rates of the quantity and quality of the productive forces and the management efficiency of the modes of cooperation. If the quality of the inputs and management efficiency are relatively constant, then the growth of total product is limited by the changing quantity of productive forces. If the appropriation of surplus product increases faster than total product, eventually either necessary product will fall, leading to non-reproduction of the base, or else some component of the mode of surplus must be reduced.

From the earliest days of Roman expansion, great landowning elites had control over the Senate and significant influence in the bureaucracy and military.

> Two aristocratic orders monopolized the most powerful and lucrative social, economic and political positions. It has been estimated that the senatorial order constituted approximately two-thousandths of one percent of the Roman people. The less powerful equestrian order (Equites) was probably less than a tenth of one percent of the population . . . . [T]he two orders owned much of the Empire's wealth and controlled most of its social and political power. Despite the autocratic position of the emperor, the aristocracy can be considered a ruling class. (Antonio 1979, 899-900).

Though the composition and direct power of this ruling class (or mode of privilege) varied, it never lost effective control over state polices. This mode of privilege was able to utilize its control of the Senate and influence within the civil and military bureaucracies to institute state policies essential to the expanded reproduction of the mode of privilege, but ultimately fatal to the mode of governance. The great estates were significantly exempted from taxation and military conscription, but more importantly, the continuous absorption of small and medium freeholdings by the privileged estates was essentially unchecked. The concentration and centralization of land and labor by the privileged estates removed taxable land from the treasury and quality citizen manpower from the military (Jones 1966, 177). Increasing portions of surplus product flowed to the mode of privilege reducing the surplus base available for expanded state reproduction. Thus the fiscal crisis of the state, which is a widely recognized aspect of imperial decline, was due to the inability of the mode of governance to fully negate the aristocratic mode of privilege upon which Rome was founded. The surplus product of the empire was never fully available to the mode of governance; the decline of the imperial state consequently involved the declining degree of state control over reproduction resources (financial and labor), not just the absolute decline of those resources.

The imperial mode of governance was progressively starved of reproduction resources because it failed to limit the expanded reproduction of the mode of privilege and it failed to promote expanded reproduction of the productive base. The limited surplus product of the formation was divided between the modes of privilege and governance in a manner that inhibited the expanded reproduction of the mode of governance to respond to increased necessities, notably the increased defense necessities from the third century forward.

The state had tried to control and reduce the mode of privilege beginning with the compromise of Augustus, i.e. the Principate. Dioclecian's reforms were primarily to bring the mode of privilege (and therefore the productive base) firmly under the dominance of the imperial state. These reforms did not successfully reduce the highest strata of the mode of privilege, but they did reduce the middle and lower strata. The decurions were heavily taxed and increasingly forced to carry the burdens of local tax collection, city financing, and in general provide social services formerly financed by state expenditures. This intensified imposition on the decurions was an attempt to increase state revenues and simultaneously reduce state expenditures; but these crushing new taxations and obligations were increasingly non-reproducing this quasi-productive stratum. The "flight of the decurions" involved the exodus of lands and labor out of the command of the state: the flight of the decurions also involved continuous reduction of the portion of surplus product available for state appropriation. The decurions were formerly taxable, but the large estates which survived were not taxable. The state did not succeed in leveling the mode of privilege, instead it crushed the productive base and productive social relations essential to state reproduction. The highest strata of the mode of privilege were not reduced; they continuously expanded through the absorption of bankrupt freeholders and decurions (Antonio 1979, 907; Anderson 1978, 92). Thus the tax and manpower base available to state reproduction was increasingly constrained by concentration and centralization of land ownership in the hands of tax-exempt privileged estates.

Bureaucratic inefficiency compounded the process by failing to allocate the system's resources instrumentally and to conserve them (Antonio 1979, 906-11). An overriding patrimonial rationality fostered corruption, self-seeking, unprofessional management, and elite dominance, all of which contributed to the squandering of state resources. The underlying fiscal contradictions of the empire became fully manifest following the third century when military expenses leaped tremendously over the staggering levels they had already attained. As spending requirements increased, the state imposed ever higher levels of taxation on the remaining tax base. Marginally profitable lands were abandoned as taxation rose; freeholders and lower stratum decurions were driven into utter poverty by taxation and indebtedness (Boak and Sinnigen 1965, 366). A vicious circle of declining tax base requiring higher tax rates forced land abandonment; this reduced the supply of taxable and draft-liable freeholders and contributed to the growth of large privileged estates, resulting in a further lowering of the tax base. As its requirements increased, the state progressively increased the rate of appropriation from the productive base such that the base was progressively non-reproduced. The state was failing to reproduce the productive base of the formation in a manner that could allow the expanded reproduction of the state. This cycle of progressive non-reproduction of the base could not be continued indefinitely; something had to give.

The Diocletian reforms attempted to rectify the crisis by a variety of revenue increasing and cost-cutting measures (Rostovtzeff 1966, 505-527; Boak and Sinnigen 1965, 426-30 and 448-69). These measures totally failed in the Western Empire, but were a solid foundation for the revitalization of its eastern portion.

> [I]f we consider the Empire as it existed at the time of Augustus, and the gradual shift in emphasis from the west to the east, culminating in the final split after the reign of Theodosius (379-95), it becomes clear that the survival of the Eastern Empire really represents the saving of one part at the expense of the other . . . . [The survival of the East] is itself a tribute to the efforts of the third century emperors and to the reorganization of Diocletian and Constantine. (Walbank 1969, 110)

An in-depth exposition of the immense geographic, demographic, cultural, economic, political, and military differences between the East and West is beyond the scope of this chapter. A general summary of the significant differences between the Western and Eastern Empires can be found in Jones (1966, Chapter 26) and Anderson (1978, 96-102). Suffice it to say that in the West the surplus over-appropriation crisis was resolved by the progressive non-reproduction of the state. The mode of privilege was reproduced, though eventually reformulated as feudalism, at the expense of the imperial mode of governance. This dominance of the reproduction of the mode of privilege supports a Marxist theory of the state/state formation. In the East, the state formation was reconfigured in such a manner as to escape the drain on surplus into privilege reproduction. The surplus product of the East no longer financed the reproduction of the aristocratic mode of privilege, but rather was reorganized to finance the reproduction of the imperial mode of governance. The East emerged as a form of "oriental despotism" in which the reproduction of the mode of governance was the overwhelming imperative. The imperial mode of governance of the Eastern Empire was monocratic to a degree never approached in the Roman West (Runciman 1956, 18-19). For example the bureaucracy of the East was squarely under the imperial office rather than being a battleground of conflicting interest groups.

> Rarely has any administration been more strongly centralized or more ably run than that of Byzantium. . . . The staff, from top to bottom of the administrative ladder, was directly dependent on the Emperor. . . . No other administration, it seems, was completely under the control of one master. (Diehl 1957, 66-68)

In the West, the bureaucracy was riddled with elite privilege, self-seeking, and competition between imperial, aristocratic, and military interests; consequently the bureaucracy of the West lacked a unity of purpose. In the East, a new bureaucracy was established with the single purpose of reproducing the state and the productive base, not the aristocracy and other privileged classes (Anderson 1978, 99). This development of the Eastern imperial bureaucracy supports Weber's emphasis on the key role that bureaucratic organization can play within a state formation in assuring above all else the dominance of the reproduction of the mode of governance.

Postscript, 2016. If analogies with regard to crises of over-accumulation and non-reproduction can be validly made between ancient Rome and the U.S. today, analogous conflicts and consequences might seem to follow. In the U.S. this could portend, on the one hand, the eventual success of *oligarchic* neoliberal and neoconservative policy and ideology, with a new type of much reduced and disempowered state apparatus. Chris Hedges has recently written of "a global form of neo-feudalism, a world of corporate masters and serfs."[1] On the other, it could result in greater concentration and consolidation of an authoritarian, bureaucratic, police-state type of power in a *proto-fascist* or *neo-fascist* manner. In either of these scenarios the labor force and democracy itself would face severe reductions, restrictions, and repression of its conditions of work and life.

Is there any de-centralized, neo-conservative, corporate rule and/or the pseudo-populism of a fascist-like dictatorship? The experience of various forms of political democracy distinguishes our age importantly from that of ancient Rome. Labor's productive capacity and power are structurally present, and—given rising expectations—can become manifest as a democratic commonwealth (even if the present explodes of its own contradictions) both by withholding labor (as in general strikes) and by a labor force offensive to free itself from its restriction to commodified relations. Under current conditions, this is feasible and foreseeable; a democratic movement for socialist/communist self-governance is both a utopian and a real possibility. *This* is the objective horizon that circumscribes the material terrain

---

[1] Chris Hedges in Mark Karlin, "Why Chris Hedges Believes That Serious Revolt is the Only Option People Have Left" *Alternet*.org, August 27, 2012, reprinted from truthout.org —See also Chris Hedges and Joe Sacco, *Days of Destruction Days of Revolt* (New York: Nation Books, 2012).

upon which we live and struggle.

Given its inadequate production potentials and social consciousness, the devolving Roman Empire lacked objective and subjective conditions to even imagine a democratic commonwealth alternative. But the modern world's productive base is objectively capable of providing universal abundance. Also, the "masses" have (some) democratic expectations and experience. Modern productivity and potential abundance are due to humanity's common heritage of technical knowledge and abilities to cooperate, i.e. *humanity's commonwealth abilities*. What is still needed is actualized awareness of the necessities for and possibilities of social arrangements that yield *humanity's commonwealth benefits*.

NB: What I see as the latent potentials for radical change *today* are outlined at the very end of this volume (pages 417-420) in response to issues raised by Peter Marcuse.

Bibliography

Anderson, Perry. 1978. *Passages from Antiquity to Feudalism*. London: Verso.

Antonio, Robert J. 1979. "The Contradiction of Domination and Production in Bureaucracy: The Contribution of Organizational Effeciency to the Decline of the Roman Empire," *American Sociological Review* 44: 895-912.

Boak, Arthur E. R. and William G. Sinnigen. 1965. *A History of Rome to A.D. 565*. New York: Macmillan.

Boren, Henry C. 1977. *Roman Society: A Social, Economic, and Cultural History*. Lexington, MA: D. C. Heath.

Diehl, Charles. 1957. *Byzantium: Greatness and Decline.* New Brunswick, NJ: Rutgers University Press.
Jones, A. H. M. 1966. *The Decline of the Ancient World.* New York: Holt, Rinehart, and Winston.
Lenin, V. I. 1961. *The State and Revolution* in *The Essential Left.* New York: Unwin Books.
Marx, Karl. [1867] 1976. *Capital, Volume 1.* London: Penguin.
Poulantzas, Nicos. 1975. *Political Power and Social Classes.*London: Verso.
Rostovtzeff, M. 1957. *The Social and Economic History of the Roman Empire.* Oxford: Clarendon Press.
Runciman, Steven. 1956. *Byzantine Civilization.* New York: Meridan.
Shaw, William H. 1978. *Marx's Theory of History.* Palo Alto: Stanford University Press.
Starr, Chester G. 1973. *The Ancient Romans.* London: Oxford University Press.
Walbank, F. W. 1969. *The Awful Revolution: The Decline of the Roman Empire in the West.* Toronto: University of Toronto Press.
Weber, Max. 1950. "The Social Causes for the Decay of Ancient Civilization" *The Journal of General Education.* 5:75-88.
Wright, Erik Olin. 1979. *Class, Crisis, and the State.* London: Verso.

MEHDI S. SHARIATI
Chapter Nine

Imperialism, Militarism & the U.S. National Debt:
"Socializing" the Costs of Globalization

This essay examines the U.S. national debt and proposes that it arises preeminently from political and military imperatives structured into the accumulation dynamics of global capitalism. Four historically overlapping and essential components of the accumulation process will be analyzed: globalization, imperialism, militarism, and what I will call social imperialism. Accumulation strategies are at the same time projects involving the internationalization of capital and production which in turn involve imperialism and militarism on a global scale.

Imperialism is understood here not only as Lenin's "highest stage of capitalism," but as an ongoing project of facilitating accumulation on a global scale with the particular ability to use "creative destruction" (per Schumpeter) in reinventing itself at a more expansive level. It seeks opportunities in every crisis, and all crises are potential military targets insofar as they adversely affect global accumulation. Militarism here is defined as the use of the actual military power and the projection of military power to implement the state's overseas expansion of the interest of the domestic capitalist classes and their overseas allies. Militarism is often associated with an ideology which presents itself as nationalism to the point that the line between the two is blurred. Successful militarism/imperialism (military-aided imperialism) abroad owes much to its fearsome armada purchased from the military industrial complex; yet this is supplemented with effective propaganda and the incorporation of the domestic working classes into the imperialistic system. Successful and effective social imperialism at home—a tradition going back to the colonialist/imperialist powers of the nineteenth century, conventionally has involved (at least until three decades ago), "concessions to the masses" in the form of "the extension of the franchise or material benefits" (Neumann 1944, 153-35, cited in Semmel 1960, 13).

Joseph Schumpeter (1919) defined social imperialism as an imperialism in which entrepreneurs and other elements woo the workers by means of social welfare. As the globalization stage in the development and evolution of capitalism proceeds, the need to utilize the military as a mechanism of subordinating the global discontent increases. Social imperialism in all of its forms has been the dominant method of co-opting the opposition to its global accumulation strategies. But the systemic contradictions stemming from the internal logic of contemporary global capitalism will continue to be its greatest nemesis. The growth of the United States' national debt (with all of its consequences) is taken as indicative of one of these contradictions, and will be analyzed as a structural imperative within global capitalism.

Theoretical Perspectives. The mapping of a truly hegemonic global capitalist system began in earnest in the period immediately after World War II—the beginning of the era of what Ernst Mandel called "late capitalism." The concerted efforts toward a strong bloc of capitalist states with overwhelming political, economic, and military power involved the incorporation of colonial and post-colonial systems, as reproducible capitalist entities, into the overall social formation. In this regard, the creation of an international capitalist class alliance equipped with modernization theory anchored in social Darwinism was indispensable. As the leader of the "free world," the United States assumed the greatest role in the implementation of the hegemonic strategy for the purpose of capital accumulation through its military, economic, and political might. Attempting to understand and to address the new world order and its contradictions, forced many to revisit classical theories of imperialism, and introduced various newer theories on the state in capitalist societies. Here an analysis of systemic contradictions took center stage. Systemic contradictions, as they relate to accumulation, have been addressed by classic and most recent theories of imperialism: the internationalization of capital, arguments about dependency in the world system, the global capitalist class alliance, and the transnational "historical bloc." A very useful perspective revisiting imperialism and global class conflict is that of "transnational historical materialism" (Murphy 1994; Augelli and Murphy 1998; Cox 1981, 1983, 1993; Gil 1990, 1993, 1995; Rupert 1995; Robinson 1998, 2001).

These various new theoretical proponents posit a world in which the global or transnational class, supported by a transnational political apparatus and military power, expands its interests on a global scale and at the expense of the international proletariat's interests. Therefore, class conflict on a national level is transformed into an international class conflict. Embedded in this analysis is an element from Gramsci (1999) and his concept of hegemony, where the new alliance is sustained—and its interests expanded—through the production and reproduction of the ideology of the dominant class and its cultural leadership. Gramsci pointed out that the Western ruling classes ensure the consolidation of their dominant position by manipulating institutions such as the media, schools, churches, and so on. The "historical bloc," composed of the capitalist state apparatus and its hegemonic intellectuals, negotiates as a cohesive unit with subordinate classes to secure the social reproduction of the structure of domination. Although the bloc seeks to maintain total hegemony, occasionally it is confronted by challenges from the subordinates (elements within the struggling masses).

To confront these challenges, the bloc attempts to coopt the anger of the opposition by changing slightly the social and economic arrangements. Social imperialism is the bloc's strategy of dealing with challenges to its domination. The strength of the bloc in the contemporary period is immense, and it enjoys the assistance of a new breed of hegemonic intellectuals well-versed in theorizing and structuring a transnational hegemonic order. Ideologically loaded phrases such as "freedom and democracy," "free trade," the "free enterprise system," the "free market," (and host of other ostensible freedoms) are embedded in a language which aims at structuring the world in the image of the hegemon. As Eagan (2003, 3) and Gill (1995) have argued, the new bloc seeks the institutionalization of the concept of "new constitutionalism." New constitutionalism has three components: "disciplinary neo-liberalism," "panopticism," and "market civilization" (i.e. the commodification) of everyday life. But it is essential that the process of "internationalization of the state"—the conversion of the state into a "transmission belt" (Robinson 1996) and an agency for the adjustment of the internal structure of the state to policy implementation needs of the global order (Cox 1987, 254) must be in place and reproducible. Cox (1987, 109) identifies three distinct world orders, each having its own hegemonic strategy, beginning with the liberal international economy (1789-1873); the era of inter-imperialist rivalries (1873-1945), and that of the post-World War II era, with the internationalization of capital and production, led by the

United States (the "Pax Americana").

Contemporary debate surrounds the concept of globalization in its historical and structural context and impact. Even opposing analytical camps have used "globalization" to mean what seem to be interchangeable combinations of internationalization, westernization, democratization, trans-nationalization, civilization, humanization, enculturation, universalization, polarization, modernization—and as the "triumph of human liberty." The connotations of these terms vary of course; on the one hand the apologists for the globalizing empires and their agents regard globalization as an economic improvement, while others see the terms as indicative of subjugation and exploitation. Somewhat reminiscent of the modernization/developmental theories of the 1940s and 1950s in the West, particularly in the American social and political sciences, projected a postcolonial world as contented family of nations pursuing prosperity through modernization (capitalist development). By reading the classic critique of imperialism based on Marx (i.e., Lenin, Luxemburg, Hilferding, and Bukharin) many have drawn a parallel between today's globalization and the imperialism of yesteryear (Harvey among others). If globalization is viewed as imperialism, this inevitably involves militarism, and militarism in most cases requires a form of nationalism. Yet the linkage of the U.S. national debt to the structural dynamics and contradictions of globalization have rarely been made.

U.S. Influence and Global Capitalism. After WWI, the United States and its European allies continued to increase their economic, political, and military influence around the world, and this only intensified with the war's conclusion. The post-WWII era became the era of American hegemony directly challenging the Soviet Union's "designs" on the rest of the world. Capitalism desired to reign supreme so as to become a dominant global system.

The components of the historical bloc of this epoch were much more sophisticated than their forbearers. The hegemonic intellectuals devised new hegemonic strategies anchored in "modernization theory." This was a strategy in collaboration of the "modernizing elites" of the less articulated social formations; it was an important component in hegemonic efforts. Social scientists theorized about the causes and the nature of a supposed "underdevelopment" and suggested policy prescription. On a mission to aid in the reproduction of capitalism in its dependent variety and prevent communist take-over of these formations, sociologists, economists, historians, anthropologists, political scientists, and psychologists began using the theory and method in their disciplines to aid the implementation of modernization policies of the western capitalist states.

Beginning with President Truman's containment doctrine in the late 1940s through the Reagan era of the 1980s, policies combating the "evil empire" through massive military spending, ruthless neo-liberal economic policy, effective propaganda, and deficit financing were key components in the policy of aiding international capitalist development and the internationalization of capital itself. This was a precondition for the successful imperialism and accumulation strategy.

The intensity of the propaganda was generally determined by the degree to which the public in the imperial centers was required to participate in the implementation of the imperial projects. It is in this context that globalization as implemented by the West, guided by neo-liberal economic policies, and aided by greater militarism with this militarism as expenditure paid from the general revenue or if the revenue is not sufficient, through borrowing—and for the purpose of capital accumulation. Precisely for this reason the general public must be coached to believe that the empire is expanding "freedom" to the non-Western world and is encouraged to view this category of expenditures not only as a matter of national security—it is also expected that we cheerfully and patriotically "help out" foreign friends while knowledge of the historical role of this imperialism in the process of accumulation is suppressed. The miseducation of the public becomes an institutional imperative and this effort includes the aid of many institutions including but not limited to schooling and higher education, sports, arts, and religion—particularly the evangelical churches.

Schumpeter (1951) argued that with the rise of the bourgeoisie, imperialism would disappear and that capitalism would not lend itself to imperialism. I argue to the contrary that contemporary global capitalism reinforces imperialism, this imperialism then requires militarism, jingoism, and the forms of nationalism sponsored by capital. It is possible that Schumpeter's observations were relevant to the capitalist mode during the era of World War I, but even he acknowledged that nationalism and militarism, while not creatures of capitalism, become "capitalized" (Schumpeter 1951, 96) and in the end draw their fullest energy from capitalism. Capitalism "keeps them alive, politically as well as economically."

The contemporary global order has a hegemonic and advanced industrialized nation at the helm. The less developed world with its "de-nationalized" state is subservient to it. At least since WWII, the United States has historically been financially, politically, militarily, and according to the proponents of the empire: culturally, the leader. This leadership has cost the United States taxpayers much on all fronts. Specifically, the financial burden of maintaining such a huge armada with sophisticated weapons systems has been enormous. As the leader of the advanced industrialized countries the United States taxpayers have been paying for the expansion of political and economic interests of the Western ruling elites. The trade-off is in the area of the political support that the U.S. receives in dealing with international crises or challenges to global capitalism's expansion presented as "coalition" or "multilateral" efforts. The foundation of which was established in the period immediately after World War II with its new Western dominated multilateral agencies such as the International Monetary Fund (IMF), the World Bank and agencies associated with the United Nations.

Globalization, both as a new form of imperialism in the era of informal empire and as a new phase in the intensification of the expansion and the development of global capitalism, demands militarism as a means of overcoming challenges to its rule. Therein lies the fiscal crisis of the state as manifested by the United States national debt. The dominant classes whose pursuit of accumulation on a global scale has created the massive debt, are also the owners and creditors carrying most of the national debt and thus the ones who receive massive income flows from the nation's debt service. In other words, the *costs* of their accumulation strategy, as O'Connor (1971) observed, are *socialized* while the benefits accrue in private fortunes. To be effective, globalization, imperialism, and the coercive mechanisms implementing the accumulation process must necessarily have the structural (and also, if possible, the conscious) support of the domestic working classes. The extent of the success of imperialism abroad does engender a concerted effort to convince the domestic working classes to support imperialistic policies abroad.

The general public is coached and manipulated to view U.S. military intervention not as imperialism, but as a "civilizing mission" reminiscent of "white man's burden," a calling from on high up above. Convincing the public in the imperial centers of their providential duties is one thing, to ask it to pay for the cost of the mission without promising any concrete reward, however, is quite another. The hard reality is that the cost must be paid by the taxpayers at the expense of their children's education, health care, pensions, and quality time with their families. The scope of imperial projects abroad dictates the needed level of internal conformity, which in turn requires effective social imperialism.

In a democratic society, authentic or not, the public must give its approval to policies involving their everyday life, their children, and their futures; therefore, it is critical that they are convinced of the "ideal" mission of their government vis-à-vis other people. Debt of this magnitude, accrued to facilitate the process of the accumulation of capital, ends up generating tremendous income and business revenue for the very wealthy creditors—who are the main beneficiaries. This debt service enhances their income and the capital accumulation process. As any other indebtedness, national debt serves as one more conveyor belt for trickle up. The American empire, like all other colonial empires before it, has its own hegemonic intellectuals—ideologues—composed of social scientists, historians, the corporate media and even religious institutions responsible for the creation of an effective agency of *soft* social control (of course it also has state agencies of *hard* social control, i.e. police power, the courts, prisons, etc.).

The right-wing side of the political spectrum, aided by mainstream social science and the corporate media, invariably considers state expenditure on social programs (welfare, health care, and in particular the Medicare and Medicaid programs) as the primary causes of the growing "debt menace" to the nation and its future generations. This group includes the vocal and partisan intellectuals at the Heritage Foundation, the American Enterprise Institute, the white supremacists, and the vigilante patriots, and a segment of academia dominated by mainstream economists, and of course the pundits appearing in the corporate media. The "left" (defined in the context of American political spectrum as composed of the socially conscious mainstream social and political activists, journalists, and economists) has also sounded the alarm about the state's fiscal crisis and the disproportionate size of the national debt. This ostensibly left analysis, however, does not benefit from being grounded in an understanding of the contradictions within the capitalist system. But it is *only* within the context of a broader view of systemic contradictions that the issue of national debt may be fully and legitimately understood.

Only when grounded in a dialectical ontology regarding the conflicted conditions undergirding our social being and the nature of human history can social science discern the system dynamics and contradictions. In this regard it is imperative that a meta-theoretical framework be utilized that includes an elaborate set of conceptual tools capable of unearthing and exposing the structural contradictions and the manner in which aspects of these contradictions, when taken in abstract isolation from one another, may be ideologically misinterpreted. The impact of military spending on the bourgeoning national debt, for example, must be understood as grounded in the state's history of imperialist exploitation and the intensified inequalities between and within nations resultant from U.S.-led globalization. First, however, let us consider the main features of the mainstream (classical and neoclassical) thinking in economics which for the most part suppresses issues arising from structural contradictions.

Classical Economics: Liberalism and Neo-Liberalism.
Classical economics began in the 18th century with the work of William Petty, Adam Smith, James Stuart, David Ricardo, J.B Say, Jeremy Bentham, and a few of their contemporaries. The revulsion against the regnant (economically nationalist) mercantilism of the time furnished the energy that drove Smith and others to consider an alternative model of political economy based on the notion of competition and the sanctity and the wisdom of the market. The classical political economists considered, at least on the surface, the "moral sentiments" (i.e., Smith) and desires for freedom of the human producer. Today it appears that human productive activity (labor) is reduced to a commodified form, and as such it is divested of its so-called surplus product before obtaining a subsistence wage. Thus, rather than personal freedom, unfreedom in the form of commodity-dependency, obtains in every facet of life (since meeting human needs for health care, education, housing, nutrition, etc. may occur only via the exchange of supposedly equivalent market values). Both the ontology and the methodology of mainstream economics reify the individual business owners' contribution to the production process at the expense of the collective contribution of labor and the rights of the collective to ownership of the product. The classical laissez-faire perspective on politics and the ostensible rationality of the individual utility calculus are components of individual-based ideology separate from the real social structure and consequently oblivious to the economy's contradictions. Based on a false ontology and employing a mathematical deductivist method, it lacks the power necessary to resolve its contradictions (Ardebili, 2005). That is, the ontology upon which it anchors its assumptions does not allow a needed penetration of the subset of causal factors beneath the veneer of what is perceived as real. The end result is that within the "closed system" (Lawson, 1999) in which it operates, economic liberalism must rely on empiricism and ideology

rather than science.

This liberalism was the dominant mode of thinking and state ideology until the Great Depression of the 1930s. With the rise of Keynesianism, public works, demand maintenance, state regulation and intervention, all became components of the new macroeconomic approach to business cycle in the form of the New Deal. The Keynesianism of the 1930s through the 1960s was used to legitimate policy for the ruling elites of the capitalist West. Keynesianism also supported the ideological struggle against the communist East. The expansion of F.D.R.'s welfare system culminated in President Johnson's "unconditional war on poverty" and the introduction of programs such as the Medicare and Medicaid, which are again today seen as controversial by the U.S. right-wing.

The bourgeoning national debt is a systemic and a structurally determined and perpetuated crisis. The contradictions within the system stemming from the class structure of society, the declining rate of profit and the crisis of legitimation, and the problem posed by managerial strengths and weaknesses is causing increases or decreases in the severity of the crisis. Commenting on the regime of monopoly capital, O'Connor (1971, 40) states that "the basic cause of the fiscal crisis is the contradiction of capitalist production itself...." And "in the long run, monopoly capital socializes most of the capital costs and the social expenses of capitalist production." Therefore we need to examine the contradictions of accumulation and legitimation during the last two decades of monopoly capital and to look at the national debt and militarism in the context of capital accumulation.

The 1970s and the Regime of Monopoly Capital Accumulation. The period between 1945 and the late 1960s was a period of expansive capital accumulation (the Golden Age of Capitalism) and the capitalist classes in the imperial countries managed to "buy social peace at home and support for imperialist policy through social reform" including, but not limited to, full employment and social security policies (Lorimar 1997, 14). Pennant Rhea, editor of *The Economist*, lamented that "the post-war welfare system was an import from Marxism forced upon the rich by the Cold War" (Lorimer 1997, 14).

During the 1960s, capital's strategy had three main components: aggregate demand manipulation through fiscal and monetary policy, productivity maximization, and investment in human capital (Phillips 1980, 129). However, by the end of the 1960s, inflationary conditions set the stage for the 1970s crisis in global capitalism in the form of stagflation (Phillips 1980, 129), leading to the break-down of Fordism as an accumulation regime and the rise of neo-Fordism with its emphasis on a greater rate of exploitation of labor. The stagflation of the early 1970s was compounded by the so-called oil embargo, and the strategists of capital viewed the increase in the price of oil as another opportunity for capital accumulation. That is, "…consumer payments for high-priced oil in the importing countries represent a diversification from other forms of consumption…creating investible funds in the hands of the OPEC countries" (Robert Roosa cited in Phillips 1980, 248). Petrodollar recycling along with reduction in wages were critical components of the accumulation process. As a tradition in the process of accumulation the lowering of the value of laborpower has always been an essential element of a successful accumulation (Phillips 1980, 250). But capital's strategy in response to working class struggle has changed.

Labor struggle in the early 1970s was in the form of strikes and the demand for higher wages and better working conditions. In 1973 and 1974 the number of days lost to strikes in the U.S. was 28 and 48 respectively (*Yearbook of Labor Statistics* 1975 cited in Phillips' Table 45, page 250). The 1960s and 70s were witness to an increasing number of strikes by public employees. The number of strikes dropped from a record high in the 70s of 470 to a record low of 29 in 1997. In the 1980s strikers were replaced with non-union workers. Strikes against wage reductions were the weapon of choice on the part of organized labor. Capital's attempt at reducing labor's earnings took three key forms: layoffs, cut-backs in social needs oriented programs, and price increases. "The failure of commodity inflation to restore the conditions favorable to accumulation left capital with little choice but to engineer a worldwide depression to stop the global wage struggle" (Phillips 1980, 251). Perhaps the most significant element in capital's war on labor took the form of global austerity (between 1976-1978) which effected lowered expectations when implemented by the IMF in many countries, including the United States and Britain.

The return of finance capital in its most ruthless form following the stagflation of the 1970s, was responsible for the deficits and the growing indebtedness of the states, as well as for the crisis of the debt of Third World countries (Duménil and Levy, cited in Epstein, 2005). The decade of the 1970s was the last in which monopoly capital negotiated the buying of social peace for accumulation purposes (Ross and Trachte 1990, 64-66).

One of the main contradictions that arose from the capital glut at the upper reaches of society was the absence of a credible consumption class to take care of the overproduction (11). A second problem was the lack of ability to valorize the over-accumulated capital. Resolving these contradictions required the expansion of the *warfare* state, but not the welfare state (O'Connor 1971, 150). The "private interests of the moneyed oligarchy" focused on "the strategic role of military spending within monopoly capitalism" because the profitable absorption of the "rising surplus" could occur "through the growth of military establishment" (Ross and Trachte 1990, 44).

Militarism and imperialism are "inherent features of capitalist economic development..." (O'Connor 1971, 151). In this context militarism often appears as nationalism, which in turn reinforces militarism, and the line between nationalistic sentiments and militaristic tendencies is blurred. Keynesianism in the form of state fiscal policy attempted the implementation of social imperialism through lower taxes on business and higher state expenditures. Fiscal policy (taxation and expenditures) must be viewed in terms of the class structure of society, and the role of fiscal policy in the reproduction of the class structure and the political economy of capitalist production and accumulation. Welfare programs then as now being the cheapest of all social expenditures, had once been the seen as a guarantor of a tension-free capital accumulation process. The accumulation process has always required an effective legitimation apparatus often appearing in the form of social welfare expenditures. O'Connor (1971) describes two categories. First, social capital expenditures (education, research etc.) and social consumption expenditures (medical care, child care, social services, and unemployment benefits). The second category sustains legitimation and that of social expenses expenditures, such as welfare and warfare expenditures (O'Connor, 1971).

Today, legitimation is as much of a concern as it was during the 60s and 70s. As then the two contradictions—legitimation and accumulation, involve the participation of nearly every state agency and are realized by "every state expenditure" (O'Connor 1971, 7). Nevertheless, welfare as a partial solution to the "under-consumption" problem while serving as a legitimacy mechanism remains and will remain (as will most of the state expenditures) because of its role in the accumulation and legitimation process. That is, the state reproduces the class system through its legitimation function which involves the cooption of popular discontent through welfare expenditures as did the Keynesianism of the 1930s in the form of the New Deal. Furthermore, as O'Connor (1971) points out, state spending on capital and consumption both contribute to accumulation. Increases in consumption are attained through the availability of credit (consumptive debt), deceptive marketing strategies, and intensified competition. Individual indebtedness has always served as a great mechanism of social control and source of insecurity. Social imperialism works accordingly to address concerns of legitimation as well as creating the domestic base of external imperialism by incorporating the working classes of the home country by presenting imperialism as necessary for the pursuit of national interests. Militarism as a form of national honor becomes the ideological point of reference. Lately this strategy has relied more on the fear factor and insecurity than the traditional means of legitimacy that adhere to welfare expansion.

By the late 1970s, the problem with accumulation raised questions regarding the viability of maintaining social welfare and of continuing with modest wage increases. In the United States, the allegedly welfare-friendly Carter Administration created the conditions for the attack by the neo-liberal camp. The working class had to go along with the global austerity by submitting to lower expectations in the face of cuts in social programs, reduction in wages, and higher rates of exploitation. In this period the rise of a global platform for increasing production forced a rethinking and a shift in the principle of "welfare state" (Teeple 2007, 1). The creation of disciplined and insecure workers was the key to the success of a restructured regime of accumulation (Lorimar 1997, 14; Phillips 1980, 250). The new regime of accumulation was extraordinarily cold, heartless, uncompromising, . . .and reckless.

The 1980s and Beyond: Neo-Liberalism on the Offensive. This period represents the rise of neo-liberalism and the worsening fiscal crisis of the state. It is the era that followed after the epoch of classic social imperialism. From the 1980s onward, the ascendency of economic neo-liberalism was accompanied by a persistent global economic crisis in the West. So-called Reaganomics in the U.S. and Thatcherism in Britain were the epitome of neo-liberalism and a direct consequence of a growing accumulation problem in the global economy.

In the 1980s temporary interruptions to the global accumulation regime were caused by the Iranian revolution, the Nicaraguan revolution, the invasion of Afghanistan by former USSR, and by domestic working class demands. These saw capital promote neo-liberalism and militarism as part of the relentless pursuit of profit through deregulation and privatization. The ideologies of rugged individualism and militarism came to define the core of U.S. foreign policy: containing the USSR and the challenges on the part of the labor and national liberation fronts to American hegemonic practices. The political ideology of this period was a rehabilitated social Darwinism and free market fundamentalism. This in turn reinforced a hyper-nationalism and demanded greater jingoism of the corporate media.

Growing U.S. military spending in the 1980s, economic growth through deficit spending, tax cuts for the rich, and the reduction in social services were manifestations of changing national and global priorities. The global context was characterized by the race for resources with Machiavellian imperialistic and hegemonic tendencies. Domestically, reinvigorated pro-business policies were hailed as a clean break with the troubling labor-dictated condition. Since the late 1970s, the eradication of the purportedly anti-business economic climate manifested itself in an all-out attack strategy by neo-liberalism with a global reach. In the post 1970s, legitimation is no longer the concern it was in the era of the Cold War. Alan Greenspan, the former Chairman of the U.S Federal Reserve System, whose statements were perceived as policy statements, once remarked that "insecure workers are good for the economy as they keep inflation low" (Congressional testimony 2/26/97). Demoralized labor, insecure labor, unorganized (de-unionized) labor, and threatened labor are necessary and effective components of struggle for legitimacy and hegemony. In retrospect the fiscal crisis of the 1970s was unique in that state expenditures for the dual purposes of accumulation and legitimation were signs of the power of the organized labor's ability to negotiate better contracts. From the late 1970s and particularly in the 1980s, labor lost its ability to regroup and maintain its ability to collectively bargain. Reaganomics and Thatcherism were the two most ideologically anti-labor attempts at restoring capital's long run hegemony.

Comparatively speaking, the current crisis has reached a point of no return for two important reasons—legitimation imperatives and the bourgeoning national debt. In order to ensure its own sustainability the capitalist state's reductions in social expenditures (the war on labor) must, out of necessity, be replaced by a set of effective legitimacy-generating mechanisms. In the 1980s, tax cuts for the rich coupled with increases in spending caused an annual increase of 13.8% in the national debt. During his two terms, Reagan increased the national debt by 200% (from under one trillion to $2.6 trillion (McGourty, 2006).

Beginning with the rise of economic neo-liberalism and the global capitalist assault on the working class in the 1980s and the uncompromising and determined policy of crushing all opposition to its rule around the world, military might became indispensable. Pouring massive resources into the military industrial complex and the massive tax cuts for the rich in the United States resulted in the first trillion dollars of accumulated deficits in 1980-81. The grand aim was the dismantling of the Soviet "evil empire" through a crippling arms race initiated by the Reagan administration in the United States and Margaret Thatcher in Britain. In the meantime, the ideology of neo-liberalism aided by militarism was to facilitate accumulation on a global scale. The two interruptions in the accumulation process, namely the Iranian Revolution of 1979 and the Nicaraguan Revolution during the 1980s, were viewed as challenges to global accumulation. The Iranian Revolution was to be at least confined within the borders, if not completely eliminated. Therefore, Saddam Hussein was called upon to respond to that challenge by attempting to invade Iran, but was bogged down in an eight year long war of attrition. The Nicaraguan Revolution was challenged by the army of Contras aided by the Reagan Administration and the rest is a story well known. The United States, however, continued with the tradition of American intervention (militarily and otherwise) in the affairs of Latin America. To meet the demands of military spending the Reagan Administration and the succeeding administrations ran high budget deficits. "Accumulation by dispossession" is the hallmark of neo-liberal economic policy (Harvey 2006, 6).

Globally, the accumulation by dispossession involved indebtedness, the privatization of state owned industries, suffocating the most vulnerable countries with "free trade," and military interventions. The attacks on the labor, the poor, and even small business, through pension raiding, declining access to social services, indebtedness, and eminent domain acquisitions to the benefitting the biggest business, are increasing (Harvey 2006, 8). Indeed, the essence of neo-liberalism globally as well as domestically involves the intensifying domination of capital's oligarchic powers. In the era of post-classic social imperialism, the implementation of globalization and the entire hegemonic and imperialistic strategy involves a violent attack on the working class and the poor of the world disguised as free trade, democracy, freedom, and civility. Inequality, both in its creation as well as its maintenance, involves violence, for it demands expropriation and exploitation and the means of coercion to achieve these ends. Around the world, neo-liberal policies in the form of austerity measures are imposed by powerful multilateral financial institutions like the International Monetary Fund (IMF), the World Bank, and WTO. Aided by these supra-national agencies, global capitalism is steered on the path prescribed by the neo-liberal economic policy (market orientation, privatization, and deregulation) for the ultimate goal of creating smooth global conditions for accumulation.

In the 1980s and 1990s, global capital mobility and trade increased, but the plight of the workers, growth and employment opportunities showed no major improvement. On the contrary what appeared to be more noticeable was the burden of national debt and declining collective bargaining power on a global scale (Cohen and Centeno, 2005). Indeed, the application of Keynesianism both nationally and globally was aided by the Bretton Woods' new International Monetary System and its two powerful supranational institutions of the IMF (through its austerity measures) and the World Bank (ostensibly under United Nations' auspices) as instruments of the centralization of capital against the global working class struggle (Phillips 1980, 126). In the American context, the neo-liberal economic strategy and the slogan of laissez-faire overshadowed all corporate accountability even to their own shareholders. The merger mania of the '80s and '90s was indicative of capital's strategy for greater consolidation and centralization. In the 1990s, globalization intensified and exceeded all prior efforts; with it came the socialization of its costs. Imperial projects such as globalization are very expensive and, according to Chalmers Johnson (2007, 63), "[t]he flow of nation's wealth from taxpayers to (increasingly foreign) lenders, through the government to military contractors" is in the tradition of what Kalecki called "military Keynesianism."

Globalization, even if it is sanitized and defined as "expansion of the free market," has been a mechanism for greater accumulation on a world scale. Effective globalization requires an international capitalist class alliance along with institutions and ideologies both at the national and global level. The significant institutions in this regard are those of finance capital and equally important the military industrial complex. To protect the alliance, and when necessary to project power, military force is required and this gives rise to the state of permanent war.

The World Trade Organization (WTO) is one component of that infrastructure charged with making sure that globalization (and therefore the accumulation process) proceeds uninterrupted. The WTO formalized imperialism of trade engineered by the old "historical bloc" through standardization. The de-nationalization of the polity of various nation-states through their participation in the process of global accumulation legitimizes the process and presents it as voluntary participation. While in the 1990s it appeared that militarism was no longer as overt as in the 1980s, in reality the military industrial complex continued to exert influence on a global scale. The militarism of the 1990s was relatively subdued, but still alive and well in an ostensibly "…demilitarized world in which business activity is primary and political power has no other task than the protection of the world free-trading system" (Lorimer 1997, 13). Throughout the 1990s, the U.S. military buildup continued as it did in the 1980s; as it does now, serving as a mechanism for greater globalization. Aided by the military, the push is for greater integration of the world capitalist system with a touch of colonialism. An unprecedented degree of social imperialism continues in its most perverse form. Increases in state expenditures on the military, mainly financed through borrowing, have created the need for an alternative means of social control.

It is not accidental that we have seen a growing reliance on the culture of fear as a mechanism to mobilize public opinion in favor of militarism abroad and domestic security actions programs and actions reminiscent of the classic form of the police-state. The psychology of living in fear on the part of the public on the one hand, and dependence on fear for the purposes of effective social imperialism on the other, have worked to replace the "enemy" of communism with the fear of radical Islam. The militarization of a specific society and of the planet requires an effective propaganda. Fred J. Cook (1964, 100), observing the late 1950s and early '60s wrote, "The crutch of the Warfare State is propaganda. We must be taught to fear and to hate or we will not agree to regiment our lives, to bear the enormous burdens of ever heavier taxation to pay for ever more costly military hardware . . . at the expense of domestic programs...." This problem has become much more severe of late and is matched only by the level of public ignorance in the U.S. Thus, a free hand in the allocation of public funds to the military and military-related activities leads to the exhaustion of credit limits as the need to borrow increases with every annual budget preparation and military action abroad.

Yet, governmental borrowing continues to be one of the mechanisms of the *upward redistribution of incomes and wealth*. And as long as the general public remains ignorant of the facts, and by extension there are no incentives for the political establishment to change course, the long-run damage to the socio-economic and the political structure will be irreversible. As James Fallows (2005) points out, the current imperial wars fought for so called "freedom" and "security" are producing results such as deficit financing and lowering the taxes on the rich, while at the same time the deficit helps government "more easily slash domestic social programs" (cited in Street, 2005). In the post-WWII period in general and the post-911 era in particular, the culture of fear has been effectively incorporated into the toolbox of jingoism and propaganda. The conditioned-to-fear Americans were "longing" in the 1990s for a "clear-cut enemy" an indisputable target for moral outrage" (Sterns 2006, 212).

> We have seen Americans increasingly take not only data ("real or imagined"), but also outright emotional cues from media promptings, using presentations for guidance not only in public fear but also public grief .... Media manipulation has been heightened, of course, by irresponsible political posturing. It was no accident that the most fear-soaked television channel after September 11, FOX News, was also closest to the Bush Administration ... (Sterns 2006, 210)

Fear dampens the spirit, demoralizes, belittles personal power, and blocks rationality. The proponents of realpolitik are not as naïve as they appear, rather they have as their brethren in economics and indeed in all fields dominated by hegemonic intellectuals, a significant role to play in the overall imperial expansion. In fact some of them, such as Fernando Teson (2005), suggest that the United States has a duty to be a "humanitarian imperialist" by crushing regimes such as that of former Iraqi dictator Saddam Hussein. The ideologues of the same genre, the hegemonic intellectuals, have revisited the Vietnam War and similar imperial wars just to present them as legitimate and "humanitarian" interventions. From the point of view of domestic classes, the demons of the foreign "other" and "enemy" are viewed as sufficient reason to cheer what the rest of the world sees as dangerous and costly militarism. Social welfare expenditures continue to be a legitimacy-generating mechanism, but increasingly the fear of the *enemy* continues, perpetuated by the sensationalist warmongering corporate media (just as in the 19th century jingoism was mobilized by the British media). This is a critical factor in establishing and implementing social imperialism. The difference was that the British jingoism defended imperialism outright with occasional references to the purportedly civilizing mission of the "superior" Anglo-Saxon race.

The contemporary jingoism of the American media uses the rubrics of *freedom, human rights,* and *defense of democracy,* etc. etc. to subdue popular discontent as the empire resorts to a great degree of the actual use of military power abroad and police action and surveillance at home. Consistent with the strategy of social imperialism, overt use of military power has been and continues to be dressed up via some noble cause—a tradition which goes back to the practices of European colonial empires. The Western colonial empires in the 19th century presented their penetration, pillage, and rape of Africa, Asia, and Latin America as *modernization* and *tutelage,* aided by the ideology of the social Darwinism (i.e., those who dominate are most "fit"). This conceit pervaded the entire bourgeois realm of social science, education, and religious institutions.

During the height of colonial domination, imperial control of the colonies occurred through formal (direct control if everything else failed) and informal mechanisms (indebtedness and comprador control). Today, Iraq is an atavism in its most grotesque form, yet it is presented as an exercise in democracy. Even in this most insincere form, this points to underlying contradictions within the imperial system. How do you maintain political system based on democratic ideals in the era of these ruthless accumulation strategies? How do you promote democracy at gun point and with the threat of annihilation and stampede of national pride and sovereignty? Even in the context of the most paranoid condition of the approach of realpolitik in international relations, survival does not warrant such expenditures unless world domination is the aim of the policy. This is precisely why neo-liberalism operates alongside militarism, war and dictatorship.

Today's global capitalism crushes all unfavorable conditions through oppression and violence (latent and manifest) in order to ensure the creation of a world in its own image. Once again colonialism—armed robbery on a global scale—is reproduced and implemented. The difference between the old form and the new form is the scale of destruction and the overt use of weapons of mass destruction, continued environmental destruction and demobilization of humanity as a potent force for change. The militarization of the globe is a natural outcome. United Fruit Company could not have flourished without the Marines and the U.S. State Department and all of their resources. The French, the German, the British, and the Belgian financiers could not have been able to suck the blood out of their colonies without their legionnaires, soldiers, mercenaries, preachers, merchants, and generals. According to Thomas Friedman (1999, 49), "McDonalds cannot flourish without McDonnell-Douglas." Friedman is correct insofar as he is pointing out the symbiotic relationship between business and the military. But empirical realities, even those which appear positive, cannot permanently gloss over structural contradictions.

Defense Secretary William Cohen, in remarks to reporters prior to his speech at Microsoft Corporation in Seattle, put it this way, "[T]he prosperity that companies like Microsoft now enjoy could not occur without having the strong military that we have" (Talbot 1999, 68). Neither militarism nor neo-liberalism ought to be viewed in isolation from each other. Neo-liberalism is perhaps curiously reinforced by neo-conservatism. Neo-conservatism is "a violent complement of neo-liberalism" and "it adds force of war to the myth of free market under modern imperialism" (Jose Maria Sisson 2004, 5). "Both neo-liberalism and neo-conservatism are intended to expand U.S. economic territory and to make the pretense at building a market economy and democracy" (Sisson 2004, 5).

The neo-conservatives and the neo-liberals have benefited from the support of resurgent evangelical Christians in the 1980s. Evangelical Christians grew in power and influence in the first half of the nineteenth century (Bigelow 2005, 34). Not only did they reject the notion of class conflict within capitalism, they "saw the new industrial economy as a fulfillment of God's plan. The free market, they believed, was a perfectly designed instrument to reward good Christian behavior and to punish and humiliate the unrepentant" (Bigelow 2005, 35). Neo-liberalism does not function under the umbrella of militarism alone; it needs comprehensive institutional support and demands that all facets of capitalism be employed. In particular the institutions of religion, education, and finance as well as the supranational organizations (i.e., the IMF, the World Bank and their form of monetary terrorism) have been effectively employed in the implementation of its policies. But, effective control, whether domestic or transnational, must involve an ideological apparatus and a coercive power as the neo-liberal policies have shown.

Gramsci identified two distinct methods of politico-social control: physical control or domination and ideological control or hegemony through consent (1999). Any fuller discussion of the distinct types of politico-social control mechanisms elaborated by Gramsci would require an epochal delineation and a global context. Suffice it to say that it is the job of the hegemonic intellectuals to decide when and what strategy is called for in particular on the basis of a realization that external control requires effective internal control. The success of the military operations overseas requires effective social imperialism. As the level of distrust against the United States increases globally, and as the domestic problems mount, "coercion rather than consensus" becomes a more viable alternative in controlling the home front (Harvey 2003, 77). "An unholy alliance between state powers and the predatory aspects of finance capitalism forms the cutting edge of 'vulture capitalism' that is as much about cannibalistic practices and forced devaluations as it is about achieving harmonious global development" (Harvey 2003, 136).

The occupation of Iraq and Afghanistan in the age of concerted and spreading challenges to global capitalism in general, and neo-liberalism in particular, attest to a global class conflict. And they remain and will continue to present the greatest imperial crises for America while in its contemporary neo-liberal and neo-conservative mode. The *human* cost at the present and the devastating impact on future generations, both in Iraq and in the United States, will dwarf the current and future *monetary* expenditures associated with the actual use of personnel and weapons in subduing and occupying Iraq. The cost of this neo-liberal/neo-conservative militarism and imperialist policy of regime change (disguised as the "war on terror" and the export of democracy) needs to be viewed in the context of greater strategy for world domination. This attempt, however, has several obstacles none of which can easily be ignored. And it is a mistake to think that only a particular party in office rather than the structure itself creates such crises and/or shows such imperialistic hegemonic tendencies.

To attribute the imperial practices to a particular political party assumes that they are a matter of management style or variations in the composition of the ruling class. Instead, modern fiscal policy was born and nurtured in the context of a military Keynesianism as a strategy for perpetuating capitalism. It did not forecast growth of national debt as entailing a fiscal crisis of the state. Endless tax breaks for the rich are one indicator of a well-entrenched "aristocracy of finance" (O'Connor 1971, 190). These tax cuts have generated massive windfalls for the rich. As expected by the proponents of the "trickle down" theory, some jobs for the working class, whose wage rate has not changed since 1972, have been created. Yet, as the interest payments on the debt must be made, the working class must pay these higher taxes as well as to likely fall victim to the austerity measures imposed by the condition of indebtedness. A tax cut for the rich, therefore becomes a coercive method in protecting and expanding the interests of the upper classes.

The national debt in terms of its determinants and size, has no political party affiliation, and is independent of the political party control of the U.S. congress. It is important to point out that since 1938, the Democrats were in control of the White House for about half the time and Republicans for the other half. Over this period, the national debt has increased at an average annual rate of 8.7 percent. For Democrats the average increase was 8.3 percent, slightly higher for Republicans at 9.7 percent (McCourty 2007). Of course, when correlated with the tax structure and the class aspect, we can see the tilt in favor of the accumulation. Prior to World War II, the wealthiest Americans paid nearly all of the federal income tax. In order to finance the war, income taxes were increased and the majority of workers had to pay income taxes for the first time. As federal tax rates on the wealthy were decreased starting in the 1960s, the tax burden on middle and low income Americans began to grow. Today, this continues to be the case, but it is rarely viewed in the context of class struggle. Similarly, the outcome of that struggle, the national debt and all of its consequences is rarely viewed in context.

In the United States the effects of neo-liberalism are more noticeable as the rich grow richer and the poor grow in numbers and poverty. Meanwhile militarization and war are intensifying, and on the other hand the position of both the lower and the middle classes is worsening within the advanced societies (Pollin 2004; Wood 2003, and Mann 2003). Furthermore, this inequality is matched by a rising culture of violence, and intensification and glorification of unrestrained consumerism through indebtedness on the one hand and the evolving seclusion of the well to do behind gated communities. Schmitt and Zepperer (2006, 16), have documented that the U.S. economy suffers from substantial "...exclusion, including high level of income inequality, high relative and absolute poverty rates, poor and unequal educational outcomes, poor health outcomes, and high rates of crime and incarceration." Recently (2007) UNICEF reported that among the developed economies, the United States and England ranked 20 and 21 respectively in worsening conditions of their children. In terms of happiness, the children of these two countries are at the bottom of the scale and the abuses of alcohol, prevalence of violence, drug abuse, sexual abuse, and poor health are major concerns.

Of course, the United States and Britain have always had many significant social problems. Nevertheless, the severity varied from period to period. However, with the advent of neo-liberal policies and the accompanying globalization, the rich have reduced their own burdens, socializing the costs of the militarism, top-heavy accumulation dynamics, and debt service, from which they benefit. U.S. corporations aided by subsidies are selling weapons systems to governments which are killing their own people. The need for the overseas expansion of "surplus" capital and the extension of American economic, political, and cultural hegemony are the root causes of the American militarism (O'Connor 1971, 152-53). The "Garrison State" (V.K. Dibble, cited in O'Connor 1971, 156) produces a culture of militarism and military-based patriotism enabled through a worldwide chain of military "colonies." According to Johnson, oil and arms barons have created "a military juggernaut intent on world domination," and are exercising "preemptive intervention" for "oil, Israel, and... to fulfill our self-perceived destiny as a New Rome" (Johnson 2001).

The relationship between globalization and militarism should be seen as two sides of the same coin. On one side, globalization promotes the conditions that lead to unrest, inequality, conflict, and ultimately war. On the other side, globalization fuels the means to wage war by protecting and promoting the military industries needed to produce sophisticated weaponry. This weaponry, and the military in turn, is used or is threatened to be used to protect the investments of transnational corporations, the agents of neo-liberalism, and their accumulation and privatization beneficiaries (Staple 2007). The military is employed to crush any resistance to neo-liberal economic policies. An example of this grotesque imperial arrogance is the Iraqi oil law. The Iraqi oil law has witnessed the wholesale privatization of Iraq oil, pushed for by foreign oil companies and private (mostly American) contractors. Since the occupation, Iraq has become one of only three nations in the world that give corporations all the rights entitled to a human being (i.e. "corporate personhood"). Naomi Klein describes Iraq as a "modern laboratory for neo-liberal experimentation" (Buckly 2005).

Similarly Duménil, and Lévy (2005) observe that "[n]eoliberalism is the ideological expression of the return to hegemony of the financial fraction of ruling classes."

As globalization continues to take effect, large powers will often use their armada in support of the globalizing agents. On November 11, 2000, Richard Haas stated that American global hegemony required an imperial power capable of extending its control formally and informally. Implicitly Haas is calling for greater social imperialism by claiming that: "Imperialism Begins at Home." To Haas, the concern ought to be with "imperial understretch, not overstretch." Full-scale military intervention, according to Haas, can lead to massive destruction, but it could also be to re-build. Of course the task of rebuilding is always left to global corporations, invariably from the imperialist countries and their allies (John Bellamy Foster 2003). In 1935 General Smedley D. Butler (Pearce 1982, 20) reflected, with palpable remorse, on his thirty-three years as a Marine Corps officer serving as "a high-class muscle man for Big Business, for Wall Street and the bankers. In short, I was a racketeer for capitalism." Bluntly put: the de facto role of the U.S. armed forces was to keep the world safe for the U.S. economy and open to a U.S. cultural assault. To those ends, the U.S. was prepared to do a fair amount of killing, according to Major Ralph Peters in *Constant Conflict* (Summer 1997, 414).

The forerunners to the modern day transnational corporations, imperial organizations like the East India Companies, used their navies alongside their merchant ships to penetrate faraway lands to grab wealth. Contemporary transnational corporations have continued with this tradition of relying on the political and military power of their national state for successful globalization and the control of production, resources, and markets. In a recent public statement, former U.S. Defense Secretary, Robert Gates, used

Korea as an analogy, and revealed that the United States has no intention of leaving Iraq anytime soon either. Nonetheless, Iraq will continue to present itself as a challenge to an uninterrupted globalization and accumulation process, and will remain as one of the greatest examples of oppressive military power coming to the aid of globalized resource extraction and wealth accumulation.

The U.S. political structure has long promoted a vengeful nationalism and military patriotism. Nationalism expressed in military terms began with the 1947 U.S. emergence of the "national security state," and has recently culminated in the "Project for the New American Century." This plan for American imperial domination of the planet envisioned a new imperialism that would not "hesitate to use force if, when, and where necessary, and… unilaterally . . . ." It anticipated what would later be formulated as follows:

> We must discourage the other industrialized nations from challenging American leadership and from bringing into question the economic and political established order. We must keep such a military supremacy that potential rivals will be dissuaded from aspiring to a larger regional or global role. (Kohl and Feldstein in Veltmeyer 2005, 9)

Paul Wolfowitz (along with Richard Perle, and Dick Cheney among others) was also the lead author of "Project for the New American Century." This is regarded at the current play book for the unilateral projection of the American military and political power in the service of the empire (Veltmeyer 2005, 14). Not too long after the script was written, the Bush administration

> used the last and only refuge of truly unchallenged American global hegemony—its

possession of a sheer preponderance of military force—precisely as a tool for shoring up its long-declining world-economic power by putting Uncle Sam's boot on that great strategic economic (and military) prize in an age of global petro-capitalism: the Middle Eastern oil spigot." (Harvey 2003)

The neo-liberal/neo-conservative fusion is personified by Wolfowitz, as deputy Pentagon leader, architect of and apologist for imperial theft and U.S. corporate patronage associated with the illegal Iraq War (Bond 2006). They were cheered by the "Israel firsters" such as Irving Kristol, Norman Podhoretz, and William Kristol among many others in the neo-con camp advocating "pre-emptive" strikes (particularly against countries like Iran). Invariably, the implementation of all of these policy components—the accumulation strategy and process—relies heavily on military power and military Keynesianism, which in turn feed the military industrial complex and creates massive indebtedness. Are there policy makers who do not see the consequences of militarism and imperialism abroad and the social imperialism inside? Few were willing to defend over $9 trillion in national debt some years ago, other than to acknowledge it as a necessary evil that needs to be addressed. Ignoring it has become a norm, and even when it reached $14 trillion in 2013, it continued to be too "abstract" to be understood.

Conclusion. Thomas Jefferson viewed public debt as one of the greatest dangers to political and economic independence. Today, as the national debt mounts, the contemporary statesmen for the most part not only seem willing to ignore the danger it poses, but they are also continuing to add to it. Though public debt is as old as institution of polity itself, it was argued in this paper that contemporary causes of indebtedness are to be found in globalization, accumulation drives, imperialism, and social imperialism. Globalization is a form of imperialism for the sake of capital accumulation; it involves militarism as the protector of globe-spanning corporations. The accumulation of capital on a global scale is an endeavor on the part of the international capitalist class, which in a solid alliance, preserves its hegemony with an armada upon a sea of hegemonic ideology. Social imperialism is a strategy adopted to meet the need of domestic control in the service global accumulation. The intensity of the internationalized accumulation drive determines the degree of social imperialism in the imperialist zones. Today, social imperialism relies less on the provision of social services, and more on fear as a control mechanism. Fear of terrorism, fear of job insecurity, fear of domestic violence, fear of gang violence, and fear of the unknown are functional to globalized capital, serving to subdue people and force their resignation to the status quo and the surrender of their rights to the agents of control (Stern 2006). In New York City in 2005, a teacher asked her sixth-grade students to draw the images that they most associate with the United States. Well over half offered military scenes (Stearn 2006, 169). A 2004 analysis of data by the U.S. Census Bureau reports that 60 million Americans lived on less than $7 per day. Twenty-five million Americans now depend on emergency food aid. Wages have remained stagnant since 1972, and for too many Americans, the litany of violence, punishment, and suffering seems unending, and the American Dream is now a uniquely Made-in-America Nightmare (William Shanley 2007). Since the mid-'90s, corporate welfare programs have outweighed spending for low-income programs by more than three to one: $167 billion to $51.7 billion (Center on Budget and Policy Priorities, FY 95 figures).

Democracy as a right and as a privilege comes with the responsibility of preserving it. Not realizing its vulnerabilities can lead to disaster. In other words democracy demands involvement in the political process and social activism. The commodification of freedom signals its demise. Even an honest and humble patriotism in this regard inadvertently serves the oligarchic interests of internationalized capital.

Bibliography

Aglietta, Michel. 1982. "World Capitalism in the Eighties," *New Left Review* I/136.

Ardebili Morteza. 2005. "Review of *Reorienting Economics* by Tony Lawson," *Review of Social Economy* 63:4.

Arrighi, Giovanni. 2005. "Hegemony Unraveling," *New Left Review* (March-April).

Augeli, Enrico and Craig Murphy. 1988. *America's Quest for Supremacy and the Third World.* London: Pinter Publishers.

Bacevich, Andrew J. 2005. *The New American Militarism: How Americans Are Seduced by War.* Oxford: Oxford University Press.

Bigelow, Gordon. 2005. "Let There Be Markets: The Evangelical Roots of Economics," *Harper's Magazine*, May, pp. 33-39.

Bottomore, T. B., and Maximilien Rubel. 1964. *Karl Marx: Selected writings in Sociology and Social Philosophy.* New York: McGraw Hill.

Buckly, Jordan. 2005. "Neoliberalism & Militarism Collide," SOA Watch, http://www.afsc.org/central/austin/NeoliberalismMilitarismCollide.htm

Butler, Smedley D. [1935] 1982. "America's Armed Forces," Part 2, *Common Sense*, Vol. 4, No. 11 in Jenny Pearce, *Under the Eagle: U.S. Intervention in Central America and the Caribbean.* Boston: South End Press.

Caves, R. 1982. *Multinational Enterprise and Economic Analysis*, Cambridge: Cambridge University Press.

Cohen, Joseph Nathan and Miguel Angel Centeno. *Neoliberalism and Patterns of economic Performance, 1980-2000.*

Cook Fred. J, 1964. *The Warfare State.* New York: Collier Books.

Cox, Robert W. 1981. "Social Forces, States and the World Orders: Beyond International Relations Theory," *Millennium: Journal of International Studies* 10(2).

_____. 1987. *Production, Power, and World Order* New York: Columbia University Press.

_____. 1993. "Gramsci, Hegemony and International Relations: An Essay in Method," in *Gramsci, Historical Materialism and International Relations*, ed. Stephen Gill, New York: Cambridge University Press.

_____. 1996. "Global Perestroika," in *Approaches to World Order*. New York: Cambridge University Press.

Dibble, Vernon K. 1971. "The Garrison Society," in *The War Economy of the United States: Readings in Military Industrialism and Economy*, Seymore Melman (ed). New York: Saint Martin's Press.

Duménil, G., and D. Lévy. 2005. "Costs and Benefits of Neoliberalism: A Class Analysis," in G. Epstein, *Financialization and the World Economy*. Aldershot, England: Edward Elgar.

Dunning, J. 1981. *International Production and the Multinational Enterprise*. London: George Allen &Unwin.

Edwards, Paul. K. 1981. *Strikes in the United States, 1881-1974*. New York: St. Martin's Press.

Egan Daniel, 2003. "Global Capitalism and the Internationalization of the State: Some Lessons from the Defeat of the Multilateral Agreement on Investment," paper submitted for the International Conference on the Work of Karl Marx and Challenges for the XXI Century, Havana.

Epstein, Gerald A. 2005. *Financialization and the World Economy*. Aldershot, England: Edward Elgar.

Fallows, James. 2005. "Countdown to a Meltdown," *Atlantic Monthly*, July-August.

Foster, John Bellamy. 2003. "Imperial America and War," *Monthly Review*, May 28.

Friedman, Thomas. L. 2000. *The Lexus and the Olive Tree*. New York. Anchor Books.

_____. 2005. *The World is Flat: A Brief History of the Twenty-First Century*. New York: Farrar, Straus and Giroux.

Gill Stephen. 1990. *American Hegemony and the Trilateral Commission*.

New York: Cambridge University Press.
_____. (ed). 1993. *Gramsci, Historical Materialism and International Relations*. New York: Cambridge University Press.
_____. 1995. "Market Civilization and Global Disciplinary Neoliberalism," *Millennium: Journal of International Studies* 25(3).
Glyn, A, and Sutcliff, B. 1992. "Global, but Leaderless? The New Capitalist Order," in Ralph Miliband and Leo Panitch (eds.), *New World Order: The Socialist Agenda*. London: Merlin Press.
Gordon, David, M. 1988. "The Global Economy: New Edifice or Crumbling Foundations?" *New Left Review*, 168.
Gramsci, Antonio. 1999. *Selections from Prison Notebooks of Antonio Gramsci*. Hoare, Q, and G. N. Smith (eds). New York: International Publishers.
Hardt, Michael, and Antonio Negri. 2000. *Empire*. Cambridge, MA: Harvard University Press.
Harvey, David., 2003. *The New Imperialism*. New York: Oxford University Press.
Hellman, Chris. 2006. "The Runaway Military Budget: An Analysis," Friends Committee on National Legislation, March, no. 705.
Higgs, Robert. 2004. "The Defense Budget Is Bigger Than You Think," *The San Francisco Chronicle*, January 18.
Hilferding, Rudolf. 1910. *Das Finanzkapital, Eine Studie über die jüngste Entwicklung des Kapitalismus*. Vienna: Wiener-volksbuchhanglung.
Hirst, Paul, and Graham Thompson. 1996. *Globalization in Question*. Cambridge: Polity Press.
Hoare, Q, and G. N. Smith (eds). 1999. *Antonio Gramsci, Selections from Prison Notebook of Antonio Gramsci*. New York. International Publishers.
Hymer, Stephen. 1979. *The Multinational Corporation: A Radical Approach*. Cambridge: Cambridge University Press.
Johnson, Chalmers. 2001. "Blowback: U.S. Actions Abroad Have Repeatedly Led to Unintended, Indefensible Consequences," *The Nation*, Vol. 273, October 15.
_____. 2001. *Blowback; The Costs and Consequences of American Empire*. New York: Henry Holt.

_____. 2007. "Republic or Empire: A National Intelligence Estimate on the United States" *Harpers*, Vol. 314, No. 1880. January.

Johnson, David. 2003. *Perfectly Legal: The Covert Campaign to Rig Our Tax System to Benefit the Super-Rich, and Cheat Everybody Else*, New York: Penguin/Putnam Group.

Kanth, R. 1999. "Against Eurocentred Epitemologies: A Critique of Science, Realism and Economics," in Fleetwood, S. (ed), *Critical Realism in Economics: Development and Debate*. London and New York: Routledge.

Kotz, David. 2003. "Neoliberalism and the Social Structure of Accumulation: Theory of Long Run Capital Accumulation," *Review of Radical Political Economics*, 35, 3.

Larrain, Jorge. 1991. "The Classical Political Economists and Marx on Colonialism and 'Backward' Nations," *World Development*, Vol. 19. No, 2/3.

Lawson Tony, 2006. "The Nature of Heterodox Economics" *Cambridge Journal of Economics*, 30.

Lenin, Vladimir I. 1969. *Imperialism: The Highest Stage of Capitalism-A Popular Outline*. New York. International Publishers.

Lochbihler, Barbara. "Militarism a Facilitator for Globalization," Women's International League for Peace and Freedom.

Magdoff, Harry. 1969. *The Age of Imperialism: The Economics of U.S. Foreign Policy*. New York: Monthly Review Press.

_____. 1978. *Imperialism: From Colonial Age to the Present*. New York: Monthly Review Press.

McCormick, Thomas. 1990. *America's Half Century: United States Foreign Policy in the Cold War*. Baltimore, MD: Johns Hopkins.

McGourty, Steve. 2006. "United States National Debt 1938-present: An Analysis of the Presidents Who Are Responsible for Excessive Spending."

McGowan, David. 2000. *Derailing Democracy*. Monroe, ME: Common Courage Press.

Murphy, Craig N. 1994. *International Organization and Industrial Change*. Cambridge: Polity Press.

Neumann, Franz. *Behemoth: The Structures and Practice of National Socialism*. London: Gollancz.

O'Connor, James. 1973. *The Fiscal Crisis of the State*. New York: St. Martin's Press.

Palloix, Christopher. 1975a. "The internationalization of Capital and the Circuit of Social Capital," in H. Radice (ed.) *International Firm and Modern Imperialism*. Harmondsworth: Penguin Books.

Petras, James and Henry Veltmeyer. 2001. *Globalization Unmasked: Imperialism in the 21st Century*. Chicago: Zed.

Phillips, Ronny Jack. 1980. *Global Austerity: The Evolution of the International Monetary System and World Capitalist Development 1945-1978*. Unpublished Ph.D. Dissertation, University of Texas at Austin.

Pollin, Robert. 2004. *Contours of Descent: U.S. Economic Features and the Landscape of Global Austerity*. London, Verso.

Ricardo, David, [1821] 2001. *The Principles of Political Economy and Taxation*. Kitchner, Ont: Batoche Books.

Robinson William and Jerry Harris. 2000. "Toward a Global Ruling Class? Globalization and the Transnational Capitalist Class" *Science & Society*, vol. 64, no. 1.

_____. 1996a. "Globalization: Nine Theses On Our Epoch," *Race and Class* 38(2).

_____. 1996b. *Promoting Polyarchy: Globalization, U.S. Intervention, and Hegemony*. New York: Cambridge University Press.

_____. 1998. "Beyond the Nation State Paradigm: Globalization, Sociology, and the Challenge of Transnational Studies," *Sociological Forum* 13(4).

_____. 2001. "Social Theory and Globalization: The Rise of a Transnational State," *Theory and Society*, 30.

Roosa, Robert. 1975. in "How Will it be Possible to Pay for OPEC Oil?" Khodadad Farmanfarmaian. *Foreign Affairs*, January.

Ross, Robert J.S., and Kent C. Trachte. 1999. *Global Capitalism: The New Leviathan*. Albany: SUNY Press.

Rupert, Mark. 1995. *Producing Hegemony: The Politics of Mass Production and American Global Power*. New York: Cambridge University Press.

Schmitt, John, and Ben Zipperer. 2006. "Is the U.S. a Good Model for Reducing Social Exclusion in Europe?" *Post-autistic Economic Review*, No. 40.

Schumpeter, Joseph A. 1951. *Imperialism and Social Classes*. Oxford: Blackwell.

_____. [1939] 2006. *Business Cycles*. Mansfield Centre, Connecticut: Martino Publishing.

Semmel, Bernard. 1960. *Imperialism and Social Reform* Garden City, New York: Anchor Books.

Shanley, William. 2007. "Poverty in America: American Dream Now a Nightmare for Millions: One in Five Lives on Less than $7 per day," *Global Research*, April 23, 2007.

Smith, Adam. [1776] 1976. *The Wealth of Nations*. Harmondsworth: Penguin.

Staples, Steven. 2000. "The Relationship Between Globalization and Militarism" *Social Justice* magazine, Vol. 27, No. 4.

Stearn, Peter N. 2006. *American Fear: The Causes and Consequences of High Anxiety*. New York: Routledge.

Street, Paul. 2005. "Bush, China, Two Deficits, and the Ongoing Decline of U.S. Hegemony," *ZNET*, July 27.

Talbot, Karen. 1999. "Backing up Globalization with Military Might," *Covert Action Quarterly*, Issue 68, Fall.

Teeple, Gary. 2000. "The Globalization and the Decline of Social Reform," New York: Garamond Press/ Humanity Books.

Thiele, Everett. 2005. "Military Spending: Cost of Iraq War is but the Tip of the Iceberg, *Global Research*, July 20.

Teson, Fernando R. 2005. "Ending Tyranny in Iraq," *Ethics and International Affairs*, http://ssrn.com/abstract=721585

_____. 2005. *Humanitarian Intervention: An Inquiry into Law and Morality*. The Hague: Martinus Nihoff.

Veltmeyer Henry. 2005. "Development and Globalization as Imperialism, http://laborinto.uma.es/articulosinpublicar/Veltmeyer, January, 2005.

Wilson, Brian S. 1999. "Who are the REAL Terrorists?" Institute for Policy Research & Development.
http://www.brianwillson.com/who-are-the-real-terrorists/

Wood, Ellen, M. 1999. "Unhappy Families: Global Capitalism in a World of Nation-States," *Monthly Review*, 51:3.

Wood, Geoffrey. 2003. *Imperialism and Disorder: The Global Ambitions and Internal Decay of the United States*. London: Verso.

Wright, Eric Olin. 1979. *Class, Crisis and the State*. London: Verso.

MEHDI S. SHARIATI
Chapter Ten

Latin America's March toward Democracy:
Challenging the Hegemon

A New Dawn in Latin America has begun. Enormous challenges and opportunities confront the region in the face of the crushing and vengeful neo-liberalism of global capitalism with all of its supportive economic, military, and political institutions. This essay examines those challenges and opportunities particularly as they are related to the possible liberation from capital's hegemony and its attempts at containing democratic aspirations and strategies in Latin America.

The contemporary challenges faced by Latin countries are no less determining now than those they were confronted with in the decades following their independence. The rise of the Bolívarian ethos,[1] was subsequently embodied in the

---

[1] Simón Bolívar of Venezuela organized the Congress of Panama in 1826 to create a united Latin American opposition to Spain, while promoting economic integration and development. It proposed a League of Hispanic American Republics with a common military, a mutual defense pact, and a supranational parliamentary assembly.

struggles for liberation and autonomy waged by guerrilla leaders such as Che, Fidel Castro, and the Sandinistas of Nicaragua, to the democratically-elected socialists such as Arbenz of Guatemala, Allende of Chile. For the contemporary, democratically-elected governments of Venezuela, Bolívia, Chile, Ecuador, Paraguay, and the quasi-populist de Silva of Brazil, the struggle remains not just a political and an economic one, but rather an existential one.

The Latin American people for most of their history have struggled for democracy and, had they been free of imperialistic interventions aided by domestic comprador classes, they would have achieved much more in the social, economic, and political arenas. This has been a very long and sordid history. Any attempt at liberation and autonomy has been forcefully confronted and decapitated.[2] Peron was discredited; Che was murdered; the Cuban revolution has been effectively contained within its shores; Arbenz was overthrown and murdered; so was the democratically elected President of Chile, Salvador Allende. The Sandinista government of Daniel Ortega was overthrown through a bloody Contra group aided by some of the Latin governments (Argentina, Honduras, and El Salvador among others) involved in the "dirty war," various organs of the United States government, Christian fundamentalists, and the World Anti-Communist League (Armony 1977).

Since independence, Latin America as a region experienced over 160 coups. During the same period, their powerful neighbor to the North often presented itself as a benevolent imperial protector by intervening when its interests warranted. In the words of former United States

---

[2] See John Perkins, *Confessions of an Economic Hit Man* (New York: PLUME/Penguin, 2005, new edition 2016).

Senator, George P. McLean, it is an "imperialism of science, peace, and justice (Congressional Record, 1927, cited in Smith 1981, 66). The United States has maintained its hegemonic control through regional treaties, agreements, and support of the elite-dominated regimes nourished through social, economic, and military means. Today, those countries which have opted for democratic socialism or are struggling against globalization and neo-liberalism are engaged in a desperate struggle to sustain themselves in the face of a very destructive and dangerous form of terrorism—financial terrorism.[3]

What do North Americans by and large think of the history of relationships between the United States and Latin America and/or the contemporary issues regarding these relationships? Much is done in the name of the U.S.-American people, and yet we are constantly reminded that not many of us know or care to know about the various regions our political, economic and social elites are operating in either in the form of war or exploitation. How many of us understand that, under the despotic regime of global capitalism, all developing countries are forced to compete for foreign investment effectively relinquishing their control over their economies to the agents of global finance. Accumulation is the alpha and the omega in the dynamism of global capitalism. Accumulation on a global scale does not allow prosperity for the majority—including North American masses. Instead the regime of global capitalism endorses and breeds dispossession. It effectively lowers wages and reduces or eliminates social services as part of the crushing austerity

---

[3] See ibid. According to Perkins, a self-described "economic hit man," corporate professionals like himself coerced Latin American governments to borrow more than they could possibly repay; leaders who did not cooperate in places like Ecuador and Panama suffered fatal "accidents."

measures administered by its powerful agents—for example, the International Monetary Fund (IMF). Accumulation through privatization has become a *core process* in the global capitalist system. Privatizing gains, while "socializing" the costs, is a constant policy associated with global capitalist transactions, free trade, globalization.

A History in Brief of U.S.-Latin American Relations. From the early part of the nineteenth century, the United States has considered Latin America all its own—the backyard. It was declared an area off-limits to foreign intervention by the Monroe Doctrine in 1823 (which has been invoked many times since its inception). It was reinforced by President James Buchanan (1857-61), who believed that the U.S. should take on the role of a policeman in the region. Police actions against Latin America continued to define the "big stick" policy of Theodore Roosevelt (another version of the "White Man's Burden," as Kipling described British imperialism's delusional self-conception). Through this type of policy Latin America suffered covert and overt military, economic and social intervention in order to "civilize" the "uncivilized." With certain modifications the big stick policy morphed into the "good neighbor" policy of Franklin D. Roosevelt,[4] but military intervention and economic imperialism along with the racism, and cultural disdain embedded in social Darwinism continued. Irrespective of the political party in control in Washington and/or the specific historical period,

---

[4] Half of century later Roosevelt's grandson, Kermit Roosevelt, engineered a coup against the democratically-elected government of M. Mossadegh of Iran in 1953. The theater of subversion and regime change was conducted from the basement of the U. S. Embassy in Tehran. This bitter history is sorely missing from the public discourse in the U.S. regarding Iran.

independent-minded Latin American governments were to be monitored, contained, or removed. All nationalists, leftists, and radicals, who opposed the domination of their economies by the hegemonic powers, were and are viewed as irritants causing political instability. The wrath of intervention and the brutality of the encounters between the mighty North and the impoverished South is a story well told in Latin America. Gabriel García Márquez's novel, *One Hundred Years of Solitude*, eloquently narrates the suffocating socio-economic and political influences on Latin American countries as exemplified by the slaughter and devastation brought to the fictional town of Macondo, Colombia.

Post-WWII, particularly during the cold war, the push for reproducible and dependent capitalist economies on the part of the dominant American political and economic classes had the ostensible aim of containing Soviet communism while at the same time containing homegrown democratic movements. This was to make sure that the U.S. penetration and domination of Latin American economies proceeded without challenge. Opposition to Soviet-style communism was used as a cover by the U.S. for its opposition to the democratic, independent, and nationalistic governments in the peripheral worlds of Africa, Asia, and Latin America. Its propaganda implied a malignancy which had to be excised while in its infancy. The biggest fear of all, however, was the fear of "losing" Latin America to its own people. This fear dictates United States' policy in Latin America today, as did then.

In 1923, the United States sponsored the Treaty of Peace and Amity with Central American governments for the primary purpose of discouraging and preventing revolutions either by the nationalists or the communists. All political appointments, organizations (especially labor unions), and individual leaders were to be monitored. Faced with challenges from radical nationalists and leftists who perceived their governments as being American puppets, the ruling elites espoused the doctrine of modernization in order to legitimize their control of state apparatus. Even when the Economic Commission for Latin America (ACLA, a United Nations Commission) introduced the idea of a Central American Common Market (ACLAC) without any structural change, the Kennedy administration made an offer of $100 million in aid trying to alter the final draft. It effectively distorted the mechanism by removing sections on regional planning and balanced growth in favor of free trade (Pearce 1982, 47). Then and now the compradors are taken care of through kick-backs and corruption disguised as bidding, competition, and mediation.

Capital Accumulation, Structural Adjustments, and Neoliberalism in the 1980s. Various strategies in the 1960s and 1970s emphasized import-substitution industrialization as a solution to economic malaise. In 1961, the Alliance for Progress was formulated to facilitate a shift in U.S. investment strategy. This involved moving away from the solely cash-crop-based economies of Latin America to import-substitution industrialization. Invariably, these industrialization policies looked to the North as the provider of technology and capital, thereby creating a new form of dependence.

During the 1950s and the late 1970s, this industrialization occurred largely in the public sector. It grew rapidly, yet with the advent of the 1980s, privatization of the major public industries accelerated. This privatization further opened up the economy to foreign investors, mostly from the global North. "Between 1985 and 1992, more than 2,000 publicly owned firms, including public utilities, banks, insurance companies, highways, ports, airlines, and retail shops, were privatized throughout the region" (Edwards 1995, 170). Privatization is a neoliberal strategy of *de*-nationalizing the national state. It invites and creates profitable investments for foreign owners and removes any credible regulation from the economic life.

Colonial empires of the 19th century, notably the British, French, and German empires, used a "debt trap" as a mechanism to reproduce their hegemony. Today, supranational and international agencies such the World Bank and the International Monetary Fund have revived indebtedness as an instrument of control. The debt trap justifies austerity measures and austerity measures guarantee higher profit margins. By 2001, the countries of Latin America and the Caribbean owed $787 billion to the U.S. and international bankers and were paying more than $150 billion/year in debt service (see the U.S. Commerce Department's "Survey of Current Business," September 2002). With indebtedness comes the massive auctioning off of public assets as a precondition to satisfy the creditors.

With the expansion of neoliberalism and the internationalization of capital came the devaluation of the national currencies and increased indebtedness. For example, following the devaluation of its currency, Mexico in 1982 saw the number of "its" maquiladoras increase astronomically. A deliberate depopulation of rural areas for the purpose of aiding the expansion of maquiladoras also began. Privatization allowed more and more foreign ownership, and in less than a decade, Mexico was forced to privatize 886 state enterprises out of a total of 1,155 with U.S. monopolies gaining control over telecommunications, airlines, banking, mining, steel, and other sectors.

Privatization invites in foreign capital, often in alliance with local capital. Once the profit is realized, it is not reinvested it in the area where the profit was made. Both the North America Free Trade Agreement (NAFTA) and the Central America Free Trade Agreement (CAFTA) are benefiting a well-to-do segment of participating countries and are expanding corporate rights at the expense of the poorest peoples in the region. The costs of privatization are thus "socialized." There is increasing scarcity of basic food items (corn) and medicine primarily because of intellectual property rights and higher prices (Weisman 2004, 13).

The General Agreement on Tariffs and Trade (GATT) considers "dumping" or selling commodities below the cost of production illegal. Yet, in 2001, "the average export price for U.S. corn was 33 percent below the full costs of production and transportation. For rice, it was 22 percent" (Ricker 2004). The loss of jobs in Guatemala alone was about 80,000 in five years. Prices of basic food items increased dramatically for Mexico (Oxfam America cited in Ricker 2004). Mexico lost 1.7 million jobs in the agricultural sector due to the influx of U.S. corn, which also meant a drastic reduction in the incomes of 15 million small farmers (Ricker 2004, 11).

The Mexican government allowed the U.S. to dump millions of tons of corn into Mexico. This policy along with greater mechanization in rural areas, forced more of the rural population to seek life in the cities and of course migrate North. Following NAFTA, Mexico reduced funding for farm programs from $2 billion in 1994 to $500 million by 2000 (Chasnoff 2004). Real wages in Mexico are lower today than before NAFTA, and 31 percent of Mexicans currently live below the poverty line while the rich have become richer. NAFTA has also cost U.S. workers over one million jobs.

Privatization is thus also a serious threat to biological diversity in Central America, and it is beginning to devastate small farmers whose condition is already a dire one. The loss of income and the threat of poverty are forcing millions to migrate to urban areas or risk their lives trying to reach the North amid its increasingly hostile mood. Current realities in the North/South relationship point to arrangements in which a handful of powerful members decide the rules, even if not all of them always play by those rules. As with the other neoliberal agreements, CAFTA's nine rounds of negotiations, for example, were held in secret. CAFTA is forcing greater privatization of state-run health care, education, electrical generation, and water systems. And it is within this context that the now common practice of privatizing the gains and socializing the costs become the norm. The costs are hunger, poverty-induced violence, degradation, hopelessness, despair, and political and economic exclusion.

For almost two centuries now Latin America, except for a few countries and for a short period of time, has been at the mercy of Anglo-American capitalism and domestic comprador groups. The end result has been the deprivation of democracy, decent living conditions, and national pride. The situation is becoming so tenuous that even the comprador groups have begun wondering how long they will last.

Central and South American workers and farmers are at the mercy of this regime of economic exploitation while the leaders, activists, and organizers for the cause of human rights, environment, and labor are arrested, tortured, and assassinated. For the time being U.S. workers are in a relatively better position than those of Latin America. But the conditions in the South are increasingly tense and potentially explosive.

A supportive political umbrella is absolutely essential for the maintenance of neoliberalism as the parasitic system that it is. It is a mistake to consider the *systemic* economic and political structures (and contradictions) that are endemic within the regime of globalizing capital in terms of *particular individuals* occupying a particular office or representing a particular political party. The reality is that in all respects, particularly with regard to the power of the big business class and U.S.-based transnationals, there are no essential differences in the political agencies representing them. The history of U.S. militarism, imperialism, and accumulation shows no pivotal dependence on any one particular individual or political party rather than another. Instead it utilizes the systemic structural allegiance of its ruling elites in general, and its ultimate goal remains the maintenance of hegemonic control over the vulnerable world.

More authentically representative democracies by their very nature do not support such a system and, therefore, from the point of view of global capitalism, are not to be tolerated anywhere. Economic democracy is antithetical to a condition in which people are denied access to basic necessities and forced to relinquish precious public/national resources, such as water, to the private sector. The demand to abandon the conditions that degrade humanity is the demand to abolish the system which imposes such degradation.

The good news is that a new chapter in the history of resistance has begun. The consequences of neoliberalism for the general public worldwide are becoming increasingly unbearable, and any attempt at cooptation without credible changes in the material conditions is not effective.

Radicalization and armed resistance on a mass scale at this stage will be obviously be severely punished, and will not accomplish the goals it desires. So what strategy is the best? It is imperative that Latin America and indeed all of the nation-states seeking to free themselves from global capitalism begin by strengthening their national democratic institutions and establishing intraregional collaboration at the level of these institutions. Latin America is in a very good position to begin to develop such a model for regional integration and development.

"Homegrown" Alternatives to U.S. Hegemony. Elements in Latin America have been struggling to find their way out of the system, characterized by alienation, powerlessness, and apathy, that holds them captive to the reproduction of its unequal material reality. Food insecurity and hunger are closely associated with extreme poverty in Latin America. The continent's income disparities, already the world's largest, have widened and millions of people have become even poorer. Today more than a third of South Americans live in poverty and, in many countries, the richest 10 per cent control more than half of all income. As a direct consequence of these measures imposed on Latin people many armed insurgent groups have emerged.

One social, cultural, and political alternative that has emerged is the "Bolívarian Alliance for the Peoples of Our America" (ALBA), founded initially by Cuba and Venezuela in 2004. This effort seeks to integrate Latin American and Caribbean economies into one viable common market, while at the same time promoting solidarity, inclusion, and respect for the diverse cultural identities involved. Its goals also include promoting peace and international cooperation, the eradication of poverty and illiteracy, the exchange of scientific and technological knowledge, and the provision of access to medicine as a basic right. As an example, Bolívia's four main languages (Spanish, Aymara, Quechua and Guarani) are taught to across the nation as a component of literacy campaign—with the aid of Cuban teachers. After the signing ceremony for ALBA, Fidel Castro said that one day, all [Latin American] countries will be members. Not long after that, Paraguayans elected Fernando Lugo, a Roman Catholic priest (referred to as the "Red Bishop" by some and "Bishop of the Poor" by others) who served as their nation's president until 2012. Evo Morales, until recently Bolívia's democratic socialist president, said the ALBA meeting was an "historic gathering of three generations and three revolutions." Morales called for the return of Latin reserves from the North; Daniel Ortega echoed the sentiment that "speculative capital" ought not to be able to ruin people's lives for the sake of profit and in the name of free trade. Morales denounced U.S. aid policy as a hegemonic tool and divisive. The leaders noted that it was no coincidence that just at the time of the ALBA Summit, Condoleezza Rice was visiting neighboring Colombia to promote a U.S.-Colombia Free Trade pact.

ALBA has as its basis and philosophy the empowerment of the economically less developed societies, while at the same time according these dignity and respect for what they have to contribute (i.e., Bolívian and Cuban knowledge in certain areas that could be used by other members). Such cultural resources as "natural medicine" on the part of Bolívia and in the case of Cuba having the capabilities of modern medicine. One significant step was also the [seductive] cancellation of nearly half of Bolívia's national debt by the IMF and World Bank.

What is crucial for any embryonic alliance with a behemoth as an enemy is to strengthen itself through "social movements from throughout the hemisphere," said Joel Suarez of Cuba's Martin Luther King Center. "Governments may be pressured not to join, but the social movements are anxious to be part of an alliance that promotes fair trade over free trade." Indeed, the proposal is to include even social movements from the United States. ALBA abjures bald market-place competition as a means of economic activity, considers trade as a mechanism toward the realization of the greater good for society, not as an end in itself, and rejects the social Darwinism and the trickle-down theory promoted within the context of mainstream economics.

Within the international arena, market competition and economic incentives have functioned to engender what Ruy Mauro Marini (1972) has called a *subimperialism*. The subimperialist exploits others while at the same time it is subject to control from the center. Subimperialism plays a role in the hegemonic structure. Take the case of Brazil in the context of Mercosur (the "Common Market of the American South," with members: Argentina, Brazil, Paraguay, Uruguay and Venezuela and associated nations, Bolívia, Chile, Peru, Colombia, Ecuador and Suriname). Although Brazil has come a long way from the decades of military governments and a repressive economic system, "instead of representing a new form of social justice . . . the country's foreign policy initiatives are structured more by the regional orientation of Brazilian elites interested in reproducing their class position in a globalized capitalist economy" (Flynn 2007). As an alternative to subimperialism, could ALBA pull other agreements such as Mercosur in its own direction? Mercosur now constitutes 75% of South America's economic activity, holds 65% of the continent's population, and contains some of the largest reserves of water and hydrocarbons on the planet. The potential for Mercosur to be a catalyst for ALBA is very good. One of ALBA's founders, Hugo Chávez, saw a dialectic at work given the "....indisputable failure of the neoliberal policies imposed on our countries, the Latin American and Caribbean peoples find themselves on the road to their second and true independence, the birth of the Bolíviarian Alternative for the Americas...."[5]

---

[5] Hugo Chávez, comments at the founding of the ALBA initiative. See https://venezuelanalysis.com/analysis/1870

What frightens the Washington bloc is the formation and reproduction of a philosophy that puts people before profit. In the context of a homegrown, regional integration the preoccupation with high profit margins cease to exist. By the very definition, regional integration strategies would eliminate intraregional competition and expensive solicitation for foreign investment from the imperialist zones. Indeed, a social democratic politics and economics and is possible only when old regulations, favoring big business, are replaced with long-term regional planning in conjunction and association with long-term planning at the national level predicated on cooperation rather than competition. Within the context of a regional common market in which each member is an equal player, the elimination of tariffs and other barriers are appropriate. In this context—an arrangement by which all members decide on the rules—development and growth (as measured by indices of social inclusion) are possible.

Within a vibrant regional economic association, a political and military (defensive) integration might well have been possible. However, there has been a lack of substantive success. The task of establishing regional economic power in Latin America should have been easier than in other geographic areas. To begin with, there are very strong cultural ties (though diverse in ethnic and racial identities) among the countries of the region. Secondly, the impulse of building a common market is much stronger since they have collectively experienced outside intervention and are aware of their common vulnerability to this. The struggle to create a common market of truly independent members operating on the basis of a charter which puts human dignity, social development, economic democracy, and political accountability, has been, is, and will be, challenged by the powerful politico-military establishment that serves the transnationals.

Chávez's utter failure was due to the absence of a solid and diversified economic base, with an accompanying commonwealth sense of social justice, by which the people could have seen the real possibilities for mutual advancement. Venezuela's over-reliance on oil hindered innovation and hampered the technological drive that might have come from its universities and elsewhere in its culture. Trade with Cuba, Bolivia, and Nicaragua remained at the level of barter since a monetary union was lacking. The Brazilian *real* was sufficiently powerful as a currency that it had the potential to be transnational, and thus a challenge to dollar and euro. Nonetheless, economic cooperation among the BRICS nations—Brazil, Russia, India, China, and South Africa, not as a defensive strategy, but as an economic necessity, has not been able to challenge the bearers of capital and technology in the global North.

Implications since ALBA for U.S. Intervention in Latin America. I have amply indicated in my historical review earlier in this essay the nature of past interventionist policies of the U.S. in Latin America. In the U.S. a corporate elite determines (of course not without internal quarrels) generally what it wants and the political establishment strategizes and packages these desires as legitimate national interests (even national security interests). Historically, if and when necessary, the U.S. has enforced those policies directly with its military or indirectly through proxies.

Today there is more of a question about the capacity of conventional U.S. military power, particularly its ability to invade and occupy multiple countries, as in Afghanistan and Iraq. The outcomes of U.S. intervention in Afghanistan and Iraq will determine the viability of greater future reliance on the military, but the real question is to what extent it is a systemic imperative. The belief that there has been a decline in the power of the United States in terms of its militarism that once it exercised in Latin America and indeed around the world is primarily based on the social and economic costs, rather than the actual preponderance of power and the proclivity to use force. Although the U. S. military has been designed to fight two and half major wars and a few small ones simultaneously, dire conditions at the present on the ground in Iraq and Afghanistan—along with massive internal contradictions—make a high-intensity military confrontation in Latin America unlikely. There are several reasons for this contention. First, the cost of undertaking another major conflict would be astronomical. Secondly, no European ally—with the possible exceptions of Britain and Israel (which has a history of military involvement in Latin America) —would join in any credible way for a war against any Latin American government.

Therefore, the likelihood of an additional front would not at the present be an option. Yet under different circumstances, the United States would not be reluctant to use force. Even if the war-making capacity exists, the idea of justifying a new war to the American public at the present would be difficult. But in the arsenal of the empire there are many other weapons which could be employed to safeguard the interests of the corporate elite: e.g., fostering internal disintegration on the basis of ethnicity and irredentist tendencies; fomenting potential intraregional conflict (as has been witnessed in Venezuela, Colombia, Ecuador and Peru among others); then there are mercenary drug lords who might be promised a better harvest and granted access to markets (as seen in the counterrevolutionary activities in Nicaragua, Colombia, Peru, Bolívia). There is a very long history of divide and conquer, and as long as there is no regional integration, it will continue. This is the least expensive of all interventionist methods.

Direct military intervention anymore would render Latin America a very troubling "backyard." The United States military strategists of yesteryear know well the potential for a Latin American backlash against overt military involvement. Still, the national security argument remains one of the most potent invocations that the U.S. has used, and it can identify just about anything as a threat to its national security—including an island nation such as Granada, which was invaded just to "rescue American medical students." The current Plan Colombia is primarily a militarization plan for the Andes and for now directed against Venezuela and Bolívia, Colombia's FARC, and similar groups. After September 11, 2001, the war on drugs in Colombia soon became a war on terror fought on the Colombian soil. Also, Colombian oil is now more than ever a reason for the United States to broaden its presence and try to eliminate rivals. Colombia is the seventh largest oil supplier to the United States. Combined with oil imports from Venezuela and Ecuador, the U.S. imports more oil from South America than from the Persian Gulf (Soltani and Koenig 2004, 12).

Even though the United States is not as likely to intervene militarily in Latin America, its power to implement neo-liberal economic policies remains intact as part of a Washington Consensus and through international agencies such as the IMF and the World Bank. This option is perhaps the most likely option to be considered. Financial strangulation would definitely lead to political upheaval and the only way to avert this scenario is to have a Latin American common market, perhaps with its own currency.

Another possible option that the United States could entertain would be the exploitation of ethnic differences in the region. Bolívia began noticing heightened ethnic tension immediately after the election of Evo Morales. There are historical precedents for supporting irredentist and separatist movements in post-colonial history. In Latin America, Colombia is illustrative of the approach to non-conformist behavior. A portion of Colombia's territory was carved out and became what is now Panama in 1903.[6] The United States was the first country to recognize the new country, and sent troops to protect its economic interests. It occurred again in the 1980s. Other options include the use of mercenaries such as the Contras, in the recent Nicaraguan past, and William Walker, who (in the period prior to the existence of Panama and the Panama Canal) organized "Vanderbilt's gang" of gunmen to assassinate, burn, and bribe their way to control rail transportation routes through Nicaragua.

Latin America's Progress toward Social Democracy / Democratic Communism. Production in the real economy cannot take place with rhetoric. It must be backed by very real and tangible measures. It must enter the realm of the attainable possibilities that have been arrested in the past, but which help a nation move toward more ideal actualities. Still, the road toward emancipation is full of traps, detours, sharp curves, bumps and bandits that can derail it toward dystopia. Equipped with knowledge of reality, energized with the absence of dogma on all fronts and a clear understanding of possibilities, various groups in Latin America can map out new collective integration strategies.

The left must be see itself as a collection of groups opposing global capitalism and neoliberalism. A common

---

[6] In November 1903, Phillipe Bunau-Varilla, a French citizen who was not authorized to sign any treaties on behalf of Panama without the review of the Panamanians, unilaterally signed the Hay-Bunau-Varilla Treaty. This granted rights to the United States to build and administer indefinitely the Panama Canal, which opened in 1914.

ground and common goal must be forged in the struggle. In Latin America as elsewhere, religious groups and movements (such as liberation theology), environmental groups, trade unions, native people, as well as the radical intelligentsia, nationalists, and Marxists can succeed only when working in concert toward emancipation and development. It is necessary for the collected multiplicity of these groups to join forces, particularly the regional groups sharing the same aspirations. Also important is to demonstrate the high costs of missing this partnership opportunity should any one nation sell-out the others through an alliance with outsiders privileging selfish interests at the expense of regional integration and development.

Liberation theology began its effort at raising awareness (conscientization) many decades ago. In the process it has allied itself with academics, labor, and environmental organizations as well. It is critical that the tradition of grassroots mobilization is incorporated into a broader strategy of change through social mobilization at all political, cultural, and leadership levels. In the context of Latin America, faith and religion on one hand, and socialism and communism on the other, have not been as antithetical as they have been in other contexts. Liberation theologians have for the most part been at the forefront of the struggle, even though their ecclesiastical institutions were historically components of the oppressive structure. As one of the founders of Latin American democratic communism, José Carlos Mariátegui (Löwy and Breña 2008) sees much convergence between faith and communism. Likewise, José Miranda of Mexico has written the influential *Communism in the Bible* (1982).

The methods of liberation theology are predicated on 1) "conscientization," i.e. an awareness of an analysis of relationships of dependency and imperialism; 2) the creation of a new church embracing self-sustaining communities and grassroots movements composed of landless peasants, workers, and the poor struggling for social, cultural, economic and political rights by opposing privatization, accumulation, and exploitation (Keucker 2007) and 3) the power of the indigenous peoples to oppose giant oil companies and multinationals as documented by Soltani and Keonig (2004), such as the power of the Zapatistas one of the most effective indigenous groups in the struggle against privatization, globalization and neoliberalism (Stahler-Sholk 2007).

It is promising that the struggle against global exploitation is very widespread and in particular that it is the working class that is in the forefront of the struggle (Almeida 2007). Why should democratic communism, religious values, and national identity collide, if each is viewed as a partner in human emancipation? Just as hegemony is context-dependent, modes of resistance must also be context-dependent. Within each context the manifestations of hegemony may require a combination of differing modes of resistance (i.e., radical democracy, socialism, passive resistance, religious values, and in cases where resistance to hegemony has been confronted with structural violence, armed struggle has also become a tactic of choice).

The "standard" and "appropriate" conduct for non-Anglo peoples and governments set by the West includes such expectations as acting "with reasonable efficiency and decency," keeping "order," and meeting debt obligations. The alleged responsibility on the part of the West led by the U.S. to "prevent chaos and anarchy," to "democratize," to "civilize," to bring "freedom," to lesser economies and peoples "prosper" by inculcating them with U.S.-American "values;" to assist them to "fight terrorism," to get rid of "dictators," and to "administer government among savages," particularly in "failed states," supposing that the U.S. has the moral authority and a providential duty to intervene, continues to justify imperial interventions. The United States ought not to be expected to abandon its long history of imperialistic intervention in Latin America. But Latin America can close that chapter of its history through greater regional integration, "radical" socio-economic and political democratization and a form of humanist socialism suitable for its own reality.

While Latin America moves toward radical democracy, it is imperative to move as far away as possible from images of the state recommended by neoliberal elites, where the few make the decisions for the many Imagining a world in which millions make collective decisions for collective goods is becoming easier. As more and more people in various regions of the world consider an alternative to the existing economic and political reality, those in control of the established systems will do their utmost to destroy the movements which challenge them. Yet the historical trajectory is pregnant with significant change, both within and without Latin America as well as in other areas struggling to overcome internal and external oppression and hegemony.

Indications are that the 21st century will be— at least for the first half—as anxiety ridden as the old century was. There is a very solid history of revolt in Latin America as indeed there are in every part of the planet subject to plunder. Arriving at a future material condition characterized by an independent Latin America seems highly probabable. Today masses of people in the core capitalist countries are as much a victim of "the political economy of predation and counterrevolution" (Reitz and Spartan, this volume) as are the masses of people in the global South. To defend the rights of the masses in the core is tantamount to defending the rights of masses in the developing world. This begins with opposition to imperialism and militarism. Real and long-term American progress requires progressive policies and responsible politics. And as long as people in the global North do not ask hard questions and take part in the process of self-governance, they will continue to erode the basis of their own "democracy." Within the existing structure of elections and politics in the U.S., individuals, even those occupying the highest offices, despite even progressive-sounding slogans, will *do* very little to resolve the structural contradictions.

A "democracy" in mainstream Western social science, particularly political science, is a democracy only if corresponds to a vision of a society based on the economics of global "free trade" and "free enterprise." In spite of this, authentic democratic struggle in Latin America is being rejuvenated. Within this context, progressive parties and their officials deserve immense credit.

Bibliography

Almeida, Paul D. 2007. "Defensive Mobilization: Popular Movements against Economic Adjustment Policies in Latin America," *Latin American Perspectives*, Vol. 34, No. 3.

Armony, Ariel C. 1977. *Argentina, the United States, and the Anti-Communist Crusade in Central America, 1977-1984*. Athens, Ohio: University Press, 1977.

Benjamin, Jules R. 1987. "The Framework of U.S. Relations with Latin America in the Twentieth Century: An Interpretive Essay," *Diplomatic History* 11 (Spring).

Chasnoff, Brian. 2004. "NAFTA's Social, Economic Consequences Brought Extremes," *The Daily Texan* online (2/12/04).

Edwards, Sabastián. 1995. *Crisis and Reform in Latin America: From Despair to Hope*. New York: Oxford University Press.

Flynn, Matthew. 2007. "Between Subimperialism and Globalization," *Latin American Perspectives*, Vol 34. No. 6.

Fredrico, G. Gil. 1971. *Latin America-United States Relations*. New York: Harcourt Brace.

Kuecker, Glen David. 2007. "Fighting for the Forests: Grassroots Resistance to Mining in Northern Ecuador," *Latin American Perspectives*, Vol. 34, No. 2.

Kuttner, Robert. 2007. "How Wall Street's Political Triumph Led to Economic Crisis—An Interview," Multinational Moniter, November/December.

Laclau, Ernesto, and Chantal Mouffe. 1985. *Hegemony and Socialist Strategy: Toward a Radical Democratic Politics*. London: Verso.

Löwy, Michael and Mariana Ortega Breña. 2008. "Communism and Religion: José Carlos Mariátegui's Revolutionary Mysticism," Latin American Perspectives, Vol. 35, No. 2: *Reassessing the History of Latin American Communism*.

Marini, Ruy Mauro. 1972. "Brazilian Subimperialism," *Monthly Review*, Vol, 23, No. 9. February.

Martins, Carlos Eduardo. 2007. "The Impasses of U.S. Hegemony: Perspectives for the Twenty-First Century," *Latin American Perspectives*, Vol 34, No. 1.

Miranda, José. 1982, *Communism in the Bible* Eugene, OR: Wipf and Stock Publishers

Pearce, Jenny. 1982. *Under The Eagle: U.S. Intervention in Central America and the Caribbean*. Boston: South End Press.

Polanyi, Karl. 1971. *The Great Transformation: The Political and Economic Origins of Our Time*. Boston: Beacon Press.

Ricker, Tom. 2004. "Competition or Massacre? Central American Farmers: Dismal Prospects Under CAFTA," *Multinational Monitor*, Vol. 25. No. 4.

Rochlin, James. 2007. "Latin America's Left Turn and the New Strategic Landscape: the Case of Bolívia," *Third World Quarterly*, Volume 28, Number 7.

Salazar, Luis Suárez. 2007. "The New Pan-American Order: The Crisis and Reconstitution of the U.S. System of Global Domination," *Latin American Perspectives*, Vol. 34, No. 1.

Shariati, Mehdi S. 2007. "Bank of the South: A New Potential Challenge to the Hegemonic Global Finance" Payvand.com

Smith, Robert F. (ed.). 1981. *The United States and the Latin American Sphere of Influence—The Era of Caribbean Intervention, 1890-1930.* Malabar, FL: Krieger Books.

Soltani, Atosa and Kevin Koenig. 2004. "U'wa Overcome Oxy: How a Small Ecuadoran Indigenous Group and a Global Solidarity Movement Defeated an Oil Giant, and the Struggles Ahead," *Multinational Monitor.* January/February.

Spronk, Susan and Jeffery R. Webber, "Struggles against Accumulation by Dispossession in Bolívia: The Political Economy of Natural Resource Contention," *Latin American Perspectives,* Vol. 34, No. 2.

Stahler-Sholk, Richard. 2007. "Resisting Neoliberal Homogenization: The Zapatista Autonomy Movement" *Latin American Perspectives* Vol 34, No. 2.

Weisman, Robert. 2004. "Dying for Drugs: How CAFTA Will Undermine Access to Essential Medicines" *Multinational Monitor.* Vol. 25, No. 4, April.

Mehdi S. Shariati
Chapter Eleven

Comprehensive Sustainable Development As a Counter-Hegemonic Strategy

The questions regarding variations in social development, economic progress, and political empowerment have produced a voluminous literature over the past century, and because of the complexity of these issues, much important reflection will continue well into the future. In the early 1980s, a United Nations' Commission coined the term "sustainable development" as a public statement regarding the deteriorating socio-economic, political, and environmental conditions. Since then, the use and abuse of the term has rendered it dubious and almost irrelevant.

This essay proposes comprehensive sustainable development (CSD) as a substitute in the hope that re-conceptualization of the term would incorporate critiques of various manifestations of capital's hegemony—its control over science and technology, particularly in the contemporary period, by way of restricting homegrown, national technological development. It is argued that in the pursuit of its interests contemporary global capitalism, as a continuation of the 19th and the 20th century colonialism/imperialism, is resorting to the policy of imperialism through the implementation of dependent industrialization (imported technology) rather than CSD.

The indices used to measure comprehensive sustainable development are diametrically different than those used to measure *dependent capitalist development*. At the core of the indices of CSD are the contribution to human development, social progress, and radical democracy. It involves the negation of atomistic indices such as rugged individualism, competition, and alienation of people dependently embedded in capitalist development. CSD is a rejection of neoliberal economic policy and its foundation: Social Darwinism. It is in favor of collective well-being as measured by indices such as national liberation, human emancipation and progress, social inclusion, and political empowerment. CSD requires an able and willing national political front and a strong public sector. It requires boldness in initiation and innovation in the development process with an awareness that there will be repercussions and consequences from hegemonic global forces.

The foundations of CSD are social justice, human emancipation, and dignity. Very few developing countries have initiated a development process which contains elements of the CSD outlook. The case of Iranian development, and its nuclear program in particular, demonstrate a clear national desire for CSD. Likewise, it has evoked a manifestation of the behavior of the hegemonic powers with regard to the control of science and technology. As a rapidly developing country Iran has concentrated its efforts on the development and expansion of basic industry while acknowledging with every development initiative the indispensability of social development, social justice, health, and a rising standard of living. To what extent Iran can deliver on the social justice front remains to be seen, but the realization that it cannot comprehensively sustain its development without regard for social justice and respect for the rights of its citizens is a promising departure. And precisely, it is with the delivery of some measure in the areas of justice and social inclusion that

Iran can be an effective player in the process of comprehensive sustainable development.

Hegemony and Under-Development. The history of the global political economy in various epochs (beginning with the rise of European colonial empires) is a history of hegemonic policies and inter-imperial rivalries on the one hand and the struggle to resist hegemony on the other. From the 19th century European colonial penetration of Africa, Asia, and Latin America in the context of a multi-polar system and its demise by the first inter-imperialist war of the 20th century (WWI), to the rise of the bi-polar system of East/West competition, to the present uni-polar world system led by Anglo-American corporate empire, the common thread has been the hegemonic tendencies and an international system based on the hegemonic rule by the economic elites.

In the 19th century, colonial powers divided the world amongst themselves. Between 1870 and 1898, Britain added 4 million square miles and 88 million people to its empire. France gained nearly the same territorial area with a population of 40 million. Germany won one million square miles and 16 million people. Belgium took close to one million miles and 30 million people. Portugal joined the race with 800,000 miles of new land and 9 million inhabitants (Heilbroner 1966). In the first 75 years of the 19th century, colonial empires added to their territories an average of 83,000 square miles every year, primarily for the purpose of economic exploitation. Between the 1870s and WWI this area of colonial control increased to about 240,000 square miles (about 85 percent of the earth's surface) by 1914 (Magdoff 1978). By 1900 Britain had fifty colonies and was in control of 450 million people while its own population was no more than 10 percent of that (45 million). France had thirty-three colonies with a population of 56 million, Germany was in control of thirteen colonies with a population of 15 million people. These extraterritorial gains were to support the development of the colonial metropolis - for the most part at the expense of the colonies. As providers of raw material and agricultural crops, the colonies were the center of an ongoing primitive accumulation.

Then as now, accumulation proceeded as an end in itself. The colonialists introduced an ecologically destructive agriculture as a means to that end and as a substitute for traditional agriculture. The German chemist and agronomist Justus von Liebig (1859) documented the case of the British destruction of the Irish ecology through surplus extraction by way of intensive agriculture. Liebig referred to this system of taking more from the land than was ever put back into it, as the "robbery system." For a century-and-a-half the English agricultural system "indirectly exported the soil of Ireland, without even allowing its cultivators the means for replacing the constituents of the exhausted soil" (Marx 1976, 638). By relying on the work of Liebig, Marx (1976, 283-290; 637-638; 1981, 949-950; 1964, 112) borrowed the concept of metabolism and subsequently utilized it to illustrate systemic dysfunction within capitalism. "Metabolic interaction" between human beings and nature conveys the realization that we live in a natural system that must be governed by the laws of that natural system itself, which involve also "systemic restoration." He went on to suggest that the process of capital accumulation has created an "irreparable rift in the interdependent process of social metabolism." This rift in social metabolism is the excessive accumulation of private wealth at the expense of the earth and the human public's well-being, a distortion which causes imbalances in social development. Sustainability requires a symbiotic relationship between humanity and the natural environment.

Concerns with the environment in the 19th century on the part of scientists in Europe and North America warned of ecological destruction and in particular soil erosion.[1] Today the same rush to increase surplus extraction through intensive agriculture is supported through the privatization of the global commons. At the present, the U.S /Mexico border where the *maquiladora* form of the factory system is destroying the environment, deforestation of the tropics, the worldwide process of corporatization of family farm, self-sufficient agriculture by the giants in agribusiness such as ADM, Cargill, Monsanto (among others) whereby uneven and unsustainable development is reproduced are illustrative modern surplus extraction.

The recent history of uneven and unsustainable development is the same time a history of colonialism and imperialism (formal and informal). It is the history of an international system in which public resources were tapped, extracted, and exploited without consent from those whose resources were being taken. National Geographic societies which were formed in the metropolitan centers of the colonial empires in the 19th century for the most part were to identify resources for their colonial metropole. Justifications and rationalizations for colonial expansion included the "civilizing" of the "savages," "saving" them by "Christianizing" them, continue to this day. But today this occurs in the form of a pre-fabricated, packaged, and

---

[1] Alfred Crosby's "Ecological Imperialism" (1986) documents the colonial destruction of indigenous people by the expansion of Europe (900-1900). The link between capital accumulation, imperialism, and environmental degradation, with significant references to the work of Marx, is delineated by John Bellamy Foster and Brett Clark, "Ecological Imperialism: The Curse of Capitalism" (2003).

superficial notion of democracy, which invariably means dependent and reproducible capitalist economies within a denationalized/crony state.

During the height of colonial expansion, the regard for the people and their environment was as dismal as it is in the era of neocolonialism. Colonialism from its inception was a violent encounter, and from its inception involved a clash of cultures, worldviews, existential questions, and philosophies of life. The European encounter thus degraded the culture as well as the environment. In the U.S. context, native Americans were described as uncivilized because they held land in common and generally lived in harmony with nature, while the conquest of the earth and its private acquisition meant being civilized (Rogin 1991, 114). In India, degradation began with the introduction of commercial cotton cultivation on a large scale in the 1850s and 1860s, linked to British colonial networks of production. Increasing global markets motivated increases in cotton cultivation which in turn increased the demand for agricultural land including wetlands. This increased the demand for grazing lands and led to deforestation, causing a decrease in rainfall and availability of water. The ultimate goal was to minimize costs of production and maximize profits even if it resulted in such social catastrophes as the devastating famine of 1899-1900 and more ecological devastation (Satya 2004).

Similarly, African famines for the most part continue to be social rather than natural disasters. Brutal colonial histories, post-colonial indebtedness, underdeveloped infrastructures, relying heavily on cash crops for debt-service payments, resulted in widespread hunger and desertification. The European colonization of Africa, and indeed in most of the colonized regions in the 19th century, drastically altered the traditional farming and herding practices which were very adaptable to changing environmental conditions. The agricultural policies of the colonial states centered on the shift to cash crop cultivation, deforestation for the grazing of export cattle, and destructive logging practices and forest product extraction (Jarosz 1999).

Colonial state policies were of course heralded as "modernization" and 'progress," and this concept of "civilization" continued to wreak havoc on the colonized. Embedded in defense of these policies was a paternalistic and condescending view of the colonized - as uncivilized, childlike and incapable of fending for themselves. Western social scientists and natural scientists constructed political and biological theories covertly predicated on the supremacy of the white race in general and the Anglo-Saxon race in particular. Racism, social Darwinism, militarism, and imperialism were the leading ideologies of the day at the service of the empires. The ownership claims over colonial territories, reached the point where the territories of defeated nations had to be legally transferred to the victor nations without any say by the inhabitants of the colonies.

The control of the colonies for the sole purpose of economic exploitation and the desire for greater access to the riches of the colonies produced hostile inter-imperialist postures leading to WWI - the first inter-imperialist war of the 20th century. The First World War ended with the defeat of smaller empires (i.e., Ottoman and Austro-Hungarian) leading to greater consolidation of power in the hands of the imperialist powers. After a short period of deceptive calm, once again the advanced capitalist countries turned their imperialist rivalries into another bloody conflict, WWII. The economic arrangements in the post-WWII era were designed to aid the developed capitalist countries striving to secure resources and markets in the context of the Cold War. In addition to the role of the provider of resources, the colonial and ex-colonial regions were drawn into the global conflict between the West and the East as tools of realignment. Economic development as a by-product of the new global order proceeded unevenly and its scope was determined by the Cold War necessities.

The regions closer to Soviet influence received substantial help from the West. Some were provided with an influx of foreign investment and technology (the East-Asian economies of Korea, Taiwan, Hong Kong and Singapore) as showcases of capitalist success. This type of development which I call defensive capitalist development would not have been possible outside of the zone where competition for proxies between the west and the East did not exist. Others continued to have access to outmoded technology and remained primarily as the provider of raw materials in the global division of labor. It is in this context that containment of communism along with the crushing of revolutionary movements took center stage in the foreign policy of the West.

Dependency and cronyism remained a structural cause of backwardness well into the 1960s. From the 1960s onward various countries in some regions benefited from the expansion of multinationals. But technology was to be controlled, and to this date major research and technological development remains in control of a handful of countries, notably in the West. The research in big science (military and all advanced non-military research) is a monopoly of the biggest powers and this remains an indisputable reality.

Countries, imperial or otherwise, have the right to control what they have developed. The issue, however, is the prevention of others from developing new technologies for use in the form of the comprehensive sustainable development. The CSD process would not be detrimental to a healthy global economy, international relations, and ecological conditions. Yet, international systems structured on hegemonic principles, whether uni-polar, bi-polar, or multi-polar, will work to the detriment of the people and their environment.

Hegemony is a multifaceted set of relations in which the prevailing political force perpetuates its domination by various means. The most notable of these are indebtedness, manifest and latent control of technology, and the brain drain. Gramsci (1996) noted that hegemony of a class is assured when that class succeeds in persuading the other classes to accept its authority—accept its "moral, political, and cultural values." In this regard, the "historical block" as a hegemonic block has a long history of fabricating national consensus for imperialist policies. This hegemony is manifested and implemented in various other ways; none is perhaps more effective than the control of technology. Hegemony is reproduced when science serves the aim of dependent social development. Perhaps the bombing of Hiroshima and Nagasaki was not merely for the immediate military purposes, but also for retarding subsequent industrial redevelopment of Japan as a potential challenger in the post war global economy.

Hegemonic policies are not limited to the assassination of potentially counter-hegemonic groups and leaders. Invasions, bombings or the threats of bombing, internal disintegration, and proxy wars are other means to stop progress. The crushing of the national liberation movements through *coupes de tat*, the subversion of democratic governments, invasions, and proxy wars have prevented sizable numbers of non-Europeans from taking control of their own socio-economic and political lives. A few examples are so infamous they hardly need to be mentioned: Che, Mossadegh, Allende, Arbenz, Lumumba, Algeria, Palestine, Vietnam, Venezuela, Cuba, Biko, Mandela, and many others. Eventually, the costs of colonial control, the rising level of consciousness of the colonized, and their struggle to end colonial rule put an end to colonialism in many places. But the anti-hegemonic struggle (both formal and informal) is today yet again entering a newer phase.

Hegemonic behavior and policies are not based on the rights of humanity, but the rights of a few whose behavior renders them anything but human. Since the rise of colonial empires and their expansion throughout the 19th and early 20th centuries, the ensuing bloody wars were fought for control of resources. Alan Greenspan (2007) explicitly writes that the "... Iraq War was all about oil ..." — hence an extension of historical Western involvement for the control of Persian Gulf oil, the overthrow of Muhammad Mossadegh, and the aborted efforts by Britain and France to take over the Suez canal.

The West's control of technology, especially maritime and military technology, enhanced its control of the resources of the world. Seyyed Jamal and others in the 19th century called for a unified Islamic front equipped with technology and science which Jamal believed were the instruments of the West's hegemonic success. He pointed out, however, the corrupt leaders in the subjugated countries are also responsible for the reproduction of hegemony. Today, this hegemony is threatened due to cracks in the fortified regions of technology control. The possibility of a comprehensive sustainable development process requires an understanding of its vulnerabilities and, given its foundation in social justice, its appeal.

CSD and Its Nemesis. As indicated above, the term "sustainable development" was originally used by the Brundtland Commission, formally the World Commission on Environment and Development (WCED). The Commission Chaired by G. H. Brundtland, was convened by the United Nations in 1983. With the rise of neoliberalism in the 1980s, organs such as the United Nations and some of its institutions such as the IMF, the World Bank, and others (the IFC, A.I.D.) invented several similar commissions to gloss over the chronic contradictions within the hegemonic neoliberal world order.

The Brundtland Commission was to address the deteriorating conditions of human life and environmental degradation. With all of its good intentions, the Brundtland Commission failed to address the key structural causes of un-sustainability in part because of its connection to the centers of power and at the service of global capitalism, and partly due to its inadequate political and ideological resources. Some of these conceptual inadequacies included privileging the production for exchange value, assigning exchange value to the environment and to labor, and the consumer's commodity dependency. Kathleen McAfee (2008), asks rhetorically: "[D]oes the commodification of ecosystem functions tend to redistribute resources upward (toward classes and enterprises with greater purchasing power) and away (toward distant sites of capital accumulation and regional growth poles) as markets of other sorts have often done?" Comprehensive sustainable development is qualitatively different: predicated instead on social justice and equity, production for human need, and respect for labor and the environment, above and beyond market values.

Countries such as China and India, with substantial commodity production growth, suffer from negative environmental conditions which threaten all of their gains. They are criticized for contributing greatly to global warming and are being pushed to curb their pollution. Countries that are struggling with industrial development under conditions of dependent sustainability find that access to cleaner sources of energy and the corresponding technology are impossible. In Iran there are annually 30,000 deaths due to pollution-related illnesses. CSD must demand access to those types of technology that can encourage forms of human activity that can provide the greater good for the greatest number—without brutally exploiting the ecosystem.

Comprehensive sustainable development may be thought of as a reasoned response to the crises caused by the uneven distribution of resources, uneven access to energy, and the consequences of using traditional commodified economic strategies with regard to the planet and people. It is also a long term approach to the earth and its inhabitants. Comprehensive sustainable development is an intergenerational issue—socialized conduct for that sustainable abundance that does not jeopardize future possibilities or deny future generations these resources. The literature often refers to the sustainable development in terms of socio-economic, political and environmental issues. Lately the cultural factor has been added and if it is to have an effective and far reaching impact, it must include anti-hegemonic concerns as well. The reproduction of underdevelopment is ensured through lack of access to technology, the brain drain, inadequate research of ideas and their development, indebtedness, and the primacy of an expanding and unbridled private sector with considerable global support from supranational organizations such as the IMF and the World Bank. The reproduction of underdevelopment also involves corrupt local, regional, and national political and economic elites in alliance with international capital.

Fossil Fuel Dependency and Under-Development. Dependency on fossil fuel is neither a matter of brute necessity or its unquestioned desirability. The underlying causes of this dependency are to be found in the power of the global petroleum industry: its control of technology for alternative sources, high profit margins, subservient political orders, and the policy of petrodollar recycling which makes the petroleum industry the only industry which benefits immensely from what it imports. This dependency has created an untenable situation for the global economy and the environment in general, and for the global south in particular. The debate within the corporate media suggests that the verdict on global warming, environmental degradation, and pollution is not a forgone conclusion. With the aid of well-paid scientists, chemists, politicians, pundits, the powerful petroleum lobby has been trying to raise doubt regarding the consequences of fossil fuel use. And when confronted with indisputable evidence, it shifts the blame to the countries of the global South (with China and India topping the list) which are said to be causing the damage. It has also attempted the cooptation of environmental concerns in the form of new profit-seeking subsidiaries and investments dealing with environmental "cleanup" and "waste management."

The increase in petroleum prices is exacerbating the already dire financial situation. Hard currencies are needed to pay debt service, and additional hard currency is required to purchase oil. This increases indebtedness further. Indebtedness has a long history in the global south. Once colonialism ended, the newly independent countries were forced by their circumstances to borrow substantial amounts at very high rates of interest. This placed them at the mercy of finance capital and the watchdog institutions such as the World Bank and International Monetary Fund (IMF) and their brutal austerity measures. The entire spectrum of economic decision-making came to be predicated on the situation of indebtedness. Most of these debtor nations relied on their cash crops (primarily agricultural products), and given the increasing demand for these crops on the international market, this has led to the abandonment of crop rotation (an ancient and effective practice of preserving and replenishing the soil by varying crop production). This cash-crop-for-debt-service situation exacerbated the already chronic food shortages, and destroyed the soil; hence desertification and intensified global climate change. The debt-trap created by colonials/imperialists, in collaboration with the comprador local groups, continues to adversely affect the global environment and in particular the global south.

In previous decades when the price of oil increased, difficult choices were created for the countries of the South. For example, Tanzania's oil imports rose from $190 million in 2002 to about $480 million in 2006. Nicaragua spent $717 million in 2006. The increases in the price of oil have been adding to already critical situations. Oil has become so expensive that rural populations have been forced to cut trees and brush as sources of energy, inadvertently aiding the process of desertification. In this context, the destruction of the environment, global warming, and the greenhouse effect caused by the industrial North has made matters worse. For example, the poor of Bangladesh in deforesting the hillsides have removed natural barriers to the destruction caused by monsoons. Mudslides now kill thousands of poor people every year in rural areas. Already, 97 percent of natural disaster deaths occur in developing countries (Watkins 2007, 17). By the year 2020, between 75 million and 250 million people are projected to be exposed to increased water stress due to climate change. In some countries, yields from rain-fed agriculture will be reduced by up to 50 percent (Watkins 2007, 18).

In the advanced industrialized countries, notably in North America and Western Europe, the petroleum industry commands considerable economic power—and this is the basis of its political power. In the United States, the fossil fuel industry (particularly the oil and gas industries) spent more on the 2004 election than ever before—$16.7 million in congressional campaign contributions, 80 percent of which went to Republicans. And in 2006 they poured $20 million into that year's congressional elections (Kretzmann 2007, 20). Of course the return has been tremendous. U.S. oil companies reported an average record profit of $40 billion for large companies in these same years while the economy was suffering from recession. This was a repeat of the capital accumulation through commodity inflation of the 1970s when a Kissinger-orchestrated oil embargo led to high oil prices and record profits. In spite of these windfall profits, the fossil fuel industry enjoys immense subsidies. At least $61.3 billion in international money has gone to subsidizing the oil and gas industries worldwide since 2000. This amount is in addition to the $150 to $250 billion in domestic subsidies that national governments provide to their oil and gas industries (UNEP: Energy Subsidy Reform and Sustainable Development, 2008).

Subsidies on oil, gas or coal are meant to help the poor by lowering the price of energy, but the United Nations' report on environment (2001) suggests that they often mainly benefitted wealthier people. The study estimated that energy subsidies, almost all for fossil fuels, totaled about $300 billion a year or 0.7 percent of the world gross domestic product. Since 2000, the United States is the top provider of aid to the oil industry worldwide, with some $15.6 billion in oil aid distributed by the U.S. Export-Import Bank, the Overseas Private Investment Corporation, the U.S. Trade and Development Agency, the U.S. Agency for International Development and the U.S. Maritime Administration. European institutions spent a total of $16.5 billion, slightly more than the U.S. in the oil and gas industries. U.S. subsidies for oil are global in scope—from Azerbaijan to the Andes, Nigeria, and Colombia. The world spends about 0.7 percent of GDP on fossil fuel subsidies.

The cost of curtailing carbon emissions to meet scientific goals by 2050 has been estimated at 1 percent of GDP. The cost of *not* curtailing carbon emissions, measured in weather calamities, mass migrations, and the like, could be 5-10 percent of GDP. The world is spending $300 billion every year to subsidize fossil fuels that pollute the air, wreck the climate ... and ruin the world's economy. If the world stopped spending $300 billion on coal, oil and natural gas, and started spending it instead on wind, sun and water as alternative sources of energy, things could improve. Russian fossil fuel subsidies at $40 billion annually are the largest on the planet, according to the U.N. report. Others that top the list include Iran, China, Saudi Arabia, India, Indonesia, the Ukraine and Egypt. Still, the U.N. report is clear: the cost of transforming an economy to run on renewable fuels always seems daunting, so ingrained are our dependencies on fossil fuels. But if you consider how much is spent to make those fossil fuels affordable in the first place, the price tag doesn't look so daunting.

The highly developed seats of empire have one fourth of the world's population, but consume three fourths of the world's energy. Annual per capita consumption of energy exceeds 300 million BTU in North America, 100 million BTU in Western Europe as compared to 25 million in most LDCs (World Energy Resources, 2007). In 1973, 74 percent of U.S. oil was sourced domestically; this was reduced to 40 percent in 2003 and it continues to shrink. Demand for oil will grow to 116 million barrels a day by 2030 and an increase of 37 percent on 2006 usage (Alternative Energy, Wind Power.com. July 17, 2008). The gap between global production and supply of oil in the late 1960s was between 3 to 5 million barrels difference and now is close to twenty million barrels per day. This in part is explained by the increase in alternative sources of energy (Energy Information Administration, U.S. Dept. of Energy, *International Petroleum Monthly*, April 2008, cited in John Bellamy Foster, 2008). The Persian Gulf and North Africa remain the principal locations of oil reserves, with 61 percent of the world's total, followed by Africa with 11 percent, South

America and Europe (including the whole of the Russian Federation) with 8 percent each and North America at just under 5 percent (2007 Survey of Energy Resources: Executive Summary, World Energy Council 2007, 6).

Major cities in the developing world are challenged by suffocating smog, noise, and overpopulation. One major reason for this, of course, is the use of and the reliance on fossil fuel that has undermined the health of millions around the globe. From the first Industrial Revolution that relied on the steam engine, to what might be called the second Industrial Revolution's dependence on fossil fuel, massive social problems have ensued, at the same time as commodity production has been enhanced many times over. While the climatic changes associated with the use of fossil fuel and the pollution of the air, water, and food are ultimately a global problem, some areas have it worse than others.

There is no good reason to rejoice if the air in Chicago, Paris, London, and Tokyo appears less polluted than the air in Cairo, Tehran, Beijing, Mexico City, Bombay, or Jakarta. For the fragile ecosystem, it does not matter where the pollution originates; what matters is that it is occurring within an interconnected system which does not recognize national, regional and ecological boundaries. Even if we assume an infinite supply of fossil fuels, the consequences of continuing to use fossil fuel to the extent that it is currently being used are unimaginable. For those countries endowed with sufficient supply, the problem of access to these sources is not an issue, but for those countries which are dependent upon these resources, the problem is much more serious. As in the case of commodity inflation (gas prices) in the industrial world, the additional burden of low income can inflict serious damage on these people. It is estimated that worldwide there are 20,000 deaths due to air pollution. In a frenzy of profit seeking, foreign-investment-attraction strategies are causing hardship to the environment of the global south. Environmental problems, such as water, air, and land pollution "contribute to 40 percent deaths worldwide each year . . ." and according to Cornell University ecologist David Pimentel' estimation, "62 million deaths per year can be attributed to organic and toxic pollutants" (cited in Thompson, 2007).

Rapidly growing countries in the global South such as China and to a lesser extent India are blamed for contributing to the global pollution. Elizabeth Economy for instance cites an IEA prediction that by 2009 China will surpass the United States as the World's biggest contributor of greenhouse gasses (Economy 2004, 2006). A Chinese official, Pan Yue, accused the developed economies of "environmental colonialism" by transferring pollution-generating industries to China (Globalization and the Environment blogspost.com 2006). In contrast to the foregoing analysis here is an example of how responsibility is portrayed in the current environmental crises from the *New York Times* (6/11/2006). Titled "Pollution from Chinese Coast casts a Global Shadow" this is a typical reflection of the attitude that China, India, and other rapidly growing economies cannot handle industrial growth.

There is no question that dependence on fossil fuel has created an untenable situation for the global south in all respects including but not limited to their inability to purchase the increasingly expensive fossil fuels. There is however, a larger issue with regard of use of fossil fuel. With the price of oil exceeding $100 a barrel, there is disproportionate and negative impact on the poor and developing economies. Impoverished nations pay a much higher price both financially, and socially/ecologically brought on by the world's dependence on fossil fuel (Watkins 2007, 15). Abdoulaye Wade, President of Senegal in an October 2006 column in the Washington Post, warned that Sub-Saharan Africa is faced with "unfolding catastrophe that could set back efforts to reduce poverty and promote economic development for years" (cited in Watkins 2007, 15).

Large-scale ethanol production led by agribusinesses such as ADM (a $44 billion a year company) is one of the world's largest buyers, sellers, and processors of grain and corn for conversion into ethanol. In 1995, 43 percent of the company's profit was from products heavily subsidized by the United States federal government, and every dollar of profit from the production of ethanol costs taxpayers $30.60 (Magdoff, 2008:14). Each gallon of biodiesel blended into regular diesel for export from the United States cost one dollar of subsidy. This has led to the following ridiculous "splash and dash" situation: "Splash and dash is where biodiesel is carried to the U.S. by ship sometimes from Europe - purely to add a drop of ordinary diesel and take advantage of public money being handed out on any refining in America" (*Guardian*, April 9, 2008, cited in Magdoff 2008, 14).

Biofuel has caused massive increases in the price of food for millions of ordinary people around the world already suffering from food shortages. Biofuel production relies heavily on fossil fuel. The environmental crisis is not limited to the shortage of food, it also includes air pollution and a serious crisis with respect to water. Asia has 66 percent of the World's population, but it has only 33 percent of the fresh water. Europe has 8 percent of the world population, but has 13 percent of fresh water. Mexico City's water usage causes a sinking of its buildings due to the loss of its underground aquifer. Sydney, Australia, is one of the world's driest cities. Australia is faced with the greatest droughts.

Palestinians under occupation are faced with a chronic shortage of water, for the water from the occupied territories is piped out by Israel. Yet Israel is major builder of desalination plants. Israel also continues to occupy Golan

Heights (a Syrian territory) ostensibly for defensive and strategic purposes, but the water resources of the area are a much more compelling reason. Currently, most of the Middle East is suffering from a drought that could render some hydroelectric dams (particularly in Iran) useless. World-wide over 300 million people get fresh water from desalination plants in 150 countries; this is a global problem.

For the regions with water, the problem is also water pollution. Water pollution is one of the most dramatic impacts of fossil fuel consumption. This is perhaps more serious than the air pollution. The reason is that water is a scarce resource, and its pollution is magnified by this scarcity factor. Advanced capitalist economies, notably North America and Europe, have been promoting carbon trading as an "incentive" to curb pollution. The allotted space to pollute is based on a variety of factors, such as the size of the company. If a company does not pollute to the extent to which it is allowed, it can sell the unused portion of the pollution quota to another company in need of a greater pollution space. Carbon trading reached $30 billion in 2006 and it is growing, but to what extent it has made a difference is unclear (States of the World 2008: Innovations for a Sustainable Economy. World Watch Institute).

Alternative Sources of Energy. Current dramatic increases in the price of fossil fuel are making the addition and the expansion of search for alternative sources more urgent. In particular, nuclear power has become an attractive alternative for many countries. Countries with no available nuclear generating capacity or with declining nuclear capability have revived an interest in nuclear development (2007 Survey, 10). There is, however, a serious problem with uranium mining and the ability to supply the needed uranium for a growing number of reactors. Shortages of uranium coupled with speculation in the market are adding to its overall price. Since the 1990s, the uranium supply has not kept up with the rising demand, therefore a variety of secondary supplies of reactor fuel are also derived from "warheads; reprocessing of spent nuclear fuel to produce mixed-oxide (MOX) fuel; recycling of uranium to produce reprocessed uranium; re-enrichment of depleted uranium tails (left over after enrichment); . . . ." (2007 Survey, 10).

The cost of generating electricity from nuclear power plants is competitive with the cost of generating electricity from fossil fuel, and even more so when the price of fossil fuel rises. As with all other production processes, location, landscape, and geopolitical factors are important elements in calculating the costs of production. Nuclear energy is also very competitive when we take into account the social and environmental costs of producing electricity from fossil fuel. The European Commission study in 1991 showed the cost per kwh of electricity from nuclear sources to be 0.4 cents/kwh, similar to electricity generated from the hydro sources. Coal was over 4.0 cents (between 4.1 and 7.3). Natural gas ranged between 1.3 and 2.3 cents.[2] Only wind showed remarkably less cost at 0.1 to 0.2 cents/kwh. Half of the cost for nuclear energy is due to the enrichment and fabrication costs and the cost associated with nuclear waste management. Uranium however has the advantage of being easily and cheaply transportable (http://www.World-nuclear.org/info/info02, html). The Finnish study in 2000 also quantified fuel price

---

[2] The European Commission launched the project in 1991 in collaboration with the US Department of Energy, Nuclear energy averages 0.4 euro cents/kWh, much the same as hydro, coal is over 4.0 cents (4.1-7.3), gas ranges 1.3-2.3 cents and only wind shows up better than nuclear, at 0.1-0.2 cents/kWh average. NB these are the external costs only (Comparative Cost of Energy Production, 2005).

sensitivity to electricity costs, showing that a doubling of fuel prices would result in the electricity cost for nuclear rising about 9 percent, for coal rising 31 percent and for gas 66 percent (World-nuclear.org).

The application of nuclear science and technology is not limited to the production of electricity, it has many major industrial and social applications. As an advanced science, it requires a set of preconditions and pre-requisites to be met and once it is mastered, it can influence the development of other technologies. It can improve the quality of tools in major industries, increase the reliability of gauges, and machines; it can diagnose metabolic abnormalities and treat cancer; it powers spaceships, space exploration and space travel. Given the diversity of applications in agriculture, medicine, and space, there is a clear need for concentrated nuclear energy. Today, about one-third of all procedures used in modern hospitals involves radiation or radioactivity. An estimated 10 to 12 million diagnostic and therapeutic procedures are performed each year in the U.S. alone involving some form of nuclear medicine. For several decades, non-food irradiation technology along with cross-link polymers used in automotives, wire insulation, printing, films, and sterilization (about 50 percent of all medical disposable materials) have been in use. And recently, a great variety of consumer products such as cosmetics, baby bottle nipples, teething rings, and so on are being sterilized using irradiation.

Close to 500 nuclear power plants operate in over 30 countries. In 1999, nuclear energy represented about 75 percent of total electricity production in France, 58 percent in Belgium, 47 percent in Sweden, 43 percent in South Korea, 38 percent in Hungary, 36 percent in Switzerland, 31 percent in Germany, 36 percent in Japan, 33 percent in Finland, 30 percent in Spain, 29 percent in the United Kingdom, 20 percent in the Czech Republic, 19 percent in the United States,

13 percent in Canada, 5 percent in Mexico, and 4 percent in the Netherlands (World Energy Council, 2007).

Typically, a doubling of the uranium market price would increase the fuel cost for a light water reactor by 26 percent and the electricity cost about 7 percent, whereas doubling the price of natural gas would typically add 70 percent to the price of electricity from that source (World-nuclear, 2008:13). Nuclear power is cost competitive with other forms of electricity generation, except where there is direct access to low-cost fossil fuels. Fuel costs for nuclear plants are a minor proportion of total generating costs, though capital costs are greater than those for coal-fired plants. In assessing the cost competitiveness of nuclear energy, decommissioning, and waste disposal costs are taken into account (OECD; European Community Studies, various years; U.S. Department of Energy; studies in Finland, Spain, the UK, and elsewhere). If the social, health, and environmental costs of fossil fuels are also taken into account, nuclear power is an outstanding alternative. And as long as carbon emissions are cost-free and not included in the calculations, the true cost of fossil fuel consumption will not be known (World-nuclear.org, 2008). These are important considerations even without attempting to include global warming. The concerns over the dangers associated with nuclear waste, radiation, and storage, however, remain legitimate and urgent ones. Nonetheless, if nuclear power held a significant share of hydroelectric generation capacity, it would provide an effective hedge against the volatility of fossil fuel prices. The trend will only be reinforced when the environmental costs associated with carbon dioxide emissions are fully internalized in the trading system. Safeguards must be put in place before the planet is faced with further dilemmas as it is faced with the dependency on fossil fuels. Unfortunate experiences at Chernobyl, Three Mile Island, and other problems with the nuclear energy apparatus must be warning signs of things to come if proper measures are not put in place. Moreover, the safe storage of nuclear waste for many countries is a monumentally expensive task.

The sun and wind are two of the most abundant sources of renewable energy. As with nuclear technology, solar and wind energy are also controlled by a handful of countries.-Every minute of the sun shining on one square kilometer surface of our planet, 1,400 megawatts of solar power is generated. Luckily "only half of that amount reaches the earth's surface. "The total radiation power of the sun varies only slightly, about 0.2 percent every 30 years" and any major "variation would alter the or end life on earth" (Solar Energy.com).

As is well known, wind energy can be converted into mechanical energy for performing work such as pumping water, grinding grain, and milling lumber. The amount of kinetic energy within the earth's atmosphere is equal to about 10,000 trillion kilowatt-hours which will remain available for what amounts to eternity. Societies have taken advantage of wind power for thousands of years. The first known use was in 500 BCE when people used sails to navigate the Nile River. Persians had already been using windmills in 200 BCE in order to pump water and grind grain. The Dutch were responsible for many refinements of the windmill, primarily for pumping excess water off land that was flooded (Wind Energy.com). The windmill was further refined in the late 19th century in the U.S.; some designs (with inefficient wooden blades) from that period are still in use today. Over the next century, more than six million small windmills were erected in the U.S. in order to aid in watering livestock and supplying homes with water during the development of the West.

Since 1999 global wind energy capacity has been doubling every three years reaching 72,000 megawatts by the end of 2006. This is approximately 120 billion kilowatt-hours of electricity which is enough to provide electricity to approximately 70 million people (2007 Survey, 18). An efficient windmill can produce approximately 175 watts per square meter of propeller-blade area at a height of 25 meters. As technology for harnessing wind energy evolves, new turbines installed on less than 1 percent of land area can produce close to 20 percent of its electricity (2007 Survey, 18). Billions of kwh of electricity produced by America's wind machines annually would eliminate the need for millions of barrels of oil and all of its consequences (smog, greenhouses, and acid rain) for the planet.

If a household used wind power for 25 percent of its needs, it would spend only $4 or $5 dollars per month and the price is still dropping. Compare this to 4.8 to 5.5 cents per kwh for coal or 11.1 to 14.5 cents per kwh for nuclear power. Germany (34 percent), the U.S. (20 percent), Spain (23 percent), Denmark (8 percent), and India (28 percent) are among the world's leading nations in the production of wind energy and expanding (2007, Survey of Energy Resources-Executive Summary). Wind power is now the world's fastest growing energy source. In 2006 an estimated $52 billion was invested in wind power, biofuels and other renewable sources. This is up 33 percent from 2005 and it is estimated that it will reach $66 billion in 2007(State of the World, 2008). The only pollution that wind farms have is noise pollution. Due to skyrocketing oil prices, many Southeast Asian countries are intensifying efforts to tap alternative sources of energy. Even oil producing countries like Malaysia, Indonesia, and Brunei are investing in renewable energy (Asia Times, 2008). Some regional initiatives have been put in place. In Africa with the help of Senegal's President Wade the Pan-African Non-Petroleum Producers Association (PANPP), with 13 member countries have taken steps toward alternative sources of energy (Watkins 2007, 16). It is through these initiatives that the global south can off-set the impact of hegemony.

CSD as a counter-hegemonic strategy. CDS is the only alternative for a fossil fuel rich country such as Iran. Iran has the geography and the climate for harnessing an abundant supply of alternative/renewable sources. Public statements by the Iranian leadership have been from the beginning of the 1979 Revolution supportive of a comprehensive plan compatible with CDS. Slogans such as collective empowerment and of late the propagation of "resistance economy" as components of a strategy of national (and indeed universal) human liberation from the yoke of hegemonic powers have permeated the state controlled media. In the formative years of the Iranian revolution of 1979 there was a substantial drive for sustainable development through a process of resource-mapping at the national level. Since antiquity Iran has regarded itself and has been considered by others as a civilized nation/empire. The national culture has long considered that it had a duty to transcend the interests of isolated private individuals in favor of the collective public interest. Iran possesses great possibilities in its people and its cultural/historical as well as its physical landscapes to narrow the gap between the potential and the actual development. Domestically in particular, it must transcend any narrow economic development which aims at private wealth generation for any comprador elite through collaboration with the leaders of capitalist globalization. Its national policy must reject the requirement as do most economies forced by globalizing agents to enhance privatization, for the labor force to make sacrifices without requiring the rich to do proportionately more. It must strive instead to create an environment in which the traditional Iranian civic ethos is reinvigorated. Diversification of energy sources would allow to ultimately reduce dependency and the elimination of dependency is one of the requirements of CSD.

Iran's regional imperative is cooperation and less sectarian tendencies it is essential that a regional integration plan devotes a large portion of its attention to meeting the rising demand for energy resources which are easily transportable, efficient, equitable, and environmentally sound. It is within this context that mutual security in all respects is assured. Indeed as CSD requires, a regional alliance must be the basis and the context, since sustainability is not merely a national issue and cannot be implemented independent of its immediate surroundings. It is to be nourished through its ability to transcend individualistic approaches.

The global imperatives are the sharing of technology with the rest of the global South, but also extending the life of the current proven oil reserves no matter what the size of potential reserves may be. A diversification of energy sources must be at the top of the agenda. Diversification reduces vulnerability, dependency, and deprivation. It is through diversity of energy sources that a nation such as Iran can sustain other production processes utilizing various sources of energy.

Comprehensive sustainable development can make a great contribution to human liberation and development only if it begins and ends with social justice as a guiding principle. On the political front, CSD would incorporate radical democracy as a force directing the process. Only through a social justice orientation can environmental degradation be reversed, basic necessities be provided for, and a culture of collective well-being be reinforced. It is in this context that racism, economic exploitation, environmental degradation, and dependent development/industrialization—the building blocks of hegemony—are removed. It is through CSD and its regard for the environment that the monopolization of technological knowledge can be broken and the right to technological invention and innovation is re-claimed. But what are the components of a strategy that can retrieve these rights to a CSD-oriented technology? Let's examine the case of Iran's nuclear program—often equated in the propaganda organs of hegemonic powers with a "nuclear weapons program." Iran's nuclear case has brought to the surface the hypocrisy of international agencies in thrall to the powerful few on the global stage.

Nuclear energy is essential in all places where concentrated energy is needed and alternative sources are scarce. But it has to be as part of a comprehensive and long term energy program. Alternative (non-fossil) sources of energy are at the moment—with the exception of nuclear and hydroelectric power—in their early stages of mass production and consumption. Solar, wind, tidal, and biomass sources continue to evolve, but the magnitude of production along with transportability and the initial capital costs have made nuclear and hydro more appealing. For instance, even if Iran gets a small percentage of its electricity from each of these renewable sources, it will be in a position to diversify home-grown energy sources while removing enormous dependency and restrictions in confronting hegemony. Iranians are the pioneers of wind energy as seen in various cities, but notably Yazd and Kashan. Today, its drive toward diversification of energy (even if criticized with good intentions) must continue. The private sector in Iran is not yet conducive to spearheading the drive toward alternative sources of energy. Public ownership must initiate this and can hasten its development, but that can happen, the rampant corruption must be addressed.

James Howarth (2008) argues that for the most part Iran's energy policy is determined by political concerns. Iran is said to be making a mistake in pursuing nuclear rather than solar and wind energy and traditional fossil fuel. Iran has the world's second largest gas reserve (measurable amounts) and perhaps in terms of potential reserve (amounts that are not discovered but thought to exist). It has the fourth largest oil reserve and perhaps much greater potential reserve. Current world consumption occurs at the rate of over 25 billion barrels per year. With a proven petroleum reserve of one trillion barrels, this will last 40 years at the current rate, and consumption is likely to increase greatly. Adding to this eventuality is the very uneven distribution of this resource and the consequences for the planet. Iran will continue to endure three problems that is suffering from now: a) pollution—carbon emissions which have increased by 240 percent since 1980 from 33.1 metric tons to almost 80 metric tons in 1998 and to 139 metric tons in 2000 (Karegar 2004, 1); b) reliance on fossil fuel as a source of earning foreign exchange; and c) greater demand for energy due to population growth.

Iran was in a relatively good position to fulfil the promise of its two revolutions (the Constitutional Revolution of 1910, and the Revolution of 1979), but global political forces stifled that drive in its infancy. Mutual hostilities between Iran and world leaders meant that Iran continued to rely on oil production and revenue to finance its expenditures. However, Iran has attempted to reduce its reliance on oil, both for export and for its particularly high rate of domestic consumption. Iran is attempting to develop alternative energy resources, albeit not really successfully.

Iran has been expanding its capacity to increase electricity from renewable sources including solar and wind, and through its planned building of more nuclear reactors. In 1994 Iran installed its first modern wind turbines, particularly in Roodbar and Manjil. The United States leads the world with an annual output of 9149 megawatts followed by India (4434), China (1266), Japan (1078) and 99 for Korea. Iran's geothermal potential, particularly in Damavand, Khoy, and Maku are promising sources of energy with adequate infrastructure (Alternative Energy Iran: Windpower for the North West. February 15, 2005). In terms of nuclear energy, Iran's results have been abysmal; hundreds of millions of dollars spent, but with nothing to show for it.

Iran has been carrying out a set of expert-level studies to set up seven wind power plants in three northwestern provinces. If the results of the studies confirm that the target regions are right for the purpose, the projects will be immediately started under private sector management. Arastou Sadeqi, the director of the wind and water energies department in the Iranian New Energies Organization had earlier said that "the government has removed basic problems" [the absence of private sector partnership] (Alternative Energy Iran...., 2005).

Canceling subsidies will reduce greenhouse gas emissions, but fossil fuel subsidies are in some cases necessary until other means of energy are made available. Iran, for example, heavily subsidizes fossil fuel, particularly gasoline, for domestic consumption. A large percentage of Iranians could not purchase gasoline without subsidies. Recent attempts at conversion to natural gas as a substitute is the first step toward alternatives. For the most part fossil fuel subsidies around the globe are a political decision to favor a very prosperous sector of the economy—the petroleum industry and related fields. For instance, liquefied petroleum gas (LPG) subsidies in India, aimed at getting fuel to poor households, totaled $1.7 billion in the first half of 2008. But the LPG subsidies are mainly benefiting higher-income households. Smarter subsidies such as tax breaks, financial incentives, or other market mechanisms could generate benefits for the economy and environment if properly targeted (United Nations Environmental Programme, UNEP). This pointed to subsidies promoting wind energy in Germany and Spain aimed at helping to shift from fossil fuels. Well-devised subsidies in Chile had spread rural electrification to 90 percent of the population from 50 percent in 12 years, it said. Nations such as China, India, and Brazil have so far won almost all of the 3,500 projects designed to develop alternative/renewable sources of energy. Therefore, subsidies could help the global south and the environment in confronting their problems.

A report titled "The Price of Power," by the New Economic Foundation (NEF) states that the costs of natural disasters linked to global warming reached $60 billion in 2007, with the warming triggered by the burning of fossil fuels, coal, oil, and gas. The report says a single year's worth of World Bank spending on fossil fuel projects could be spent instead on small-scale solar installations in sub-Saharan Africa providing electricity for 10 million people. And a year's worth of global fossil fuel subsidies could "comfortably" pay off sub-Saharan Africa's entire international debt burden, leaving billions of dollars to spare ("The Price of Power," NEF). The report says these subsidies amount conservatively to about $235 billion a year and they distort the global economy, damage the environment and hold back the development of renewable sources. Andrew Simms of NEF points out, as long as dependency on fossil fuels continues, "corruption and violence," climatic changes, and increasing poverty are expected. And the solution to these problems lies in the removal of that dependency. If indeed the world is serious about reducing the greenhouse gasses and further destruction of the environment, then the renewable energy and the technology of harnessing it must be made available to all. Sharing of the technology for an abundant source of energy would reduce hegemony and would move the world closer to achieving CSD. Yet for the control of fossil fuel, more wars will be fought as we are witnessing now and the environmental degradation and the subjugation of people will continue until there are unified forces equipped with technical know-how and homegrown technology.

Nuclear Testing and Environment Destruction. On July 16, 1945 the United States tested the first nuclear weapon in the desert of New Mexico, at the Trinity site. Between 1945 and 1996, the world's nuclear powers tested over 2000 nuclear devices (the U.S. conducted 1032 between 1945-1992; the Soviet Union 715 between 1945-1990; England 45 between 1952-1991; France 210 between 1960 and 1996; China 45 between 1964-1996; India and Pakistan have conducted two tests (ctbto.org/nuclear-testing/history of nuclear testing). Several tests have been conducted by Israel, which possess up to 200 warheads; it also has a second strike capability via German-supplied submarines capable of launching missiles with nuclear warheads.

Israel is the most secretive nuclear state whose relentless pursuit of nuclear weapons and other WMDs goes back to 1948. The French conducted their first atmospheric nuclear test, Gerboise Bleue (Blue Jerboa), on February 13, 1960 in the French Sahara, during the slaughter of Algerians (1954-62). This took place at 40 km south of the Sahara in Mali. France tested a hydrogen bomb in French Polynesia. France possesses the third largest stockpile of nuclear warheads. In 2006 Jacque Chirac declared that as a matter of policy the French would use nuclear weapons against states using terrorism against France. The United States has used the bomb and now is developing a new class of smaller nuclear weapons for tactical use. Israel has likewise publicly threatened that they would "turn Iran into a nuclear wasteland" and "bomb them back to the stone age." Republican Presidential Candidate John McCain arrogantly rephrased the Beach Boys' song entitled Barbara Ann to "bomb Iran" (*bomb bomb bomb eye-ran*) and he was sadly and pathetically cheered on. Of course, the administration of Iranian president, Mahmoud Ahmadinejad, was equally aggressive in creating enemies without regard for people's sensibilities, such as by denying the holocaust, and through the wide-spread corruption exhibited by its financial elites.

On February 1, 2007, President Chirac of France commented on the nuclear ambitions of Iran, hinting at possible nuclear countermeasures from Israel: "Where will it drop it, this bomb? On Israel? It would not have gone 200 meters into the atmosphere before Tehran would be razed" (Sciolino and Bennhold, Feb, 1, 2007). Iran and the rest of the world believe that Israel has close to two hundred nuclear warheads and a second strike capability, even though Israel has not admitted that it possesses weapons of mass destruction.[3] As long as the NPT maintains a double standard in this regard, and further has no power to enforce on the signatories and/or non-signatories, proliferation will continue. How else do we account for the fact that there are "new generation" nuclear weapons, even if these are said to be for deterrence or for "limited" use. The international concern over the contamination of the planet by the countries equipped with nuclear weapons goes back to the 1950s, beginning with the radiological disaster caused by the hydrogen bomb test in Marshall Islands. The Bravo test had many victims including U.S. servicemen and a Japanese fishing trawler. Even though there have been nuclear test ban treaties, France and China refused to join. France conducted its last atmospheric test in 1974. Radioactive contamination, nuclear waste disposal, and the use of depleted uranium in a weaponized form continue to be global threats.

---

[3] Precisely for this reason Iran would not likely be the first to attack. It is a fact that Iran has never attacked anyone, yet Iranians have historically endured savagery at the hands of Macedonians, Arabs, Mongols and others.

Conclusion. Globalization, militarism, colonialism, imperialism, and the structure within which these forms of violence are taking place—contemporary capitalism—have created a tragic human and planetary conditions. Measures taken to remedy these problems must delve into the causes. There are tens of millions of land mines killing and maiming people around the world. The price of food has increased by 83 percent in the past three years. Over 1 billion people live on one dollar a day. One billion suffer from hunger and close to one billion are malnourished. Most surface water on the planet is polluted. Two to three billion have tuberculosis and half of billion have malaria every year mostly in Africa. Worldwide, seven hundred people die of malaria every hour, and respiratory diseases along with the destruction of the environment kill millions. As the advanced countries of the global North march on, they devour resources much beyond their real needs and pollute the planet. Those who are lagging behind will continue to suffer a worsening condition. This process can be reversed only if the global South reaches a certain level of internal solidarity, values social justice, and practices radical democracy. Blaming others goes only so far, and excessive finger-pointing will divert the attention from forging alliances toward overcoming hegemony. Repeating the same claim that the West is harassing and controlling and has sinister design is useful up to a point and it is a well known historical fact. Why then spend so much time and energy repeating that which is known to your audience? A healthy future for the world requires a global strategy for comprehensive sustainable development and its prerequisites.

Bibliography

Crosby, Alfred. 1986. *Ecological Imperialism: The Biological Expansion of Europe*. Cambridge, Cambridge University Press.

Congressional Budget Office May 2008 Nuclear Power's Role in Generating Electricity. ctbto.org/nuclear-testing/history of nucledar testing.

Economic Research Council. 2008. New Nuclear Build in the UK - the criteria for delivery.

Economy, Elizabeth. 2006. "Blame Game China Needs to Stop" *Washington Post*.

_____. 2004. *The River Runs Black: The Environmental Challenges to China's Future*. New York. Cornell University Press.

Energy Information Administration, U.S. Dept. of Energy, International Petroleum Monthly, April 2008. eia.doe.gov/ipm/supply.html, tables 1.4d and 4.4.

Farr, D. Warner. 1999. "The Third Temple's Holy of Holies: Israel's Nuclear Weapons." Counterproliferation papers USAF. www.au.af.mil/au/awe/awcgate/

Foster, John Bellamy and Brett Clark. 2003. "Ecological Imperialism: The Curse of Capitalism." *The Socialist Register*. Vol. 40.

Foster, John Bellamy. 2008. "Peak Oil and Energy Imperialism," *Monthly Review* July -August.

Greenspan, Alan. 2007. *The Age of Turbulence: Adventures in a New World*. New York. Penguin Group.

Gramsci, Antonio. 1996. *Prison Notebooks*. New York. Columbia University Press.

Hasna, A. M. 2007. "Dimensions of Sustainability," *Journal of Engineering for Sustainable Development: Energy, Environment, and Health* 2 (1): 47-57.

Heilbroner, Robert. 1966. *The Worldly Philosophers*. New York: Simon & Schuster.

Howarth, James. 2008. *The Quiet Revolution: Energy Futures in Iran, the Gulf, and Israel. South East Alternative Sources of Energy*. United Nations

Jarosz, L. *Defining and explaining tropical deforestation: shifting cultivation and population growth in colonial Madagascar, (1896-1940)*.

Karegar, Kazemi H. A. Zahedi, V. Ohis, G. Taleghani, and M. Khalaji. 2004. "Wind, and Solar Energy Development in Iran" Center for Renewable Energy Research and Application. North Amir Abad, Tehran Iran. http://www.itee.uq.edu.au/~aupec/aupec02/Final-Papers/H-Kazemi1.pdf

Kretzmann, Steve. 2007. "The Best Congress Oil Could Buy" *Multinational Monitor* September/October. Vol. 28, No. 4.

———. 2003. "Oil, Security, War: The Geopolitics of U.S. Energy Planning," *Multinational Monitor*. January /February. Vol. 24. Nos 1 &2.

Liebig, Justus Von. 1859., *Letters on Modern Agriculture*. London: Walton and Maberly.

McAfee, Kathleen. 2008. "Sustainability and Social Justice in the Global Food System Linking Conservation, Agro-ecology, and Food Security." http://www.kmcafee.com/gegee.php (Retrieved Sept 9, 2008).

Magdoff, Fred. 2008. "The Political Economy of Biofuels". *Monthly Review*, July-August.

Magdoff, Harry. 1969. *The Age of Imperialism: The Economics of U.S. Foreign Policy*. New York: Monthly Review Press.

———. 1978. *Imperialism: From the Colonial Age to the Present*. New York: Monthly Review Press. New York.

Marx, Karl. 1976. *Capital*. Vol. I. New York: Vintage Books.

———. 1981. *Capital*. Vol II. New York: Vintage Books.

———. 1964. *Economic and Philosophical Manuscripts of 1844*. New York: International Publishers.

Percebois J. 2003. "The Peaceful Uses of Nuclear Energy," *Energy Policy* 31, 101-08, Jan 2003.

Rogin, Michael Paul. 1991. *Fathers and Children: Andrew Jackson and the subjugation of the American Indian*. Piscataway: Transaction Publishers.

Royal Academy of Engineering. 2004. *The Costs of Generating Electricity*. ExternE web site.

Satya, Laxman D. 2004. *Ecology, Colonialism and Cattle: Central India in the Nineteenth Century*, New Delhi: Oxford University Press.

Sciolino, Elaine and Katrin Bennhold. 2007. "Chirac Strays From Assailing a Nuclear Iran," reprinted in *The New York Times*, February 11.
Simon, John. 2008. "Ecology: The Moment of Truth: An Introduction," *Monthly Review*
Speth, James Gustave. 2008. Bridge at the Edge of the World: Capitalism, the Environment, and Crossing From Crisis to Sustainability.
Survey of Energy Resources, 2007. Executive Summary, World Energy Council.United Nations. 2007a. "Report of the World Commission on Environment and Development." General Assembly Resolution 42/187, 11 December 1987.
United Nations. 2007b. *Sustainable Development Issues* Division for Sustainable Development.
Watkins, Neil. 2007. "Fueling Another Debt Crisis," *Multinational Monitor,* September/October. Vol. 28, No. 4.
Will, Allen. 2007. "Learning for Sustainability: Sustainable Development." http://www.World-nuclear.org/info/info02,htm1.
World Summit. 2005. *Outcome Document*, World Health Organization, 15 September.
WorldWatch Institute. 2008. *Innovations for a Sustainable Economy.* States of the World.

CHARLES REITZ
Chapter Twelve

Global Capitalism and Radical Opposition: Herbert Marcuse's *Paris Lectures* at Vincennes University, 1974[1]

Herbert Marcuse's recently discovered *Paris Lectures* ([1974] 2015) possess an uncanny relevance today. Now more than ever, given the current crisis of global finance capital, higher education must encourage students and faculty alike to examine the conditions that serve to perpetuate the increasingly stressed and volatile realities of political, economic, and cultural life in the U.S. and the militarized processes of U.S.-led global polarization. Marcuse's analysis discloses the fatal vulnerabilities of corporate capitalism—how its very development "invalidates its own production relations, . . . invalidates its own way of life, its own existence" (48). Most important, he shows that there are attainable and realistic economic alternatives—including those that have political dimensions once derided as utopian. His in-depth examination of the social dynamics of wasted abundance, economic disintegration, political violence, workforce alienation—and radical praxis—is a vital part of critical pedagogy.

---

[1] Herbert Marcuse, *Paris Lectures at Vincennes University, 1974*, edited by Peter-Erwin Jansen and Charles Reitz (Frankfurt and Kansas City: Jansen-Reitz, 2015).

On U.S. Political Economy. Marcuse sees American society as representing the "highest stage in the development of monopoly capitalism" (21) in the following terms:

1. Economic power is more highly concentrated in the U.S. than among other advanced capitalist countries.

2. U.S.-dominated multinational corporations have penetrated in a neo-imperialist fashion into the developed as well as undeveloped countries. The U.S. is exporting *production itself* from the metropolitan countries to other capitalist and pre-capitalist countries with lower production costs.

3. There is a fusion of *political, economic, and military power* in which the representatives of particular corporate interests have become key leaders in the government and administration.

4. The population, generally managed without overt force through advanced forms of political economic manipulation, is now controlled through *the systematic and methodical increase in the power of the police*. This enforcement keeps itself within the framework, although reduced framework, of the patterns of unfreedom that pass for American democracy. Further, "You know too well, I suppose, the progress which by virtue of the electronic industry has been made in surveilling an entire population secretly, if desired" (23).

This fourth point, especially, is quite prescient given the nation's new awareness of the regularity of police killings of unarmed black men in the U.S. after incidents such as Ferguson and Baltimore and Edward Snowden's revelations forty years after Marcuse's lectures.

Political and philosophical tendencies that are often referred to as "neoliberalism" and/or "neo-conservatism" in much analytical work today are treated in depth by Marcuse in these lectures. One significant insight is that "At the highest stage of its development, capitalism reproduces itself by devoting a growing portion of socially-necessary labor time to labor outside of the material production of goods and to the work of commercial and financial operators, professional supervisors, and so on." He thus recognized the incipient tendencies toward the outsourcing of manufacturing and the growth of the financialization of the economy. Speculation on fluctuations in asset prices is displacing the production of goods or services as a source of capital accumulation, and this has come to dominate what passes for "investment" in the U.S. political economy today.

Increasing capitalist difficulties, today only worse. Marcuse discerned in these 1974 lectures a dialectic of the *ripening and rotting* of the productive forces:

> Capitalism retains [its] stabilizing power in a reorganized form, reorganized on the national as well as global scale. A few indications of this reorganization: On the national scale, in the recent years we have witnessed a considerable and still growing restriction on civil rights and liberties by the courts, by administrative decree, by legislation. We have observed a continued and a growing manipulation of the still-existing democratic process, as if it would not have been manipulated enough already before. If it is impossible to become a candidate in the elections without disposing of a fortune of around a million dollars, this is in any case a strange form of democracy. (5)

Clearly the development of U.S. capitalism involves advancing economic and political dysfunction.

> I suggest to analyze this problem in the classical Marxian terms, namely, that the very forces which make for the preservation and for the growth of the capitalist system are also the forces which make for its decline and eventual collapse. This is the classical dialectical conception, and I've found that it is the only one that gives, or may give us, an adequate understanding of what is going on. (37)

Ten years after *One-Dimensional Man* (1964), where Marcuse had stressed the nearly total absorption of the populations of advanced industrial societies within in a completely administered political universe of a liberal welfare/warfare state, he contends in dialectical contrast that at this "stage of unprecedented social wealth and unprecedented growth capacity . . . this contradiction threatens to explode" (48). Marcuse emphasizes nonetheless that the future direction of system change hinges on the alternatives of socialism or neo-fascism.

Marcuse's unique analytical perspective stressed in 1974 that "it is not the threat of impoverishment, it is not dire material privation and need, but on the contrary, it is the reproduction and re-creation of increasing social wealth, it is the high standard of living on an enlarged scale, which ushers in the end of capitalism" (48).

> This is the Twentieth Century form of the contradiction. On the one hand, the increasing production of goods which could constitute a realm of freedom, joy, and creative work. And on the other hand, the perpetuation of toil and alienated labor in

order to be able to purchase and sell these goods to be enjoyed in a realm of freedom. (52)

Transvaluation of Values and the *Radical* Goals of Socialism. Marcuse sees as crucial "the emergence in the individual of needs and satisfactions which can no longer be fulfilled within the framework of the capitalist system, although they were generated by the capitalist system itself" (53). These include the struggle for the restoration of nature, women's equality, racial equality, reduction in profitable waste. Here he is developing the perspective presented two years earlier in *Counterrevolution and Revolt* (1972, 16-17):

> [W]hat is at stake in the socialist revolution is not merely the extension of satisfaction within the existing universe of needs, nor the shift of satisfaction from one (lower) level to a higher one, but the rupture with this universe, the *qualitative leap*. The revolution involves a radical transformation of the needs and aspirations themselves, cultural as well as material; of consciousness and sensibility; of the work process as well as leisure.

Marcuse was attracted to the New Left during this period because the radicals were conscious of the economy's potential to eliminate want and misery, and they had a new emphasis on quality of life, not just a secure subsistence. Their subjective and radical consciousness was way ahead of the objective conditions. This New Left was *radical* and not merely utopian: it projected the potentialities in the objective conditions; it anticipated possibilities not yet realized.

In his 1974 *Paris Lectures* he articulates an even broader view of the Left seeing in it:

the opposition in the labor movements, the opposition among the intelligentsia, and the opposition in the women's liberation movement. They all have one thing in common, namely, that we can detect in them new motives for revolution, new needs for revolution, and new goals for revolution. (53-54)

The key question he poses is whether oppositional forces are gaining power. In his estimation increasing numbers of individuals are no longer adhering to the operational values that essentially help keep the system going. He believes there are warranted prospects for radical change and that the "possible advent of a free socialist society" (69).

So we see that Marcuse discusses the historical agents and subjects of social change under three headings, each of which he sees as having now a primarily preparatory, educational function:

1. *The working class.* "What is actually happening at this stage of capitalist development is not the emergence of a new working class but a vast extension of the working class, an extension of the working class to strata of the middle classes which at previous stages of capitalism have been independent" (46). Within this, in 1974, wildcat strikers and small groups of blacks and Chicanos were the most radical. "This small minority may very well be the beginning of a process which may well threaten the system as a whole" (67). Working class for Marx and Marcuse meant all those, whether employed or unemployed, whose income is dependent upon wages and salaries in exchange for labor, rather than those whose income flows primarily from property holdings, in the form of as dividends, interest, profit, or rent, i.e. as returns to capital.

Despite attempts by "capital to intensify and enlarge the division within the working class itself," (67) . . ." . . . a potentially revolutionary attitude expresses itself outside and against the trade union bureaucracy" (62-63). "In the place of a still not actually revolutionary working class, the preparatory educational political work of such groups as students assumes all-important significance" (8).

2. *The intelligentsia*, mainly the student movement. "I have never said that . . . students could be a replacement" (8) for the working class. In fact Marcuse recognizes that the student movement of the 60s and 70s had quite collapsed; that it needed to regroup after disappointment and prepare for the long-haul. Yet movement students and public intellectuals as independent and critical thinkers could educate the nation! Marcuse warned against the theory that "knowledge workers" were becoming a new class. While knowledge was becoming a decisive productive force,

> the application of knowledge in the process of production remains dependent on the actually ruling class. The vast majority of these so-called knowledge workers do not by themselves make decisions which actually would control the development of the economy. Their knowledge and at least the application of their knowledge remains subordinated to this interest . . . (15)

3. *The women's liberation movement.* Marcuse also underscores his belief that the women's movement is potentially one of the most important political movements. This movement is seen as key in the transformation of civilization's traditionally patriarchal values, and this is central to what he sees as the "context of the enlarged depth and scope of the revolution, of the new goals and possibilities of the revolution," (60) such that the movement for the

liberation of women finds proper political significance.

Marcuse makes clear that he never said that the working class could be replaced by any other force (i.e. a "knowledge class") in the transition from capitalism to socialism. His discussion here is lengthy and makes his analytical position absolutely clear. He sees the composition of the workforce as changing (which I will discuss below) and its opposition is still not organized on a mass scale. Yet within it there were in 1974 evident forms of unorthodox opposition: absenteeism, sabotage, unauthorized strike actions by militant autoworkers, etc. Labor's recognition of the obsolescence of alienated toil has become more and more palpable, even if workforce rebellion has noticeably quieted. Of the proletariat Marcuse said in 1979 (in the last publication during his lifetime): "Can there still be any mystification of who is governing and in whose interests, of what is the base of their power?"[2] There is a wide-spread "new sensibility," which could come to herald and constitute a "realm of freedom, joy, creative work" (52). "No specific group can substitute, can replace the working class as the subject and agent of radical social change" (60).

Intellectuals and students in the late 1970s were increasingly likely to see their task as political education as well as radical opposition to oppressive educational and political realities. Since the culture wars of the 1980s this has tended to decline. Yet this was also the period of the most intense and successful reform movement in education, especially higher education: the multicultural education reform movement. Henry Giroux and Peter McLaren were

---

[2] Herbert Marcuse, "The Reification of the Proletariat" *Canadian Journal of Political and Social Theory / Revue canadienne de théorie politique et sociale*, Volume 3, Number 1, Winter/Hiver, 1979.

prominent voices in this regard, with revolutionary multiculturalism a major feature of revolutionary critical pedagogy. This was effort was supplemented by the worldwide anti-globalization movement whose "teamsters and turtles" made much headway—until September 11, 2001. Struggles re-emerged globally and very dramatically in 2011, a year Douglas Kellner described as perhaps as significant as the social upheavals of 1968.[3]

On the possible role of "an *avant-garde* today . . . and the question of who is or could be the avant-garde today" —Marcuse emphasizes this must be understood "only in a preparatory way [having] *educational* functions in the activation of the existing tendencies of radical, or for radical, social change" (11).

Wasted Abundance:
Contemporary Warrants for *Radical* Goals of Socialism

Marcuse foresees the end of capitalism precisely at a time of its greatest productive capacities and its greatest wealth accumulations. He believes he can discern U.S. societal disintegration from what is actually happening in the process of production itself. First, is the increasing unproductivity of those who control the destructive and wasteful productive forces today" (33). He points out that in 1974 the Pentagon is the nation's biggest single industrial enterprise with 14.2 million workers directly or indirectly dependent on military spending. "[I]f you throw together—which as an orthodox Marxist you might well do—unemployment and employment for the military services, you arrive at the following figures: a total of over 25% of the labor force, i.e. 22.3 million, were either unemployed or dependent on military spending

---

[3] Douglas Kellner, *Media Spectacle and Insurrection, 2011: From the Arab Uprisings to Occupy Everywhere* (London and New York: Bloomsbury Press, 2012).

directly or indirectly" (42). This is a capitalism of a different stripe, one in which the preponderance of congealed labor (capital goods) over living labor is intensifying the tendency of the rate of profit to fall. This a capitalism with a frantic bourgeoisie that that has become more and more militarist and predatory; profits are still generated by wasteful war production. Likewise, any limited prosperity among war production workers is eluding masses of people whose conditions of life are becoming increasingly precarious.

With the shift from employment in the material production to employment in services and financialization, there is likewise a decline of the formerly well-paid blue collar labor force and proportional growth of pay polarization in the increasingly itinerant and hierarchical and white collar labor force. Capitalism is at the same time creating needs and satisfactions which come necessarily into conflict with the necessity of incessant alienated labor, even of its most highly paid workforce. The production of luxuries and waste, planned obsolescence, is an indication that capitalism is producing its own negation, that a society of authentic abundance requires liberation from the logic of capitalist accumulation.

> In other words, it is not the threat of impoverishment, it is not dire material privation and need, but on the contrary, it is the reproduction and re-creation of increasing social wealth, it is the high standard of living on an enlarged scale, which ushers in the end of capitalism. This is the Twentieth Century form of the Marxian concept according to which the law of capitalist development is at the same time the law of the decay and eventual breakdown of capitalism. (48-49).

> If this is correct, it would mean that we have to become aware of the real possibility of a revolution in the most advanced industrial countries taking place not on a basis of poverty and misery, but rather on the basis of wasted abundance. And if this paradoxical concept is correct, it would mean that we have to become aware of new motives for revolution—new motives for revolution and new goals of revolution. (49)

In a mock statement that he pretended was "off the record, because all of these things [recording devices in the Vincennes lecture hall] are on," Marcuse made a clear declaration:

> . . . I do believe, as I said, there will be a socialist revolution. I do believe that in order to be really global and successful it will have to occur, as Marx foresaw, in the most highly-developed industrial country in the world, and in order to come about it will take a time of at least 75 to 150 years. Now there you have it. (34)

The final paragraphs of Marcuse's *Paris Lectures* conclude with a question that appears to refine the form of radical opposition that he had previously called the "Great Refusal"—with his revolutionary admonition to work for the *radical* rather than the *minimal* goals of socialism:

> Is this opposition in any demonstrable way really tending towards a revolution which would not only do away with capitalism but also bring about, perhaps, a new form of socialism, namely socialism as in any and every respect qualitatively different and a break with capitalism, again the radical transformation of values of which I spoke? And it

seems to me that only a decisive redirection of production itself would in this sense be a revolutionary development. A total redirection of production, first of all, of course, towards the abolition of poverty and scarcity wherever it exists in the world today. Secondly, a total reconstruction of the environment and the creation of space and time for creative work; space and time for creative work instead of alienated labor as a full-time occupation.

One only has to formulate these goals in this way in order to see what is involved here, namely, such a revolution, which would truly replace the capitalist system with a true socialist system, may well, and perhaps with necessity, mean a lower standard of living for the privileged population in the metropolitan countries. The abolition of waste, luxury, planned obsolescence, unnecessary services and commodities of all kind may well mean a lower standard of living, which may not be a price too high to pay for the possible advent of a free socialist society. (69)

Marcuse's overall perspective in these lectures valorizes a classical Marxian characterization of the U.S. political economy. We can see that it was Marcuse who, forty years ago warned of the global economic and cultural developments that are now much more obvious given capitalism's crescendo of economic failures since 2008. Today this has won wide acceptance among a range of anti-globalization activists and in the more radical circles of the Occupy movement and Black Lives Matter.

CHARLES REITZ
Chapter Thirteen

Education *As* Alienation; Education *Against* Alienation

"We submit to the peaceful production of the means of destruction, to the perfection of waste, to being educated for a defense which deforms the defenders and that which they defend."

—Herbert Marcuse, *One-Dimensional Man* (1964)

As one of this nation's most visionary social commentators, Herbert Marcuse's critical social theory needs to be reclaimed—in particular on matters of the theory and the politics of education. We need to revisit his philosophy of the emancipatory power of education *against alienation* and *for the cosmopolitan re-humanization of culture.*

"A comfortable, smooth, reasonable, democratic unfreedom prevails in advanced industrial civilization, a token of technical progress" Marcuse wrote in *One-Dimensional Man* (ODM, 1964) formulating one of his most vivid and synoptic statements about our contemporary mode of social existence (ODM, 1). He warned against a form of "repressive desublimation" (ODM, 56)—a type of contented, but false, consciousness—where the manipulated pleasures of popular entertainment enhance the economic system's mechanisms of control. By the late 60s, Marcuse famously became a proponent of an activist politics against capitalist culture, war, and imperialism. What remains relatively unknown, though it is arguably the core element of his overall theory and practice, is the profound challenge he asserted against the systems of schooling and higher learning in the U.S., specifically opposing ". . . the overpowering machine of education and entertainment . . . [which unites us all] . . . in a state of anaesthesia. . ." (*Eros and Civilization*, 104).

It should be recalled that, as Marcuse was publishing these and subsequent critical cultural observations, alternative forms of society and politics were being sought for, and fought for, by individuals and catalyst groups within larger oppositional social movements around the world. In student, worker, and guerilla movements around the globe, the goal *of emancipation from alienation* motivated a considerable quantum of resistance. In Paris 1968, for example, the workforce engaged in a general strike that united with the "Great Refusal" (EC, 149) of vast numbers of rebellious students—much as the sizable protests in recent years in Seattle, Genoa, and Paris are testimony to resurgent worker/student/immigrant uprisings; as are also the Occupy Movement and Black Lives Matter today. Radically democratic organizations emerged then as now, and a wide variety of people worked to challenge the institutional inequalities of race, gender, and class in order to end the fundamental injustices of, and dehumanization within, the global political economy.

Marcuse believed that there was a real possibility that education could act *against* this alienation and oppression. The general framework of his critical social theory dialectically transformed (through negation, preservation, and elevation) a central assumption of classical European philosophy. The continuing appeal of Marcuse's writings stems especially from his work on the nature of learning and the political implications of different types of knowledge, particularly his critique of the alienating effects of the prevailing modes of education in the United States, Germany, France, and elsewhere, and from his theory of the dis-alienating power of the aesthetic imagination.

This *educative power* of struggle is illustrated in a recent high profile showdown between students and administrators over institutional racism and related conflicts at "Mizzou," the University of Missouri, Columbia. Here *theoretical deficiencies* on the part of the top administration, especially their lack of familiarity of features of the multicultural educational reform movement, led to swift disaster for the system President, Timothy Wolfe. After a semester of student protests—against cost-cutting measures (proposals to eliminate the University of Missouri Press and fighting the drastic cuts in health care and other benefits for graduate teaching assistants); against administrative decisions to eliminate the privileges of Planned Parenthood doctors at the university hospital; against administrative cultural insensitivity to issues arising from bigotry on campus; and against the university's passivity regarding lethal racism in law enforcement at nearby Ferguson, Missouri,—system President Wolfe (one of the new corporate kind of university CEOs with no academic background) was cell-phone-videoed responding ineffectually when challenged directly by black students to define "*systematic oppression.*"[1] When he said this was a matter of the

---

[1] Joe Nocera, "Athletes' Potential Realized in Resignation," *The New York Times*, November 10, 2015 p. B13. See also John Eligon and Richard Perez-Peña, "Campus Protests at Missouri Spur a Day of Change," *The New York Times*, November 10, 2015, A1. The impact of the Mizzou action has sparked a nation-wide campus movement with multidimensional issues and concerns. See http://www.thedemands.org/

perceptions of discrimination held by the black students, the protesters were aghast, and regarded his response as dismissive victim-blaming. When the video went viral, the struggle widened dramatically with black members of the university's Division 1 football team announcing that they would strike until Wolfe resigned or was removed from office. A key economic pressure point had been found. The coach and concerned faculty supported the student strikers, and system President Wolfe and campus chancellor, R. Bowen Loftin, resigned seemingly unassailable positions of power in a matter of days.

The social movements of our age have been its civilizing forces. Black Lives Matter, with whom the Mizzou students were allied, has effectively educated the nation about the real nature of undemocratic governance (in municipalities and higher education institutions), and the cavalier use of racist deadly force (on and off the campus). The organized social struggles against racism, sexism, poverty, war, and imperialism, have educated wide swaths of this country's population outside traditional classrooms about alienation and oppression, power and empowerment. The professoriate, as such, certainly did not lead in these educational efforts, although many individual college teachers, like Peter McLaren and Herbert Marcuse, played key roles.

I have been a sometime student radical and a faculty activist, and the studies assembled here may be taken, in lieu of a memoir, as a retrospective on my own self-education efforts along the way on matters related to radical practice. Over the course of a lengthy teaching and research career, the latter intermittent given my usual workload of five courses each semester in my community college setting, I have investigated theories of knowledge in science and history-writing, higher learning, emancipatory politics and ethics, and have sought a form of free social/political organization that is also attainable, as I have researched the parameters of a revolutionary critical pedagogy and a multicultural commonwealth. A signature leitmotif of socialist humanism runs throughout my reports and essays in this volume.

Insights from struggle as a radical student and as a radical teacher combine in these explorations, and have infused my interdisciplinary teaching of logic, ethics, social problems, multicultural education, and labor studies. In this volume my colleagues and I offer a set of studies in philosophical, social, and political theory as incitements to readers who are building *their own* perspectives on critical theory and praxis, materially imagining laboring humanity's future of freedom. Central chapters will examine the essentially *dialectical* features of the human condition. These include the *unity-within-difference principle* of concrete thinking that undergirds any evaluation of moral practice, social goods in common, and related criteria that can build a *critical appreciation* of the emancipatory power of philosophy and political action.

Marcuse's initial cultural impact in the U.S. was connected closely to the intellectual and political, campus-based turmoil of the 1960s, and was related to his theoretical influence on the global radical student movement and to his addressing key educational issues involved. Marcuse examined, for example, the questions of science and research in service to the "logic of domination" (ODM, 144) of advanced industrial society. He also spoke to the almost infinite facets of alienation and domination in everyday life, i.e., at school, on the job, and in recreational activities, where these were thought to be regulated by a "total administration" (ODM, 7). He stressed the emancipatory potential of a renascent sensuality under the guidance of the most rational and legitimate goals of art. A new form of liberal arts education could act against one-dimensionality and cultural alienation, re-humanizing political life.

Marcuse's philosophy of protest within higher education decades ago was prescient, especially in its devastating, albeit latent. criticism of the multiversity vision of Clark Kerr. Kerr's educational philosophical point of view represented a decisive departure from the traditional collegiate self-conception as an autonomous ivory tower or grove of academe, one step removed from the practical realm, and stressed instead a logic of corporate and government involvement in higher education. Institutionalized during the 60s among other places at Columbia, Harvard, Berkeley, and at the State Universities of Wisconsin and New York, this philosophy of the extended, service university has now been implemented almost everywhere in the U.S. system of higher education, as well as in Europe, where the U.S. model is displacing traditional higher education structures at an ever accelerating pace since the events of 1989. As far back as the post-Sputnik, early-Vietnam era, critics of the U.S. multiversity pointed out that the phenomenal growth of these conglomerate higher education systems was heavily subsidized by grants from the federal government and corporations for research into areas such as aerospace, intelligence, and weapons. A massive expansion of Reserve Officer Training Corps programs also occurred. What today would be called neoliberal or market interests characteristically influenced higher educational policy giving priority to many of the needs of the business and military establishments. Many objected also to the dehumanization displayed in the multiversity's new and increasing commitment to behavioral objectives in teaching and learning and performance-based criteria for intellectual competence, as well as the growing predominance of managerial language and thinking in the organization of higher education.

As head of the University of California, Clark Kerr was a major liberal spokesperson who thereafter became chairperson of the Carnegie Commission on Higher Education. Kerr's ideological and institutional innovations represented one of the most articulate and authoritative administrative points of view in the intense educational philosophical debates that occurred on this nation's campuses during the late 1960s and early 70s. Marcuse on the other hand acquired a reputation in the U.S. and in Europe as a spokesperson for radical university reform and for the militant new left's analysis of (and resistance to) the foreign and domestic policies of the U.S. government and its allies in Europe and Southeast Asia.

Alienation, in Marcuse's estimation, was thought to be the result of training people to forget their authentic human potentials—by educationally eradicating the realm where this knowledge was considered to be best preserved, i.e., in the humanities and social sciences (Geisteswissenschaften). Marcuse was appalled at what he saw as the displacement of these studies in the 1970s by Kerr's vision of higher education that had become mainly scientific and technical and that primarily stood in service to the needs of commerce, industry, and the military. Marcuse's theory contends that capitalism is obsessed with efficiency, standardization, mechanization, and specialization, and that this fetish involves aspects of repression, fragmentation, and domination that impede real education and preclude the development of real awareness of ourselves and our world. Alienation is seen as the result of a mis-education or half-education that leads people to accept sensual anaesthetization and social amnesis as normal. Conditioned to a repressive pursuit of affluence, making a living becomes more important than making an abundant, alienation-free life.

Marcuse (in some ways very much like Allan Bloom) valued high art and the humanities precisely because they teach the sublimation of the powerful urge for pleasure that in other contexts threatens destruction. Marcuse was never a sheer advocate of a *Bildungshumanismus,* however. He had been more than dubious of the traditionally conservative quality of high-serious German art and university education in a 1937 *Zeitschrift* piece, "On the Affirmative Character of Culture" (AC). Still, he did believe that the traditional liberal arts philosophy also had a *critical* dimension. The liberal arts and humanities make possible the development of critical thinking and human intelligence itself. Here the arts relate to higher education not merely in terms of "arts instruction," but as the very basis of a general educational theory. In both his earliest and latest writings Marcuse directs special attention to the emancipatory power of the intelligence gained through a study of the humanities and social sciences. Marcuse's understanding of the cognitive value of art and philosophy, particularly the great literatures of classical Greece and modern Europe, thus needs also to be more fully appreciated. It is within this context that we may perceive an overarching theme in his philosophy—its several, interconnected attempts to extract reason from art and the aesthetic dimension.

Marcuse stresses the educational value of the arts because of the qualitative difference he finds between the multi-dimensional kind of knowledge thought to be produced by the aesthetic imagination and the unidimensional kind of knowledge attributed to what he describes as the controlled and repressive rationalities of achievement, performance and domination. Marcuse theorizes that art provides a deeper kind of cognition—not through mimesis or by replicating worldly objects—but by recalling *the species-essence of the human race* from philosophical oblivion (EC, 232). He contends that the reality of death and human suffering assert themselves as pivotal phenomena in the educative process of recollection, even where the artist and the work of art draw away from them in pursuit of an eternity of joy and gratification.

Since the venerable liberal arts tradition has been historically (and inseparably) tied to a realistic and normative concept of eidos and essence (as per Plato, Aristotle, Augustine, Thomas, Hegel, and Husserl), we should not be surprised to find some modification of classical realism within Marcuse's aesthetics and ontology. This stands in sharp contrast to the value relativism fallaciously posited by conservative culture warriors (like Allan Bloom, et al.,) when setting up Herbert Marcuse as their straw man. Indeed, chapter eight of ODM argues the historical reality of universals, and his third chapter highlights the importance of the aesthetic Form as the dimension where both reality and truth are disclosed. Marcuse also generally shares with Plato and Schiller the philosophical conviction that the most meaningful and beautiful works of art are also the soundest foundation for an education to political justice.

Marcuse's valuable philosophical excursion into a discussion of the nature of newer and older forms liberal arts education has been largely ignored in U.S. academic circles. On those occasions where the humanities do become thematic the discussion is routinely swamped by nationalism, conservative moralism, and provincialism at the hands of William Bennett, E.D. Hirsch, Jr., Allan Bloom, Dinesh D'Souza, et. al. Marcuse does occasionally articulate a view of the world that seems primarily grounded in an *aesthetic of history* where political, social, and educational issues are considered best understood *from the perspective of the aesthetic dimension* (Reitz, 2000). Nonetheless, in the larger context, Herbert Marcuse's thought is permeated with a multifaceted concern for the societal implications of art, especially its power as an educative and productive force linked to radical engagement for our future of political-economic freedom.

I contend that Marcuse has contributed substantially to a deprovincialization of what he saw as the uni-dimensional technocratic imperative in post-war U.S. culture. "Deprovincialization" is a concept I borrow from Egon Schwarz (1992), who like Marcuse was also a German-Jewish refugee to the Americas during the Nazi period. As a literary artist, he used this term in his autobiography to describe the cultural impact of the German exile community in the U.S. With regard to the life and theory of Herbert Marcuse, I take deprovincialization to mean the replacement of an essentially single-dimensional view of the world with an analysis of culture and philosophy that is profoundly multi-dimensional and multicultural. Marcuse theorized as single-dimensional those cultural or philosophical perspectives that are oblivious to the problematic nature of the social and economic relations that still prevail today. One-dimensionality is constituted, now as then, by the suffocation and repression of society's internal conflicts and contradictions such that this culture simultaneously witnesses (a) the triumph of a happy consciousness and (b) a repressive tolerance of brutal forms of racial and other kinds of oppression (including crusading military invasions in order to extend, hypocritically, U.S. "democracy and human rights").

Marcuse proposes that a philosophy is worthy of the name only if it is sceptical of simplistic visions of the good life or good society and also aware of questions of complex causality with regard to society's deepest problems and prospects. Philosophy must confront "the power of positive thinking," which Marcuse holds to be destructive of genuinely emancipatory theory with "the power of negative thinking." This *illumines "the facts" in terms of the real possibilities which the facts deny*. Philosophical reflection, as he sees it, is thus essentially always multi-dimensional, dialectical, and generative of expanded societal scope and cultural transformation.

Marcuse's efforts to deprovincialize culture in the U.S.A. have actually led to a *recovery of philosophy* today, especially among a new generation of scholars in the humanities and social sciences who are more conscious than ever of issues arising from conflicts involved in the context of our political, moral, and academic culture. After WW II, logical positivism had attained a near monopoly in U.S. graduate schools of philosophy and generally prevailed as the underlying scholarly methodology within the undergraduate curricula as well. European approaches such as phenomenology, existentialism, Marxism, and critical theory tended to be severely marginalized, especially at the most prestigious private and the largest state universities. The philosophical upheavals, which developed throughout the 80s in the American Philosophical Association, for example, splitting "analysts" and "pluralists," were substantially, if not directly, due to the influence of his critique of analytical philosophy (ODM) and advocacy of alternative traditions, positions that gained prominence in the 1960s and 1970s but were then attacked from the 1980s through the present in attempts by analytic philosophy to regain hegemony with American philosophy while marginalizing alternative traditions.

Marcuse also emphasized the potential of an internal political factor within general education to become emancipatory. This occurs when reason is permitted to pursue the real possibilities embedded within the established cultures that can enhance and protect universal human rights and socio-economic equality. In Marcuse's view in "Lecture on Education, Brooklyn College, 1968 (2009), what the future needs most is higher education in the liberal arts and sciences *with critical civic purpose* that can politically transcend the established culture. Critical education, for Marcuse, is education that by its own inner dynamic *"leads beyond the classroom* . . . and may define action and behavior patterns *incompatible* with those of *the Establishment*" (Marcuse [1968] 2009, 35).

> The *voice of the Establishment* is heard day and night over the media of mass communication—programs as well as commercials, information as well as advertisement—and it is heard through the machine of each of the two parties. The voice of the *radical* opposition is also heard:—sometimes, and through no machine. It has no promising jobs to give, *no money* to buy adherents and friends. Within this structure of basic inequality the radical opposition can be tolerated *up to the point* where it *tries to break through* the limits of its weakness, through the illusion of democracy, and then it meets the reality of democracy, as the police, the National Guard, the courts. Institutionalized violence . . . confronts any action by the opposition which transcends the limits set by, and enforced by established Law and Order. (Marcuse [1968] 2009, 36)

Marcuse's educational philosophy emphasizes that, if democracy means the institutionalization of freedom and equality and the abolition of domination and exploitation, then in this sense democracy nearly everywhere still remains "to be created" ([1968] 2009, 38). Traditional liberal arts education must be renewed, must become actively engaged for social justice.

In 1929, while Herbert Marcuse was a post-doctoral student working under Martin Heidegger in Freiburg, he was assigned to attend and transcribe one of Heidegger's major lectures on educational philosophy. Entitled "Einführung in das Akademische Studium [Introduction to Academic Study, Summer Semester 1929]" (Heidegger 1929), this presentation centered on Heidegger's interpretation of the theory of learning and political empowerment in Plato's myth of the cave. According to Marcuse's German language notes (available at the Frankfurt archive), Heidegger stressed that academic study was increasingly becoming a cause for considerable consternation: "Die Universität hat immer mehr Warenhauscharakter . . ."— the university was becoming more and more like a department store, where students mindlessly pursued credentials (in law, medicine, and even the liberal arts) without ever examining philosophically weighty questions such as the nature of crime, guilt, death, sickness, or unfreedom. Such matters, Heidegger stressed, are not the prerogatives of any specific field of scientific study, but are rather of universal relevance. "Haben wir nicht alle die Gemeinschaft und Gemeinsamkeit verloren, die wir als Studierende haben sollten [Haven't we all lost the community and the commonality that we are supposed to have as academics?]. And if education is preparation for political leadership and civic freedom, "[t]oday we do not even know *what* we are to be liberated *from*. Yet it is exactly this knowledge that is the condition of every genuine emancipation."

Heidegger's lecture emphasizes what he sees as the core intellectual and political deficiencies of modern academic study. Plato's *Republic* was of course first and foremost a discussion of the polis and the nature of social justice. In 1927 Heidegger's *Being and Time* had indicated that we must be liberated from our *alienation* in everyday, factical modes of being, by being redeemed through an authentic awareness of death as our own most particular possibility and by choosing authentic possibilities for a self-determined and authentic life, i.e. by becoming philosophically and intellectually mature. Douglas Kellner (1973) has emphasized that Heigegger's concept of authenticity involves both being-toward-death *and* resolute choice of self from traditional and contemporary possibilities.

In his 1929 lecture, Heidegger characterizes academic study (albeit in a preliminary fashion) as arising from our "need in common [den gemeinschaftlichen Drang] to get near to the world as a whole" (Heidegger 1929, 2). In his estimation, we need to free ourselves from the comfort and security afforded by pre-scientific forms of consciousness, illusions internal to the cave, like religion, which offer protection by being socially accepted and conventional though they are also inauthentic/alienated frames of mind.

In contrast to Weber's strategy of demythologizing the world, however, Heidegger argues that *Plato's own cave myth* discloses that, to accomplish one's own freedom, a person must look inward and pose the question it took the Greeks four centuries to discover—not what are the gods?, or what is the fundamental substance of the earth?,—but "was bin ich selbst?," what [authentically —C.R.] am I? Self-examination, Heidegger contends, is the *action of a mind determined to be free*. This determination permeated the life of Socrates, and Plato understood that we must strive to see not merely with our eyes, but with the light of intelligence that brightens comprehension, as the *Republic*'s myth of the cave teaches. Heidegger emphasizes that the Platonic myth of the cave is about both the essence of the human condition and about *paideia* (Heidegger 1929, 3) and/or the *lack of paideia* (*Republic*, Steph. *VII* 514a) as an attribute of consciousness. Often translated as the quality of *humanitas,* Heidegger's definition of *paideia* emphasizes being enlightened rather than unenlightened, educated rather than uneducated (or miseducated) with regard to the human condition.

Building also on Aristotle, but breaking through his formal logic, Heidegger's approach (as I understand it from this lecture) holds that though we were once imprisoned in a world of seeming things, we must ultimately learn that we (and the world) are not things: we are intellectual and political capacities or powers, social beings who can know the good life and the good society (i.e. learn the master art of politics), and who can thus decide to conduct ourselves morally. Liberated in this manner, we must continue to act to help others learn about the cave, and the chains, and to *actualize* our latent function and virtue (to become theoretically accomplished through science and philosophy and to dwell in the truth of a social life and social world whose authentic worth and meaning is no longer hidden). Only in this fashion do human beings act resolutely for their freedom. Heidegger devotes substantial subsequent work to these themes in *Platons Lehre von der Wahrheit mit einem Brief über den "Humanismus"* (1947). Marcuse's subsequent writing, especially his discussion of Plato in ODM, clearly owes much to this 1929 Heidegger lecture on the nature of higher learning. "[T]he original link between science, art, and philosophy . . . ," he writes there for example, ". . . is the consciousness of the discrepancy between the real and the possible. Between the apparent and the authentic truth" (ODM, 229).

The crisis of educational theory today requires a transformation of the frayed academic credo of liberation through the arts into a more philosophically and sociologically advanced form of critical theory of the sort constructed by Marcuse. Educational philosophy must be set free from the tendency to reduce it to an ahistorical aesthetic enterprise. Both art and society must be understood historically, and our economic system liberated from the commodity fetish and the unequal distribution of life chances that ensues from it. Education cannot legitimately be considered merely an affair of inwardness or the supposedly unchanging nature of the human essence or condition.

Marcuse's political-philosophical vision and cultural critique make a powerful contribution to the emancipatory analysis of *ongoing* social circumstances of corporate control of the economy and U.S. global domination. His militant social theory continues to shed light on current debates in both education and society especially where issues of alienation, war, racial oppression, critical media literacy, civic action, and critical thinking are involved. As U.S.-led corporate globalization intensifies social inequality, alienation, and cultural polarization today worldwide, Marcuse's many caustic condemnations of U.S. military aggression and the irrationality of the U.S. economy deserve to be reiterated across this nation's campuses as well as in higher education circles world-wide.

A fateful crisis of the global capitalist system is upon us. So too is a crucial opportunity for a new political beginning. There are openings at every level for educators with ingenuity and motivation to challenge the processes of wealth *production* and resource *commodification* through forms of radical pedagogy. Yet the goal of building a universal human community on the foundations of universal human decency and dignity cannot be accomplished by education to emancipatory consciousness alone.

Herbert Marcuse privileged at one phase of his theoretical development the political potential of aesthetic education. Great art in his estimation always disclosed a realm of freedom and the *promesse du bonheur*, art's promise of happiness. Still, he emphasized that this promise could not be realized by art alone: our *new aesthetic sensibility* must be accompanied by revolutionary struggle and inspired by the most radical goals of socialism. Here the *de*commodification of social-needs-oriented resources, like health care, education, food, child care, transportation, housing, and a guaranteed income, represents socialism's *minimal* goal. *Radical* socialism means *creating the most encompassing conditions of human flourishing*. Commonwealth is living labor's promise. Marcuse acknowledges—as we all must—the fundamental role of *the* *labor process* in the liberation and realization of this new form of human community, despite our grief at the multiform ways in which labor and the realm of necessity have been dehumanized and degraded. *Sensuous living labor*—by collectively struggling to overcome its commodification and deformation—can bring to fruition, *within* the realm of necessity, an intercultural architecture of equality, disalienation, ecological balance, freedom, and abundance.

Peter McLaren and Herbert Marcuse: *Toward a Revolutionary Multicultural Humanism.* During this period of the intensifying global crisis of capitalism, Peter McLaren and Nathalia Jerimillo have co-written *Pedagogy and Praxis in the Age of Empire: Toward a New Humanism* (2007). They denounce "the rising tide of belligerence" and "the emblematic war on the poor" (2007, 3-21), and call for a world economic system based on socialist equality and democracy, without which there can be no peace and no survival. Furthermore, McLaren (2000, 1997) develops a *pedagogy of revolution* and *revolutionary multiculturalism* —that is, teaching in a critical manner that refuses to replicate class exploitation, racism, gender inequality, empire, and war.

McLaren urges educators to "take the struggle over the social division of labor as seriously as we do the struggle over meaning and representation" (McLaren 1997, 13). Similarly, radical educationist Michael Apple contends: "There are gritty realities out there, realities whose power is often grounded in structural relations that are not simply social constructions created by the meanings given by an observer" (Apple 2001, 56).

Reconfiguring educational institutions overall in the direction of *multicultural organizational transformation* involves the struggle under current conditions for multicultural changes in *curriculum* (including also social action components), teaching *methodology,* school *climate* (emphasizing support for student academic success and social justice activities), as well as into effective diversity initiatives in *staffing, sourcing, supervision,* and *governance.* All of this must be infused into a more emancipatory educational system.

The movement and struggle for multicultural organizational transformation recognizes that entrenched patterns of *institutional* racism and discrimination undergird attitudes of *interpersonal* racism. Race and racism must be brought to the forefront of critical educational theory, and we need to heed ethnic minority scholars (Calderón, 2009). Prejudice and bigotry are *not* simply a result of an individual's attitude of disrespect or disregard (or *Anerkennungsvergessenheit* [being unmindful of the dignity of others] Honneth 2005, 62-77).

Reductions in mindless bigotry and/or interpersonal expressions of bias are best facilitated through the reduction and elimination of *institutional* inequalities in the economy, law, and education, etc. Thus, it is insufficient for multicultural education reform merely to "celebrate diversity!" Necessary as that is, it is also necessary to pursue social action projects and educational strategies to ensure equality and revolutionary empowerment.

Marcuse anticipated the counterrevolutionary tendencies now raging in the neoconservative culture wars to reinsinuate an elitist, Eurocentric program for the liberal arts in U.S. general education. He nonetheless saw within the classical liberal arts philosophy critical impulses toward multiculturalism, social history, and critical social theory. Marcuse stressed that traditional liberal arts education must be renewed with an aesthetic sensibility and multicultural empathy that can help us become actively engaged for social justice. There needs to be a key unity in education of critical thought and radical action; radically changed systems of schooling must come to evoke the visceral need for fairness and equality on questions of gender, race, and class. Educational activity can and must represent the *negation* of exploitation, inequality, alienation. Revolutionary critical educators and students need to continue to take risks and struggle to infuse education (both K-12 and higher education) with analyses of the "critical, radical movements and theories in history, literature, philosophy" (Marcuse [1968] 2009, 37).

Education must afford a world-historical, international, and multicultural perspective that examines the pivotal social struggles that have led to the emergence of various standards of criticism in ethics, in logic, in the worlds of art, physical science, production, and technology. These standards constitute the *criteria* of judgment which intelligence requires, and critical education, thus grounded in the rational kernel of the Hegelian educational philosophy, emphasizing *critical theorizing*, must necessarily also have an *emancipatory action* component (Reitz 2002). Learning occurs in communities that help one another to apprehend the dialectic of the historical and material world and the changing social condition of humanity within it. Learning from real world struggles aims at an understanding of the principles of action required for human beings, as sensuous living labor, to grasp theoretically, and possess politically, the economic processes that today divest us of our own creative work and communal power.

Peter McLaren's Pedagogy of Insurrection. Peter McLaren's most recent book, *Pedagogy of Insurrection [PoI]* (2015), highlights a political economic focus early on. Its leading section, "Solving the Problem of Inequality: The Market Is Not a Sustainable or Livable Community," begins with the foundational recognition that "Schools in the main reflect the inequality found in the structure of capitalist society" (PoI, 19). He makes clear: "the market is not a community. It is only possible to realize your humanity if you are educated in an authentic community . . . . Critical educators assume the position that equality is both a precondition and outcome for establishing community, and a community is a precondition for deep democracy" (PoI, 21, 23).

> Revolutionary critical educators question capitalist concepts—such as wage labor and value production—alongside their students in order to consider alternative ways of subsisting and learning in the world so as to continually transform it along the arc of social and economic justice. . . . As such, critical pedagogy calls for a movement that is anti-capitalist, anti-imperialist, anti-racist, anti-sexist, anti-heterosexist and pro-democratic. (PoI, 35)

This is classic McLaren. Yet much in *Pedagogy of Insurrection* takes a surprising and visionary "turn." To "enrich the debate about the future of humanity" (PoI 395), McLaren breaks new ground with several daring and controversial, and well-founded, essays on—

"Comrade Jesus,"—linking his work to that of Cornel West and Chris Hedges, both radical socialist Christians, and to Thomas Piketty's contributions in rethinking inequality. "I do not suddenly mention this [the teachings of Jesus] out of some otherworldly penchant, but for a concern for the here and the now. The majority of American citizens are Christians of some denomination or other, and it is important to point out as an incontrovertible fact that the message of Jesus in the Gospels is focused on the liberation of the poor from captivity and oppression" (PoI 103).

"Comrade Chávez"— McLaren's long-standing appreciation for the political praxis of Che Guevara and Fidel Castro animates his earlier writings and continues in this volume. And now a discussion of the nature of the socialist leadership of Hugo Chávez is elaborated. "Venezuela's ongoing Bolivarian Revolution [does not] seem hindered by a lack of poststructuralist insight" (PoI 197). "Chávez was not about to let the business sector set the priorities for public education and thereby colonize the commons with the ideas of the transnationalist capitalist class in which the knowledge most valued is that which is the most exploitable in a capitalist economy, and where knowledge becomes fragmented, instrumentalized and narrowly specialized, and is destined to produce self-alienating subjectivities" (PoI 171). The electoral successes of Chávez offer strategic lessons.

Revolutionary eco-pedagogy and the concept of *planetary comunalidad*—"Critical educators, who have addressed for decades and with firm commitment topics of race, class, gender, sexuality, disability and other social justice issues are now casting their eyes to the antagonism between capitalism and nature to ask themselves how we can rationally regulate the human metabolic relation with nature. In our struggle for a 'transformed economy founded on the nonmonetary values of social justice and ecological balance' we don't follow a productivist socialism or capitalist market ecology. We emphasize use value, not exchange value and 'a liberation from the alienating economic 'laws' of the growth-oriented capitalist system'" (PoI 301). "[Vandana] Shiva's general principle of 'earth democracy' (2005) is congruent with the idea that the foundations of the means of production in land, seed, water and so on, need to be kept in perpetuity by an arranged social commons" (PoI 316). Following Mayer, et al. (2010), McLaren contends "'*Comunalidad* is a Oaxacan concept that serves as a type of cosmovision, and it deals with 'the complex intertwining of history, morality, spirituality, kinship and communal practices' [derived from] '[t]he concept of reciprocity . . . that requires the other or others to make . . . equivalent response[s], and it is meant to be a permanent relation and inclusive of all members of the community'" (PoI 328). My own concept of *green commonwealth* finds a profound resonance here.

Radicalizing education in and through music—McLaren confesses: "My imagination . . . is surrealist and situationist, my spirit is ecumenical and my soul has been humbled by the martyrdom of saints such as Archbishop Óscar Romero. But I can say firsthand that my heart perpetually sings the blues" (PoI 337-38). "Approaching music education from the perspective of revolutionary critical pedagogy will require music educators . . . [to engage] with the notion of the proletarian subject, given that what we stand to lose today is the entire human race (and non-human life as well) and the planet through capital accumulation, war and environmental catastrophe . . . We do this through our protagonistic identification with the oppressed and by enacting a praxis of interculturality" (PoI 350). "What song and *musicing* can do—along with theater and other 'unorthodox' approaches to teaching and learning—is to provide alternative and oppositional ontologies and epistemologies that can then serve as mediating languages for reading the word and the world dialectically. This is certainly true in the music of Rage Against the Machine" (PoI 344-45).

Guns in the service of capital—"Regardless of rhetoric, guns are mass-produced to kill . . . ." (PoI 357). The idea that guns preserve democracy constitutes an unconscionable and egregious swindle of benevolence that is unfathomable in the face of continuous bloodshed" (PoI 355). "[G]uns form part of the broader military-industrial complex that encompasses our military, the prison system, the law enforcement industry, the border patrol industry, weapons manufacturing corporations, marketing strategists, training schools and gun safety and crime prevention programs" (PoI 357). "We see the interests of the elite capitalist class too clearly in the failure to restrict guns even after such atrocious events as the recent massacre at Sandy Hook Elementary in Newtown, Connecticut" (PoI 358).

The praxis of negation—"We do not want to fit into this destructive society of commodified, monetized relations of capitalism. We refuse to live within relations of subordination wrought by capital with its ever-increasing rate of exploitation. We will not let capital define and redefine us according to its need to maintain its rate of profit" (PoI 341). McLaren generously cites my own work on dialectics: "In the language of dialectical materialism, a knowledge that enables the social negation of the social negation of creative labor constitutes the foundation of all critical knowledge (Reitz, 2000)" (PoI 343).

In its conclusion *Pedagogy of Insurrection* offers *a script to be performed* primarily on college campuses, complete with stage directions, expressing the utter revulsion and disgust many of us, educators and students (and especially those of undergraduate age), feel at how *perfectly "f..."-ed* most of us are in this society. McLaren calls this dramatic theater piece *"critical rage pedagogy."* "We are the children of 1968 and of hip-hop; we will not accept bribes; we will not accept financial compensation; we refuse to let our subjectivities be cooked in the ovens of the state; we refuse to ask permission for anything; we refuse to be colonized or to colonize; we refuse to be exiled from our own flesh; we refuse to let our languages, our songs, our histories and our dreams be expropriated by the mass media. We will not let capital disfigure us" (PoI 392-93). McLaren is reminding us that, like Hamlet, we must harken to the ghosts of those murdered with impunity by sovereign powers (Laquan McDonald, Michael Brown, Eric Garner, Sandra Bland, Tamir Rice, and unnamed thousands in Iraq, Afghanistan, Syria). We are consigned *to consider and to act* against the disgrace and dishonor of passivity or complicity with a rotten (vile and grotesque) system. Even if there are more things on heaven and earth than are dreamt of in our philosophy, we are, like Prometheus, entrusted to care for the prophetic fire—through perpetual engagement in cultural action for freedom.

Bibliography

Apple, Michael W. 2001. *Educating the 'Right' Way: Markets, Standards, God and Inequality.* New York & London: RoutledgeFalmer, 2001.
Bennett, William J. *Why We Fight: Moral Clarity and the War on Terrorism.* Washington, DC: Regnery Publishing, 2003.
Bloom, Allan. 1987. *The Closing of the American Mind.* New York: Simon & Schuster.
D'Souza, Dinesh. 1992. *Illiberal Education: The Politics of Race and Sex on Campus.* New York: Vintage Books.
Heidegger, Martin. 1967. *Sein und Zeit.* Tübingen: Max Niemeyer Verlag.
_____. 1929. "Einführung in das Academische Studium. Sommer 1929" Herbert Marcuse (ed.) unpublished outline to lecture in the Frankfurt Marcuse Archive (Stadt- und Universitätsbibliothek), manuscript #0013.01. 1929
Honneth, Axel. 1994. *Kampf um Anerkennung.* Frankfurt a. M.: Suhrkamp.
_____. 2005. *Verdinglichung.* Frankfurt a. M.: Suhrkamp.
Kellner, Douglas. 2012. *Media Spectacle and Insurrection 2011: From the Arab Uprisings to Occupy Everywhere.* London: Bloomsbury.
_____. 2008. *Guys and Guns Amok.* Boulder, CO: Paradigm Publishers.
_____. 2003. *From 9/11 to Terror War: The Dangers of the Bush Legacy.* Lanham, Boulder, New York, and Oxford: Rowman & Littlefield Publishers.
_____. 1998. *Technology, War, and Fascism, The Collected Papers of Herbert Marcuse,* Vol. 1. New York and London: Routledge.

_____. 1995. *Media Culture: Cultural Studies, Identity and Politics Between the Modern and the Postmodern*. London and New York: Routledge, 1995.

_____. 1989. *Critical Theory, Marxism, and Modernity*. Cambridge and Baltimore: Polity Press and Johns Hopkins University Press.

_____. 1973. "Introduction to 'On the Philosophical Foundation of the Concept of Labor,'" *Telos*, No. 16, Summer 1973.

Kerr, Clark. 1963. *The Uses of the University*. New York: Harper & Row.

Marcuse, Herbert. [1974] 2015. *Paris Lectures at Vincennes University: Global Capitalism and Radical Opposition*. Peter-Erwin Jansen, Charles Reitz (eds). Frankfurt a M. / Kansas City: Jansen/Reitz.

_____. [1968] 2009. "Lecture on Education, Brooklyn College, 1968" in Douglas Kellner, Tyson Lewis, Clayton Pierce, K. Daniel Cho. *Marcuse's Challenge to Education*. Lanham, MD: Rowman & Littlefield.

_____. 1964. *One-Dimensional Man: Studies in the Ideology of Advanced Industrial Society*. Boston: Beacon Press.

_____. [1955] 1960. *Eros and Civilization*. Boston: Beacon

McLaren, Peter. 2015. *Pedagogy of Insurrection*. New York and Bern: Peter Lang Publishing.

_____. 2005. *Capitalists & Conquerors: A Critical Pedagogy Against Empire*. Lanham, MA: Roman & Littlefield.

_____. 2000. *Che Guevara, Paulo Freire, and the Pedagogy of Revolution*. Lanham, Boulder, New York, and Oxford: Rowman & Littlefield.

_____. 1997. *Revolutionary Multiculturalism: Pedagogies of Dissent for the New Millennium*. Boulder: Westview Press, a Division of HarperCollins.

_____. 1995. *Critical Pedagogy and Predatory Culture*. London and New York: Routledge.

McLaren, Peter, Macrine, S., and Hill, D., (Eds). 2010. *Revolutionizing Pedagogy: Educating for Social Justice Within and Beyond Global Neo-liberalism*. London: Palgrave Macmillan.

McLaren, Peter (co-editor with) Nocella, A., and Best, S., 2010. *Academic Repression: Reflections from the Academic Industrial Complex*. San Francisco: AK Press.

McLaren, Peter (co-editor with) Martin, G., Houston, D., and

Suoranta, J. 2010. *Havoc of Capitalism. Educating for Social and Environmental Justice.* Rotterdam: Sense Publishers.

McLaren, Peter (co-editor with) Sandlin, J. A. 2009. *Critical Pedagogies of Consumption: Living and Learning in the Shadow of the "Shopocalypse."* New York and London: Routledge.

McLaren, Peter and Nathalia Jarimillo. 2007. *Pedagogy and Praxis in the Age of Empire: Toward a New Humanism* Rotterdam: Sense Publications.

McLaren, Peter and Ramin Farahmandpur. 2005. *Teaching Against Global Capitalism and the New Imperialism.* Lanham, MA: Roman & Littlefield.

Reitz, Charles. 2016a. "Celebrating Herbert Marcuse's One-Dimensional Man." *Radical Philosophy Review.*

⸺. 2016b. *Philosophy & Critical Pedagogy: Insurrection & Commonwealth.* New York and Bern: Peter Lang Publishing.

⸺. 2015a. "Accounting for Inequality: Questioning Piketty on National Income Accounts and the Capital-Labor Split," *Review of Radical Political Economics*, forthcoming.

⸺. [2013] 2015b. *Crisis and Commonwealth: Marcuse, Marx, McLaren.* Lanham, MD: Lexington Books.

⸺. 2009a. "Herbert Marcuse and the Humanities: Emancipatory Education and Predatory Culture," in Douglas Kellner, Tyson Lewis, Clayton Pierce, K. Daniel Cho, *Marcuse's Challenge to Education.* Lanham, MD: Rowman & Littlefield.

⸺. 2009b. "Herbert Marcuse and the New Culture Wars," in Douglas Kellner, Tyson Lewis, Clayton Pierce, K. Daniel Cho, *Marcuse's Challenge to Education.* Lanham, MD: Rowman & Littlefield.

⸺. 2002. "Elements of Edu*Action*: Critical Pedagogy and the Community College," in *The Freirean Legacy: Educating for Social Justice.* New York, Bern, Frankfurt: Peter Lang.

⸺. 2000. *Art, Alienation, and the Humanities: A Critical Engagement with Herbert Marcuse.* Albany NY: State University of New York Press.

CHARLES REITZ
Chapter Fourteen

Decommodification & Liberation:
Social Labor's Aesthetic Form—Commonwealth

> The socialist universe is also a moral and aesthetic universe: dialectical materialism contains idealism as an element of theory and practice.
> —Herbert Marcuse, *Counterrevolution and Revolt*

> [M]an also produces in accordance with the laws of beauty.
> —Karl Marx, "On Alienated Labor" *Paris Manuscripts 1844*

Global finance capital is in crisis. So too are the economic worlds of "the 99 percent" in the United States, Europe, Latin America, Asia, and Africa. Now more than ever we must examine the conditions that perpetuate the increasingly stressed and volatile realities of our political, economic, and cultural lives.

In Herbert Marcuse one encounters what is lacking in other members of the Frankfurt School: an analysis of advanced industrial society. Marcuse's critical social theory has special relevance to U.S. culture today centering on his analysis of the *commodified labor process* as a structural source of social inequality and economic crisis, and the *power of labor* to liberate itself from commodification and exploitation to make commonwealth the human condition. Herbert Marcuse's caustic condemnations of U.S. military aggression, its need for an "enemy," the irrationality of U.S. economic waste, destruction, and wealth distortions, etc., are particularly timely and deserve invigorated attention across this nation's campuses as well as in other cultural and political circles today. His political-philosophical vision, cultural critique, and social activism continue to offer intelligent strategic perspective on such current concerns as repressive democracy, political and racial inequality, education as social control, and the radical meaning of socialism—especially where issues of alienation, war, oppression, critical inquiry, critical media literacy, and civic/revolutionary action are involved. He maintained that the most important duty of the intellectual was to investigate destructive social circumstances—and be engaged in activities of transformation toward justice and peace.[1]

Marcuse's philosophy, practically from the beginning, addressed the deep roots of the capitalist system's functioning and its crisis: the commodification of labor. He developed a critical study of work and social alienation looking at economic activity within the total complexity of other human activities and human existence in general.

If living labor creates all wealth, as John Locke and Adam Smith have maintained, then it creates all the value that is under capitalism distributed as income to labor (wages and salaries) and to capital (rent, interest, dividends, and profit). Marx and Marcuse stressed that labor is a *social* process, that the value created through labor is most genuinely measured by socially necessary labor time, and its product rightfully *belongs* to the labor force as a *body*, not to individuals as such, i.e. grounding a *socialist labor theory of ownership and justice*.

---

[1] Herbert Marcuse, *Zeit-Messungen, Herbert Marcuse Schriften 9.* Frankfurt: Suhrkamp, 1987) p. 182.

My contributions to this volume and also to *Crisis and Commonwealth* (2015) have sought to recover Marcuse's philosophy of labor from its relative obscurity, and defend his view that the felt needs of sensuous living labor insist upon political movement from the minimal to the radical goals of socialism. I have also attempted in an earlier chapter of this volume to develop a labor theory of ethical action and commonwealth and to show how this undergirds Marcuse's desire to *rehumanize* the labor process and our very mode of existence.

Marx and Marcuse encompassed the theories of Locke and Smith within a larger philosophy of labor. Where Locke and Smith saw individual labor as the source of private property, in an atomistic (Robinsonian) manner, Marx recognized that all humans are born into a social context. Humanity's earliest *customs*, i.e. communal production, shared ownership, and solidarity assured that the needs of all were met, i.e. including those not directly involved in production like children, the disabled, and the elderly. This right of the commonwealth to govern itself, and humanity's earliest ethic of holding property in common, derive only secondarily from factual individual contributions to production; they are rooted primarily in our essentially shared species nature as humans, as sensuous living labor.

Real structured interconnection exists in our economic lives. Theory can be called critical only if it penetrates beneath empirical economic facts and discerns generative economic and labor structures that are neither obvious nor apparent. Usually concealed, the structure and dynamics of the value production process are to be made visible in their material form. This crucial dynamic undergirds the over-appropriation of capital and the intensifying dehumanization accompanying the maldistribution of wealth in the U.S. These economic structures are at the root of this country's recurring recessions and economic depressions, including finance capital's crescendo of economic failure in 2008. The recent global economic dislocations demand a re-thinking of critical theory with greater focus on issues of our economic alienation and dehumanization, the powers of our commonwork and commonwealth, and the rehumanization of world politics.

The critical analysis presented earlier in this volume by Stephen Spartan and me—utilizing U.S. Census Bureau data from the *2011 Statistical Abstract of the United States*—emphasizes that labor has a reality and a capacity beyond its theoretical and practical confinement within its commodified form (i.e. a wage or salary). The fuller potential and power of labor, as recognized by Locke and Smith, challenges the presumption that capital produces value, the view that profit *unilaterally* accrues as a reward for the contribution of the investor/employer. Labor provides the total value added in the production process. Profit is a *subtraction* from the overall value produced. Our *critical* appreciation of work turns right side round the empiricist assertion that employers are paying their employees, and demonstrates that *employees are paying their employers.*

Inequalities of income and wealth have been increasing over the last three decades in the United States, a tendency established well before the current economic fiasco in the banking and real estate industries. Middle range households have lost the most in absolute terms, about 20% of their wealth between 1984 and 2004. In large part this is the toll of capitalist globalization. Yet, even after the crash of 2008, in November 2010 U.S. corporations reported their best quarter ever, after seven consecutive quarters at the highest rates of growth in history.[2]

---

[2] *The New York Times*, November 24, 2010, p. B-2.

The Americanization of the world-wide economy aims at the overall reduction of payrolls on the global assembly line, no matter the greater levels of manufacturing employment in developing countries. Our thesis is that *inequality is not simply a matter of the gap between rich and poor, but of the structural relationships in the economic arena between propertied and non-propertied segments of populations.* The crisis conditions which afflict the U.S. economy today need to be understood not only in terms of predatory financialization dynamics but also as *a war on labor.*

This society is fully capable of abundance as Marcuse recognized in *One-Dimensional Man,* yet the material foundation for the persistence of economic want and political unfreedom is *commodity-dependency.* Work, as the most crucial of all human activities, by which humanity has developed to its present stage of civilization, can be and should be a source of human satisfaction. Under capitalism it is reduced to a mere means for the receipt of wages. Sensuous living laborers are reduced to being mere containers for the only commodity they can bring to the system of commodity exchange, their ability to work. This represents the commodification of the most essential aspect of human life. Necessities of life are available to the public nearly exclusively as commodities through market mechanisms based upon ability to pay.

Commodified existence is not natural; it is contrived. Significant portions of commodified social life need to be rethought. What are the most intelligent/wisest uses of labor? We emphasize here how the transformation of commodified human labor into *public* work, i.e. work that aims at the public good rather than private accumulation (Boyte and Kari 1996), would undergird progressive political advance. Work in the public interest in the public sector expands areas of the economy traditionally considered the public domain, the public sphere, the commonwealth: social needs oriented projects like libraries, parks, utilities, the media, telephone service, postal service, transportation, social services, especially care for the young and the elderly.

The decommodification of services in these areas, along with a guaranteed minimum income, would supply a socialist alternative its viability. So too the decommodification of health care, housing, and education. Already we see that areas within the field of information technology are pregnant with the possibility of decommodification: public-domain software and shareware on the internet, market-free access to Skype, etc. The demand for decommodification sets Marcuse's analysis—and ours—distinctly apart from a *liberal* call for a "politics of recognition" that features primarily *attitudinal* or only *redistributive* remedies.

While recognition and redistribution are certainly necessary, they are not sufficient. The slogan "tax the rich," while fundamentally helpful in *liberal* terms, misses the *revolutionary socialist* point that the cure for the harsh distributional inequalities cited above lies in a *new mode of property ownership* that restructures the very process of value creation, as well as the inextricably interconnected processes of exchange and consumption. No non-socialist theory of education or society has any profound quarrel with wage labor or the general system of commodity dependency. Marx admonishes workers: "…instead of the *conservative* motto '*A fair day's wage for a fair day's work!*' they should inscribe on their banner the *revolutionary* watchword, '*Abolition of the wages-system!*'"[3] Marx clarified capitalist society's obsession with production for profit rather than human need: its structurally generated fetish/addiction to production for commodity exchange rather than for use-values. Production

---

[3] Karl Marx, *Wages, Price, and Profit* (Beijing: Foreign Languages Press, 1965), p. 78. Emphasis in original.

for use rather than exchange would optimize living conditions within the social formation as a whole. Capitalist productive relations are driving global labor to its knees. Only the abolition of wage labor and commodity fetishism in the economy can restore satisfaction and dignity to an uncommodified labor process. Communal labor sustained communal human life and human development. When commodified, labor's wealth-creating activity is no longer a good in itself. The overall "value" of the activity of the workforce, governed by capitalist property relations, is reduced to its aggregate payroll. It is never fully remunerated for its contribution to the production process precisely because its contribution, when commodified through the labor market, *is reduced to the equivalent of the cost of labor force reproduction,* and the "surplus" is appropriated as property by powerful non-producers. Classical political economy (Ricardo, then Marx) called the pressures upon the "value" of commodified labor to drop to bare subsistence income the iron law of wages. As Marcuse clearly saw, there can be no rehumanization of society and social philosophy without the decommodification of labor.

Marcuse articulated his own definition of Marxist socialist humanism: "In the Marxian conception, socialism is humanism in as much as it organizes the social division of labor, the 'realm of necessity' so as to enable men to satisfy their social and individual needs without exploitation and with a minimum of toil and sacrifice."[4] I would add that in this manner socialism also becomes the aesthetic form of a liberated society.

Our colleague Fred Whitehead, co-editor of a volume

---

[4] Herbert Marcuse, "Socialist Humanism?" in Erich Fromm (ed). *Socialist Humanism: An International Symposium.* (Garden City, NY: Doubleday, 1965) p. 98.

on the historical examples of utopian socialist efforts at community-building, *Freethought on the American Frontier*, has noted especially the necessity of the aesthetic moment in these lived experiments in communal labor, ownership, and freedom: "The power politics cynics, who are not only on the Right but on the Left, dismiss Utopian communities as expressions of misguided fantasy and romanticism. Yet those communities often created lovely small towns and villages, such as at the Amanas in Iowa, New Harmony in Indiana, the Shakers, etc. Many of these were religious, but not all of them. I think their experiences are important because they demonstrated how to develop territories governed by Beauty, productivity, and justice. To be sure, some were led by cranks, but again, not all of them."[5]

Marcuse urges education and art as counter-movements to alienation: an aesthetic rationality is thought to transcend the prevailing logic of performance and achievement in the one-dimensional society and to teach radical action towards justice and human fulfillment. He even sees a possible reconciliation of the humanistic and technological perspectives via the hypothesis that art may become a social and productive force for material improvement, re-constructing the economy in accordance with aesthetic goals and thus reducing alienation in the future.

The most militant and adversarial dimensions of Marcuse's philosophy emerge especially in ODM and EL. In the latter, the aesthetic ethos becomes also *gesellschaftliche Produktivkraft*, a social and productive force (EL, 126).

As Marcuse sees it, art offers the promise of liberation, and the experience of beauty furnishes the "promesse du bonheur" (*Soviet Marxism*, 115). This is the promise of bliss,

---

[5] Private communication, December 9, 2015.

good fortune, genuine civic satisfaction, and success in life. Yet art, understood most fully and concretely, is deeply dialectical. It unites the opposites of gratification and pain, death and love, freedom and repression. Only because of this can art honestly represent what Marcuse takes to be the conflicted, tragic, and paradoxical substance of human life. Addressing the *promise of art for life*, he notes in *The Aesthetic Dimension* (AD, 1978), his final book, that:

> If art were to promise that at the end good would triumph over evil, such a promise would be refuted by the historical truth. In reality it is evil which triumphs, and there are only islands of good where one can find refuge for a brief time. Authentic works of art are aware of this: they reject the promise made too easily; they refuse the unburdened happy end. (AD, 47)

Art alone cannot fulfill the promise of liberation, yet in Marcuse's view, the insights provided by study of the humanities are the intellectual precondition to any political transformation of alienated human existence into authentic human existence.

In *An Essay on Liberation* (EL, 1972) Marcuse writes about what the aesthetic dimension *does* offer: a *new sensibility* (El, 23) and insight into an *aesthetic ethos* (EL, 24) that subvert the existing one-dimensional order.

The aesthetic reality is a concrete reality which recovers a sense of the human species essence in its universal aspects. "The universal comprehends in one idea the possibilities which are realized, and at the same time arrested, in reality" (ODM, 210). In Marcuse's view, the concrete and critical dimension of art discloses the inevitably conflicted condition of human culture. At the same time, the aesthetic ethos restores humanity's most rational enterprise: seeking the convergence of gratification and universal human need, society and human dignity, art and politics: ". . . the development of the productive forces renders possible the material fulfillment of the *promesse du bonheur* expressed in art; political action—the revolution—is to translate this possibility into reality" (SM, 115).

> Released from the bondage to exploitation, the imagination, sustained by the achievements of science, could turn its productive power to the radical reconstruction of experience ... the aesthetic ... would find expression in the transformation of the *Lebenswelt*—society as a work of art. (EL, 45)

Economic processes today divest us of our own creative work, yet these also form the sources of our future social power. A comprehensive critical social theory must stress the centrality of labor in the economy. It must help us to apprehend the dialectic of the historical and material world and the changing social condition of humanity within it. It must theorize the origins and outcomes of economic and cultural oppression and be engaged politically by the labor force to end these abuses.

Critical education, embodied in a new multicultural approach to the liberal arts and sciences, must in practice disclose the *real need for* and *revolutionary possibility of* re-humanized and egalitarian forms of productive relations, relations to nature, and interpersonal dynamics, such that these can cultivate the aesthetic and moral worth of civilized life. This is the logic and manifesto of materialism, dialectics, and liberatory education today.

A critical examination of the social dynamics discussed in this volume on the material human condition is a vital part of radical pedagogy. Anyone who has grown up in the U.S.A. typically has little awareness of the nature of wealth or the pattern of its distribution in society. We also lack insight into the connection of income flows to relations of capitalist property ownership and the commodification of labor and life.

In addition to his contributions to critical social and economic theory, Herbert Marcuse deserves to be recognized as a practitioner/theorist of revolutionary critical pedagogy, paving the way decades ago for some of today's most eloquent and radical educational theorists: Henry Giroux, Angela Davis, Douglas Kellner, and others, including Peter McLaren. These writers bring to bear critical pedagogy's most radical elements in a variety of ways.

First and foremost McLaren asks educators to "take the struggle over the social division of labor as seriously as we do the struggle over meaning and representation."[6] "As it stands, the major purpose of education is to make the world safe for global capitalism. . . . [R]evolutionary educators *refuse* the role that global capitalism has assigned to them: to become the supplicants of corporate America and to work at the behest of the corporate bottom line."[7] (McLaren 2000, 196-197 emphasis added). He turns our attention toward capitalism's incompatibility with democracy, and combines a critique of the logic of capital accumulation and global predation with a critique of schooling as a mechanism of social control and the reproduction of the unequal social division of labor.

---

[6] Peter McLaren, *Revolutionary Multiculturalism: Pedagogies of Dissent for the New Millennium* (Boulder: Westview Press, HarperCollins, 1997) p. 13.

[7] Peter McLaren, *Che Guevara, Paulo Freire, and the Pedagogy of Revolution*. Lanham, Boulder, New York, and Oxford: Rowman & Littlefield Publishers, 2000) pp. 196-197.

McLaren's stress on the *refusals* required of the revolutionary critical educator derives from Marcuse's concept of the "Great Refusal." McLaren (2015) presented a *Manifesto* for *socialist* teaching in *Crisis and Commonwealth*.[8]

A few years ago I came across two documents in the Marcuse Archive at Frankfurt each of which reads like a contemporary manifesto of educational philosophy and politics (Reitz 2000, 191, 246). These have been published for the first time in *Marcuse's Challenge to Education*[9] as "Lecture on Education, Brooklyn College, 1968" and "Lecture on Higher Education and Politics, Berkeley, 1975." As an assessment of general education and its relationship to social change, the former lecture confronts the ideals of U.S. general education with its social reality.

Education is "*not* general even today."[10] Access to general education, he says, remains confined to the privileged few and is an upper class phenomenon, not only because it is an expression of underlying structures of social inequality, but because it contains a potentially dangerous critical dimension. In the existing U.S. social order, general education tends to be socially and institutionally restricted, he emphasizes, because of "the 'subversive' element . . ."[11] in this education. In theoretical education ". . . knowledge, intelligence, reason are catalysts of social change. They lead to the projection of the

---

[8] Peter McLaren, "Revolutionary Critical Pedagogy for a Socialist Society: A Manifesto," in Charles Reitz (ed.) Crisis and Commonwealth: Marcuse, Marx, McLaren (Lanham, MD: Lexington Books, 2015.

[9] Douglas Kellner, Tyson Lewis, Clayton Pierce, and K. Daniel Cho (eds.), *Marcuse's Challenge to Education* (Lanham, MD: Roman & Littlefield, 2005).

[10] Ibid., 33.

[11] Ibid.

possibilities of a 'better' order; violation of socially useful taboos, illusions."[12] Opposition to this general theoretical education arises "from below *and* from above" due to a deeply seated anti-intellectualism in U.S. history and culture. Marcuse stressed that reform efforts toward general education were gaining momentum back in 1968, and this was occurring . . .

> . . . on a very *material basis*: the need of industrial society to increase the supply of skilled workers and employees, especially the need for scientists, technicians, etc. for the efficient development of the productive forces and their apparatus and, more recently, the need for psychologists and sociologists for analyzing and projecting and stimulating economic and political demand.[13]

In the intervening years since Marcuse addressed the material forces impelling U.S. education toward a new emphasis on the general and the theoretical, the world has witnessed the full-fledged coming of the information age and the ascendancy of the internet and electronic technologies for information processing. We have also seen the resurgence of a culturally conservative general education movement in the U.S. with the advent of the culture wars in the mid-1980s under Reagan, and their continuation in contemporary neoconservatism. Still, Marcuse stressed that the social dynamics at work in higher education have a dialectical character: they require that education must permit (for some) unrestricted access to high quality knowledge in the humanities, natural sciences, and social sciences in order to be competitive in the global economic market and to guide the

---

[12] Ibid., pp. 33-34.
[13] Ibid., p. 34.

political cultures of nations in a sophisticated manner. Yet education must also shield this information-based global society against radical change. Marcuse anticipated in *Counterrevolution and Revolt* (1972) the now raging tendencies, on the one hand, to reinsinuate an elitist program for the liberal arts in American general education against the critical cultural impulses and radical political potential within it. On the other hand, general education was being increasingly displaced by vocationalism. In Marcuse's view:

> To create the subjective conditions for a free society [it is] no longer sufficient to educate individuals to perform more or less happily the functions they are supposed to perform *in this* society or extend 'vocational' education to the 'masses.' Rather . . . [we must] . . . educate men and women who are incapable of tolerating what is going on, who have really learned what *is* going on, has always been going on, and why, and who are educated to resist and to fight for a new way of life.
>
> By its own inner dynamic, education thus *leads beyond the classroom*, beyond the university, *into the political* dimension, and into the *moral*, instinctual dimension.[14]

Teachers and students in the liberal arts and sciences were admonished to be critically engaged with the materials under study, and to "*become partisan*, that is, *against* oppression, moronization, brutalization" (2009a, 38). These themes were reiterated at Berkeley a few years later with an emphasis on community impact projects outside the university as well:

---

[14] Ibid., p. 35.

To attain our goal, we need *knowledge*. It is still true that *theory* is the guide of radical practice. *We need history* because we need to know how it came about that civilization is what it is today: where it went wrong. And we need the history not only of the victors, but also of the victims. *We need a sociology* which can show us where the real power is that shapes the social structure. *We need economics* which are not "sublimated" to mathematics. *We need science* in order to reduce toil, pain, disease, and to restore nature. It is still to a great extent up to you to get such teaching and learning, to insist on the "missing courses" and persons, on class discussion and criticism, and the like.

And *outside* the university? "Community work," based on grass roots discontent is easily ridiculed by the super-radicals as "social work" for the Establishment. But under the counterrevolution, and in the present situation of monopoly capitalism, what was formerly harmless becomes increasingly intolerable for the power structure. The space for concessions increasingly narrows! And there is still room for *political* activity. A resumption of the tradition of the sixties: boycotts, pickets, *demonstrations*, against the brutal support of fascist regimes, the policy of soaking the poor, racism and sexism, and the destruction of our life environment. Demonstrations at the right time and on concrete issues![15]

Catalyst groups of students and faculty within higher education institutions have quite remarkably moved educational theory and practice forward in recent decades,

---

[15] Ibid., p. 43.

especially through the anti-racist and anti-sexist multicultural education reform movement.

Marcuse advises: "Today radical opposition can be considered only in a global framework."[16] "All the material and intellectual forces which could be put to work for the realization of a free society are at hand. That they are not used for that purpose is to be attributed to the total mobilization of the existing society against its own potential for liberation."[17] The 1 percent's enormous accumulation of private property has not led to the self-actualization of the human species or its individual constituents, as the neoliberal business utopians assert, but to the continuation of war and poverty, and to the delusions of grandeur and self-destruction on the part of our current Masters of the Universe on Wall Street. The radical goal of socialism is to reclaim our common humanity through public work for the public good. Sensuous living labor, through its own agency and revolutionary humanism, has within its power the transformation of the social wealth production process into the production of our *common wealth*.

A commonwealth counter-offensive is the political challenge today. Under system duress, continuing allegiances to crumbling structures of power will be seen as fatally misguided, because they entail real material loss and suffering; they can and will swiftly shift. The fundamental role of the labor process in the sustenance of the human community, on the other hand, is a lodestone not to be disparaged or displaced, even if the labor force is being dehumanized and degraded.

---

[16] Herbert Marcuse, "The Problem of Violence and the Radical Opposition" in *Five Lectures*. Boston: Beacon Press, 1970) p. 83.
[17] Herbert Marcuse, "The End of Utopia" in *Five Lectures*. Boston: Beacon Press, 1970) p. 64

Over the last several decades there has been a regression in the comprehensiveness and materiality of critical philosophy. Returning to Marcuse's work filled-in some of the key and notable economic deficits of contemporary forms of cultural commentary stemming from postmodern literary, aesthetic, and political theory. Marcuse tied his labor theory of humanism also to Marx's historical and dialectical theory of socialist revolution as having the *essential purpose* of labor's supersession of "capitalist commodity production." He likewise honors Marx's philosophical humanism as "the foundation of historical materialism." He repeatedly identifies a genuine concept of communism with a humanist worldview, and looks to the supersession of alienation through the actualization of the human essence. Commonwealth has the power to reclaim our common humanity. Its "radical" goal is decommodification: public work for the public good. Humanity's *rights* to a commonwealth economy, politics, and culture reside in our commonworks. This involves sensuous living labor authentically actualizing itself through humanist activism and creativity—humanity remaking itself through a social labor process in accordance with the commonwealth promise at the core of our material reality. This requires *a new system of shared ownership*, democratized ownership, common ownership. Commonwealth is humanity's (that is, sensuous living labor's) aesthetic form: workmanship and artistry, emancipated from repression, taking place not only "according to the laws of beauty," but also according to the labor theory of ethics and justice that I have endeavored to develop in my chapter 6 earlier in this volume.

Bibliography

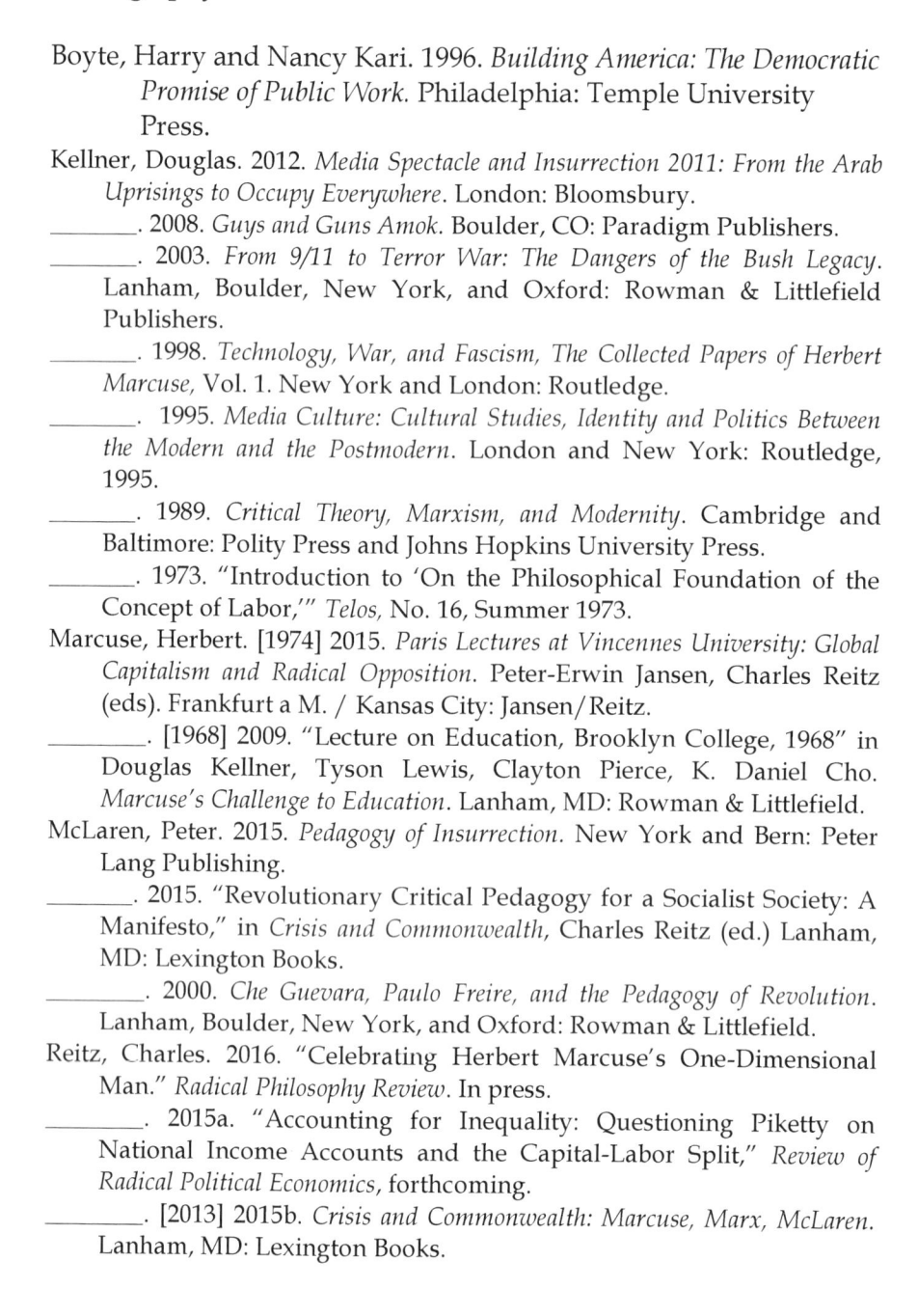

Boyte, Harry and Nancy Kari. 1996. *Building America: The Democratic Promise of Public Work.* Philadelphia: Temple University Press.

Kellner, Douglas. 2012. *Media Spectacle and Insurrection 2011: From the Arab Uprisings to Occupy Everywhere.* London: Bloomsbury.

———. 2008. *Guys and Guns Amok.* Boulder, CO: Paradigm Publishers.

———. 2003. *From 9/11 to Terror War: The Dangers of the Bush Legacy.* Lanham, Boulder, New York, and Oxford: Rowman & Littlefield Publishers.

———. 1998. *Technology, War, and Fascism, The Collected Papers of Herbert Marcuse,* Vol. 1. New York and London: Routledge.

———. 1995. *Media Culture: Cultural Studies, Identity and Politics Between the Modern and the Postmodern.* London and New York: Routledge, 1995.

———. 1989. *Critical Theory, Marxism, and Modernity.* Cambridge and Baltimore: Polity Press and Johns Hopkins University Press.

———. 1973. "Introduction to 'On the Philosophical Foundation of the Concept of Labor,'" *Telos,* No. 16, Summer 1973.

Marcuse, Herbert. [1974] 2015. *Paris Lectures at Vincennes University: Global Capitalism and Radical Opposition.* Peter-Erwin Jansen, Charles Reitz (eds). Frankfurt a M. / Kansas City: Jansen/Reitz.

———. [1968] 2009. "Lecture on Education, Brooklyn College, 1968" in Douglas Kellner, Tyson Lewis, Clayton Pierce, K. Daniel Cho. *Marcuse's Challenge to Education.* Lanham, MD: Rowman & Littlefield.

McLaren, Peter. 2015. *Pedagogy of Insurrection.* New York and Bern: Peter Lang Publishing.

———. 2015. "Revolutionary Critical Pedagogy for a Socialist Society: A Manifesto," in *Crisis and Commonwealth,* Charles Reitz (ed.) Lanham, MD: Lexington Books.

———. 2000. *Che Guevara, Paulo Freire, and the Pedagogy of Revolution.* Lanham, Boulder, New York, and Oxford: Rowman & Littlefield.

Reitz, Charles. 2016. "Celebrating Herbert Marcuse's One-Dimensional Man." *Radical Philosophy Review.* In press.

———. 2015a. "Accounting for Inequality: Questioning Piketty on National Income Accounts and the Capital-Labor Split," *Review of Radical Political Economics,* forthcoming.

———. [2013] 2015b. *Crisis and Commonwealth: Marcuse, Marx, McLaren.* Lanham, MD: Lexington Books.

CHARLES REITZ
Chapter Fifteen

The Commonwealth Counter-Offensive:
Political Economy, Pedagogy, Praxis

Material force can only be overthrown by material force; but theory itself becomes a material force when it is seized by the masses. Theory is capable of seizing the masses when it demonstrates *ad hominem,* and it demonstrates ad hominem as soon as it becomes radical. To be radical is to grasp things by the root. But for man the root is man himself. . . . The criticism of religion ends with . . . the *categorical imperative to overthrow all those conditions* in which man is an abased, enslaved, abandoned, contemptible being. . . . Theory is only realized in a people so far as it fulfills the needs of the people.

—Karl Marx, *Critique of Hegel's Philosophy of Law*

We would therefore suggest that *Gemeinwesen* [commonwealth] be universally substituted for *state*; it is a good old German word that can very well do service for the French "Commune."

—Frederick Engels, Letter to Bebel, March 18-24, 1875

A group of radical scholars with whom I have worked has attempted to assess our contemporary political-economic conditions in a tentative and provisional manner in order to re-frame and reconstruct, through the dialectical methodologies of critical theory, keener insights into the generative mechanisms that undergird intensifying inequality, alienation, cultural polarization, and war. We are grappling with the critical intellectual traditions of Marcuse and Marx, and we explore in particular the potentials and latent powers of an incipient radical opposition.

We assembled our views in a collection of essays titled *Crisis and Commonwealth.*[1] The distinctive quality of the volume is its desire to oppose the intensely precarious crisis conditions today and to propose a *commonwealth counter-offensive*. The political voices represented in it are all to the left of center, and range from radically democratic to explicitly socialist/communist. My work as editor was grounded in Herbert Marcuse's philosophy of labor, a perspective that I call *critical work*, because it penetrates beneath empirical economic facts and discerns generative economic and labor structures that are neither obvious nor apparent.

Fred Whitehead, a long-time socialist and labor advocate, emphasized to us at the outset the need for a new strategic political-economic *offensive*. In his estimation "while the Right wing has had strategic plans in place since before Reagan became President, the Left has failed to come up with anything that can take them on. Failure to have a strategy at all means failure in the long run, and often in the short run too." His words reflect a daunting task, but one indispensable for the future success: "Any person or team that only has a defense is doomed to defeat eventually. In part, lacking an offense, you don't ever score any points. Also, if you are only defensive, your opponent on the offensive not only has the momentum, but he can study your defense and pick out the weaknesses in it. In a purely defensive strategy, however good that may be, there is, then, an inherent weakness. Of course, in

---

[1] Charles Reitz (ed.), *Crisis and Commonwealth: Marcuse, Marx, McLaren* (Lanham, MD: Lexington Books, 2003) first paperback edition 2015 with a "Foreword" by Peter McLaren. https://rowman.com/ISBN/9781498515351

any sport, great defense is critically important. And having a poorly designed or executed offense has its perils as well."

Building upon this insight, David Brodsky presents a discussion of a common ground political platform that he and others in our loosely-organized circle have developed that is meant to serve as a comprehensive *counter-offensive* against the epoch's ongoing war on labor. "It is in the interest of all people who must work for a living, and those dependent on them—in other words, everyone except the privileged classes—to mount a counter-offensive against the intensified assault on labor now occurring around the world." We call this planning and discussion document *Charter 2000,* and it encompasses an eclectic mixture of reformist and radical ideas serving as "a proposal for labor to make gains, rather than preserve its status quo." *Charter 2000*'s core is a highly detailed provisional program for what will doubtless still be a long-term project of discussion and organization as we start to rethink the shape of human society. Its compendium of universal rights and entitlements helps us re-imagine labor's humanist future, i.e. *what we are for, not just what we are against.* These are spelled-out in detail under headings such as: peace (peaceful, nonviolent, and civilian economy and society; teach nonviolent conflict resolution; foreign relations based on peaceful cooperation and international grass-roots solidarity; end U.S. aggression against other nations and peoples; end military sales to foreign countries, especially repressive regimes; eliminate U.S. military bases in foreign countries and territories); justice (a democratic economy producing for human needs, legitimate aim of economic activity is to optimize the common good; equal rights; democratic and fair distribution of wealth, property, and power; an end to classism, racism, sexism [gender and sexual orientation], ageism, xenophobia, domination by single culture or religion, whether institutionalized or informal, including the scapegoating of immigrants and non-citizens; end racial profiling; support affirmative action); solidarity/community; basic freedoms, privacy, civil and human rights, women's rights, rights of children and youth, rights of gays, lesbians, bisexuals and transgenders; robust democratic process and structure, electoral reform, democratic outcomes; stout public domain and public services; sustainable abundance; ecological and environmental stewardship; sustainable agriculture; humane treatment of animals/animal rights. The discussion of rights is expanded into a discussion of *assured entitlements* to: jobs and income; housing, accommodations, food, clothing, utilities; health care; transportation; communication/media; education; culture/the arts; child care; science and technology in the public interest; citizen/consumer power; safe, clean sustainable environment; and security and emergency services. The full text of *Charter 2000* is available on the internet.[2]

It is unique among U.S. progressive platforms and programs in its focus on universal human rights, especially social, economic, and cultural rights, which are excluded from the U.S. constitution and slighted in statutory law. It is also unique in its insistence that U.S. democracy expand to embrace these universal human rights, which *Charter 2000* calls democratic outcomes, and that they be guaranteed through constitutional amendments.

The emphasis on praxis here is clear as Brodsky apprises us that: "*Charter 2000*['s]. . . 'Preamble' reads: 'We prefer flexibility: any strategy that furthers the broad progressive transformation of American society is a good one. There are many effective ways of advancing progressive goals, ranging from educational efforts to testimony before public bodies, community and labor organizing, electoral and media

---

[2] At http://www.progressiveplatform2000.org/

campaigns, and actions in the streets (rallies, marches, demonstrations, picketing, and civil disobedience).'" On the strategy of winning new constitutional amendments guaranteeing rights — Brodsky rightly admonishes: "Implementation will depend on a permanent, militant mass movement insisting on enforcement."

Another contributor, a much-honored radical voice in academe, Douglas Dowd, emeritus professor of economic history at Cornell, presses upon us a legitimate sense of urgency: "as the world now spins it increasingly becomes obvious that unless sane and decent people take over U.S. politics that our indecent politics will bring an end to life on earth." Looking back to summer 2011 he recounts that "beginning on Wall Street, protests took hold throughout the nation. . . . The protests are beginning to take hold again. Three cheers for that, but we also need *a nationally coordinated movement* for the substantial improvement of all social problems and possibilities at home: and peace abroad." He asked: "As the rich and powerful go about their dirty work, what should *we* be doing?" and he suggested that, for one thing, a campaign should be waged as a left within the Democratic Party focusing on six major issues: "the economy, inequality, big business, taxes, wars, and the environment. The 'six' interact and are interdependent; to rid ourselves of what's harmful in any one of them, all must become substantially undone in ways to serve *all*, instead of a few." The recent U.S. presidential campaign of Bernie Sanders certainly embodies this broad-based and radical (for the U.S.) approach.

In recent years the Occupy Movement captured the nation's imagination by standing up to Wall Street and holding the financial district responsible for most of the poverty and suffering on the planet. So too have the uprisings in Madrid and the massive demonstrations and general strike last year in Athens against the austerity budgeting required by its biggest public and private creditors (i.e. the European Central Bank, and other national banks, Germany's in particular, mediated through the IMF). Synchronized workforce actions, like the general strike of November 14, 2012, that linked the opposition in Spain and Greece with forces in Italy, Portugal, Belgium, and France challenge the notion of the loss of the revolutionary subject. The demonstrators have connected with the key power base: labor. Yet these challenges must grow from revolt to revolution.

The workforce is *the resource* with programmatic power. It is *the* creative force in the economy. *Everything* depends on labor. Yet today labor is supervised and controlled by finance capital. Marx and Marcuse emphasized that, in and of itself, labor has the capacity to act freely. Labor occurs in social relationships, and it is a communal project of social beings to meet human needs and promote human flourishing.

Marx and Marcuse built upon Locke and Smith, but stressed that labor is a *social* process; that the value created through labor is most genuinely measured by socially necessary labor time; and its product rightfully *belongs* to the labor force as a *body*, not to individuals as such, i.e. grounding a theory of commonwealth ownership and justice.

Herbert Marcuse knew that because capitalism exists, so too does exploitation, and that *system change* is necessary and *possible* if we comprehend and refuse the system. He stressed that system change requires a twofold refusal: of its mode of production and the repressive satisfactions that replicate it.

Our common work is the source of our common wealth. Only the labor force, as a group, has a legitimate right to the political leadership of the commonwealth system of governance upon which it is built. This *right of the commonwealth to govern itself*, and *humanity's earliest ethic of holding property in common*, derive only secondarily from factual individual contributions to production; they are rooted primarily in our essentially shared species nature as humans, as empathic beings whose condition is that of *sensuous living labor*, a perspective that I have discussed in detail above in chapter 6. Richard Leakey (1994, 60-63; Leakey and Lewin 1978) and Frans de Waal (2013, 2009) stress that the historically earliest cultural context of cooperation and caring fostered interdependence and an awareness of the power of partnership. These customs and behaviors had the capacity to ensure survival. Subsistence needs were met with relatively little time spent in the collaborative acquisition of necessities (3-4 hours a day); thus the foundation was established for the fuller species life to flourish within the human community. This included the development of language as a derivative of the communal human condition (Leakey 1994, 124).

The *commonwealth vision*—and the *practice* flowing from it—have the power to reclaim our common humanity. Political activism has been emphasized above as I have explained by three of the authors in *Crisis and Commonwealth*. Several more crucial and diverse proposals will be summarized below in a series of excerpts and echoes from the volume itself.

Critical reasoning and analysis have formulated an alternative vision for labor grounded in a critical theory of work, wealth, and the historical human condition. The *politics of critical work* begins with an understanding of the legitimacy of this philosophy of labor as the foundation upon which to develop strategy and tactics on a number of fronts that can also be coordinated into a proto-revolutionary movement tending toward socialism's most radical goals. The *critical work of politics* stems of course from Marcuse's Great Refusal and his *reality-based* utopianism.

For these reasons we wish to argue, as Marcuse clearly saw, that there can be no rehumanization of society and social philosophy without the decommodification of labor. Communal labor sustained human life and human development. When commodified as it is today, labor's wealth-creating activity is no longer a good in itself. The overall "value" of the activity of the workforce, dominated by capitalist property relations, is reduced to its aggregate payroll. The workforce is never fully remunerated for its contribution to the production process precisely because its contribution, when commodified through the labor market, *is reduced to the equivalent of the cost of labor force reproduction,* and the "surplus" is appropriated as property by powerful non-producers. Classical political economy (Ricardo, then Marx) called the downward pressures upon the "value" of commodified labor to drop to de-humanized levels of bare subsistence "the iron law of wages." Douglas Kellner called Marcuse's notion of labor decommodification the *"liberation of labor"* (Kellner 1973, 3 emphasis in original). Rehumanization cannot be accomplished without a form of justice grounded in commonwealth ownership.

Herbert Marcuse describes the nature of *humanist* socialism as follows: "In the Marxian conception, socialism is humanism in as much as it organizes the social division of labor, the 'realm of necessity' so as to enable men to satisfy their social and individual needs without exploitation and with a minimum of toil and sacrifice." As Marcuse saw it in the late 1960s, a new, more generalized, type of communism in Europe, "Eurocommunism," was being fueled by an *ascendant intercultural anti-capitalist counter-consciousness* that philosophically and politically negated the veiled mechanisms of domination. Critical clarity had come to the striking *workers* and *students* of Paris 1968, for example. In 1979 Marcuse asked: "Can there still be any mystification of who is governing and in whose interests, of what is the base of their power?"[3] The dominant European and American political tendencies at that time were tending to the right, but the development of Eurocommunism, which had much in common with the broadly activist socialist humanism of Marcuse, meant that the rightward drift was "meeting an enlarged opposition."[4]

The decommodification of social-needs-oriented resources, like health care, education, food, child care, transportation, housing, and a guaranteed income, represents socialism's *minimal* goal. *Radical* socialism means *creating the most encompassing conditions of human flourishing.* Commonwealth is living labor's promise. This involves sensuous living labor authentically actualizing itself through humanist activism and creativity—humanity remaking itself through a social labor process in accordance with the commonwealth promise at the core of our material reality. This is the radically socialist logic of commonwealth production and ownership: bring to fruition, *within* the realm of necessity, an intercultural architecture of equality, disalienation, ecological balance, freedom, and abundance.

Herbert Marcuse's son, Peter Marcuse, himself an emeritus professor of urban planning at Columbia University, has outlined a strategy of moving toward *socialism one sector at a time*. If revolution in its classic form is unlikely to take place all at once, its goals might best be approached strategically piece by piece, built on those elements of the existing system that already rested on socialist-aspects. Spaces of Hope exist for socialist political action, as in the housing sector for example where cooperatives, land trusts, public ownership,

---

[3] Herbert Marcuse, "The Reification of the Proletariat," *Canadian Journal of Political and Social Theory / Revue canadienne de théorie politique et sociale*, Vol 3, No 1 (Winter/Hiver) 1979.
[4] Ibid.

mutual housing associations raise the question of whether the for-profit market is really the best way to allocate housing, one of the necessities of life. Similarly anti-capitalist alternatives in education, health care, and even the financial sector, raise the option of an aggressive posture that would not only defend the existing islands of non-commodified production but call for their expansion. This would deepen the debate: to go from private vs. public, to open up the socialist vs. capitalist choice. In practice, it would mean a kind of progressive economics of decommodification and liberation from the market dependency, moving towards socialism one sector at a time.

Steve Spartan and I presented an analysis earlier in this volume of the income accounts for the U.S.A. which has demonstrated that incomes are structurally determined, and that structural, that is socialist, changes to the economy (e.g. decommodification of the labor process and production, expropriation of the expropriators) can reconfigure the patterns of wealth creation and distribution in accordance with the radical goals of equality and justice. Such changes are really *possible*, and *not only* possible; they are *feasible*: worldwide we have a system ripe with abundance, yet obsolete economic mechanisms—based on ownership or non-ownership of private property—are driving most of humanity, the labor force internationally, to its knees. The Marxist conceptions of *wage-labor* and *commodity fetishism* are the key analytical criteria that measure the underlying dehumanization and commercialization of education and life itself under capitalism. Abolition of these phenomena will be the hallmark of humanist advancement in society and culture. Critical philosophy and radical pedagogy must theorize the origins and outcomes of economic and cultural oppression, and be engaged politically with the labor force to end them. To liberate the fullest potential of any critical theory of society this must be its logic and manifesto.

Our vision of re-humanized social action and social ownership is a mature philosophy of human freedom and fulfillment grounded in the human capacities of sensuous living labor. Authentic freedom is ours when we grasp intellectually and hold politically the resources that we have produced, and which can be possessed by all, within a de-commodified and re-humanized world. We emphasized the transformation of commodified human labor into *public* work, i.e. work that aims at the public good rather than private accumulation. Work in the public interest in the public sector expands areas of the economy traditionally considered the public domain, the public sphere, the commonwealth: social needs oriented projects like libraries, parks, utilities, the media, telephone service, postal service, transportation, social services.

Henry Giroux takes up one of *Crisis and Commonwealth*'s key issue areas—schooling—as a political point of engagement, in addition to Dowd's "six." He makes a powerful case for critical pedagogy as a force against inequality and for social transformation. "In this conservative right-wing reform culture, the role of public education, if we are to believe the Heritage Foundation and the likes of Bill Gates-type billionaires, is to produce students who laud conformity, believe job training is more important than education, and view public values as irrelevant. Students in this view are no longer educated for democratic citizenship. On the contrary, they are now being trained to fulfill the need for human capital."

Giroux states sharply that: "privatization, commodification, militarization and deregulation are the new guiding categories through which schools, teachers, pedagogy and students are defined. The current assault on public education is not new but it is more vile and more powerful than in the past." Teachers can spearhead a new social movement as a powerful force for critical consciousness and societal reconstruction. As he sees it:

> Pedagogy is a mode of critical intervention, one that believes teachers have a responsibility to prepare students not merely for jobs, but for being in the world in ways that allow them to influence the larger political, ideological and economic forces that bear down on their lives.
>
> Schooling is an eminently political and moral practice, because it is both directive and actively legitimates what counts as knowledge, sanctions particular values and constructs particular forms of agency.

Teachers are being put on the defensive by neoliberal reformers in education like Michelle Rhee. Giroux, like Whitehead, stresses that the teacher corps needs to go on the offensive: "...educators need to start with a project, not a method. They need to view themselves through the lens of civic responsibility and address what it means to educate students in the best of those traditions and knowledge forms we have inherited from the past, and also in terms of what it means to prepare them to be in the world as critically engaged agents." This means that: "educators will have to focus their work on important social issues that connect what is learned in the classroom to the larger society and the lives of their students. Such issues might include the ongoing destruction of the ecological biosphere, the current war against youth, the hegemony of neoliberal globalization, the widespread attack by corporate culture on public schools, the dangerous growth of the prison-industrial complex, the ongoing attack on the welfare system, the increasing rates of incarceration of people of color, the increasing gap between the rich and the poor, the rise of a generation of students who are laboring under the burden of debt and the increasing spread of war globally." "[E]ducators need to do more than create the conditions for critical learning for their students; they also need to responsibly assume the role of civic educators willing to share their ideas with other educators and the wider public by writing for a variety of public audiences in a number of new media sites."

Giroux is thoughtful about the teacher's necessary political engagement, and suggests: "One useful approach to embracing the classroom as a political site, but at the same time eschewing any form of indoctrination, is for educators to think through the distinction between a *politicizing pedagogy*, which insists wrongly that students think as we do, and a *political pedagogy*, which teaches students by example and through dialogue about the importance of power, social responsibility and the importance of taking a stand (without standing still) while rigorously engaging the full range of ideas about an issue." Further, "political education foregrounds education not within the imperatives of specialization and professionalization, but within a project designed to expand the possibilities of democracy by linking education to modes of political agency that promote critical citizenship and address the ethical imperative to alleviate human suffering." In sum: "[I]n opposition to the privatization, commodification, commercialization and militarization of everything public, educators need to define public education as a resource vital to the democratic and civic life of the nation."

In her article Patricia Pollock Brodsky presented an historical account, remarkably consonant with Giroux's analysis and experience, of exactly how her institution of higher education "faced a series of relentless attacks on academic freedom, faculty governance, and the public status of the university." Her assessment of the ordeal is upbeat: "In response to this multi-pronged attempt to corporatize and privatize much of UMKC (the University of Missouri at Kansas City), faculty, students, and the community together mounted a successful defense of public higher education." The details were these: "Threats to UMKC initially came from a group of local big businesses trying to gain access to public funds, particularly from research in the lucrative fields of health sciences and biotechnology." The university's Chancellor advocated the neoliberal agenda of transformation and technology transfer: "Deals were floated to sell off part of the highly rated Dental School to a private company, and to transfer teacher training and degree granting from the School of Education to a private "Institute for Urban Education . . . . The biggest prize coveted by [the Chancellor] Gilliland and her backers, however, was the biotech industry. UMKC, with its medical, dental, pharmacy and nursing schools and its large-grant-funded research-oriented School of Biological Science (SBS), seemed to offer a ready-made institutional framework." The School of Biological Science, seeing itself as doing fundamental scientific research in the public interest, refused to be partnered with a private local institute that sought to commercialize and commodify its work. To defeat the Chancellor's agenda, "the faculty used a variety of strategies to realize the principles of informed resistance and outreach to all potential allies." In the end the Chancellor was felled by a vote of no confidence from within five of the university's Schools. Brodsky said her account "has been written in the hope that the successes at UMKC can serve as an example of, if not an inspiration for, what can be accomplished through principled action and solidarity. To fight back, the academic workforce need not be unionized, or even have an AAUP chapter, though some organizational focus is necessary. Conditions since 2005 have worsened significantly in our society in general, and attacks continue on public higher education and on UMKC, but campus resistance and mobilization showed that victories are possible."

John Marciano, like Henry Giroux, has also written about the need for civic literacy, civic activism, and social justice education. He raises the issue of whether a push for a left in the Democratic Party is a dead end. While there are definitely some progressives within the party to be supported, he believes past history has shown that at the national level the Democrats from Wilson to Obama are "a criminal gang." Herbert Marcuse would fundamentally agree, yet he also concedes (and here Dowd might well agree) that: "Radicalism has much to gain from the 'legitimate' protest against the war, inflation, and unemployment, from the defense of civil rights ... The ground for the building of a united front is shifting and sometimes dirty—but it is there."

Arnold L. Farr's essay on repressive and emancipatory education utilizes Jonathan Kozol's *Savage Inequalities* to get at class and race issues. Kozol's work documents the material inequalities in school resources, and of course unequal resources translate into unequal life chances for children in class and race terms. Farr shows how Kozol's radical perspective investigates the causes of the underlying inequalities and injustices, while the liberalism of John Rawls's famous theory of justice provides a deceptive ideological veil rendering the basic structure of society invisible. Emancipatory education requires an intellectual and historical re-contextualization of the facts with "what the facts have denied," as Marcuse says, to build a multidimensional context for interpretation. Only this type of historical and multicultural learning can undergird radical political action for freedom and equality.

A final lesson from Farr's essay is a reminder of the dangers of repressive tolerance. Here I would also build on one of Kevin Anderson's insights warning against the destructive cultural toleration of misogyny in his overview of "Year Two of the Arab Revolutions." Certainly sexism is an ongoing global phenomenon fueling violence against women that knows no class or ethnic boundaries: from Kansas City to India, to South Africa. Witness the world-wide records of sexual assaults, rapes and murders, genital mutilations, sex trafficking and sex slavery, against which the "V-Day" and "One Billion Rising" movements have campaigned and protested. Male-dominated cultural patterns must be replaced with patterns of partnership power: males must be liberated from misplaced aggression and any sense of entitlement in relations with women.

Poet and essayist Lloyd C. Daniel, a former elected state representative in the Missouri House, often reads his material at public arts events with jazz and hip hop inflections, but in the address transcribed in our collection he turns seriously indignant: "We've gone down a military road to control the world. You can follow them if you want to but Dr. King wouldn't have. We can't presume to know exactly what he would have said about what's going on now, but we know what he said about Vietnam. If you read, you know what he said about the Congo, about South Africa. A third of his *Chaos or Community* book was about foreign policy and he points to how it's not about democracy, it's about protecting a handful of rich corporations, military interests and American arrogance, so they can somehow run the world, be policeman of the world and can't run their own affairs. Oppress their own people." Like Dr. King, Daniel admonishes the U.S. government: "Stop your invasions. Stop your oppression of your own people. Then think about telling somebody else something. The United States of America does not have the right, wisdom or ability to run planet Earth. God is not dead. Dr. King in fact said he could hear God saying to America, 'You're too arrogant and if you don't change your ways, I'll rise up and break the backbone of your power and I'll place it in the hands of a nation that doesn't even know my name. Be still and know that I'm God.'"

Daniel emphasizes that most Black leaders at the time told MLK, Jr, "stay with civil rights Dr. King, don't mix civil rights with foreign policy and the economic system. Don't do that." But Dr. King said, "I have to"—echoing the phrase of his famous namesake after posting his ninety-five theses on the Church door at Wittenberg in 1517: "Ich kann nicht anders [I cannot do otherwise]."

Daniel stressed the radical nature of Dr. King's political philosophy: "He said he couldn't come out against violence in the ghettos, unless he came out against what he called, 'the greatest purveyor of violence on planet Earth, my own government." He concludes: "The point is this, let us live Dr. King's dream. Please don't trivialize Dr. King. Please don't make him into just another okey-doke handkerchief head Negro leader. If that were all he was, he'd be on one leg, sliding around the stage with his collar whipped backwards, collecting money now. He was much more than that."—"They had to kill the brother."

Alfred T. Kisubi has introduced us to the too-little-heralded philosophical and literary traditions of socialism and humanism in post-colonial Africa, providing a wealth of political leadership information for critical study. He also documented the secular African approach to cooperative economics, *Ujamaa,* and the traditional roots of labor cooperation and the moral power of partnership conduct that resonate deeply with views I have myself presented.

Peter McLaren's writings on critical pedagogy have long been an inspiration to me and several of my colleagues, not to mention the many co-conspirators in the critical pedagogy movement far and wide. He stresses here that the radical approach to teaching that we have chosen is a necessary, yet certainly insufficient vehicle for transforming the world; nonetheless we can strengthen our work anew by emphasizing the intended societal impacts of our project with a militant manifesto proclaiming our practice as "revolutionary critical pedagogy for a socialist society." He explains: "The work that we do has been adapted from the pathfinding contributions of the late Brazilian educator, Paulo Freire, whose development of pedagogies of the oppressed helped to lay the foundations for approaches (feminist, post-structuralist, Marxist) to teaching and learning that utilize the life experience of students in and outside of traditional classrooms to build spaces of dialogue and dialectical thinking." Today critical educators are faced with a heightened political urgency: "The fact is, surely, that we are faced with two [loaded] choices about how to live our humanity—the liberal model of pleading with corporations to temper their cruelty and greed, and the reactionary model that has declared war on social and economic equality. And on the evidence that each of these models is fiercely and hopelessly entangled in each other's conflictual embrace, we can accept neither." McLaren makes the most fundamental of radical proposals: "as we participate in an analysis of the objective social totality that we simultaneously struggle for a social universe *outside the commodity form of labor. If we are to educate at all, we must educate for this!* McLaren is calling upon us to challenge, creatively and militantly, the prevailing forms of educational administration and pedagogical practice in the U.S. which ultimately *reproduce* the unequal social division of labor through the acceptance of wage labor and capital's fetishism of commodities. These must no longer be taken as natural and normal—as both the overt economic function of education and the covert hidden curriculum of schools. Yet schools and society today are also confronting crises of institutional failure: the massive over-appropriation of GDP by elites dialectically translates into crises of non-reproduction for society's laboring base.

Crisis and Commonwealth repeatedly turns to Marx and Marcuse as crucial sources for a critical understanding of the commodification of life and learning. Liberation requires decommodification and social action consistent with standards of justice that are intercultural and humanistic. Peter McLaren's concluding piece in *Crisis and Commonwealth* indicates his belief (and mine) that an explicitly socialist strategic offensive is indispensable for liberation. The socialist humanist nature of his manifesto is clear: "We need to reclaim the power of critique as the sword arm of social justice and not relinquish it. For in doing so we reclaim our humanity and the world." McLaren, in contradistinction to the united front strategic recommendation of Marcuse and others, warns against "forming enfeebled and enfeebling popular fronts that fall like spent cartridges on the heels of any real challenge to capitalism." So this aspect of strategy formation is an issue yet to be conclusively resolved.

In "The Communist Horizon" Jodi Dean introduces us to the radical perspectives of literary critic Bruno Bosteels (Cornell University) and the once-imprisoned revolutionary theorist, Álvaro García Linera, who subsequently became the Bolivian vice-president under Evo Morales. Dean acknowledges Bosteels as having brought Linera to her attention through his recent monograph, *The Actuality of Communism* (London: Verso, 2011). Bosteels quoted Linera's fundamental thesis: "The general horizon of the era is communist." Dean found this absolutely remarkable and elaborated: "García Linera invokes the communist horizon 'as if it were the most natural thing in the world,' as if it were so obvious as to need neither explanation nor justification. He assumes the communist horizon as an irreducible feature of the political setting. 'We enter the movement with our expecting and desiring eyes set upon the communist horizon.' For García Linera *communism* conditions the actuality of politics."

Dean explains her understanding of this "horizon" as having relevance both for the anti-communist Right as well as for the non-communist Left: "Communism is that against which they construct their alternative conception of the economy. It's a constitutive force, present as a shaping of the view they advocate." Speaking of a spate of new publications and conferences on radical social theory and practice, Dean comments: "Over the last decade a return to communism has re-energized the radical Left. Communism is again becoming a discourse and a vocabulary for the expression of universal, egalitarian, and revolutionary ideals. A vital area of philosophy considers communism a contemporary name for emancipatory, egalitarian politics and has been actively rethinking many of the concepts that form part of the communist legacy." In her estimation, communism "is reemerging as a magnet of political energy because it is and has been the alternative to capitalism." She is optimistic about revolutionary possibilities today: "As recently became clear in worldwide rioting, protest, and revolution, linking multiple sites of exploitation to narrow channels of privilege can replace melancholic fatalism with new assertions of will, desire, and collective strength. The problem of the Left hasn't been our adherence to a Marxist critique of capitalism. It's that we have lost sight of the communist horizon, a glimpse of which new political movements are starting to reveal." "Instead of a politics thought primarily in terms of resistance, playful and momentary aesthetic disruptions, the immediate specificity of local projects, and struggles for hegemony within a capitalist parliamentary setting, the communist horizon impresses upon us the necessity to abolish capitalism and to create global practices and institutions of egalitarian cooperation." Dean offers an exemplary form of the offensive strategic thinking: "For over thirty years the Left has eschewed such a goal, accepting instead liberal notions that goals are strictly individual life-style choices or social-democratic claims that history already solved basic problems of distribution with the compromise of regulated markets and welfare states—a solution the Right rejected and capitalism destroyed . . . . In light of the planetary climate disaster and the ever-intensifying global class war as states redistribute wealth to the rich in the name of austerity, the absence of a common goal is the absence of a future. The premise of communism is that collective determination of collective conditions is possible if we want it. *The communist horizon appears closer than it has in a long time.*"

In her most recent essay Dean emphasizes that "at a minimal level, if we are to have a chance of taking power, of reformatting the basic conditions under which we live and work, *we have to share a name in common*. . . ."[5] Where she is proposing the formation of a revolutionary party, I am suggesting we need to form a prefigurative *alliance of working groups* with the character of a *Commonwealth Counter-Offensive*. This is as it happens one of the prefigurative forms of party organization she endorses: "Trusting others' skills and knowledge is essential if we are to form ourselves into a political force capable of addressing global capital. This suggests the utility of working groups in multiple locales and issue areas—groups with enough autonomy to be responsive and enough direction to carry out a common purpose, which itself would have to be hashed out and to which all would have to be committed."[6]

Inspired by Dean's crucial contributions as well as the work of Zvi Tauber, I took up the material force and scope of *a labor theory of ethics and commonwealth* in *Crisis and Commonwealth* (republished as chapter 6 in this volume) as the

---

[5] Jodi Dean, "The Party and Communist Solidarity," *Rethinking Marxism, A Journal of Economics, Culture & Society*, Volume 27, Issue 3, 2015, emphasis added.
[6] Ibid.

larger political reality that encompasses all our engagement and action. I argued that a demythologizing and humanist reading of the history of ethical thought in the world's great wisdom traditions yields trans-historical insights. Humanity's oldest moral customs rooted in specific-historical conditions and practices, reflected communal ideals of sharing, cooperation, empathy, mutual regard, respect and reciprocity, partnership power, etc. These norms were themselves *practical:* aiming at the transformation and pacification of everyday tumult. Partnership practices and commonwealth customs, raised to a higher, ideal, level as proverbs and principles, provided a critical negation of conflictual social realities. In non-religious and sociological terms: Life depends on labor. Social labor is the source of social wealth. The labor force has the power to reclaim it from any who have unjustly appropriated it.

Marcuse and Marx emphasized the underlying identity of communism, socialism, and humanism. Philosophical humanism was seen *not* as impossibly utopian and politically powerless, but the "other way 'round:" *practical* struggles for human dignity, respect, and empowerment, against infamous encroachments of man's inhumanity to man, have led to significant intercultural learning and social progress. The force of the material needs of sensuous living labor may, of course, be distorted by a mobilization of bias and/or subdued by the ongoing clash of class interests within the established capitalist order resorting to police state measures. The future is open. Capitalist class predation will stand or fall depending on whether political-economic institutional foundations continue to support accumulation for private gain or are revolutionized in the public interest. Battles by labor have been and will be lost, but the war? The material pressures toward commonwealth are irrepressible. The overarching aim of the classical humanist traditions, like that of the praxis-oriented authors in *Crisis and Commonwealth,* has been to offer an apt contribution to the project of *re*-humanizing a *de*-

humanized material culture. Labor is humanity's mode of being in the world. Commonwealth culture remains the venerable, and today thoroughly viable, means of survival for humanity as sensuous living labor. It is ultimately, as I argue in Part Nine of this volume, also labor's (and thus humanity's) emancipatory aesthetic form.

My belief is that the tremendous mass of corporate political-economic capital has reached its half-life limits; its forms of domination and power are outdated and gyrating dangerously. An intercultural labor force humanism, is not only necessary and feasible, it provides the gravitational center that holds real group life together despite other flare ups and explosions. Labor's humanism in this sense defines not only an emancipatory ethos, but the type of economic, social, and political structure that is needed for justice and peace to be accomplished and sustained.

Herbert Marcuse also knew the paradox persists: our options are socialism or barbarism. Convinced that counterrevolution was underway in the U.S. with politics veering to the extreme Right, he concluded with a statement of our contemporary crisis and challenge: "The life and death question for the Left is: Can the transformation of the corporate State into a neo-fascist State be prevented? The question, as well as the possible answers to it do not arise from a *revision* of Marxian theory, they are posed by Marxian theory itself!" (1979, 23).

Stephen Spartan and *Peter* Marcuse: Final Comments. Peter Marcuse cautions us that radical change does not come about by itself, no matter how radical the goals. Change can be held back on the one hand by 1) the strength of the forces materially dominating and benefiting from the status quo; on the other it can be inhibited by 2) the weakness of the radical opposition. He asks us to think about 3) who the agents of change are who will actually achieve these goals.

Stephen Spartan responds: With regard to 1) we are seeing today the beginning of the end of a decaying system whose productive base is not being reproduced. Reproduction resources have been shifted from the middle class—the American system's vaunted citizenry—toward the financial sector and the society's "1 percent." The growth in income of society's upper echelons of privilege (11.2 percent for uppermost 1 percent)[7] is dramatically out of proportion to the slow growth of GDP and the real economy (1.8 percent),[8] not to mention the reductions in income flow (down 0.4 percent)[9] experienced by everyone else throughout the society (so much for "trickle-down"). Over-accumulation at the top is occurring at the expense of labor force reproduction, whose economic expectations are continually being leveled-down, and whose members are increasingly being treated with oligarchic disdain as expendable and dispensable. The demise of the system is occurring, including the very state which liberal policy-making would traditionally utilize to pacify and control the masses. The veneer of democracy is melting away in the heat of a new military nationalism. This can be viewed with horror, yet there is also the possibility of liberation. A world of abundance is possible and feasible given the system's productive potential.

With regard to 2) what is lacking is the *commonwealth*

---

[7] Annie Lowery, "Incomes Flat in Recovery, but not for the 1%," *The New York Times*, February 16, 2013, p. B-1.
[8] Bureau of Economic Analysis, U.S. Department of Commerce, "Growth in Goods and Services Industries Slowed in 2011," November 13, 2012. Retrieved February 27, 2013 from http://www.bea.gov/newsreleases/industry/gdpindustry/gdpindhighlights.pdf
[9] Lowery, op. cit.

vision, an awareness of the alternative. Prosperity is a collective product, this establishes the claim to *common wealth*. We have a *right* to a commonwealth economy, politics, and culture. The benefits of prosperity require cooperation, planning, a democratic commonwealth ethos, and an end to commodity-dependency. While the objective productive forces have ripened such that the global economy can be seen as pregnant with abundance, the *subjective* element matters. Without an adamant ideology of commonwealth, there is no sufficient negation, no sufficient transformation. *The labor theory of ethics and commonwealth raises expectations: there is a world to win!* Hence the need for revolutionary critical pedagogy for a socialist society.

With regard to 3) the question of the agents of change, multiple groups internationally already recognize that commodified existence and economic want are not natural, but rather contrived; groups like the public domain software development communities producing shareware and freeware; groups like Adbusters, Greenpeace, the participants on the militant anti-globalization movement from Seattle (1999) to Genoa (2001), the *indignados* of France and Spain from 2010 forward, and the coordinated anti-austerity general strikes in five European countries November 14, 2012, as well as many others. They advocate that significant portions of commodified social life need to be rethought and reconstructed. Human essentials need to be met. Large swaths of working men and women around the globe have rising expectations and are aware of the need to end corporate rule and shift power to those who will prioritize human needs over private accumulation. The ideological justifications for capitalism have significantly eroded, as well as its major mode of control: commodity-dependency. In the riveting words of Chris Hedges and Joe Sacco in *Days of Destruction, Days of Revolt* (2012): "The game . . . is up. . . . Even our corporate overlords no longer believe the words they utter. . . ." (2012, xii). Hedges and Sacco had to admit, however, that when they began writing their book, "the nation-wide revolt was absent;" that is, until the Occupy Wall Street movement flared-up up in dozens of U.S. cities. Their ultimate conclusion is that oppositional forces are real, not speculative: "There comes a moment in all popular uprisings when the dead ideas and decayed systems, which only days before seemed unassailable, are exposed and discredited by a population that once stood fearful and supine. . . . Astute observers know the tinder is there, but never when it will be lit" (2012, 226-227).

Our sense of the reality of right persists within a world of wrong. It infuses our theory and politics and the commonwealth counter-offensive. It presses humanity forward toward a future worth living—a rehumanized future that is clearly, but not easily, within our grasp. In accordance with this sensibility, we hope that our *Reflections on Science and the Human Material Condition* have offered timely and insightful perspectives on our politics, praxis, and pedagogy. The essays presented here give some indication of the explorations and struggles in which its authors have been engaged, primarily as pathfinders. It is my hope, as general editor and publisher, that their efforts resonate and converge with *your own* intimations and experiences to advance socialism's most radical goals in a global revolutionary movement. Our work is not done, but as Marcuse's bold letters admonish us: "IT CAN STILL BE DONE!"[10]

---

[10] Herbert Marcuse, "Lecture on Education, Brooklyn College, 1968" in Douglas Kellner, Tyson Lewis, Clayton Pierce, K. Daniel Cho, *Marcuse's Challenge to Education* (Lanham, MD: Rowman & Littlefield, 2009) p. 43.

Bibliography

Charter 2000: A Comprehensive Political Platform. 2011. Kansas City Progressive Network. Ratified 1996. Additions 2002. Integral version 2011. http://progressiveplatform2000.org/Charter-2000-Platform.htm

Leakey, Richard. 1994. *The Origin of Humankind.* New York: Basic Books.

Leakey, Richard and Roger Lewin. 1978. *People of the Lake.* Garden City, NY: Anchor/Doubleday.

De Waal, Frans. 2013. *The Bonobo and the Atheist: In Search of Humanism among the Primates.* New York: W.W. Norton.

———. 2009. *The Age of Empathy.* New York: Random House.

———. 2006. *Primates and Philosophers.* Princeton, NJ: Princeton University Press.

Kellner, Douglas. 1973. "Introduction to 'On the Philosophical Foundation of the Concept of Labor,'" *Telos,* No. 16, Summer 1973.

Marcuse, Herbert. 1979. "The Reification of the Proletariat," *Canadian Journal of Political and Social Theory / Revue canadienne de théorie politique et sociale,* Vol 3, No 1 (Winter/Hiver).

Reitz, Charles. [2013] 2015. *Crisis and Commonwealth: Marcuse, Marx, McLaren.* Lanham, MD: Lexington Books.

Chapter Fifteen: Charles Reitz

About the Co-Authors

The co-authors of this volume have worked together as faculty colleagues at Kansas City Kansas Community College (KCKCC). In addition to teaching in their areas of specialization, their academic careers have included special leadership efforts with regard to multicultural educational reform (i.e. curriculum revision and institutional development) and in their engagement as faculty leaders in the shared governance process. All partnered closely with the college's Intercultural Center and were involved in the activities of the faculty bargaining unit. Morteza Ardebili and Stephen Spartan each served as faculty negotiators; Curtis V. Smith and Charles Reitz each served multi-year terms as President of the Faculty Association (KNEA). Both Smith and Spartan worked as switchmen in the rail yards of Kansas City before entering into their community college teaching careers.

Morteza Ardebili, Ph.D. in sociology from the University of Kansas, was instrumental in the creation of the college's Intercultural Center, and was its first Director. He led the campus-wide effort at multicultural curriculum revision. He regularly team-taught in the PACE Program (Program of Adult Career Education) with professors Reitz and Spartan. He undertook administrative duties for several years before his retirement in 2009, serving as the college's Vice President for Executive Services and as the college's chief academic officer, the Provost.

ABOUT THE CO-AUTHORS

Charles Reitz studied philosophy at the University of Freiburg, Germany, from 1969-71. He obtained his Ph.D. in philosophy of education from the State University of New York at Buffalo in 1983. Teaching duties at KCKCC included German, ethics, logic, and foundations of education. He served as Co-Director of the Intercultural Center with Melanie Jackson Scott, then also as Director of Intercultural Education until his retirement in 2006. He is the author of *Art, Alienation, and the Humanities: A Critical Engagement with Herbert Marcuse* (SUNY Press, 2000); *Crisis and Commonwealth* (Lexington Books, 2015); and *Philosophy & Critical Pedagogy* (Peter Lang Publishing, 2016).

Mehdi S. Shariati earned his Ph.D. from the University of Missouri at Kansas City (UMKC) and regularly teaches economics, geography, and sociology. His research interests center on global political economy, social change, and sustainability. He has also been involved in developing techniques of critical pedagogy. He has published his own textbooks for Macro- and Micro-Economics, and has been the faculty advisor to student groups such as the Econ Club, Public Achievement, and the Campus Forum, each of which hosts speakers and addresses debates on contemporary issues. He has widely published critical political commentary in several venues, including the *Monthly Review Online.*

Curtis V. Smith, holds an Interdisciplinary Ph.D. in Urban Leadership and Policy Studies in Higher Education with Minors in Political Economy and Social Theory from the University of Missouri at Kansas City (UMKC). He regularly offers coursework and labs in the biological sciences, and coordinates the biology faculty on campus. He also teaches history of science in the social science division, and is the coordinator and treasurer for the Wyandotte County Ethnic Festival, an annual community-building, multicultural event. Smith has published over a dozen articles on a wide range of topics in the *Kansas City Kansas Community College eJournal,* most notably, "The Impact of Part-Time Faculty on Student Retention," and "A Short History of Shared Governance."

Stephen Spartan earned his BA and MA in economics from the University of Missouri at Kansas City (UMKC) and his MA in social psychology from UMKC. He earned his Ph.D. in sociology/political economy from the University of Kansas. Before his retirement in 2007, he taught economics, geography, and sociology, and co-taught with Morteza Ardebili and Charles Reitz in the Kansas City Kansas Community College PACE Program as well as graduate classes in the Labor Studies Institute at UMKC.

About the Co-Authors

Made in the USA
Charleston, SC
01 November 2016